MW00425783

Higher Education in the American West

HIGHER EDUCATION & SOCIETY

Series Editors:

Roger L. Geiger, Distinguished Professor of Education, Pennsylvania State University

Katherine Reynolds Chaddock, Professor of Higher Education Administration, University of South Carolina

This series explores the diverse intellectual dimensions, social themes, cultural contexts, and pressing political issues related to higher education. From the history of higher education to heated contemporary debates, topics in this field range from issues in equity, matriculation, class representation, and current educational federal acts, to concerns with gender and pedagogy, new media and technology, and the challenges of globalization. In this way, the series aims to highlight theories, historical developments, and contemporary endeavors that prompt critical thought and reflective action in how higher education is conceptualized and practiced in and beyond the United States.

Liberal Education for a Land of Colleges: Yale's "Reports" of 1828
By David B. Potts

Deans of Men and the Shaping of Modern College Culture
By Robert Schwartz

Establishing Academic Freedom: Politics, Principles, and the Development of Core Values
By Timothy Cain

Higher Education in the American West: Regional History and State Contexts
Edited by Lester F. Goodchild, Richard W. Jonsen, Patty Limerick, and David A. Longanecker

Public Policy Challenges Facing Higher Education in the American West
Edited by Lester F. Goodchild, Richard W. Jonsen, Patty Limerick, and David A. Longanecker

Higher Education in the American West

Regional History and State Contexts

Edited by

Lester F. Goodchild

Richard W. Jonsen

Patty Limerick

David A. Longanecker

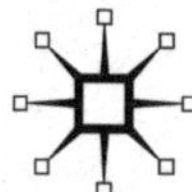

HIGHER EDUCATION IN THE AMERICAN WEST

First published in 2014 by
PALGRAVE MACMILLAN®
in the United States—a division of St. Martin's Press LLC,
175 Fifth Avenue, New York, NY 10010.

Where this book is distributed in the UK, Europe and the rest of the world, this is by Palgrave Macmillan, a division of Macmillan Publishers Limited, registered in England, company number 785998, of Houndmills, Basingstoke, Hampshire RG21 6XS.

Palgrave Macmillan is the global academic imprint of the above companies and has companies and representatives throughout the world.

Palgrave® and Macmillan® are registered trademarks in the United States, the United Kingdom, Europe and other countries.

ISBN: 978–1–137–38194–1

Library of Congress Cataloging-in-Publication Data

Higher education in the American West : regional history and state contexts / edited by Lester F. Goodchild and others.
pages cm.—(Higher education & society)
Includes bibliographical references and index.
ISBN 978–1–137–38194–1 (hardback)
1. Education, Higher—West (U.S.)—History. 2. Education and state—West (U.S.)—History. 3. Universities and colleges—West (U.S.)—History. 4. West (U.S.)—History. 5. West (U.S.)—Social life and customs. I. Goodchild, Lester F.

LA230.5.W48H54 2014
378.00978—dc3 2013047588

A catalogue record of the book is available from the British Library.

Design by Newgen Knowledge Works (P) Ltd., Chennai, India.

First edition: March 2014

10 9 8 7 6 5 4 3 2 1

Contents

Part III A Concluding Commentary

Figures and Tables

Figures

Tables

Editors' Preface

American public higher education is at a crossroads; its future is uncertain. The twenty-first-century financial demands on states for improved services to their citizens have outstripped the public determination and will to support postsecondary education during the recent Great Recession. Many states have reduced their funding for public universities and colleges in the face of the current difficult times. To overcome the current economic difficulties, a new consensus needs to be built around one of their most powerful public and private resources—their universities and colleges. The higher education development engine has succeeded in the past to boost the economic productivity of the states. If the current public leadership had an understanding of higher education's past successes and a vision for appropriate policy strategies to progress using these great educational plants, a more productive way forward might emerge.

Two comprehensive books on higher education in the western states seek to provide this understanding and vision through analytical and researched studies. The first volume, *Higher Education in the American West: Regional History and State Contexts*, offers the first regional overview of the history of postsecondary education in the United States. In this book we crafted a new portrait of the development of western higher education to show how the peoples of the West created its colleges and universities to educate its citizens, and to analyze how in previous eras these institutions provided part of the means to overcome tough times. Its companion volume, *Public Policy Challenges Facing Higher Education in the American West*, explores seven major public policy directions needed to utilize this higher education enterprise to educate and train the West's citizens for future careers and to move the state economies forward. National policy experts have made assessments of postsecondary access, finance, federal funding, governance, institutional tuition, technology and distance education policy, as well as community college issues for 15 western states and their systems of higher education in thoughtful and data rich chapters. In this way, postsecondary history in the first volume provides a context and a vision that informs public policy directions in the second companion volume.

This two volume project thus offers an overview and assessment of public and independent higher education in the West, from the very earliest American efforts to bring scholarship along the overland migration trails and sea routes to the Pacific and beyond to create a future that built the region's higher education sector. Subsequent major immigrations to the West over the past 50 years have made it the most diverse region of the country. Now its 71.5 million citizens support nearly 1,000 universities and colleges to educate its people, to train its professionals, and to advance knowledge through its researchers and scholars. The West's historic importance in supplying natural resources for the country and the world as well as its more recent history of dynamic technological innovations makes what happens in the West, and how its colleges and universities develop, important signals for the future of the nation's economy, society, and culture.

These books are intended for a variety of audiences and to those interested in higher education, particularly in the western states. State and higher education policymakers will be especially interested in the second companion book, which focuses on the difficult issues facing higher education policymakers in the West and indeed the nation. They will find that the first book provides a valuable context for understanding these policy commentaries and seeing how different eras used higher education to foster state development. State political leaders will find this comprehensive treatment of postsecondary education a useful study for crafting new public policy directions. Faculty and graduate students in the field of higher education will find this regional history and policy overview a useful addition to their study of public policy and the development of American higher education. Those engaged and interested in higher education in other parts of the country will find this portrait helpful in seeing their own regional postsecondary needs and directions.

One major initial question perplexed this project: How should one define what states constitute the American West? The scope of this two-book project was influenced initially by the fiftieth anniversary celebration of the 15-member state compact, the Western Interstate Commission for Higher Education (WICHE), which occurred in 2003. The 15 states comprising WICHE's membership are: Alaska, Arizona, California, Colorado, Hawaii, Idaho, Montana, Nevada, New Mexico, North Dakota, Oregon, South Dakota, Utah, Washington, and Wyoming. This WICHE West and its states' higher education stories, traditions, histories, and policies became the main focus of the project's undertaking. With a view toward this anniversary, the late Michael Malone, president of Montana State University, proposed in 1998 to engage a collaboration of scholars, policy researchers, and administrators associated with or interested in WICHE and its state higher education systems to initiate a book project, and discussed the idea with the then Executive Director Richard Jonsen. Malone hoped they would write a history of higher education in the western United States. They then consulted with Patty Limerick, director of the Center of the American West and Professor of History at the University of Colorado at Boulder who joined the collaboration. David A. Longanecker, who succeeded Jonsen at WICHE in 1999, warmly endorsed the project. After Jonsen's invitation, Professor Lester F. Goodchild, then director of the Higher Education Program at the University of Denver, assumed the leadership of the project. Goodchild's coedited book *Higher Education and Public Policy* (1997) suggested a way of doing policy history and analysis as its key framework. With the untimely death of Malone, Goodchild, Jonsen, Limerick, and Longanecker became the gang of four editors who oversaw this two-book project to its conclusion. Discussions with members of the Western Historical Society also aided in identifying themes, possible authors, and the western scope for the project. Most of the early chapter drafts of the book were vetted at a WICHE symposium in 2002, and then presented at an authors' conference the following year to mark the anniversary. Along the way, the William and Flora Hewlett Foundation provided generous support for the project, and additional funds came from the Wyss Family Foundation of Portland, Oregon.

Over the next 13 years, Les Goodchild and Richard Jonsen worked closely with authors to obtain the final versions of the chapters for the books, and divided them into two manuscripts. Their efforts were greatly enhanced by the very able work of our content editor, Jason Hanson, at the Center for the American West, our copy editor, Paul Albright, formerly with WICHE, and our graphic designer, Candy Allen, currently at WICHE. Their work with policy leaders, researchers, historians, and administrators led to this extraordinary collaboration, the outcome of which is these two companion volumes. Eventually, 22 authors have written 18 chapters and have produced this first regional history and public policy study of higher education in the western United States, which blends the historical character, current status, and policy problems and perspectives into a narrative picture that is unique, both in the West and among the other regions of the country. Many thanks are owed to the authors and editors who have made these volumes possible.

In fall 2010, critical support for publishing this extensive project initially came from Professors Roger L. Geiger of Pennsylvania State University and Katherine E. Chaddock of the University of South Carolina who believed the work was highly appropriate for their Palgrave Macmillan series "Higher Education and Society." At the November 2010 History of Education Society meeting in Boston, Goodchild met with them there, and with their endorsement discussed the project with Burke Gerstenschlager, Palgrave Macmillan's senior editor. Gerstenschlager liked it and welcomed a full prospectus. His continued encouragement of the project over the next two years and then further support from his successor, Associate Editor Sarah Nathan, enabled the project to be realized. The four editors extend their grateful thanks and appreciation to the Palgrave Macmillan and its Editorial Board for their endorsement of this two-companion volume project. Finally, the editors would like to thank Social Explorer for the use of the US census data as well as the National Parks Service and the Bureau of Land Management for the cartography data to create the College Foundings and Western Trails map in this book's first chapter. With the project's completion in 2013, the editors see the work now as part of the sixtieth anniversary celebration of the founding of WICHE.

A Critical Commentary

In his new appraisal of America in a "post-American world," Fareed Zakaria (2008, p. 186) called higher education "America's best industry." Perhaps. However, the political consensus to support this growth and development industry has always been a struggle. Nevertheless, higher education in the American West represents a new wave of responsive postsecondary education. Zakaria focused on the global predominance of the major research universities, and this is surely true of the West. Five of the top ten US universities with the most research and development revenues—all world-class institutions, as noted in Arthur Cohen's chapter (p. 63) —are located in the West. Of course, there are pinnacles of excellence in the West among the public and private institutions at each level and of each type. Community colleges are undoubtedly portals of opportunity to millions of western students, where the 15 WICHE states have some 259 of them or 25 percent nationally. Among the fewer primarily baccalaureate public institutions and the many master's and limited doctoral level institutions, there are numerous exemplary institutions. Twenty-three of the 37 Tribal Colleges and Universities (TCUs), or 62 percent nationally, the West's truly unique institutions serve the distinctive needs of Native American students on their tribal lands, both with respect to deepening their cultural knowledge and preparing them for further education. The 119 Hispanic-Serving Institutions (HSIs) in the West represent approximately one-half of the US institutions enrolling more than 25 percent Hispanic students. Finally, alternative higher education has a significant home in the West with nonprofit online higher education being represented by the Western Governors University, Regis University, and National University or with for-profit higher education being led by the University of Phoenix and Jones International University in Denver. In total, according to Cheryl Blanco's demographic Chapter 1 in *Public Policy Challenges Facing Higher Education in the American West*, the West is home to nearly 1,000 colleges and universities, whether they are public, independent, proprietary, or for-profit.

It may be best to depict the West as a region of regions, and look at common qualitative comparisons in this higher education landscape. However, even within those subregions (such as the Pacific West with its states of Oregon, Washington, Alaska, and Hawaii), there exist huge differences among and within the states regarding the development and strength of higher education. History, culture, demography, wealth, and, surely, the role of visionary and strong leaders, all have affected those western subregions and their institutions, as can be seen in the chapters that review the Southwest states, the Middle Border States, or the Pacific West.

What is at stake for these various kinds of institutions and their constituents in each part of the West? Looking at the future, Roger Geiger claimed: "Despite recurrent financial pressures and demographic pressures looming in the next century, the immeasurable contribution of colleges and universities to American life should sustain them through the inevitable challenges lying ahead" (Altbach, Berdahl, and Gumport, 2005, pp. 65–66). However, at the close of the twentieth century, Clark Kerr was less sanguine about future prospects or their predictability. In the final edition of his classic work *The Uses of the University* (2001) Kerr wrote, referring to accurate predictions in the first 1963 edition, "I wish that today I might again be so prescient about the shape of things to come, but I cannot... I think having a clear view of the future is now much more difficult, perhaps impossible. We live in an age of too many discontinuities, too many variables, too many uncertainties, as almost any university president today can certify" (p. 201). And, considering the economic conditions at the time of this writing (in mid-2012), those uncertainties seem daunting indeed.

True, there are commonalities and common strengths among our western institutions. The land-grant institutions are of high quality, close to their constituents, and oriented to public service. The famed "Wisconsin Idea"—that of a progressive, collaborative relationship between that land-grant university and its state and community—during the first half of the twentieth century surely inspired the later development of those institutions in the West. There are world-class research institutions in the public and private domains, and among smaller private institutions, enormous diversity, especially in value-oriented and church-sponsored institutions. The West took leadership early on in the community college "movement," possessing some of the first and some of the best. Our western institutions serve an increasingly diverse population—the most diverse in the country. Some have done so admirably, some fall far short of reflecting their communities or states. In fact, the TCUs and HSIs represent unique examples of institutions serving specific clienteles, and most of these institutions are in the western WICHE states. Initially, the classical New England–inspired liberal arts model existed in only relatively limited numbers in the West, because many of that genre sprang out of untilled colonial soil some 350 or more years before the West's development. While some early institutions may have "looked like" the small liberal arts colleges of New England, there was too much of a gap in time and geography for that model to be widely replicated here.

Public higher education became dominant in the West currently. For this reason, the future of higher education in the West remains largely in the hands of state government and public higher education decision makers.

Summing Up

There are major differences between the West and other regions of the United States in terms of higher education institutions, faculty, students, and curriculum, although there are elements within institutional types that are more "uniform" when compared with other parts of the country. Western higher education is a complex enterprise: over 1,200 institutions overlay the enormous and magnificent landscape and the political history of the states. Those institutions, collectively and individually, have a distinctive history that includes thousands of leaders, faculty, and students. It took a myriad of individual decisions in public and private higher education to create and comprise this world.

The enterprise is magnificent, but many of its promises remain unfulfilled. Access is far from universal, and far from equitably distributed across socioeconomic groups. Access is greatly hampered by weak links between higher education and K-12 education. Financial resources, whether sufficient or not, are distributed unevenly across institutional types. Institutions carrying the greatest burdens of access seem to be those least well financed, especially the community and tribal colleges. Though much attention has been paid to striking the "right" balance between research and undergraduate education, we have much more to achieve. Similarly, efforts to revise and renew curricula are often victims of entrenched interests, or at a deeper level, the absence of a contemporary consensus among the state and campus leaders of higher education. Its resolution will involve new purposes for all three levels of undergraduate, graduate, and professional education that have yet to be realized.

So, what we may have originally intended to mark the "celebration" of western higher education and the rise of WICHE some years ago has become a more ambiguous and ambitious exercise. It may be that the uniqueness and spirit of innovation in western higher education lies more in how these institutions of higher learning confront their challenges than in their triumphs, as Patty Limerick discusses in chapter 3, the challenges of a vast area to serve (one-half of the landmass of the United States, larger than all but six of the world's nations); the diversity of a population that includes more than one-half of the US Asian Americans, more than one-half of the Native Americans, and more than one-half of the non-Cuban and non-Puerto-Rican Hispanics; and, most critically, a political landscape that includes several of the country's most restrictive state tax-limitation laws.

To confront these challenges, much work needs to be done at a time when it looks like the country's resources will be seriously constrained in the short or even medium-range future. We encourage our readers to review both the history of western higher education book here and the public policy issues facing state and higher education leaders that is analyzed in our companion volume, Lester F. Goodchild, Richard A. Jonsen, Patty Limerick, and David A. Longanecker's *Public Policy Challenges Facing Higher Education in the American West* (2104). There our authors address policy concerns related to postsecondary access, federal research funding, state higher education governance, fiscal challenges facing states and public higher education systems, rising costs of tuition, distance education and technology, as well as challenges facing community and tribal colleges. In spite of these concerns, the West has always been a land of hope, promise, and innovation. There is no reason why it should be different for higher education tomorrow.

REFERENCES

Altbach, P. G., R. O. Berdahl, and P. Gumport. *American Higher Education in the Twenty-First Century: Social, Political, and Economic Challenge*, 2nd ed. Baltimore, MD: Johns Hopkins University Press, 2005.

Goodchild, L. F., R. W. Jonsen, P. Limerick, and D. A. Longanecker (eds.). *Public Policy Challenges Facing Higher Education in the American West.* Higher Education and Society series. New York: Palgrave Macmillan, 2014.

Goodchild, L. F., C. D. Lovell, E. R. Hines, and J. I. Gill (eds.). *Public Policy and Higher Education.* Association for the Study of Higher Education Reader Series. Needham Heights, MA: Simon and Schuster, 1997.

Kerr, C. *The Uses of the University*, 5th ed. Cambridge, MA: Harvard University Press, 2001.

Zakaria, F. *The Post-American World.* New York: W. W. Norton, 2008.

Dedications

With great affection, this book is dedicated to the memory of Michael P. Malone, president of Montana State University from 1991 to 1999, whose idea this book was, to Phillip Sirotkin, executive director of WICHE from 1976 to 1989, whose leadership improved western higher education during his important tenure in office, to Thomas T. Farley, Colorado legislator and board member, who was a generous supporter of both public (the Colorado State University System) and private (Santa Clara University) higher education, and to Loren Wyss, whose leadership as commissioner and chair took WICHE to the next stage.

The words and works of leaders like these echo throughout the companion volumes of this new western regional history and policy study of American higher education:

> *With the economic downturn of the 1980s, westerners came more and more to realize that education was the key to their social, cultural and economic future—just as, in truth, it always had been.*
>
> Michael P. Malone and Richard W. Etulain, *The American West: A Twentieth Century History* (1989, p. 214)
>
> *Sirotkin proved himself the right person for the WICHE directorship at the right time. His convictions about the needs and potential for regional interstate collaboration and his energy and courage in dealing with governors and legislators inspired responses from commissioners and other WICHE friends and transformed threat to opportunity.*
>
> Frank C. Abbott, *A History of the Western Interstate Commission for Higher Education: The First Forty Years* (2004, p. 247)
>
> *Thomas T. Farley...dedicated himself to public service and to helping the underdog... (and) in the death of Thomas T. Farley the people of Pueblo and the State of Colorado have lost an outstanding citizen and dedicated public servant.*
>
> House Memorial 11–1001, State of Colorado, August 23, 2010.
>
> *When scholars of the future compile a list of Oregon's most wise, passionate and effective citizen leaders, the name of Loren Wyss will surely be prominent on the list...Loren will be missed for his good-natured wit, generous and caring spirit and his unyielding integrity.*
>
> Bill Allen, from tributes on Loren Wyss, Obituary Notice in the *Portland Oregonian*; Loren Wyss became involved in WICHE programs in 1977,

and served as a WICHE commissioner from 1984 to 1990 and as chair of the commission from 1988 to 1989.

In Grateful Appreciation

Our grateful thanks to The William and Flora Hewlett Foundation for its generous support of the project that produced this book, and to Sally Tracy for her personal support and patience in approving an interminable journey to its conclusion. We would note the role played by the foundation and also by the Hewlett family in their support of western higher education. That generosity, as well as William Hewlett's pioneering role in Silicon Valley, has greatly strengthened the economy of the West, as well as its colleges and universities. The Wyss Foundation of Portland, Oregon, also made a generous contribution in the memory of Ann M. Jonsen, late wife of one of the editors, to support the publication of these volumes.

We wish also to acknowledge the valuable assistance of the University of Denver's staff of its Sponsored Programs Office and Mordridge College of Education in assisting with the management of the Hewlett Foundation grant.

We would be remiss not to acknowledge the support of WICHE and the assistance and participation of David Longanecker, its president, in helping to bring this two companion volume project to completion.

Introduction

Lester F. Goodchild, Richard W. Jonsen, Patty Limerick, and David A. Longanecker

Higher Education in the American West: Regional History and State Contexts and its companion volume, *Public Policy Challenges Facing Higher Education in the American West*, are the first regional history and public policy studies of higher education in the United States. These two companion volumes consist of multiple chapters written by a variety of higher education scholars, university administrators, and policy experts. The first book provides a broad historical overview from the beginnings of the westward expansion in North America down to the present condition of higher education, especially its state systems. It examines the West as a region, and how higher education has both shaped and been shaped by the distinct character of the West. It answers the question: "Is there a unique western higher education?" The second book focuses on public policy studies, providing a background through demographic data, institutional and student statistics, and a report-card approach to how western higher education "measures up." It also looks at the seven critical public policy issues facing higher education today. The afterwords in both volumes discuss the distinctive character of western higher education as well as its challenging future with various higher education scenarios that might unfold in the current millennium.

This first volume with its subtitle *Regional History and State Contexts* focuses specifically on history and state contexts of the trans-Mississippi West and the 15-state WICHE West. Through a number of detailed and subregionally analyzed researched chapters, the book provides the background for understanding how higher education developed in the West. While not explicitly discussed, this early history in the first chapter builds upon the invasion from all directions of the indigenous people: from the south marched Spanish conquerors and their evangelizing padres; from the east rushed Euro-American pioneers and gold-seekers; and from the west sailed the English and Russians. These pioneers were deeply interested in establishing institutions of higher learning for their progeny and for this new western society. The chapters in this volume present the evolution of these western colleges and universities from their beginnings and provide subregional multistate portraits. Each chapter offers a new lens on how and why higher education blossomed in the West. This hope for riches or better lives may have been intensified by the grandeur and variety of the land: stunning coastlines, endless deserts, fertile valleys, majestic mountains, and rippling rivers that flow both to the Pacific and the Gulf of Mexico. "Something in the soil," to use Patty Limerick's evocative phrase, inspired these settlers and their successors to found over 1,200 colleges and universities, as they spread out across the West.

In chapter 1, Lester Goodchild and David Wrobel look at the first 125 years of building higher education in the American trans-Mississippi West up to World War II, observing that religious colleges predated public institutions in most western states as the early pattern of institutional establishment basically followed the pioneer trails, seaport migrations, rivers, railroads, and population migrations across the land. Following the genius of D. W. Meinig's four volumes of *The Shaping of America: A Geographical Perspective on 500 Years of History* (1986, 1993, 1998, 2006) on the geographic history of the United States, this history of higher education offers a new geographic approach to understand the roles that religious evangelization and state boosterism played in raising higher education. Their interpretations somewhat puncture the more romantic and heroic sagas of institutions being started by rugged educational pioneers seeking to provide the education and training necessary to create the economy and the society of this region in its fledgling years.

In chapter 2, Arthur Cohen surveys the developmental sweep of higher education in the 15-state WICHE West up to the present day, pointing to some of its distinctive characteristics. Following his more sociological institutional patterns in his widely acclaimed *The Shaping of American Higher Education: Emergence and Growth of the Contemporary System* (2010), he identifies some of the unique problems and aspects of the character of western higher education by exploring: institutional types; their organization and governance; finances; students and curricula; private, tribal, and Hispanic Serving Institutions; innovative higher education; and the effects of the Great Recession. Critically, he notes the beginnings of higher education regional compacts, including the launching of the Western Interstate Commission for Higher Education (WICHE) in 1953, and their role in western higher education. He further makes some important comparisons between higher education developments in the WICHE West and that of the Midwest and the East.

In chapter 3, western historian Patty Limerick offers an invitation to explore how the West shaped higher education in its states and concludes with a more regional view of this part of the country. As cofounder of the Center for the Study of the West at the University of Colorado Boulder in 1986, she has received acclaim nationally for her work, including the prestigious MacArthur Fellowship from 1995 to 2000 and the university's recognition of her extraordinary scholarship on and teaching about the West with its Hazel Barnes Prize, and offers a distinctive treatment here of the West and its higher education. Following her major western commentaries, such as *The Legacy of Conquest: The Unbroken Past of the American West* (1987) and *Something in the Soil: Legacies and Reckonings in the New West* (2000), she paints a vivid portrait of the West and then recounts vignettes about western institutions and their denizens to illustrate some contemporary dilemmas facing its colleges and universities. She offers some prescriptions for reform in the twenty-first century drawn from her 45 years of professorial experience in the academy. These prescriptions play themselves out through an indepth analysis of higher education and its development in various parts of the West.

Moving to more focused state cluster chapters in the WICHE region, chapters 4 through 7 look at subregional pictures from 1945 to the present, with each author or team of authors having a distinctive focus and voice in this series. In chapter 4, Jason Lane and Francis "Frank" Kerins describe the vastly different evolution of what they call the "middle border" states of Idaho, Montana, Wyoming, and the two Dakotas. They highlight public and private higher education, tribal colleges, community colleges, and professional education before delving into focused explorations of individual state profiles and their combined 133 institutions of higher learning. They conclude with a critical discussion on the five-state high school graduation rates and their possible impacts on higher education. In chapter 5, William "Bud" Davis describes the postwar southwest "boom states" of Arizona, Colorado, Nevada, New Mexico, and Utah and how the influx of returning veterans and the G. I. Bill propelled the expansion of higher education in those states. He examines the 262 institutions of higher learning in these states by discussing their institutional types, tribal colleges, and community colleges with particular attention to state governance issues. In chapter 6, Bud Davis, Lester Goodchild, and David Tandberg explore the development of 168 institutions of higher learning in the Pacific West with its diverse group of states: Alaska, Hawaii, Oregon, and Washington. In these state profiles, they examine: (1) the development of state universities, (2) the creation of state higher education governance systems, and (3) the recent conditions within the state's system of higher learning. Attention is also given to private higher education, tribal colleges, and community colleges. Each subregional history chapter notes some of the WICHE activities in these states and the impact of the recent Great Recession on state higher education budgets. The diversity of those states is representative of the entire western region; though there are commonalities, there are more disparities.

The next two chapters offer a taste of public policy issues within the historical context of the 15-state WICHE West region, and in some ways foreshadow the companion volume. In chapter 7, Patrick Callan analyzes California as a subregion with its 666 postsecondary institutions and surveys the state's higher education public policy process over the past 60 years with particular attention to the California Master Plan and more recent political changes. He concludes that the most recent era of policymaking due to political volatility, decline of state finances, and student population growth does not bode well for the future development of public higher education there. In chapter 8, WICHE President David Longanecker looks at the long relationship between the federal government and western higher education, and the critical roles played by the Morrill Land Grant Act, as well as federal financial aid and research dollars on many leading research universities in the region.

Finally, Lester Goodchild in the Afterword discusses how this first regional history of American higher education provides valuable insights on how western lands, state cultures, and diverse populations affected its developing 1,229 higher education institutions and state systems. Recalling how Patty Limerick characterized the West as having a spirit of innovation, he points to how many higher education developments were unique and embodied this spirit. He comments on how regional compacts, such as WICHE, seek to provide system data and to convene state leaders to make better policy decisions—noting some high points during its 60 years. Furthermore, such a history provides policy researchers and state leaders with a rich contextual narrative for developing state higher education system policies.

REFERENCES

Cohen, A. M. and C. B. Kisker. *The Shaping of American Higher Education: Emergence and Growth of the Contemporary System.* San Francisco, CA: Jossey-Bass, 2010.

Limerick, P. *The Legacy of Conquest: The Unbroken Past of the American West.* New York: W. W. Norton, 1987.

———. *Something in the Soil: Legacies and Reckonings in the New West.* New York: W. W. Norton, 2000.

Meinig, D. W. *The Shaping of America: A Geographical Perspective on America.* Vol. 4: *Global America, 1915-2000.* New Haven, CT: Yale University Press, 2006.

———. *The Shaping of America: A Geographical Perspective on 500 Years of History.* Vol. 3: *Transcontinental America, 1850–1915.* New Haven, CT: Yale University Press, 1998.

———. *The Shaping of America: A Geographical Perspective on 500 Years of History.* Vol. 2: *Continental America, 1800–1867.* New Haven, CT: Yale University Press, 1993.

———. *The Shaping of America: A Geographical Perspective on 500 Years of History.* Vol. 1: *Atlantic America, 1492–1800.* New Haven, CT: Yale University Press, 1986.

Part I

Regional, Historical, and Comparative Views

1

Western College Expansion: Churches and Evangelization, States and Boosterism, 1818–1945

Lester F. Goodchild and David M. Wrobel

A simple question frames this book: How did American higher education begin and develop in the West? Initially, the geographical expansion of the American West led frontier settlers to create towns and schools and even more. Town boosters then sought to lure other prospective settlers to their territories, states, and counties. Their hopeful and optimistic words reflected both their sense of promise and their anxiety about the future of their hometowns and regions.[1] Seeking to educate their own children as well as Native American, Chinese, African American, and Mexican peoples in higher studies, these pioneers sometimes built academies, colleges, and nascent universities to attract others along the western trails. Unfortunately, these migrations and developments came at the expense of indigenous peoples, as the pioneers gradually moved indigenous tribes off their historic lands.

This chapter begins with an introduction and a discussion of the meaning of the West—beyond the more well-known idea of the frontier—offering an explanation of those historic educational realities from a more recent interpretive perspective on boosterism and evangelization. The second and third sections focus on the nature of boosterism whether to advance economic gains in building up the town or from religious groups to advance evangelization goals of Christianity. The fourth large section explores three major immigration movements in the 125-year development of western higher education from 1818 to 1945: (1) its developing era, 1818–1860; (2) its expansion era, 1861–1900; and (3) its service era, 1900–1945. Moving the discussion to a more contemporary focus in the fifth and sixth sections of the chapter, some comparisons of higher education with other parts of the country are broached with notes on the perils and promises in the region. A concluding coda overviews this expansionary era, describing how these beginnings led to more modern institutions of higher learning in the West, which is described more fully in succeeding chapters. This chapter lays the foundation for the first regional history of western higher education in the United States, and offers a developmental context for the demographic portrayal and public policy analyses of this region in the companion volume, Lester F. Goodchild, Richard W. Jonsen, Patty Limerick, and David A. Longanecker's *Public Policy Challenges Facing Higher Education in the American West* (2014).

Moreover, in exploring how western colleges and universities were established since so little is known about their western development, this study draws on historical geographer D. W. Meinig's ground-breaking four-volume study *The Shaping of America* (1986, 1992, 1995, 2006) and examines the flow of western migration and settlement patters of various groups.

These major migrations led to the founding of colleges, following three major geographic patterns. First, western migration accounted for the development of St. Louis, the so-called Queen City to the West. Initial schools began there as early as 1818 and provided the first educational opportunities for the new groups heading west. Missouri would be the "Gateway to the West" for three major trails (namely, the Lewis and Clark, the Oregon, California, and Mormon, as well as the Santa Fe and Old Spanish). In addition, two important shorter trails (Trail of Tears and El Camino Real de Los Tierra Adentro) advanced institutional foundings to educate new peoples there. Perhaps just as critically, the region's major rivers, such as the Mississippi, Missouri, and Columbia, provided waterways to create towns, schools, and colleges. Along these trails (shown in figures 1.1, 1.2, and 1.3), newcomers founded colleges in their towns, thus spreading higher education across the continent (Peters, 1996). Various motivations led to these developments. Among these early groups were Catholic and Protestant missionaries who sought to Christianize the native Pawnee, Shawnee, and Kansa Indian tribes, as well as some Cherokees forcibly moved from the East (Meinig, 1993, pp. 78–103; Hine and Faragher, 2000, 174–179). The initial success of these evangelization efforts led to the founding of schools (Malone and Etulain, 1989, p. 206). Although these schools were accessible to Indians, more often than not they were used for the new emigrants from the East (Elliott et al., 1976a, b; Patton, 1940, pp. 29–49, 141–191). Often neglected in historical educational research are the strong church calls for missionary work among the Indian tribes and how easterners encouraged extensive organizing and funding of these religious groups to go to the Middle West and eventually the Far West (Findlay, 2000, pp. 115–116).

Subsequently, as western populations grew (as shown by the increasing density reflected in the US Census data from 1860, 1900, and 1940 and displayed in figures 1.1, 1.2, and 1.3), they soon followed the practice of developing state templates to augment their early town building along these trails or rivers: a college, a prison, and in some locations a state capital. Such civic boosterism occurred simultaneously or shortly thereafter with these earlier movements of religious and ethnic pioneer groups to a particular place, creating public colleges (Boorstin, 1965; Potts, 1977). Robert L. Church and

Michael W. Sedlak in "The Antebellum College and Academy" in *Education in the United States: An Interpretive History* (1976, p. 140), described the process well:

> Colleges were often founded right on the frontier line—not a generation after the founding of a town or of a state, but at the same moment as the founding of the town or state. Thus in states like Kentucky, Kansas, and Minnesota, colleges were founded before the population of the state rose above the 100,000 mark—if the 18 in 10,000 figure for college trained people can be said to apply uniformly across the country, each of these states established colleges before there were 200 college-trained residents in the state.

Similarly, western migration and town boosterism along these five trails or rivers accounted for most of the initial college building in the West.

Second, a much smaller southern migration brought schools to Arkansas and Louisiana in 1834, as new settlers crossed the Mississippi River or traveled up from New Orleans, and resolved their disputes with the native Osage, Creeks, and Choctaws, as well as some of the Cherokees immigrating from the East (Meinig, 1993, pp. 78–103). The Methodists established the Centenary College of Louisiana in Shreveport in 1825, while the Presbyterians founded the University of the Ozarks in 1834. Texas and Oklahoma would later benefit from this population surge toward the West.

An interior, eastern third migration occurred from coastal Washington, Oregon, and California. Clipper ships and steam ships brought passengers to the West who sought to discover gold, buy land, and create towns in the northwestern or in the old Spanish territories, as they moved toward the Rocky Mountains (illustrated by increasing population density, according to the US Census data, figures 1.1, 1.2, and 1.3). Their efforts led to both the Jesuit founding of Santa Clara College and the Methodist founding of the University of the Pacific in 1851, as the first institutions of higher learning in California (Elliott et al., 1976b; Giacomini and McKevitt, 2000; McKevitt, 1979) and later public colleges and universities.

These three migrations were the major forces for founding colleges in the West, before the transcontinental railroads in the 1870s changed western settlement patterns and increased population movements and densities (Milner, O'Conner, and Sandweiss, 1994, pp. 213–224; Nugent, 1999, pp. 77–80). In this fashion, and not surprisingly, Euro-American westward expansion (along with interior movement from the West Coast) forged a distinctive pattern of college development (Goodchild, 1999, 2002; Powell, 2007, Chapter 5, especially pp. 190–191). Churches, ethnic groups, and states celebrated their emerging towns with a hearty religious or civic boosterism that founded colleges. For example, St. Louis University, founded by the Catholic community of that town, began higher education in 1818, followed by a state mandate leading to the creation of the public University of Missouri in 1839. Similarly, the Methodist community having come across the Oregon Trail founded Willamette College in 1842, while Oregon State

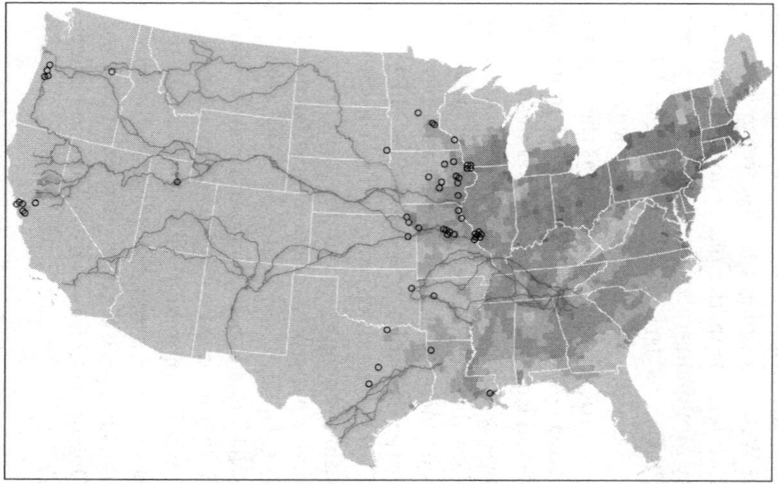

Figure 1.1 United States, Higher Education Developing Era, 1818–1860.

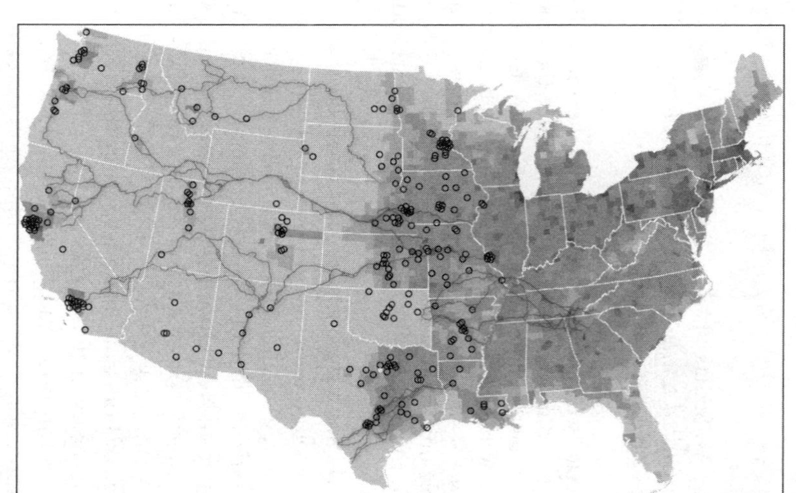

Figure 1.2 United States, Higher Education Expansion Era, 1861–1900.

Western Colleges Founded Near Wagon Trails and with Population Migrations

Including the Eastern Migration from the Pacific and the Southern Migration toward Texas and Oklahoma

Historic wagon trails

Institution founded in area

Population per square mile

0 10 20 40 80 160 320 640 1,280 2,560

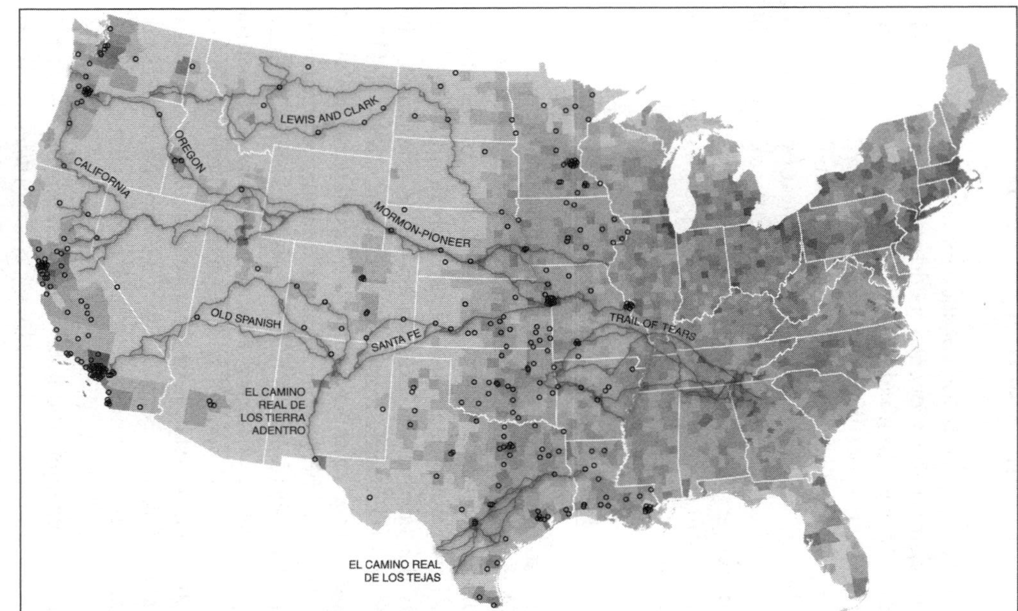

Figure 1.3 United States, Higher Education Service Era, 1901–1940.

Sources: All three maps by Archie Tse.
Data on institutions for the three maps from Lester F. Goodchild,University of Massachusetts Boston. Wagon trails data from the Bureau of Land Management and the National Parks Service. Population density from Andrew Beveridge, Queens College/Social Explorer (U.S. Census data from 1860, 1900, and 1940).

University opened in 1868. Demands for coeducation also found a home in the West, as the University of Iowa opened its doors to women in 1855 (Solomon, 1985). Many other western public institutions followed its lead. The 22 western states and territories in the continental United States thus comprise an interesting pattern of religious and civic college building development in the initial "boom" phase of western higher education during this national period (Thelin, 2004, pp. 41–42) (see the appendix for a list of the first religious and state college foundings in the 22 western states and those of Alaska and Hawaii). For our purposes, it is critical to discuss the meaning of the West at this juncture.

The Idea of the West

How did the West come to hold such importance for these educational pioneers? The place is understood to be the land located west of the Mississippi River, which now comprises some 22 states. Beginning with the Louisiana Purchase in 1803, the new western lands were eventually bounded by "the forty-ninth parallel to the north, the Mexican border to the south, the Mississippi to the east, and the Pacific to the west" (Dippie, 1991, p. 115). However, the remaining chapters of this book focus on a different idea of the West—what we have designated here as the Western Interstate Commission for Higher Education (WICHE) West. WICHE, now a 15-state compact, was created in 1951 to assist state higher education leaders and institutions through consulting, mutual policies and programs, and other activities (Abbott, 2004). Its member states are: Alaska, Arizona, California, Colorado, Hawaii, Idaho, Montana, Nevada, New Mexico, North Dakota, Oregon, South Dakota, Utah, Washington, and Wyoming. The WICHE West is thus different from the historic West.

For our purposes in this chapter, the meaning of the historic West can be better understood by using *The Oxford History of the American West*'s (Milner, O'Connor, and Sandweiss, 1994, p. 2) definition of the West as the "trans-Mississippi West," bounded by the Mississippi River to the east and the Pacific Ocean to the west. Yet the meaning of this place has always resisted easy definition. Frederick Jackson Turner's 1893 essay, "The Significance of the Frontier in American History" (reprinted in 1962), presented the West as a transitory frontier process through which Euro-American settlers brought their ideas of American civilization westward. They aggressively pursued the avowed right of manifest destiny in claiming all lands to the Pacific Ocean.

Yet, in their path stood other peoples: indigenous plains and mountain tribes, Spanish settlers and their government, and later the new republic of Mexico. Historical research in the past 30 years has shifted away from the triumphalist model of white westward expansion and toward a more critical framing of the western past. A critical figure in this transition, Patricia Nelson Limerick, in her 1987 book, *The Legacy of Conquest: The Unbroken Past of the American West*, emphasized the conquest of peoples of color and subjugation of the land. Deemphasizing the ethnocentricism and hyper-nationalism of Turner's frontier thesis (p. 21), Limerick argued that the West was better understood as a process of conquest, that was much in keeping with the practices of other empires (e.g., Great Britain) in other parts of the world. More specifically, Limerick reenvisioned "the history of the West [as] a study of a place undergoing conquest and never fully escaping its consequences" (p. 26). Exploring the continuity between the West in the nineteenth century and the region in the twentieth, she paid special attention to core tensions that illuminate both the western past and present, noting that:

> the contest for property and profit has been accompanied by a contest for cultural dominance. Conquest also involved a struggle over languages, cultures, and religions; the pursuit of legitimacy in property overlapped with the pursuit of legitimacy in way of life and point of view. (p. 27)

Soon after the publication of *The Legacy of Conquest*, Limerick took the lead in launching the New Western History movement with the mission "to widen the range and increase the vitality of the search for meaning in the western past" (Limerick, 1991b, p. 88). In this project of creating a regional history, the New Western Historians viewed: "first, the contesting groups; second, their perceptions of the land and their ambitions for it; third, the structures of the power that shape the contest" (White, 1991, p. 37; also see Limerick, 1991a, p. 77). Furthermore, responding to the power of a deeply embedded set of national stereotypes centered on the notion of a thoroughly positive frontier heritage as the wellspring of American exceptionalism, Limerick insisted that "in western American history, heroism and villainy, virtue and vice, nobility and shoddiness appear in roughly the same proportions as they appear in any other subject of human history." She added that this observation would only be "disillusioning to those who have come to depend on illusions" (Limerick, 1991a, p. 77). Others took up her project as can be seen in Robert V. Hine and John Mack Faragher's *The American West: A New Interpretive History* (2000), where the legacy of conquest stands clearly at center stage as groups contested for western lands.

This chapter explores the legacies of this western conquest. Indeed, the history of western higher education reflects how the results of this conquest led to Euro-American conquerors creating their own "western" culture in these lands. Town building led to school building that eventually led to the creation of colleges, schools of advanced learning. These initial log colleges were religious and civic backwaters, sometimes involving both conquerors and those conquered, although they were generally reserved for what would become the new majority in these western lands.

Building on Meinig's model and Limerick's definition then, we suggest that the meaning of the West be understood as the legacy of conquest, exploration, and assimilation of the western region (i.e., the geographical context of plains, mountains, coast, and islands, and their peoples) by outside persons, groups, and cultures. Once established, these new settlers promoted these lands and their opportunities. It is abundantly clear that such a legacy endures today. It is also true that new generations of peoples on this land are forging a new compromise, a new society where its multicultural fabric may enrich and enliven and enhance its developing cultures and peoples. In the process, colleges and universities, as social institutions of higher learning, have and will play an important and critical role in this development as the regional history of the West evolves.

Promoting Western Education: Claims and Concerns

After these initial college developments, parts of the Far West saw significant settlement before the Civil War—the Oregon Territory (present-day Oregon and Washington states), California, and Nevada are good examples—but the pace of settlement into the Far West as a whole quickened in the decades following the Civil War, especially with the expansion of the railroads throughout the West. Then, after a comparative lull in westward migration during the depression years of 1893–1897, the migratory streams were in full flow again by the beginning of the twentieth century, fueled by renewed economic prosperity and a second great wave of promotional activity. Indeed, it is interesting to note that the peak year for homesteading in the United States was 1913, when more land was "proven up" than in any year before or since. Nonetheless, most of the migrants moved to western cities and surrounding areas, as can be seen in figures 1.1, 1.2, and 1.3, not homesteads; by 1910, the West had four cities with populations exceeding 200,000: San Francisco (607,000), Los Angeles (319,000), Seattle (237,000), and Denver (213,000), and three more—Portland, Oakland, and Spokane—with more than 100,000 residents each. In the first 13 years of the twentieth century, the population of the West as a whole increased by two-thirds (Nugent, 1999, p. 172).

While it is impossible to establish a direct causal relationship between the magnitude of promotional efforts to prompt migration to the West and the actual demographic growth of the region, it is worth considering that from around 1870 to 1920, a mountain of promotional books, pamphlets, and posters was produced by local chambers of commerce, state immigration bureaus, land companies, and railroads to draw people to the West's "promised lands" (Wrobel, 2002). These "booster" publications shared many commonalities, among the most important of which was their tendency to present relatively sparsely settled western places as already settled regions, brimming over with the comforts and conveniences, the essential infrastructure of civilization, and even high culture that potential migrants hoped to find. In short, western promoters, often shamelessly, placed the future in the present, depicting still undeveloped, embryonic towns as places that were already thriving.

Combating a common eastern regional bias against the West in this period, a bias that rested on the notion that the nation's newest region was a cultural wasteland (a view not entirely absent among some residents of the East even today), late nineteenth-century western promoters worked hard to present their towns as aesthetically pleasing municipal havens graced with neat, tree-lined streets, which in turn were home to beautiful buildings—courthouses or state capitols, fine houses, churches, and, of course, schools.

Development of Education in the West

As a key indicator of cultural advance, education featured prominently in promotional works on the region and big claims were made by town and state boosters. The inside front covers of town and county promotional publications often featured a picture of the most impressive structure in the vicinity—the public or local school building. Similar to back East, these schools, initially usually offered through the churches, could be academies where more advanced reading in English and some Latin was taught; other subjects could have been offered, such as history or geography. Curriculum was dependent upon the teacher and the community (Cremin, 1980, pp. 388–390, 428). On the other hand, "booster colleges" developed extensively in the West and offered more formal curriculum with Latin and Greek as well as some science with the granting of a bachelor's degree (Thelin, 2011, pp. 68–70). State-level publications often featured a picture of the state university or normal school. Tremendous emphasis was placed on the quality of the educational facilities. An 1870 publication from the State of Oregon made the very broad, effusive claim that "[f]or its population, there is no state in the Union more liberally provided with educational facilities" (Board of Statistics, Immigration and Labor Exchange of Portland, Oregon, 1870, p. 55). The sentiment was echoed again and again in the 1870s and 1880s. In 1884, former Civil War correspondent and then Golden State booster Benjamin Cummings Truman confidently claimed for California that "no State in the Union spends more relatively on its common schools, or has a better educational system or more competent teachers" (Truman, 1885, p. 51).[2] Robert Strahorn, a promoter in the employ of the Union Pacific Railroad, insisted in 1889 that "no state in the Union makes a more generous provision for its public schools, or has more complete or effective system" than Oregon (1889, p. 50).[3]

Over time, the claims became still more grandiose and more specific. In 1887, the Boise City Board of Trade boldly proclaimed that "it is conceded by *all* that between the Missouri River and the Pacific Coast there is no school superior to, if any equals, our city school either in discipline, equipment or any other advantages" (emphasis added). One would, of course, have to exclude from the "all" category those promoters who made essentially the same claim for every other trans-Missouri western town. The Boise Board of Trade further noted that "citizens always say to strangers, 'You've not seen the city unless you've been to the school house.'"[4]

In 1889, T. E. Farish, Arizona's commissioner of immigration, emphasized that "no state or territory spends so much per capita in the education of its youth" (1889, p. 29). Western locales simply could not afford to be perceived as educational wastelands. Elevated claims about educational facilities were designed to serve as evidence for potential settlers that they would lose nothing in the way of cultural amenities by moving to more westerly places and that the prospects for their progeny would not be compromised.

The quality of schools continued to be a primary emphasis of the boosters' promotional pitch in the early twentieth century. A 1903 promotional publication claimed that "it is a statistical fact that Oregon stands third from the top in freedom from illiteracy." The statistics were there in the publication for all to see: with 99.58 percent of its population literate, Oregon was outpaced only by Nebraska at 99.66 percent and Iowa at 99.63 percent (Hall, 1904, p. 11). These were the percentages of children from 10 to 14 years of age who were able to read and write, perhaps not the definitive measure of a region's cultural development and the extent of its cultural amenities; but the figures must have seemed striking to some readers nonetheless.[5]

A 1909 essay on "Western Advantages and Opportunities" noted that the schools and educational facilities of the Northwest "put many of the older sections [of the country] to shame when a comparison is made" (Wilhelm, 1909, p. 71). A few years later, Wyoming's State Board of Immigration claimed that the state employed "a much larger number of teachers...in proportion to population than in most of the states." Furthermore, the reader learned, "[a] school is established wherever as many as five pupils can attend." Careful reflection on the claim might have led readers to the accurate conclusion that Wyoming needed to provide so many teachers for so few pupils, because the state had a very sparse population spread over a rather large area (Schenck, 1912).[6] Had student/faculty ratios been part of the education-related dialogue of the era, Wyoming's boosters would surely have claimed the most favorable ratios in the nation for their lightly peopled places.

Evangelization as Religious Boosterism

As the American Revolution marked a new beginning for the English colonialists, their descendants sought to create a new country west, especially after the Louisiana Purchase in 1803. Central in this dynamic were the roles played by the old and new Protestant churches. Mark Noll's *The Old Religion in a New World: The History of North American Christianity* describes the strong "white evangelical Protestants" who had become "an expanding religious force, the strongest shaper of manners and morals in the country, and a major influence on public events" (2002, p. 108). During this Federal Era, revivalism through the "Great Awakenings" would strongly influence church growth across the new country among mainline Protestant churches until 1835, when the challenges of slavery sapped much of this evangelical spirit in the East and the South from then through the Civil War. Nevertheless, the older mainline Protestant churches pushed for greater evangelization efforts on the western frontier for the next 60 years. Under this idea of evangelization as a form of religious boosterism came all types of religious activities devoted to spreading the Christian gospel of salvation through camp meetings, gaining church membership with the building of log churches, and creating institutions of higher learning to further these efforts as quickly as possible (Marty, 1986, p. 209; Finke and Stark, 1992, pp. 87–104). They were joined by more evangelical Methodist and Baptist churches, which were aggressively growing in midcentury.

Demographically, Congregationalists, Episcopalians, and Presbyterians constituted 54.7 percent of the church-going members in 1776, but by 1850 these mainline groups constituted only 19.1 percent. A dramatic religious shift was occurring in this young country as Methodists and Baptists comprised 54.7 percent by 1850. Catholics were also increasing, as they went from only 1.8 percent to a significant 13.9 percent by midcentury (Finke and Stark, 1992, pp. 54–56). Among these changes came new citizens of color as African Americans, Chinese, and Mexicans entered the western territories and states, although their numbers were relatively small at 10 percent or less; problematically, census figures grouped Mexicans with Anglo-Americans (De León, 2002, pp. 18–22). These changes among all groups signaled the success of the camp meeting revivals and preaching on the wagon trails, leading to the building of new churches in the western towns of Ohio throughout the trans-Mississippi West region.

Exploring these developments, Ferenc Morton Szasz blazed a new scholarly trail with his book *Religion in the Modern American West* (2000), as he reflected on the growth of religion through the preaching of the Christian gospel in the West from 1890 forward. Importantly, he claimed that "a religious template realigns all the traditional categories used to understand the western past: ethnic, political, economic, social, the traditional westward expansion, and the new triad of race-class-gender" (p. xii). His scholarly accomplishment offered new perspectives on how Protestantism, Catholicism, Mormonism, and Judaism provided the "ethnic glue" that fused immigrant national groups, western expansion, and new town life. Significantly, while many early nineteenth-century settlers were Protestant or Mormon—estimates of mainline Protestant members put the number at 9 million across the country, or some 18 percent of the population—many family members and relatives also considered themselves to be part of these churches in this predominantly Christian nation (Handy, 1991, pp. 8–9). Yet, by the first decade of the new century, the full extent of other religious groups, especially in the West, was clear:

> In 1909 a *World's Work* tabulation of religious statistics concluded that Catholics maintained the largest percentage of church members in sixteen states and territories, half of which lay in the West: New Mexico, 88.7 percent; Montana, 73.1 percent; Nevada, 66.7 percent; Arizona, 66.2 percent; California, 58 percent. The Catholics also held the largest proportion, although not the majority, in Washington, Wyoming, and Colorado . . . In North and South Dakota, Catholics and Lutherans were approximately equal, each larger than all other Protestant denominations combined. Only Kansas, Texas, Oklahoma, and to

some extent Nebraska boasted significant mainline Protestant numbers...San Francisco formed a Catholic-Jewish enclave, with only about 15 percent of the claiming membership in Protestant churches. (Szasz, 2000, pp. 4–5)

These western state religious demographics reflected another significant shift in Christian churches in the United States from 1890 to 1906. As Catholic immigration skyrocketed, this church became the largest, going from 12 percent to 14 percent of the population during this period, or from 7 to 14 million Catholics, slightly surpassing the Methodists numerically (Finke and Stark, 1992, pp. 112–113).

These growing Christian and Catholic church communities fostered religious education and social gospel activities through the establishment of school systems or hospitals in the developing cities. The *Denver Post* put it well in 1902: "If a new hospital is wanted or a new college is wanted, it is the church people of the locality who are called upon to meet the expense of it" (Szasz, 2000, p. 21). Importantly, the settlers first built churches in their frontier towns, which then became "the social center for rural immigrant life" (pp. 36–37), followed by other institutions. This is why the denominations often founded the first colleges in the western territories and states, as is discussed below, which were then followed by state institutions of higher learning.

These churches founded colleges to provide advanced education for the pioneer families and for new ministers. L. Glenn Tyndall's extensive essay on Methodist higher education put it accurately for the West: "the small church college has...been essentially a frontier institution" (1996, p. 456). Prominent examples include California Wesleyan College (now the University of the Pacific), which was one of the first colleges in California in 1851, and the University of Denver in 1864. The church's evangelization goal for its higher education activities resulted in some 123 educational institutions nationwide and reflected the power of its mission to see the educational value of these institutions as primary as opposed to "religious indoctrination." In this sense "United Methodists have always had a broader concept of higher education than that—blending spiritual values with a concern for the whole person, and seeing higher education from the earliest times as much more than educating clergy" (Tyndall, 1996, pp. 457, 477). This idea of evangelization was linked to improve the spiritual life of the individual, allowing for the freedom to respond to such an invitation to be Christian in everyday life. This broad evangelization spirit fostered initial western higher education.

The following Missouri Methodist Central College's statement of major purposes reflected well this mainline "pan-Protestantism" in 1891 that came to characterize western religious related higher education:

> The Christian religion we endeavor to make the basis on which our system of education rests. All that is truly noble and substantial in human character must rest on this basis: and we make constant efforts to bring our students to a

> saving knowledge of the truth as it is in Christ Jesus, that they may early in life be established upon this immovable foundation...Put your son into the care and keeping of Christian teachers, if you value his soul. (Patton, 1940, p. 56)

These college purposes were anchored to classroom teaching and campus activities seeking to develop students' Christian character and moral training, while encouraging attendance at religious activities in these schools. This Christian liberal education encouraged student mental discipline by studying the classics as was encouraged by the 1828 Yale Report (Potts, 2010), emphasized citizenship and social responsibility, and enhanced mental and physical health (Patton, 1940, pp. 58–59). Gradually, Christian colleges became more nondenominational, as religion courses and activities became more voluntary rather than mandatory. Another Christian college in North Dakota, Jamestown College, put this different ideal of evangelization over indoctrination this way in its 1937 catalogue: "No denominational doctrine is taught or required, but the religious life is guarded as life's highest aim." Most religious-related colleges thus were becoming more "nonsectarian in teaching," although open to students of all religious persuasions (pp. 76–77). As a form of religious boosterism, evangelization among mainline and newer Christian churches thus fueled the development of western towns, schools, and their colleges as the frontier became the fertile ground.

Western College Development along the Westward Trails and Rivers

The geographic patterns of migration to the West accounted for the development of its towns, schools, and colleges. With the development of western schools came the urge for more advanced education. Between 1818 and 1940, 655 colleges and universities were founded that still existed by 2010. Table 1.1 offers a state-by-state inventory of the number of higher education institutions.

Certainly, many "ghost colleges" were lost during this 120-year period (Milner, O'Conner, and Sandweiss, 1994, p. 371). We do not know how many such institutions were closed. Historian Richard Hofstadter's "Great Retrogression" thesis claimed there was a dramatic decline of the eastern and midwestern "old-time" colleges between 1800 and 1860 (Hofstadter and Metzger, 1955, pp. 209–274). His evidence for this claim was rather weak (following the 1932 Tewksbury research) and subsequently was overturned with the revisionist research from Colin Burke's *American Collegiate Populations* in 1982 (Geiger, 2000, pp. 5–6). While no substantial research study has been able to comprehensively determine how many colleges were lost in the West, an interesting 1976 national survey of former Methodist colleges and academies points perhaps to a need to reassess Hofstadter's contention (Elliott et al., 1976b, pp. 95–140). The Methodists alone closed a total of 473 institutions from 1784 to 1976—some 221 colleges and universities, 146 academies and high schools, 5 normal schools, and 101 seminaries

Table 1.1 Higher education expansion in the west, 1818–1940

	AR	AZ	CA	CO	IA	ID	KS	LA	MO	MN	MT	NE	ND	NM	NV	OK	OR	SD	TX	UT	WA	WY	Total
Developing Era																							
1818–1839	1	0	0	0	1	0	0	2	5	0	0	0	0	0	0	0	0	0	0	0	0	0	9
1840–1859	0	0	6	0	12	0	3	0	9	4	0	0	0	0	0	1	4	2	5	1	1	0	48
Expansion Era																							
1860–1879	6	0	20	6	4	0	5	2	12	13	1	5	0	0	1	1	3	1	10	2	1	0	93
1880–1899	3	5	22	4	10	4	10	5	8	8	4	10	5	6	0	8	4	7	22	7	12	1	165
Service Era																							
1900–1919	6	1	36	4	7	2	9	7	12	18	1	5	5	1	2	17	5	1	16	1	1	0	158
1920–1940	4	2	52	7	7	2	14	14	9	7	6	3	1	1	0	5	7	1	30	1	10	0	182
Total	**20**	**8**	**136**	**21**	**41**	**8**	**41**	**30**	**55**	**50**	**12**	**23**	**11**	**8**	**3**	**32**	**23**	**12**	**83**	**12**	**25**	**1**	**655**

Source: Institution founding dates are noted in Burke, J. M. (ed.). *2003 Higher Education Directory*. Fall River, VA: Higher Education Publications, 2003.

(excluding all "schools" from this compilation). Critically, 46 colleges, 55 academies and high schools, 1 normal school, and 30 seminaries—some 132 of these 473 institutions—shut their doors between 1800 and 1860—Hofstadter's era of the old-time college. What is problematic about this period is what constituted a college, an academy, or even a seminary, since all may have offered postsecondary studies. Only further study on this church's collegiate foundations and other religious groups would again support or discard Hofstadter's contention, at least in the West or elsewhere.

Returning to our analysis here, three major population movements brought about these social institutions of higher learning in the West: (1) the western trails emanating from Missouri to the Pacific Ocean; (2) the southern migration across the Mississippi moving into Arkansas and Oklahoma, as well as Louisiana and Texas; and (3) the eastern migration flowing from primarily Washington, Oregon, and California back toward the Rocky Mountains.

Let's explore each of these main trails in greater detail. First, the western migration from the Mississippi River toward the Pacific Ocean began at St. Louis and Independence, Missouri. Here, the pioneers created three crucial trails: the Lewis and Clark expedition of 1803–1806; the Oregon overland trail leading to the Pacific in 1841 and then to California in 1844; and the Santa Fe and Old Spanish Trails toward the southwest in 1821 (see figure 1.1). As these groups moved west on these trails, they established towns along the way. In the developing period of higher education from 1818 to 1859 (table 1.1), these towns sought to develop their own schools and some 57 colleges. The founding of St. Louis College in 1818 by Catholic bishop William DuBourg was the first college in the trans-Mississippi West. The Society of Jesus took over this struggling college in 1832 and received a state charter for it to become a university. It would be the oldest university west of the Mississippi (Power, 1972, p. 38). This first religious college reflected a tremendous desire on the part of easterners to bring religion to the West and its peoples. Priests of the Catholic dioceses and religious communities followed the Lewis and Clark Trail or shipped up the Mississippi River to establish Loras College, a diocesan college, in Dubuque, Iowa, in 1839, Clarke College (an all-women's institution operated by the Sisters of Charity) in the same town in 1843, and later St. Ambrose University, a diocesan seminary and college, in Davenport, Iowa, in 1882. The Jesuits later used the Oregon Trail to establish initially a mission presence and later a college, Creighton University, in Omaha, Nebraska, in 1878 (Cadigan, 2001; Garraghan, 1938, pp. 3:435–511).

Similarly, Protestant home missionary societies from various churches mobilized people and funds for western evangelization. The Methodists founded a series of colleges along and extending from the St. Louis trails. From the Lewis and Clark Trail, and later the railroads, they began seven colleges: Iowa Wesleyan College in Mount Pleasant, in 1842; Cornell College in Mount Vernon, Iowa, in 1852; Westmar College in Lemars, Iowa, in 1855; Simpson College in Indianola, Iowa, in 1860; Dakota Wesleyan University in Mitchell, South Dakota, in 1883; Rocky Mountain College in Billings,

Table 1.2 Higher education expansion on the Lewis and Clark Trail

State	Missouri	Iowa	Minnesota	South Dakota	Montana
First College Foundings	1818	1839	1851	1858	1878
1818–1839	5	1	0	0	0
1840–1859	9	12	4	2	0
1860–1879	12	4	13	1	1
1880–1899	8	10	8	7	4
1900–1919	12	7	18	1	1
1920–1940	9	7	7	1	6
Total	**55**	**41**	**50**	**12**	**12**

Source: Burke (2003).

Montana, in 1878; and Morningside College in Sioux City, Iowa, in 1889 (Elliott et al., 1976b, pp. 35–82). Travel up the Mississippi River brought about Hamline College in St. Paul, Minnesota, in 1854. Similarly, the Baptists launched the Northern Baptist Seminary in South Dakota in 1858, while the Lutherans began Augustana College in South Dakota in 1860. Further north, the Presbyterians established Jamestown College in North Dakota in 1884, as the Northern Pacific Railway reached the Dakota Territory in the late 1870s (Nugent, 1999, p. 72).

Alternatively, public higher education also arose in Missouri. The University of Missouri in Columbia was founded in 1839 (Stephens, 1962). As the first western public university, it represented the boosterism of the local state communities to establish their own state universities following the pattern in the East. Public institutions of higher learning were established at the University of Iowa in 1847, the University of Minnesota in 1851, the University of South Dakota in 1862, the University of North Dakota in 1883, the University of Idaho in 1889, and the University of Montana in 1893 (Burke, 2003). Thus the Queen City of the West became the gateway for future western exploration and avenues for migration.

As populations grew along the northwestern trails and rivers, originally explored by Lewis and Clark, and upper Mississippi, colleges were founded in Iowa in 1839, Minnesota in 1851, South Dakota in 1858, and Montana in 1878. Catholics, Lutherans, and Baptists led the way with religious colleges to further the evangelization of the Indians or the new settlers. Only in the case of Minnesota was its state university founded before religious schools. As wagon trains and river boats gave way gradually to the transcontinental railroad in the 1870s, some 64 extant colleges had been established from 1818 to 1879 that continue today (see table 1.2 and figures 1.1 and 1.2).

Already opened in the early 1840s, the Oregon Overland Trail became the main thoroughfare to Oregon and California in the West. Missionaries soon located log churches for evangelizing along the trail. With the discovery of gold in California in 1858, thousands of easterners traveled west on this trail—often religion became an important part of this growing frontier society. For example, the Methodists established Willamette College in Oregon in 1842. Its story offers an insight into the nature of conquest and religious evangelization. Two groups traversed the Oregon Trail. First, Jason Lee arrived in the Willamette Valley in Oregon and began a religious school for Indians, sponsored by the Methodists, in 1834; soon he shifted his work to educating the new settlers who needed education. In 1836, another group came across the Oregon Trail and created a settlement a few miles from Walla Walla in Washington. Marcus and Narcissa Whitman, one of the pioneer Presbyterian families, created a medical mission and school near the Cayuse Indians, who had befriended and assisted them with their new life in the Northwest. Unfortunately, they were killed by these Indians in 1847, and the expanding white community imposed itself on the Native Americans and the forces of a severe winter, sickness, Christian morality, and overcrowding led to conflict and tragedy (Meinig, 1993, p. 113; Limerick, 1987, pp. 37–41; Hine and Faragher, 2000, pp. 184–185). In 1859, a state charter was granted to Whitman Seminary, which became a four-year college in 1883. The other school begun by Jason Lee became Willamette College, when he organized a board of trustees and bylaws in 1842. The school represented Methodist missionary educational efforts. By 1875, six other colleges had crowded into the Willamette Valley with their 166 college students and 761 preparatory students (Sheldon, 1940, p. 26).

Log schools and colleges began at both ends of the Oregon Trail. The Methodists founded the University of the Pacific initially in San Jose in 1851 and later moved it to Stockton, California; Central Methodist College in Fayette, Missouri, in 1854; and Nebraska Wesleyan University in Lincoln, Nebraska, in 1887 (Elliott et al., 1976b, pp. 35–82). Perhaps, the most well-known effort occurred when the Mormons left Nauvoo, Illinois, and followed the Oregon Trail, and then branched south to enter their promised land in 1847. They quickly established the University of Utah in 1850 and then a more explicit religious school, Brigham Young University, in 1875. Since almost all of the citizens in this territory were of Mormon faith in these early decades, these schools were religious; Utah did not reach statehood until 1896. As western migration encroached further into western lands, more public colleges were founded. They typically were established later than these first religious colleges, as the foundings of the University of Washington in 1861, Oregon State University in 1868, the University of Nebraska in 1869, the University of Wyoming in 1886, and finally the University of Idaho in 1889 show (Burke, 2003). In two states in this area, however, public universities were founded first—Washington and Wyoming. As wagon trains gave way to the transcontinental railroad in the expansionary era, 17 colleges were established along the Oregon and California Trails from 1842 to 1879 (see table 1.3, excluding Missouri, which was used in table 1.2 for the Lewis and Clark Trail; see figure 1.2).

Table 1.3 Higher education expansion on the Oregon and Mormon Trails

	Oregon						Mormon
State	Missouri	Oregon	Washington	Nebraska	Wyoming	Idaho	Utah
First College Foundings	1818	1842	1859	1867	1886	1888	1850
1818–1839	5	0	0	0	0	0	0
1840–1859	9	4	1	0	0	0	1
1860–1879	12	3	1	5	0	0	2
1880–1899	8	4	12	10	1	4	7
1900–1919	12	5	1	5	0	2	1
1920–1940	9	7	10	3	0	2	1
Total	**55**	**23**	**25**	**23**	**1**	**8**	**12**

Source: Burke (2003).

Table 1.4 Higher education expansion on the Santa Fe Trail

State	Missouri	Kansas	Colorado	New Mexico
First College Foundings	1818	1858	1864	1888
1818–1839	5	0	0	0
1840–1859	9	3	0	0
1860–1879	12	5	6	0
1880–1899	8	10	4	6
1900–1919	12	9	4	1
1920–1940	9	14	7	1
Total	**55**	**41**	**21**	**8**

Source: Burke (2003).

The Santa Fe and Old Spanish Trails opened a third way for easterners to go west. William Bucknell led a group west in 1821. The Methodists, with their highly funded home missionary society, led educators by opening Baker University in Kansas in 1858, followed by the University of Denver in Colorado in 1864, and Southwestern College in Winfield, Kansas, in 1885 (Elliott et al., 1976b, pp. 35–82). State universities followed respectively with the University of Kansas, in 1861; Colorado School of Mines, in 1869; and the University of Arizona and Arizona State University, both in 1885. New Mexico State University, founded in 1888, was one of the last state universities to open along the old trails (Burke, 2003). Public universities were founded first in Arizona and New Mexico. As wagon trains gave way to the transcontinental and mainline railroads after 1870, 14 colleges

Table 1.5 Historic pathways and locations of Western College Foundations

	Eastern Migration by Ship	Five Western Trails	Rivers	Western Migration to the Pacific	Total
1818–1859	6	24	16	11	57
1860–1899	46	73	21	118	258
1900–1940	95	64	29	152	340
Total	**147**	**161**	**66**	**281**	**655**

Source: Goodchild analysis of institutional foundings and locations (zip codes) in three eras, based on geographic locations, institutional histories, and state histories, especially related to the development of the wagon trails and railroads; institution founding dates are noted in Burke (2003).

were established along the Santa Fe Trail from 1858 to 1879 (see table 1.4, excluding Missouri, which was used in table 1.2 for the Lewis and Clark Trail), while several were founded along the Old Spanish Trail in Utah or along old Southern and Gila Trails into Arizona (see figure 1.2).

The main western trails thus provided new routes to the West. Two smaller ways, the Trail of Tears and the El Camino de los Tierra Adentro Trail, augmented these main thoroughfares. Some 50,000 easterners, mostly from New England, wagoned west to Oregon from the 1840s to the opening of the transcontinental railroad in 1869, when the population reached more than 100,000 (Nugent, 1999, p. 77). Yet this growth is somewhat relative, for during the same period, the population of the state of Iowa increased to some 1.2 million, which accounted for the development of many colleges there (Hine and Faragher, 2000, p. 189). Indeed, it was not the frontier that held the real promise for both private and public higher education, but the growing density of population in the western territories, lands, and states, as they became the new fertile land of choice. As wagon trains and riverboats gradually gave way to the railroads, the 5 western trails more than any other way had contributed to the founding of 24 out of 57 collegiate and university institutions by 1860 in the developing era, another 73 out of 258 by 1900 in the expansion era, and 64 out of 340 institutions in the service era or 161 overall. Rivers also played a major role for these new colleges in towns, cities, and open lands as 16 out of 57 colleges were founded along or near them by 1860 in the developing era, another 21 out of 258 by 1900 in the expansion era, and 29 out of 340 institutions in the service era or 66 overall (see figures 1.1, 1.2, and 1.3 and table 1.5). While figures 1.1 through 1.3 show the approximate location of the colleges using their zip code locations, table 1.5 offers a more precise identification of the "pathways" (Meinig, 1993, pp. 311–334) that institutional founders used to determine and reach their college locations. Using an approximate 50-mile radius from either a trail or a river indicates a historic geographic way by which the institution became founded. This determination was more difficult in towns and states in places with overlapping major trails and rivers, such as St. Louis and Missouri with the Mississippi, Omaha and Nebraska with the Missouri, as well as Davenport and Dubuque and Iowa with the Mississippi. In these three states, designations were given to the rivers, since they were the start of the trails in some cases. Conversely, eastern migration toward the Rocky Mountains or western migration toward the Pacific, irrespective of trails or rivers, suggests alternative means of location by ship, road, or rail. In the 15 WICHE western states where these three main trails passed, religious groups had begun 9 of the first 15 colleges and universities, while the states had founded 6 of them. Thus, 60 percent came from Christian churches and their desire to evangelize and educate, while 40 percent occurred from state's obligation to further the higher education of their pioneer citizenry.

College Development and the Southern Migration

A second major way by which institutions became founded came from the southern migration across the Mississippi River toward and in Texas, as is evidenced by the population growth from the early 1800s through 1940 (see figures 1.1, 1.2, and 1.3). Groups from the South moved across the river and began colleges as early as 1825, following the last part of the historic Spanish El Camino Real de Los Tierra Adentro Trail that came up from Mexico City and the multiple trails associated with the Trail of Tears where Cherokee, Creek, Chickasaw, and others were forced from their lands west to Oklahoma after the Indian Removal Act of 1830 (Hine and Faragher, 2000, pp. 174–179, 373–379; Limerick, 1987, pp. 192–196; also see figures 1.1, 1.2, 1.3). These southern trails enabled the new settlers to establish their towns, schools, and colleges. Following the typical pattern, the Methodists launched Centenary College of Louisiana in 1825. Begun as the College of Louisiana in Jackson, north of Baton Rouge and slightly east of the Mississippi, it often had enrollments of 300 students—larger than even Harvard at this time. However, it struggled to survive in its remote wooded location. Not until the Methodists combined it with Centenary College and its newer buildings did it further expand in 1845. After the Civil War, it languished until the Methodist leaders of Shreveport moved it northwest to that city in 1908 (Lee, 2000). Following this early college founding, the Presbyterians opened the University of the Ozarks in 1834 in Arkansas. On the other hand, Tulane University in New Orleans has a much more complicated history. It began as the privately founded Medical College of Louisiana in 1834 and then became the University of Louisiana, a public university from 1847 to 1884. Later, Paul Tulane gave a million dollars to the school and made it a private institution in 1884. In Arkansas, the Methodists founded Hendrix College in Conway in 1876, while the Baptists opened Ouachita Baptist University in Arkadelphia in 1886. Finally, in 1891, the Catholics began St. Joseph Seminary College in St. Benedict, Louisiana. Moving to Texas, the Methodists established

Southwestern University at Georgetown in 1840, and the Baptists founded Baylor University at Waco in 1845 (Elliott et al., 1976b, pp. 35–82). By 1900, about nine Texas colleges were founded by immigrant groups leaving their ships at Galveston and heading toward West central Texas on the Upper Road trail that went to El Paso (see figure 1.2). Finally, the opening of state universities was begun first in Oklahoma with Northeastern State University in 1851, followed by Louisiana State University in 1860, University of Arkansas in 1871, and Texas A&M University in 1876 (Burke, 2003). Of course, these initial developments were greatly hampered and delayed by the southerners' loss during the Civil War. Between 1825 and 1860 in the developing era (see table 1.5), 3 colleges in the states of Louisiana and Texas out of 57 across the trans-Mississippi West came about through southern migration going west. In the expansion era up to 1900, 24 colleges opened in the states of Louisiana, Arkansas, Texas, and Oklahoma, while in the public service era up to 1940 significant development took place as some 84 institutions began in these states (tables 1.1 and 1.5, figures 1.1, 1.2, and 1.3, and appendix).

College Development Eastward from the Pacific

A third major immigration pathway for western college founding occurred when people came west by ship. These pioneers migrated east toward the Rocky Mountains and established colleges along the way. Clipper ships and steam ships came to Oregon, Washington, and California bringing easterners, especially with the Gold Rush of 1849 (Milner, O'Conner, and Sandweiss, 1994, pp. 208–209). Religious groups again started schools and colleges by generally traveling across country on wagon trains on the trails. As private and public institutions began on or near the western coast, or later in Alaska or Hawaii, they increasingly depended on personnel and equipment coming by sea. For example, after traveling across country on wagon trains in the 1850s to Christianize the Flathead Indians along the Oregon Trail in Oregon, Washington, Montana, and Idaho, the Italian Jesuits later took a ship from Oregon to San Francisco. They then moved to San Jose and opened Santa Clara College as the first operating postsecondary institution in California in 1851 (Garraghan, 1938, pp. 2:396–397, as cited by McKevitt, 2007, n. 12, p. 349; Garraghan, 1938, pp. 2:365–375; McKevitt, 2007, pp. 92–96). A Golden Jubilee story from the Jesuits 50 years later in 1901 related the confined and cramped aspects of these log colleges on the frontier:

> Life at a pioneer College . . . had its inconveniences with all of its romance . . . As yet only the low adobe structure was in use, every corner of which was utilized to meet the most pressing needs . . . There was no washroom, for the open space where now the interior garden is was certainly roomy and airy enough, especially on winter mornings; and a well near where the Sacred Heart Statue stands supplied the water with which the boys filled their basins,

> and after resting them on wooden framework, performed their daily ablutions. Classrooms were utilized wherever found, and one of the professors of modern languages might be constantly seated on a trunk in the northwest corner of the garden, his pupils seated on trunks around him... Frs. Masnata and Messea, although professors of classics and of the sciences, the former afterwards president of the College, had for quite a while no room, but slept wherever they could find a place, rolled up their mattress every morning, not knowing where they would unroll it at night. (Giacomini and McKevitt, 2000, p. 28)

Earlier that year, the Methodists had received a charter for California Wesleyan College, also in San Jose, which later became College of the Pacific in 1911 and subsequently moved to Stockton in 1924. They further expanded their educational efforts along the coast of Washington, as they opened the University of Puget Sound in Tacoma in 1888 (Elliott et al., 1976b, pp. 69–70). By 1868, the University of California at Berkeley provided the first public instruction of higher learning in the state (Douglass, 2000). Similar developments occurred in Washington and Oregon, where the University of Washington began in 1861 and Oregon State University in 1868 (Burke, 2003). In one state of the three coastal states, a public university opened first—in Washington. Between 1842 and 1859, 11 colleges were established among these coastal states of California, Oregon, and Washington. By 1900, 62 other colleges were founded during the expansion era. Yet the greatest growth occurred during the service era as 111 colleges and universities trained many people for jobs and professions (see table 1.1, figures 1.1, 1.2, 1.3, and appendix).

Before they entered the union, the territories of Alaska and Hawaii followed this third migration pattern, as ships brought founders of more entrepreneurial types of institutions to these remote places. The first postsecondary institution in Alaska was Sheldon Jackson College, an independent school, in 1878, while the state University of Alaska was formed in 1917. The reverse happened in Hawaii. The state University of Hawaii began in 1907, followed by a proprietary postsecondary school, Cannon's International Business College of Honolulu in 1917, and three other University of Hawaii campuses in Honolulu, Kauai, and Maui in 1920, 1926, and 1931, respectively (Burke, 2003). Statehood did not occur in these territories until 1958.

Significant college development took place through eastern migration as groups moved toward the Rocky Mountains. Between 1825 and 1860 in the developing era (see table 1.5), 6 colleges were founded in California out of 57 across the trans-Mississippi West. In the expansion era up to 1900, 46 colleges out of 258 were established in the two states of California and Washington, while in the public service era up to 1940 significant growth happened as 98 out of 340 institutions opened in Arizona, California, Idaho, Nevada, Oregon, and Washington (tables 1.1 and 1.5, figures 1.1, 1.2, 1.3, and appendix). Alaska and Hawaii contributed seven additional colleges during these three eras.

In these developments, three migration patterns led to the early collegiate foundings after 1818. Initially, many groups followed the three major wagon trails westward or traveled along rivers to create institutions of higher learning in the new towns that developed across these 22 trans-Mississippi states. Another pattern developed in the southern migration with two major trails that were formed across four states. Finally, an eastern pattern formed as groups gradually founded institutions in the three coastal states, especially after the California Gold Rush. Ultimately, three eras may thus be seen in the forming of western higher education. During the developing period from 1818 to 1859, 57 private and public institutions of higher learning began. After the Civil War, increasing migration expanded higher education opportunities, as some 258 institutions were founded between 1860 and 1900. Yet it was in the third period of their development from 1900 to 1940 when 340 institutions were established that their public service to the nation was fully demonstrated. Importantly, the wagon trails were the major means of college foundings in the first era with 24 out of 57. In the second era, greater western migration came about through the use of railroads and developing roads as 118 were founded out of 258. Nevertheless, the old wagon trails and rivers still brought about 94 collegiate foundings. Only during the public service era up to 1940 did population expansion by the railroads seem to account for most foundings with some 152 out of 340 (see table 1.5).

DIFFERENTIATING HIGHER EDUCATION IN THE WEST

With the founding of some 655 collegiate institutions in the contiguous United States by 1940s, there were considerable concerns, too, accompanying the heady claims for public education in the West. Most members of elite society continued to send their sons and daughters to prestigious universities in the East, even after very reputable institutions of higher learning, such as the University of Colorado (1861), University of Washington (1861), University of California Berkeley (1868), and Stanford University (1891) were established in the West.[7] Western editors even expressed their concern that the region could not really claim to be the cultural equal or superior of the East until its universities grew in prestige.

Perhaps these concerns are still borne out today. Nearly a century and a half after the founding of those early trans-Mississippi western state universities, it is still often the case that even the best students from the West are more likely to select the Ivy League institutions of the Northeast as their first choices than their own regional institutions. With long traditions to build on prior to the founding of the West's major institutions (Harvard was founded in 1636 and Yale in 1701), it is perhaps inevitable that the West is still playing catch-up in the higher education arena, or at least in the arena of perceptions of institutional quality.

However, one advantage that the West may have had at the dawn of the twentieth century—and we define the region broadly here, from Wisconsin or even Chicago to the West Coast (as most Americans of the time would have)—was a strong tradition of university faculty viewing themselves as public intellectuals and acting accordingly. John Dewey at the University of Chicago or Frederick Jackson Turner, Richard T. Ely, and others at the University of Wisconsin, just to name a few, were scholars who spoke to the public and viewed their institutions as centers for public concern and public policy formation. They fostered the Wisconsin idea where the university and state collaborated in doing public service and research—to assist the state's citizens. This spirit affected this "western" generation of university leaders and faculty beyond the Appalachian mountains in the Midwest and further (Thelin, 2011, pp. 137–138). Perhaps it was the comparative lack of tradition, the lack of ivy on the walls, or the Wisconsin idea that facilitated this close connection between college/university faculty and the public in the West.

Certainly, this healthy tradition continues today and is clearly evident in the proliferation of centers based at western colleges and universities and engaged in significant community outreach efforts. For example, the successful Center of the American West based at the University of Colorado is involved in outreach to the local community, in initiatives to enhance the undergraduate and graduate learning experiences at the university, and in shaping public policy through publications on such vital western topics as energy use, abandoned mines, water use, and immigration. This vital engagement with the immediate community and the larger region is also a key component of the New American University model recently developed at Arizona State University. Such community and regional engagement are defining a number of universities in the West and becoming a major part of their promotional campaigns. Whether western institutions have been and still are more engaged with their communities than is the case with other colleges and universities in other parts of the country is, of course, debatable. Nonetheless, it is certainly the case that this wise engagement with the public and beyond the bounds of traditional academic fields has been and continues to be a real strength of western higher education. These strong connections between the faculty at western colleges and universities and the broader public remain a vital foundation of western higher education and offer some hope in an era of funding difficulties.

PERILS AND PROMISES OF THE FUTURE

While the West is still the fastest-growing part of the country and no longer needs to work as hard as it did in the late nineteenth and early twentieth centuries to attract population, that very success has brought a new set of concerns in recent decades. The rapid population growth and demographic diversity of the region are placing enormous strains on the educational resources of the states. Increased state funding is vital to the expansion of the higher education infrastructure (from campus construction and maintenance), to attracting new professors, to creating language immersion, and/or postsecondary bilingual education programs for newly arrived students from non-English speaking countries.

The West's cultural diversity will over time, we believe, be its greatest strength in the educational arena. However, in the immediate present, the deeply embedded fiscal conservatism of much of the West, the reluctance of voters to support additional revenues for K-12 and higher education through increased taxes, whether in income, property, or purchasing (sales tax), has hampered the ability of western educational institutions at all levels to develop and mature at anything approximating the same pace that new suburban housing divisions were springing up in parts of the region. What is more, the cultural conservatism in parts of the West that have experienced rapid population growth and growth in cultural diversity in the late twentieth and early twenty-first centuries has proven an impediment to the development of the language-learning infrastructure necessary for success in K-12 and higher education.

In those parts of the West that have experienced particularly rapid demographic growth in the past two decades—the greater Phoenix metropolitan area and the Las Vegas Valley are two of the best known examples—new elementary, middle, and high schools have been built at an astonishing rate, and the area community colleges and universities have expanded at a similarly frenetic pace to meet the higher education needs of these enlarged populations.

To illustrate this, Clark County, Nevada, which encompasses Las Vegas, Henderson (the state's second largest city), Summerlin (its most famous master-planned community), and North Las Vegas, had 277,230 residents in 1970. A decade later, the county had 463,087 residents. In 1990 the population was up to 770,280. By 2000, it had virtually doubled again, to 1,394,440. By 2008, the Clark County population had passed the 2-million mark. In the past decade or so, the full-time equivalent (FTE) student population of the county's main university, the University of Nevada Las Vegas (UNLV), has doubled to approximately 28,000. The College of Southern Nevada (formerly the Community College of Southern Nevada) educates 70,000 students at 20 locations spread across 42,000 square miles, including 3 main campuses and 12 learning centers. And a new institution, Nevada State College, located in Henderson, opened its doors in 2002.

However, Clark County, like other fast-growing parts of the West, was hit hard by the subprime mortgage crises of the late 2000s and early 2010s, and higher education was hit particularly hard. Indeed, the entire state educational system was at the epicenter of the fallout from the crisis. As housing sales slowed and home values (which had risen at even higher percentage rates of increase than the county's population did in the early to mid-2000s) had begun to fall, revenues from the Real Estate Transfer Tax (1 percent paid by the buyer and 1 percent by the seller) have dropped precipitously. As a consequence, there has been less revenue in the state treasury for all state-run and state-assisted programs. The Nevada System of Higher Education, which had developed new programs and constructed new buildings in a dynamic fashion from the 1990s to the mid-2000s (particularly in the southern part of the state), was forced to respond creatively to significantly reduced budgets.

This is a classic example of the educational perils that can accompany demographic prosperity. In the late nineteenth and early twentieth centuries, population growth was generally considered a sign of national good health and vitality. New western towns and cities boasted of their booming populations and relied upon continued population growth for the very construction of their built environments. It was common for promotional publications to feature pictures of new school buildings and courthouses that were "projected," rather than actually in place. Rather than adopting a "build it and they will come attitude," the boosters of a century ago often had to adopt a "convince them to come and then we will be able to build" attitude. The persistence of this emphasis on "population first, infrastructure later" still seems evident in many parts of the West where the infrastructural development is barely keeping up with new population demand, let alone planning for the likely future increase in demand.

Population growth alone does not guarantee the health of higher education in the West. Larger populations necessitate growth in every area from the provision of basic utilities to the growth and development of transportation systems, health care systems, K-12 education, and higher education. However, the growth part of the equation fulfills only one part of the original booster's vision for the West. Regional boosters a century ago and today have envisioned western places that will grow in "cultural capital," as well as raw numbers, thus becoming attractive communities in which to live and work and learn. When periods of unusually high growth come to an end, it is surmised that recently arrived residents will want to remain. Economic and demographic booms have been commonplace in the history of the American West; but the busts that almost inevitably seem to follow them have been commonplace, too. Boosters from the late nineteenth and early twentieth centuries to the present have been much better at precipitating the booms than they have been at planning for the subsequent busts.

The western region needs to grow responsibly, placing as much effort into planning for its future needs in the educational area as it does into attracting new homeowners. There are encouraging signs that some western states have chosen to do this. For example, the Wyoming State Legislature recently took advantage of the new revenue streams generated by the latest mineral boom to permanently enhance the ability of the University of Wyoming to rise to regional and national prominence in a wide range of fields. The legislature in 2006 established the Excellence in Higher Education Endowment, investing $70 million to create dozens of new endowed chairs for distinguished senior faculty whose presence will attract graduate students from around the country and thus enhance the university's research profile.

Higher education remains no less vital to the region's health today than it was to the promoters a century earlier. With the 150th anniversary of the Morrill Land Grant Act of 1862—which provided support for state universities and land-grant colleges—just passed, it is important to remember that this legislative landmark was merely a beginning in laying the foundations for higher education in the West. It would take decades for these institutions to attract even 500 to 1,000 students (Johnson, 1981). Nevertheless, the growth of these universities in the twentieth century points to how regionally based initiatives might have a similarly transformative impact on western higher education today.

A CONCLUDING CODA

The first era of college building brought higher education west of the Mississippi from 1818 to 1860. These colleges and universities dramatically advanced in the second era of expansion because of new enthusiasm for practical college learning with greater state and federal funding due to the Morrill Land Grant Act of 1862 and with the expansion of the railroads in the late 1870s and thereafter (Blackmar, 1890; Mayo, 1900). Moreover, the second Morrill Land Grant Act of 1890 secured state colleges for African Americans in the South and West, including in Arkansas with the University of Arkansas at Pine Bluff, in Louisiana with Southern University at Baton Rouge, in Texas with Prairie View A&M University, and in Oklahoma with Langston University (Christy and Williamson, 1992; Williams, 1991).

Nonetheless, the development of higher education continued in the early twentieth century as newer social institutions arose to meet their higher and practical education needs of western citizens. In the final era, service to the state played a growing role as land-grant universities, state colleges, and junior colleges began to provide postsecondary education to a growing culture of aspiration (Cohen, 1998; Levine, 1986). The growth of federalism beginning in 1933 through World War II portrayed western higher education as a greater public service to and defense of the nation. Federal and state grants to universities for research, particularly at the University of California at Berkeley, Stanford University, and the University of Washington, placed these three universities well ahead of all others in the West (Gates, 1961, pp. 163–164, 175–176; Geiger, 1986, pp. 211–214, 230–233; Thelin, 2004, pp. 272–273). World War II and its defense spending led to these western universities becoming national centers for scientific research not only to enable the nation to win the war but also to provide greater opportunities for its citizens to obtain postsecondary education. Succeeding chapters in this volume describe how western higher education expanded dramatically after the war.

Overall, the health of this western region depended in no small part on the success of its systems of higher education. The claims made in the present for western higher education will become the source material for historians a century hence, when they try to make sense of the hopes and concerns of early twenty-first-century westerners. The lesson higher education leaders might take from those hopeful but anxious optimists of a century ago is that there is nothing inherently wrong in regional boosterism, but promotional efforts on behalf of western higher education are likely to secure greater dividends over the long term if campus and state higher education leaders are responsible in what they say and write. They need to plan carefully for the future, rather than proclaiming that it has already arrived; they need to identify the shortcomings in our higher education systems as well as its achievements.

In summary, western collegiate foundings reflected the various patterns of migration across the West, including Alaska and Hawaii, during the past two centuries. Early settlers and town leaders were influenced by the spirit of evangelization or civic boosterism to create institutions of higher learning. Religious institutions were generally founded first, as churches began missionary and educational activities in these new lands. Thirteen of the first 24 institutions, or 54 percent, were so sponsored. Later, as populations in various regions increased and states were formed, public colleges and universities were created. Nine of the first 24 institutions, or 38 percent, were so authorized. Finally, 2 of the first 24 institutions were launched as independent schools, or just 8 percent. During this period of settlement and institutional expansion, some 655 institutions of higher learning were founded in the American West that still exist—a sure foundation for the region to build on in the future.

Appendix

Private and Public Institutional Development of Higher Education in the Western States

The list of the first private (church-related), public, proprietary, local, or independent institutions of higher education that still exist is presented in order of founding dates and by state. They are arranged according to the western expansion from the Mississippi River, southern expansion across the Mississippi, and then from the western coasts of California, Oregon, and Washington eastward, including Alaska and Hawaii.

Western Expansion of Institutions (From the Mississippi River toward the Pacific Ocean)

1. Missouri—St. Louis University (Catholic), 1818; University of Missouri, 1839
2. Iowa—Loras College (Catholic), 1839; University of Iowa, 1847
3. Utah—University of Utah (Mormon), 1850; Brigham Young University (Mormon), 1875—statehood not reached until 1896
4. Minnesota—University of Minnesota, 1851; Hamline University (Methodist), 1854
5. Kansas—Baker University (Methodist), 1858; University of Kansas, 1861
6. South Dakota—Augustana College (Lutheran), 1860; University of South Dakota, 1862
7. Colorado—University of Denver (Methodist), 1864; Colorado School of Mines, 1869
8. Nebraska—Doane College (United Church of Christ), 1872; University of Nebraska, 1869
9. Nevada—University of Nevada, 1874; Morrison College (proprietary), 1902
10. Montana—Rocky Mountain College (Interdenominational/Presbyterian/Methodist), 1878; Montana State University, 1893/University of Montana, 1893

11. North Dakota—Jamestown College (Presbyterian), 1883—charter petition date; University of North Dakota, 1883
12. Arizona—University of Arizona, 1885/Arizona State University, 1885; Frank Lloyd Wright School of Architecture, 1932
13. Wyoming—University of Wyoming, 1886; Casper College (local), 1945
14. Idaho—Ricks College (Mormon), 1888; University of Idaho, 1889
15. New Mexico—New Mexico State University, 1888; Parks College (proprietary), 1895

SOUTHERN EXPANSION OF INSTITUTIONS (FROM THE MISSISSIPPI RIVER TOWARDS TEXAS)

16. Arkansas—University of the Ozarks (Presbyterian), 1834; University of Arkansas, 1871
17. Louisiana—Centenary College of Louisiana (Methodist), 1825; Louisiana State University, 1860
18. Texas—Southwestern University (Methodist), 1840; Texas A&M University, 1876
19. Oklahoma—Northeastern State University, 1851; St. Gregory's College (Catholic), 1875

EASTERN EXPANSION OF INSTITUTIONS (FROM THE PACIFIC OCEAN TOWARD THE ROCKY MOUNTAINS)

20. Oregon—Willamette University (Methodist), 1842; Oregon State University, 1868
21. California—Santa Clara University (Catholic), 1851; University of the Pacific (Methodist), 1851; University of California, 1868
22. Washington—University of Washington, 1861; Gonzaga University (Catholic), 1887
23. Alaska—Sheldon Jackson College (Independent), 1878; University of Alaska, 1917
24. Hawaii—University of Hawaii, 1907; Cannon's International Business College of Honolulu (proprietary), 1917

NOTES

1. A fuller discussion of the promotional efforts of western states and territories in the late nineteenth and early twentieth centuries is provided in Wrobel's book (2011) chapters 1 and 2.
2. For more on education in California boosterism see Dumke (1944, pp. 244–258).
3. It is worth noting that Strahorn was more restrained in his section on "Educational Advantages" in *Washington: A Complete and Comprehensive Description*, when he

wrote merely that "Washington Territory enjoys a good common school system, and is splendidly supplied with higher institutions of learning. An increasing interest is manifested in education, the schools are well attended, and the standard of scholarship is steadily improving" (p. 54). For Idaho he could say only that "the cause of education is keeping pace with the material development of the state," though given his optimistic account of Idaho's material development, the claim was not overly modest; see *The Resources and Attractions of Idaho Territory* (p. 117).

4. Map of "The Inter-Mountain District." This publication includes an extensive description of the Boise City Public Schools, including the claim that its high schools are superior to those in the East because they prepare students for direct entry into college without a preparatory course of study.
5. With the influx of large numbers of southern and eastern European immigrants in the late nineteenth and early twentieth centuries, literacy rates would drop. However, large numbers of unassimilated immigrants from non-English speaking countries were not moving to Iowa, where land prices were relatively high, compared with states and territories in the semiarid West where homesteading and railroad lands were more readily available. It is worth noting that Iowa at the turn of the century was one of the nation's more culturally homogenous states, and it should be remembered that this was the tail end of a period of tremendously high literacy in the United States. The state's high rate of "freedom from illiteracy" was not necessarily a measure of the extent of cultural amenities in the state or the quality of its educational system, but more likely the consequence of a mix of fortuitous circumstances. Savage (1901, p. 25) claimed that Kansas had the lowest literacy rate in the country. The reliability of the claims is less significant in the present context than the fact of the sheer frequency with which they were made. Savage's work is a mixture of boosterism, history, and reminiscence. This mixing of genres occurs occasionally; see also, for example, Meeker (1921).
6. For more on the problems of providing educational facilities in the sparsely settled High Plains, see Fite (1979, pp. 187–203), especially pp. 192–193. This problem has continued to hamper educational efforts in the High Plains to the present.
7. For more on the early history of higher education in the West, see Whitehead (1998, pp. 233–235) and Etulain (2006, pp. 273–298).

REFERENCES

Abbott, F. C. *A History of the Western Interstate Commission for Higher Education: The First Forty Years.* Boulder, CO: Western Interstate Commission for Higher Education, 2004.

Blackmar, F. W. "State Education in the Western States." In *The History of Federal and State Aid to Higher Education in the United States.* Contributions to American Educational History, no. 9. US Bureau of Education, Circular of Information, no. 1. Washington, DC: Government Printing Office, 1890.

Board of Statistics, Immigration and Labor Exchange of Portland, Oregon. *Oregon: Its Advantages as an Agricultural and Commercial State.* Portland, OR: Walling Book and Job Printers, 1870.

Boorstin, D. J. *The Americas: The National Experience.* New York: Vintage Books, 1965.

Burke, C. *American Collegiate Populations.* New York: New York University Press, 1982.

Burke, J. M. (ed.). *2003 Higher Education Directory.* Fall River, VA: Higher Education, 2003.

Cadigan, M. *Directory of Catholic Colleges and Universities*, 3rd ed. New York: Paulist Press, 2001.

Christy, R. D., and L. Williamson (eds.). *A Century of Service: Land-Grant Colleges and Universities, 1890–1990*. New Brunswick, NJ: Transaction, 1992.

Church, R. L., and M. W. Sedlak. *Education in the United States: An Interpretive History*. New York: Free Press, 1976.

Cohen, A. M. *The Shaping of American Higher Education: Emergence and Growth of the Contemporary System*. San Francisco: Jossey-Bass, 1998.

Cremin, L. A. *American Education: The National Experience, 1783–1876*. New York: Harper & Row, 1980.

De León, A. *Racial Frontiers: Africans, Chinese, and Mexicans in Western America, 1848–1890*. Histories of the American Frontier Series. Albuquerque: University of New Mexico Press, 2002.

Dippie, B. W. "American Wests: Historiographic Perspectives." In P. N. Limerick, C. A. Milner, II, and C. E. Rankin (eds.), *Trails: Toward a New Western History*. Lawrence, KS: University Press of Kansas, 1991.

Douglass, J. A. *The California Idea and American Higher Education: 1850 to the 1960 Master Plan*. Palo Alto, CA: Stanford University Press, 2000.

Dumke, G. S. "Encouragement for Education." *The Boom of the Eighties in Southern California*. San Marino, CA: Hunnington Library, 1944, pp. 244–258.

Elliott, M. T., D. Dillard, R. G. Loeffler, and K. M. Weeks. *A College-Related Church: United Methodist Perspectives*. Nashville, TN: National Commission on United Methodist Higher Education, 1976a.

Elliott, M. T., D. Dillard, R. G. Loeffler, and K. M. Weeks. *To Give the Key of Knowledge: United Methodists and Education, 1784–1976*. Nashville, TN: National Commission on United Methodist Higher Education, 1976b.

Etulain, R. W. "Culture in the Frontier West." In *Beyond the Missouri: The Story of the American West*. Albuquerque: University of New Mexico Press, 2006.

Farish, T. E. *Central and Southwestern Arizona: The Garden of America*. Phoenix, AZ: 1889.

Findlay, J. "Agency, Denominations, and the Western Colleges, 1830–1860." In R. L. Geiger (ed.), *The American College in the Nineteenth Century*. Nashville, TN: Vanderbilt University Press, 2000.

Finke, R., and R. Stark. *The Churching of America, 1776–1990: Winners and Losers in Our Religious Economy*. New Brunswick, NJ: Rutgers University Press. 1992.

Fite, G. C. "The Great Plains: Promises, Problems, and Prospects." In B. W. Blouet and F. C. Luebke (eds.), *The Great Plains: Environment and Culture*. Lincoln: University of Nebraska Press, 1979.

Furstenberg, F. "The Significance of the Trans-Appalachian Frontier in Atlantic History." *American Historical Review*, 2008, 113, 647–677.

Garraghan, S.J., G. *The Jesuits of the Middle United States*. 3 Vols. New York: American Press, 1938.

Gates, C. M. *The First Century at the University of Washington, 1861–1961*. Seattle: University of Washington Press, 1961.

Geiger, R. L. "Introduction: New Themes in the History of Nineteenth Century Colleges." In R. L. Geiger (ed.), *The American College in the Nineteenth Century*. Nashville, TN: Vanderbilt University Press, 2000.

———. *To Advance Knowledge: The Growth of American Research Universities, 1900–1940*. New York: Oxford University Press, 1986.

Giacomini Jr., G. F., and G. McKevitt, S. J. *Serving the Intellect, Touching the Heart: A Portrait of Santa Clara University, 1851–2001.* Santa Clara, CA: Santa Clara University, 2000.

Goodchild, L. F. "History of Higher Education in the United States." In James J. F. Forest and Kevin Kinser (eds.), *Higher Education in the United States: An Encyclopedia.* Denver, CO: ABC-Clio Press, 2002.

———. "Transformations of the American College Ideal: Six Historic Ways of Learning." In J. D. Toma and A. J. Kezar (eds.), *Reconceptualizing the Collegiate Ideal.* New Directions for Higher Education, no. 105. San Francisco, CA: Jossey-Bass, 1999.

Goodchild, L. F., R. W. Jonsen, P. Limerick, and D. A. Longanecker (eds.). *Public Policy Challenges Facing Higher Education in the American West.* New York, NY: Palgrave Macmillan, 2014.

Hall, R. M. *Oregon, Washington, Idaho and Their Resources: Mecca of the Homesteader and Investor: A Land of Promise and Opportunity, Where the Soil, Climate and All Conditions Are Unsurpassable for the Successful Pursuance of Varied Industry.* Portland: Passenger Department of the Oregon Railroad and Navigation and Southern Pacific, 1904.

Handy, R. T. *Undermined Establishment: Church-State Relations in America, 1880–1920.* Studies in Church and State Series. Princeton: Princeton University Press, 1991.

Hine, R. V., and J. M. Faragher. *The American West: A New Interpretive History.* Lamar Series on Western History. New Haven, CT: Yale University Press, 2000

Hofstadter, R., and W. P. Metzger. *The Development of Academic Freedom in the United States.* New York: Columbia Press, 1955.

Johnson, E. L. "Misconceptions about the Early Land-Grant Colleges." *Journal of Higher Education,* 1981, 52 (4): 333–351.

Lee, M. "A Brief History of Centenary College of Louisiana," 2000. Retrieved from www.centenary.edu/about history, on April 29, 2009.

Levine, D. O. *The American College and the Culture of Aspiration, 1915–1940.* Ithaca, NY: Cornell University Press. 1986.

Limerick, P. N. "Turnerians All: The Dream of a Helpful History in an Intelligible World." In *Something in the Soil: Legacies and Reckonings in the New West.* New York: W. W. Norton, 2000.

———. "The Unleasing of the Western Public Intellectual." In P. N. Limerick, C. A. Milner, II, and C. E. Rankin (eds.), *Trails: Toward a New Western History.* Lawrence: University Press of Kansas, 1991a.

———. "What on Earth Is the New Western History?" In P. N. Limerick, C. A. Milner, II, and C. E. Rankin (eds.), *Trails: Toward a New Western History.* Lawrence: University Press of Kansas, 1991b.

———. *The Legacy of Conquest: The Unbroken Past of the American West.* New York: W. W. Norton. 1987.

Limerick, P. N., C. A. Milner II, C. E. Rankin (eds.). *Trails: Toward a New Western History.* Lawrence: University Press of Kansas, 1991.

Malone, M. P., and R. W. Etulain. *The American West: A Twentieth-Century History.* Lincoln: University of Nebraska Press, 1989.

Marty, M. E. *Modern American Religion: The Irony of It All, 1893–1919.* Vol. 1. Chicago: University of Chicago Press, 1986.

Mayo, A. D. "The Development of the Common School in the Western United States from 1830 to 1865." *Annual Reports of the Department of the Interior,* no. 5. US Bureau of Education, Report of the Commissioner of Education. Vol. 1. Washington, DC: Government Printing Office, 1900.

McKevitt, S. J. G., *Brokers of Culture: Italian Jesuits in the American West, 1848–1919.* Palo Alto, CA: Stanford University Press, 2007.

———. *The University of Santa Clara: A History, 1851–1977.* Palo Alto, CA: Stanford University Press, 1979.

Meeker, E. *Seventy Years of Progress in Washington.* Seattle, WA: Allstrum, 1921.

Meinig, D. W. *The Shaping of America: A Geographical Perspective on America.* Vol. 4: *Global America, 1915–2000.* New Haven, CT: Yale University Press, 2006.

———. *The Shaping of America: A Geographical Perspective on America.* Vol. 3: *Transcontinental America, 1850–1915.* New Haven, CT: Yale University Press, 1998.

———. *The Shaping of America: A Geographical Perspective on America.* Vol. 2: *Continental America, 1800–1867.* New Haven, CT: Yale University Press, 1993.

———. *The Shaping of America: A Geographical Perspective on America.* Vol. 1: *Atlantic America, 1492–1800.* New Haven, CT: Yale University Press, 1986.

Milner II, C. A., C. A. O'Connor, and M. A. Sandweiss (eds.). *The Oxford History of the American West.* New York: Oxford University Press, 1994.

Noll, M. A. *The Old Religion in a New World: The History of North American Christianity.* Grand Rapids, MI: Eerdmans, 2002.

Nugent, W. *Into the West: The Story of Its People.* New York: Knopf, 1999.

Patton, L. R. *The Purposes of Church-Related Colleges: A Critical Study—A Proposed Program.* Teachers College Columbia University Contributions to Education, no. 783. New York: Teachers College, Columbia University, 1940.

Peters, A. K. *Seven Trails West.* New York: Abbeville Press, 1996.

Potts, D. B. *Liberal Education for a Land of Colleges: Yale's Reports of 1828.* Higher Education and Society series. New York: Palgrave Macmillan, 2010.

———. "'College Enthusiasm!' as Public Response: 1800–1860." *Harvard Educational Review,* 1977, 47 (1): 28–42.

Powell, D. R. "Scholar Holler: Critical Regionalism and the University." In *Critical Regionalism: Connecting Politics and Culture in the American Landscape.* Chapel Hill, NC: University of North Carolina Press, 2007.

Power, E. J. *Catholic Higher Education in America: A History.* New York: Appleton-Century-Crofts, 1972.

Savage, I. O. *A History of Republic County, Kansas.* Beloit, KS: Jones and Chubbic, 1901.

Schenck, R. W. "Map of Wyoming Resources, Showing at a Glance the Harvest of Gold which Awaits the Settler and Investor in Wyoming." Wyoming State Board of Immigration. Denver, CO: Clason Map, c1912.

Schulten, S. *The Geographic Imagination in America, 1880–1950.* Chicago: University of Chicago Press, 2001.

Sheldon, H. D. *History of University of Oregon.* Portland, OR: Binfords and Mort, 1940.

Solomon, B. M. *In the Company of Educated Women: A History of Women and Higher Education in America.* New Haven, CT: Yale University Press, 1985.

Stephens, F. F. *A History of the University of Missouri.* Columbia: University of Missouri Press, 1962.

Strahorn, R. E. *Washington: A Complete and Comprehensive Description*, 6th ed. Chicago: Rand McNally, 1893.

———. *Oregon: A Complete and Comprehensive Description of the Agricultural, Stockraising, and Mineral Resources of Oregon; Also in Regard to Its Climate, etc., Compiled from the Very Latest Reports of 1888*, 2nd ed., revised. Chicago: Rand McNally, 1889.

———. *Idaho: A Complete and Comprehensive Description: The Resources and Attractions of Idaho Territory: Facts Regarding Climate, Soil, Minerals, Agricultural and Grazing Lands, Forest, Scenery, Game and Fish, and Reliable Information on All Other Topics Applicable to the Wants of the Homeseeker, Capitalist, and Tourist.* Boise City: Idaho Legislature, 1881.

Szasz, F. M. *Religion in the Modern American West*, Modern American West Series. Tuscon: University of Arizona Press, 2000.

Tewksbury, D. G. *The Founding of American Colleges and Universities before the Civil War.* New York: Teachers College Press, 1932.

Thelin, J. R. *A History of American Higher Education*, 2nd ed. Baltimore, MD: Johns Hopkins University Press, 2011.

———. *A History of American Higher Education.* Baltimore, MD: Johns Hopkins University Press, 2004.

Truman, B. C. *Homes and Happiness in the Golden State of California: Being a Description of the Empire State of the Pacific Coast: Its Inducements to Native and Foreign-Born Emigrants; Its Productiveness of Soil and Its Productions; Its Vast Agricultural Resources; Its Healthfulness of Climate and Equability of Temperature; and Many Other Facts for the Information of the Homeseeker and Tourist*, 3rd ed. San Francisco, CA: Crocker, 1885.

Turner, F. J. *The Frontier in American History.* Foreword by R. A. Billington. New York: Holt, Rinehart, and Winston, 1962. (Originally published in 1893)

Tyndall, L. G. "Higher Education in the United Methodist Church." In T. C. Hunt and J. C. Carper (eds.), *Religious Higher Education in the United States: A Source Book.* Source Books on Education, vol. 46, Garland Reference Library of Social Science, vol. 950. New York: Garland, 1996.

White, R. "Trashing the Trails." In P. N. Limerick, C. A. Milner, II, and C. E. Rankin (eds.), *Trails: Toward a New Western History.* Lawrence: University Press of Kansas, 1991.

Whitehead, J. S. "Colleges and Universities." In H. R. Lamar (ed.), *The New Encyclopedia of the American West.* New Haven, CT: Yale University Press, 1998.

Wilhelm, H. L. "Western Advantages and Opportunities." *Coast*, 1909, 18: 69–75.

Williams, R. L. *The Origins of Federal Support for Higher Education: George W. Atherton and the Land-Grant College Movement.* University Park: Pennsylvania State University Press, 1991.

Wrobel, D. M. *Promised Lands: Promotion, Memory, and the Creation of the West.* Lawrence: University Press of Kansas, 2002.

———. *The End of American Exceptionalism: Frontier Anxiety from the Old West to the New Deal.* Lawrence: University Press of Kansas, 1993.

2

The Evolution of Institutions in the Westward Expansion

Arthur M. Cohen

The American migrants who settled in the trans-Mississippi territory in the nineteenth century established colleges much like those that had been formed in the East dating from the earliest years of the English colonies. This chapter covers the major influences on the development of institutions in the West, events and trends in the early years, the dominant institutional types and models of organization, and similarities and differences with higher education outside the region.

The main consideration regarding the westward expansion is that social institutions, government, and child-rearing practices are all transported with only minor modifications during the first generations. When the English colonists landed on the Eastern Seaboard, they brought all these social forms with them. And so did the migrants who traveled from the East Coast, establishing towns, businesses, institutions that looked much like those they left behind as they traveled west.

Thus, the major influence on early institutional development in the West was imitation. The colleges formed in the English colonies had a similarity that was repeated, as the United States expanded across the continent along the wagon trails, rivers, and eventually railroads. That initial model included the isolated campus built away from the city and its temptations; often a preparatory school as a feeder for the college, the four-year baccalaureate degree; a curriculum centering on the liberal arts; the lay governing board; and a pattern of student residence designed as much for character formation as for instruction.

The formation of new colleges as the American population expanded into the West was stimulated by several forces. First was the sheer number of people as the nation's population increased tenfold in the 80 years after the first census of 1790. Second was a steady expansion in the number of years of schooling for most of the population, which led to the establishment of preparatory schools on college campuses initially and independent high schools later to fill the gap between the elementary and college years.

Settlers brought families having all levels of education and only a general school could offer the education needed to prepare students for postsecondary subjects. Such preparatory programs had their origins with the very ideal of the liberal arts college and arose as local educational needs arose (Pfnister, 1984, pp. 148–150). Many, if not most, American colleges offered by 1870 "integral college preparation" on their campuses until the rise of accredited high schools and compulsory admissions testing (Rudolph, 1962, pp. 281–283). Boosterism was another influence as land speculators and community leaders sought status for their expanding towns. And each of the Protestant religious organizations, splintering and reforming as numerous sects took root, desired to have its own college as a way of establishing itself as a legitimate group and to perpetuate the faith by passing on its tenets through education.

As the western territories were formed, they developed higher education institutions that exhibited a few differences but a great many more similarities with those in the East. The societal context differed in several ways. Industrialization was not as prominent in the West but mining and timber harvest, extractive industries, were important influences. The populations were different in that considerably fewer people of African American descent, a significant minority in the East, were seen in the early years of the West, while those of Native American or Hispanic heritage were widespread. Asian American groups eventually became prominent but not until the latter half of the twentieth century.

Institutional Differences and Types

These patterns led to institutional differences. The western institutions were more likely to enroll both women and men. Their governance patterns were different not in kind but in magnitude as the publicly supported institution with a governing board appointed by the state's governor or legislature quickly became the dominant form. Federal land grants and state support were more prominent in their funding. Western institutions were also slower to build residence halls. For example, the first large dormitory at the University of California was opened more than 50 years after its first class was enrolled.

The federal government was considerably more prominent in affecting higher education in the West early on. Grants of federal land for higher education dated from the Northwest Ordinance of 1787, which set aside two townships of land for support of schools in each territory. When the Morrill Act was passed in 1862 awarding federal land that the states could sell to support public colleges emphasizing agriculture and the mechanical arts, the West benefited proportionately more than the East because it had a lower ratio of private institutions.

The major state universities in most of the western states became the flagship institutions and retained that prominence (see table 2.1). And

Table 2.1 WICHE state universities

State	Statehood Date	State University Established
Alaska	1959	1917
Arizona	1912	1885
California	1850	1868
Colorado	1876	1870
Hawaii	1959	1907
Idaho	1890	1889
Montana	1889	1893
Nevada	1864	1874
New Mexico	1912	1889
North Dakota	1889	1883
Oregon	1859	1868
South Dakota	1889	1862
Utah	1896	1850
Washington	1889	1861
Wyoming	1890	1886

Source: Torregrosa (1990).

access for higher percentages of young people was stimulated by the public sector in the West as community colleges became prominent, as will be noted later. Still, the colleges in the East and the Midwest were the models for those developed in the West. Through the first half of the nineteenth century, these were denominational colleges, primarily, with Princeton, Yale, and Harvard being the most prominent. In fact, the private institutions spawned most of the people who would become leaders of western institutions; six of the first nine presidents of the University of California were graduates of Yale or Harvard. By the time the western universities began to form in the latter part of the nineteenth century, the idea of public higher education had gained momentum. Accordingly, the denominational colleges in the West never gained the prominence that they had in the states east of the Mississippi, even though they were often the first institutions founded in each of the western states, as noted in the appendix in chapter 1.

The dominance of public institutions in the West has continued throughout the history of the region. By the end of the twentieth century only two western states, Hawaii and Idaho, had enrollment in private colleges one-fourth as large as that in public institutions. Public institution enrollment exceeded 80 percent in Alaska, New Mexico, and Wyoming. This is quite in contrast to the ratio for the United States as a whole where about one-fourth of the students are in the private sector.

The development of institutions for special groups of students was retarded in the West. Women's colleges and colleges for ethnic and racial minorities were slow to take hold even though in the East those types of institutions became quite prominent in the latter third of the nineteenth century. Relatively few women's colleges developed in the West because the state universities were early to admit female students. Missionary groups formed colleges in the Southeast for the recently freed slaves, but no such institutions were formed in the West, because of the paucity of African Americans. A few manual training schools for Native American populations were formed in the West, but it was not until the 1960s that higher education institutions focused on educating Native Americans in their own vernaculars. A few such institutions, modeled on community colleges, were formed and the group gained impetus after the federal Tribally Controlled College Act of 1978 provided support.

The Ivy League schools were models both for denominational colleges and state institutions because they epitomized higher learning. The Yale Report of 1828, which praised the liberal arts and sciences as necessary for the development of young people, was cited by curriculum organizers in all types of institutions for more than 50 years after its publication. Its precepts appeared almost verbatim in the 1885 University of Oregon catalogue: "The aim of college is to cultivate the mind in a general way of disciplining the faculties, to make the young strong in intellect, to give them acute, polished, well balanced minds...The mind may afterwards be applied to any subject, to the study of any profession, art, or business" (quoted in Sheldon, 1940, p. 59).

The Morrill Act was particularly important in encouraging state universities west of the Mississippi. Twenty-one institutions benefiting from Morrill funds were in the West. Conditions were placed on the use of funds derived from the federal land grants. The states were to develop institutions that would further agriculture and the mechanical arts, an intention slow to be realized. Instead, classical studies, a thread of religious orientation, and the superior professions of law and medicine guided their efforts along with basic instruction in the three Rs for students who matriculated without having had the benefits of sufficient prior schooling. The institutional leaders who were not in a hurry to organize agriculture programs were in concert with the majority of the citizenry who, although their occupations may have centered on agriculture, had little idea of how farming could be taught or improved within the confines of a college. Even so, the state colleges had to contend with legislators who argued that higher education should not ignore the precepts of religion, and compulsory chapel attendance was a feature in several western state institutions.

The state universities in the West were prominent in accrediting newly emergent secondary schools. Because of the dominance of private higher education in the East, collegiate accreditation of public secondary schools was hardly on the screen. However, in the Middle West, beginning with the University of Michigan (the model public institution), close relationships between secondary schools and state universities became a natural outgrowth after the turn of the twentieth century. Even so, there was a gap between the secondary school curriculum and the liberal arts based admissions requirement at the universities. Accordingly, remedial studies were manifest in the western public institutions until two trends had advanced: (1) a strengthening of secondary school curriculum and graduation requirements and (2) a relaxation of the university expectations that incoming students would be prepared in classical languages and the higher reaches of mathematics.

The differences between higher education in the West and in the East became less pronounced as the two sections were blended into a more homogeneous nation. By the latter part of the twentieth century it was difficult to see obvious differences, although one remained in the development and maintenance of colleges for special populations. The historically black colleges and universities were confined to the East, while colleges for Native Americans, stimulated especially by federal support, were almost exclusively in the West. A new category of so-called Hispanic-Serving Institutions (HSIs) also became a western phenomenon.

ORGANIZATION AND GOVERNANCE

Writing for the US Bureau of Education in his 1890 report on western colleges, F. W. Blackmar traced developments: "Following the example of the early colonists of the Atlantic coast, the settlers of the West have scarcely provided shelter and food for their families before plans were made for schools and education" (1890, p. 311). He wrote that it had become "settled policy" among western states to adopt a system of public education that included a university. State universities are considered "as a sacred trust, essential to the public schools and to be guarded with jealous care" (p. 285). And so it was, across the region, as most of the territories authorized or chartered their universities before being granted statehood, by as much as 25 years (Arizona, Colorado, Washington) or 50 years (Hawaii and Utah).

Nevada's first state constitution in 1864 asserted that "the legislature shall encourage by all suitable means the promotion of intellectual, literary, scientific, mining, mechanical, agricultural, and moral improvement" (Blackmar, 1890, p. 315). (Interestingly, this phrase was taken from the Morrill Act practically verbatim.) It further stipulated the "establishment of a State University, which shall embrace departments for Agriculture, Mechanical Arts, and Mining" (Hulse, 1974, p. 16). California's 1879 constitution named the university as a "public trust" that should "be perpetually continued in the form and character prescribed by the Organic Act creating the same..., subject only to such legislative control as may be necessary to insure compliance with the terms of its endowments"

(Stadtman, 1970, p. 82). Idaho, with fewer than 90,000 inhabitants spread across 83,000 square miles, established a university and two normal schools within a couple of years prior to or after being admitted to the Union. Because the territorial legislature had "located the insane asylum, the capital, and the penitentiary in the South," it set the university in the North "to appease that region" (Fisher, 1985, p. 119). Washington's legislature formed the university to "provide the inhabitants of this territory with the means of acquiring a thorough knowledge of the various branches of the literature, science and arts" (Gates, 1961, p. 14). The first legislative assembly held in Colorado in 1861 patterned a school of law after the one existing in Illinois. When the Colorado constitution was framed, a proviso was included embracing "normal, preparatory, and university departments; but no religious institution of a strictly sectarian character shall receive the aid of the State" (Blackmar, 1890, p. 311). The 1886 bill establishing the University of Wyoming at Laramie also placed the state capital at Cheyenne and was followed within a week by legislation setting the prison and the insane asylum in different towns (Veal, 1986, p. 9).

The degree of state-level control varied. Some states placed all of public education from grade one through the university under a single board. Others created individual boards for each institution. Overall, the tendency was to keep the university as a democratic institution, as for example, in the University of Colorado, which was governed by a board of regents elected by the people. In Idaho, separate boards for each institution were superseded in 1913 by a constitutional amendment providing for just one body to govern the university, public postsecondary schools, and the public school system. The University of California's 23-person board of regents included 7 state officials and 16 appointed by the governor. In Washington, the legislature appointed the nine regents, to serve in a staggered cycle of three-year terms, but until 1943 the governor had the power to dismiss them at will (Fisher, 1985, p. 114). The governor of Oregon appointed the university's nine regents for 12-year terms. The first regents in Nevada were state officials named in the constitution, but since 1888 they have been elected by popular vote. The 12 original regents of the University of the State of Deseret (Utah) were named by the legislature.

FINANCE

Federal land grants and university formation proceeded apace. Each territory received a grant of 46,000 acres for university purposes and the Morrill Act provided varying additional amounts. When statehood was achieved, the enabling act provided around 250,000 acres if the state constitution stipulated that the proceeds from the sale of such land would be used for postsecondary education. Nevada used its land grants to support the university that opened 10 years after that sparsely populated area became a state. But in most of the other states the funds were spread among the university and other educational structures, including normal schools, schools of mining, and vocational schools. Washington supported an agricultural college and three normal schools in addition to the university. The California legislature approved an agricultural, mining, and mechanical college (that did not open) in order to satisfy the provisions of the Morrill Act before it established the university.

The funding that was derived from the sale of public lands proved barely enough to get the institutions started. The interest on the fund established by the sales of land did not even cover the salary of the first presidents of the University of Washington. The state legislatures had to make direct appropriations and pass laws providing that funds from special taxes be set aside for university support. Furthermore, the contributions made by citizens in the schools' locale were important and decisions about where to locate the university were often persuaded by the amount of local funding that was promised. In Washington "the normal school at Cheney remained open most of the time only because of financial contributions by local citizens" (Fisher, 1985, p. 114). The University of Oregon was barely surviving in its early years until Henry Villard, president of the Northern Pacific Railroad, donated funds equivalent to several times the legislative appropriation.

The 46,000 acres that Congress awarded to California in 1853 yielded but $1.25 per acre, when it was sold, and the income from the university's endowment rarely covered operating expenditures. The regents had to find money from a variety of sources, such as the sale of water from university lands, land rentals, and collecting nonresident tuition fees from out-of-state students. The legislature provided a fund coming from one cent of every $100 worth of taxable property in the state, an amount that proved inadequate even when it was raised to two cents and subsequently to three cents. The university growth was so rapid that the regents continually had to go to the legislature asking for operating money and special funds for constructing buildings. By 1887, only about one-third of the total funds that had been spent by the university were derived from the income on a permanent endowment; the remainder had been appropriated by the legislature.

Other state universities similarly had to petition the legislature continually. Early on, the Colorado legislature voted a tax of one-fifth of a mill on the assessed value of all property in the state to provide a permanent funding base. In 1877, the Congress began appropriating funds annually to states that maintained agricultural experiment stations, and additional funds in 1890 came from the Second Morrill Act. That helped, but nowhere was it enough to sustain the growing higher education system. In the wealthier states, the universities could petition for funding on the basis of demonstrable need but then, as now, the funding was never enough to match university growth. The California legislature agreed to "augment the annual appropriation by 7% each year" but enrollment was increasing by 13 percent per year and costs were rising even faster (Stadtman, 1970, p. 189).

STUDENTS AND CURRICULUM

Curriculum centering on the liberal arts dominated the early universities, with mining and other occupational programs either ignored or relegated to vocational schools. The University of Oregon, founded in 1873, began as did most others with a classical curriculum. Because the pressure to establish a scientific or practical program was pointed, the university established parallel programs. But the classical curriculum remained the basis for scientific studies, and not until a student was well along in the third or fourth year did science classes enter. This then yielded a six-year program, too long for most of the students who wanted to get into the workforce as soon as possible. A letter written to an Oregon newspaper in 1882 complained: "The students of this university... must plod for four, five, or six of those years that are best as far as acquisition is concerned through the musty vaults of Greek and Roman mythology, to the utter disregard of what is going on about them" (quoted in Purdy, 2003, p. 44).

The University of Oregon eventually revised its curriculum but not until the end of the nineteenth century did the regents remove the required two years of preparatory courses. At the time the university established a shorter sequence of classes in English, literature, and grammar along with practical courses in shorthand, typing, and penmanship. The University of California curriculum was typically classical courses required for freshman and sophomores with students allowed to take electives only beginning in the junior year.

As was the case nationwide before the opening of junior colleges in the twentieth century, the universities were involved also with post-high-school basic education. The University of Nevada opened at Elko in 1875 but during the first decade of its existence its classes looked more like high school. More than one-half of Oregon's first class was precollegiate. When Washington became a state in 1889, most of its 273 university students were in preparatory courses for secondary-school-type music and art classes, which were not dropped finally until 1902. Even in California, which was early in forming junior colleges, the University of California Los Angeles had a program leading to the associate in arts degree until well into the 1940s.

Actually, California was better off than the other western states. After statehood in 1850, it grew so rapidly that by the time the University of California (UC) opened in 1868 more than half a million people were living in the state, this at a time when few western states had as many as 100,000. Furthermore, the population composition differed from other states: only 20 percent were farmers compared with 47 percent nationwide. This explains also why agriculture courses were slow to develop. The farmers and the mechanics had an outspoken support group but they were less influential than the other professionals. The prominent UC professor, Alexis Lange, mentioned: "The common schools are to prepare for life in its individual and social aspects; secondary schools and the universities are to have the same aim exactly" (Clifford, 1992, p. 45). Nonetheless, as was the case in most of higher education at the time, UC awarded the bachelor of arts degree only to graduates of its classical curriculum and awarded bachelor of philosophy or bachelor of science to graduates from its other programs. Still, "only 17 of 130 new students admitted in 1888 took the Classical course; the Colleges of Letters and Political Science and Civil Engineering each had more" (p. 47).

The University of California grew rapidly by absorbing professional schools that had been formed in the San Francisco Bay area. The first was the San Francisco medical college in 1873. The same year, the California College of Pharmacy became affiliated with the university. The dentistry department was opened in 1881, and the California Veterinary College was absorbed in 1894. These professional school affiliates stimulated early growth. "There was virtually no limit to the number of professional affiliates the University of California could accommodate. They were no drain on the University treasury; required little attention from the Regents or faculty at Berkeley, and gained the University instant identification with professional education in the state. Affiliation was attractive to the founders of professional schools because it meant that their ventures would enjoy the moral, if not financial, backing of the state" (Stadtman, 1970, p. 133).

Several gifts from wealthy people of the area not only enhanced the university but also enabled it to expand into further pursuits. Nearly $1 million coming from two bequests in the middle of the 1890s saw UC helping to organize a trade school for boys, something not within the university's primary mission, but the regents felt compelled to accept the money. Donations also included the world's largest telescope and support for studies of marine biology. "The significance of such action and generosity is found less in the monetary value of the gifts received than it is in the fact that they pushed the University into new endeavors" (Stadtman, 1970, p. 86).

Even in its first 25 years UC was among the "highest ten universities in the country ranked according to such quantitative criteria as enrollment, size of faculty, income and number of graduate students" (Stadtman, 1970, p. 85). In the last 30 years of the nineteenth century, the enrollment rose from less than 100 to more than 2,500. When Stanford University opened in 1891, it forced UC faculty and regents to realize that they were not alone in maintaining a strong university in the region. By 1915, competition from public institutions including junior colleges and state normal schools had become a factor in university planning.

The University of North Dakota was understandably slow in getting started because of the sparse population in the Dakota Territory, which included what became several states: Wyoming, Montana, North Dakota, and South Dakota. Still, prior to North Dakota's becoming a state, the University of North Dakota was approved by the territorial legislature. When it opened in the 1880s it included three programs: bachelor of arts, bachelor of science, and a three-year program leading to a teaching credential. Requirements for the BA degree looked much like those in other institutions: three years each in the classical languages, two modern foreign languages, English, and mathematics, along with studies in history, psychology, philosophy, and political science. Few electives were in the program. Students seeking the bachelor of science degree were excused from more than one year of Latin and for them Greek was not required, but they were expected to do more work in biology, astronomy, physiology, and the other sciences. The teaching program offered bookkeeping, elocution, and school law. The university modified its curriculum in the late 1890s, but it was teacher training that kept the university afloat because few farmers wanted to see their children in a classical curriculum and the growing population needed public school teachers. At the end of the 1890s, the university had around 225 students. And North Dakota did open a school of mining in 1897.

Arizona launched a college of agriculture early on, stimulated by the federal Hatch Act that was passed in the same year that the university opened; the regents wanted to qualify for federal funds that were thus made available. Fifty years before Hawaii achieved statehood, its university was set up as a college of agriculture and the mechanical arts, enabling it to qualify for federal funds under the Morrill Land Grant Acts of 1862 and 1890. It offered bachelor of science degrees in agriculture and engineering but had very few students; its first graduating class in 1912 comprised four people. The act that established the University of Colorado in 1877 specified that the institution would provide "to young men and women, on equal terms, a liberal education and a thorough knowledge of the different branches of literature, the arts, and the sciences with their various applications" (Blackmar, 1890, p. 312). Subsequently, an agricultural college and a school of mines were added as supplemental higher education institutions.

As in the East, vocational curricula were slow to reach parity with classical studies but student access was considerably more open. The University of California's Board of Regents authorized the admission of women in its second entering class. In 1870, nine women attended, representing 9 percent of the enrollment; dramatically, by 1900, 46 percent of the student body would be female (Gordon, 1990, p. 52)! When Lucy Sprague arrived as the new dean of women in 1906, there was much to be done to address women's place in California's leading institution. Struggles for equality in many areas were difficult. In fact, only with World War

I and male students' departure for war by the fall 1914 did the campus become 53 percent female. Nevertheless, equal rights and social standing still suffered for women. Resolutions would await the 1960s (pp. 70–84). From its inception, the University of Washington was "to be open to all residents" (Gates, 1961, p. 14). Everywhere, the issue of student residence on campus was controversial because of conflicting ideas of the extent to which student life should be managed by the institution, as tempered by the cost of constructing dormitories and by the proximity of alternative housing. Where the institution was established in a rural area, the necessity for on-campus residence was apparent. Where it was near a city, the case for dormitories was more difficult to make. Even in the case of California community colleges, which were organized as extensions of the public school districts, those located far from population centers constructed residence halls while they were never considered in the colleges opened in the cities. In the University of California, one-half of the students at the turn of the twentieth century commuted to campus from Oakland or San Francisco, while the others roomed in the community of Berkeley surrounding the institution. At the University of Washington, dormitories were constructed early in the twentieth century primarily because the university president wanted to attract students from parts of the state other than Seattle. At most other universities, the construction of dormitories was limited because of the paucity of available funds, and students were forced to find lodging in private homes or apartments. The first women students at the University of Washington roomed at the president's house.

Problems and opportunities in the organization of fraternities and sororities in the western institutions were similar to those in the East. Some universities went as far as the University of Michigan did in the 1870s in attempting to abolish fraternities. At the University of California, the regents determined to require freshmen to pledge that they would not join a fraternity but never went through with the threat. One reason was that the living quarters maintained by the fraternities were useful at a time when the institution had not built its own residence halls. Similarly, at the University of Washington the fraternities and sororities were providing living arrangements for a sizeable portion of the student body; early in the twentieth century as many as one-third of the student body were fraternity or sorority members.

Admissions remained restricted, although by the 1890s the legislatures in California and Washington had mandated that students graduating from high school in those states would be eligible for admission to the universities. This could not have happened if the universities had not previously begun accrediting the secondary schools even to the point of requiring them to adhere to a list of approved textbooks. Early in the twentieth century, the UC created a set of entrance requirements that included English, mathematics, science, and foreign language. By 1918, the university no longer required Latin for its matriculants. The University of Washington also was admitting graduates of high schools that it had accredited.

PRIVATE AND SPECIALIZED INSTITUTIONS

Independent institutions in the West often were established earlier than the public universities. They were founded for the same reasons as private colleges elsewhere: civic pride, especially as promoted by vigorous civic leaders; religious organizations; and the philanthropy provided by local citizens and industrialists. Seven colleges in Oregon, set up by as many different Protestant churches, opened before the state's public university. The University of California was preceded by several denominational colleges that opened in the 1850s. The Protestant sects were not alone in building colleges. Catholic colleges were among the first higher education institutions organized in California (Santa Clara University) and Washington (Gonzaga University). Other early denominational institutions include Brigham Young University, formed by the Church of Latter-Day Saints more than 20 years before Utah became a state.

Civic pride was as influential as religious expansion in establishing new colleges. The West at the turn of the twentieth century was the region with the largest percentage of its population living in or near cities. Where civic leaders had been successful in gaining the state university, as in Seattle, they were not as concerned with building new institutions. However, in cities where the state university had built elsewhere, as in Portland and in Los Angeles, new institutions were considered desirable.

The formation of Reed College in Portland in 1908 came about when a local wealthy resident and his wife left a portion of their estate to the community, and their trustees decided the city needed a college. When Reed College opened, it boasted a Harvard alumnus as president and faculty that had worked in other Eastern institutions. "Even the president's secretary was recruited from Mount Holyoke Seminary" (Purdy, 2003, p. 61). This disaffected the local citizenry just as did the college's determination to abjure intercollegiate athletics.

The Los Angeles area saw several private colleges formed from the same impulses of civic pride and religious affiliation. Pomona College, Occidental, and the University of Southern California had religious connections but these were considerably less prominent than the ecumenical attitudes that brought forth support from local boosters. A major contributor to the University of Southern California, which had been established as a Methodist institution, described his action as follows: "I donated to them property in Los Angeles which probably could bring a million dollars at the present time. The Catholic bishop sent for me and wanted to know if I left the church. I told him no, but the work that these men were doing was just as acceptable in the sight of God as the work of our church" (Serving and Wilson, p. 11, quoted in Purdy, 2003, p. 62). Early in the twentieth century, Occidental

College, whose first board comprised Presbyterian laymen and ministers, changed its status to nonsectarian. Pomona College, the first of the group eventually known as the Claremont colleges, was founded originally as a Christian college but it had become quite secularized in 1925 when it joined together with Scripps College and Claremont Graduate School as a set of institutions in a cluster.

Because these colleges were located in rapidly growing municipal areas, their student body expanded often beyond what the founders had hoped for or expected. From a small liberal arts college of just over 300 students at the beginning of the twentieth century, the University of Southern California (USC) had an enrollment of 4,600 by 1920. By the time the University of California got around to establishing a branch in Los Angeles, USC was providing professional education in medicine, law, dentistry, and education.

In the meantime, Stanford University was expanding. Because of its handsome endowment and firm determination to be a university on a Germanic research model, it organized its curriculum around professors in each of the major fields. Freshmen had a few basic required courses, and by the beginning of their second year of study, they had to choose a major and electives. It did not offer a variety of undergraduate degrees except the bachelor of arts. It quickly became the most prestigious independent university in the West and retained that position throughout the twentieth century.

Public junior colleges or later community colleges date from the formation of Joliet Junior College in Illinois at the turn of the twentieth century in 1901. But these institutions achieved the most spectacular growth in the West. Built with the same impulses that formed public universities, the community colleges expanded to provide a place in postsecondary education for the rapidly growing number of high school graduates who found it difficult to leave home and attend a university in a distant city. Civic pride led the leaders to petition for state and local support that would allow community colleges to be organized as extensions of high schools or as freestanding institutions. For the first half of the twentieth century, more than one-half of their financial support came from local taxes and one-fourth from the state. Subsequently the proportion of local support diminished and state funds increased to nearly one-half, with tuition rising toward one-fourth of the total. Immensely popular, they reached a position such that by the beginning of the twenty-first century, 8–10 percent or more of the population aged 18–44 were enrolled in community colleges in Arizona, California, New Mexico, Washington, and Wyoming (Cohen and Brawer, 2008, p. 61). Community college expansion was furthered not only by students seeking the first two years of baccalaureate studies but also by the emphasis on programs preparing students for immediate employment. As they added adult education and remedial studies, community colleges expanded even further.

Freshman and sophomore studies were provided not only through public community colleges but also through the universities that established two-year branches, such as those in New Mexico, and by universities such as California, which in 1907 began offering a junior certificate similar to the associate in arts degree at Fresno Junior College. The colleges received political support from some of the prominent university leaders, including Stanford's President Jordan and California's President Sproul, both of whom shared Chicago President Harper's belief that freshman and sophomore work should be provided by other colleges, thereby freeing universities to concentrate on upper division, graduate, and professional training, and research.

The community colleges had their greatest growth in California where in 1930 one-third of all community college students in America were enrolled. The California colleges achieved this early lead because of the state's rapid population growth and because the legislature had authorized the public school districts to receive state support for students in post-high-school courses. Furthermore, by the 1920s, California began authorizing new college districts to be organized independent of lower schools and to levy their own taxes and to issue their own bonds for capital improvement. The state never relinquished this early lead; in 2004 its full-time student equivalent enrollment was well over double that of the next largest state (Cohen and Brawer, 2008, p. 15).

Only a few of the western states—Alaska, Montana, North Dakota, and South Dakota—lagged in developing community colleges. A primary reason was that the difference in cost for a student attending the public university or the community college in those states was not great. Furthermore, the scattered population made it difficult for those states to sustain freestanding community colleges with an expectation of sufficient enrollment or support. Subsequently, community colleges throughout the nation were able to capitalize on the federal government's expanding support for vocational education. Since the institutions had occupational programs dating from the second quarter of the twentieth century, by the time the federal Vocational Education Act was passed in 1963, they were in position to receive a sizeable proportion of the funds that were provided.

Public community colleges in the 15 Western Interstate Commission for Higher Education (WICHE) states number 259 or some 25.9 percent of the 1,000 nationally. Not surprisingly, California is the regional leader with 112 institutions, followed by the state of Washington with 27, Arizona and New Mexico with 20 each, Oregon with 17, Colorado with 15, and Montana with 12. Nationally, California leads the country with its 112 community colleges, followed by Texas with 64, Illinois with 48, and New York having 35. The WICHE states' dedication to community college education is also reflected in the 2,441,421 undergraduate students enrolled in these institutions in fall 2009, comprising 34.3 percent of the 7,101,445 million students at all public community colleges nationally. Western regional state leaders in undergraduate education at these institutions are: Wyoming with 66 percent attending community colleges, California with 62 percent, New Mexico with 54 percent, Oregon with 46 percent, Washington with 42 percent, and Hawaii with 39 percent. Of course, California has the largest community college enrollment of all the WICHE states with some 1,629,609 students or 66.7 percent of the community college students in the region. Similarly, these community colleges provide initial undergraduate education for students of color. The highest minority undergraduate populations are in Hawaii with 79.4 percent, New Mexico with 55.1 percent, California with 51.5 percent, and Arizona with 34.6 percent (see table 2.2). These institutions play a vital force in how states are educating their undergraduates with a number of them maximizing their transfer mission to four-year institutions.

Table 2.2 WICHE state community colleges, undergraduate and minority enrollments in Fall 2009–2010

State	Public Community Colleges	Public Community College Enrollments	Percentage of State Institutions Undergraduate Enrollment (%)	Percentage of Community College Minority Enrollment (%)
Alaska	2	820	3	33
Arizona	20	218,072	28	34.6
California	112	1,629,609	62	51.5
Colorado	15	96,793	31	26.3
Hawaii	6	28,089	39	79.4
Idaho	3	14,678	19	9.7
Montana	12	11,032	22	22.4
Nevada	1	12,942	13	28
New Mexico	20	81,369	54	55.1
North Dakota	6	6,623	13	14.9
Oregon	17	107,241	46	16.3
South Dakota	5	6,173	12	10.9
Utah	6	47,278	21	16.8
Washington	27	157,447	42	18.5
Wyoming	7	23,255	66	9.9
Total	**259**	**2,441,421**	**30% Average**	**28.4% Average**
	25.9% of 1,000 US public community colleges	34.3% of the 7,101,445 US public higher education enrollment		

Source: US Department of Education for fall 2009 for enrollments and fall 2010–2011 for institutions as cited by Editors, "Almanac of Higher Education, 2011–12." *Chronicle of Higher Education*, 2011, 58 (1), August 26.

America's attempts to provide higher education for its indigenous population began in the colonial era on the Eastern Seaboard but achieved its greatest emphasis in the West. The colonists who founded Harvard, William and Mary, and Dartmouth were determined to, as they put it, "Christianize and civilize" the Native American peoples. These efforts were largely unsuccessful. Few Native Americans enrolled; for example, at Dartmouth, which had begun with a specific intention to bring Indians into the fold, hardly 50 students had enrolled between the institution's founding in 1769 and the end of the nineteenth century. The other colonial colleges fared even worse. Even so, the college's intentions of assimilating the Native Americans into the dominant culture and converting them to Christianity survived as a pattern for Native American education well into the twentieth century.

The early schools established especially for Native Americans were founded by missionaries and were devoted to teaching trades and the manual arts. This was similar to the programs of the colleges for African Americans that were formed by missionaries in the years following the American Civil War. Accordingly, instead of full-fledged universities or colleges with a liberal arts curriculum and graduate programs, the institutions appeared more as vocational schools. The federal government followed this pattern with heads of the Bureau of Indian Affairs commenting repeatedly on how schools for the Native Americans should center on programs enabling them to learn the trades. These impulses guided the formations of the Carlisle Indian Industrial School in Pennsylvania and similar institutes in the West.

Not until the post–World War II era did the colleges for Native Americans turn their attention to other goals. Haskell Institute in Kansas obtained federal sponsorship in the 1960s. Other colleges formed with federal support during that time included the Navajo Community College in Arizona in 1968. In 1978, the Tribally Controlled Community College Act led to the formation of more than two dozen other colleges, nearly all in the West. The emphasis on the manual arts was not lost as the colleges focused on preparing people for jobs in the local economy. In attempting to have the Native American students graduate with skills enabling them to work on the reservations or nearby communities, the colleges offered specialized training in forestry management, mining, livestock management, and other degree programs, depending on the resources of the region. The colleges also sought to preserve Native American culture by centering a significant portion of their curriculum on tribal government and language along with typical collegiate courses taught with a Native American perspective. Although not sizeable in terms of enrollments, the two-year and four-year institutions developed by and for the various tribes represented a focal point both for training and for cultural pride.

One of the most distinctive characteristics about western higher education thus has been the major presence of Native American tribal colleges in the 15 WICHE states. The American Indian Higher Education

Table 2.3 Native American tribal colleges in WICHE States, 2011

WICHE States	Native American Community Colleges, Colleges, and University	Bachelor's or Graduate Degrees Offered	Institutions Offering Degrees
Alaska	1		
Arizona	2	1 BA	Diné College
Montana	7	1 BA	Salish Kootenai College
New Mexico	3	1 BA	Institute of American Indian Arts
North Dakota	5	3 BA	Sitting Bull College Turtle Mountain Community College United Tribes Technical College
South Dakota	3	1 BA	Oglala Lakota College
		23 BA, 2 MA	Sinte Gleska University
Washington	1	1 BA	Northwest Indian College
Wyoming	1		
Total	**23 of the 37 tribal colleges or 62%**		

Source: www.aihec.org/colleges/TCUmap.cfm; www.indiancountrytodaymedianetwork.com. Retrieved on January 31, 2012.

Consortium (AIHEC) comprises 37 community colleges, four-year colleges, and one university (www.aihec.org). Twenty-three, or 62 percent of these institutions, are in WICHE states (see table 2.3). During the past 50 years, these institutions have moved from the early years of all community colleges to some nine four-year collegiate institutions, offering baccalaureate and graduate level learning—as may be seen dramatically at Sinte Gleska University in South Dakota. Begun in 1970, the university confers 25 associate degrees, 23 bachelor degrees, and 2 master of arts degrees. These developments made a major advance in 1994 when the US Congress passed the Equity in Educational Land-Grant Status Act that raised 29 of these institutions to land-grant institutional status and provided an endowment for their advancement (Reyhner and Eder, 2003; Boyer, 1997). Federal support for these institutions has remained a priority with the creation of the Office of the White House Initiative on Tribal Colleges and Universities, which began under President George W. Bush in 2002 through Executive Order 13270 and has continued under President Barack Obama.

The WICHE states also have the greatest number of HSIs in this region with some 119, or some 50 percent of the 234 such institutions nationally, according to the Hispanic Association of Colleges and Universities. Institutions with at least 25 percent Hispanic students are members (www.hacu.net/hacu/HSI_Definition.asp). Regional state leaders are California with 82 designated institutions, New Mexico with 17, and Arizona with 11 (www.hacu.net/assnfe/ CompanyDirectory.asp). Continuing immigration and growth of Latino populations in the West will see this institutional expansion continuing.

Because most of the western colleges and universities enrolled women either from the beginning or soon thereafter, single-sex institutions were not nearly as prominent as they were in the East. Although the idea of women enrolling in college had first borne fruit in the second quarter of the nineteenth century, it was slow to spread. But by the time the western colleges opened, the notion that women could be admitted was rather well established. Only a few women's seminaries or colleges were organized in the West. Mills College opened early in California's history and has remained a single-sex institution. But in the main, women's education was well served by institutions such as the University of Southern California where, early in the twentieth century, 10 percent of the students in its law school were women. There were some limitations, however, such as at Stanford, where a quota system holding women to no more than one-fourth the student body was officially established early on and remained in place until the 1930s.

Rise of Interstate Higher Education Compacts

As American higher education state systems developed, university leaders wanted better state coordination. They believed the older government idea of an agreement or compact between legislatures and governors to coordinate interstate issues offered a mechanism for improving public higher education. In 1948, the Southern Governors' Conference approved the Southern Regional Education Board (SREB) and launched it the following year to resolve higher educational matters initially and later in all levels of education. Sixteen southern states constitute this compact dealing with educational policy issues, data collection, and student access concerns (www.sreb.org pages/1068/who_we_are/html). When the former president of Mississippi State University, George D. Humphrey, became president of the University of Wyoming in 1946, he proposed this regional compact idea for the West. His initial rationale was for improving professional medical education opportunities in his state, which lacked a medical school. He wanted his state's prospective professional students to benefit from existing medical schools in Colorado and New Mexico through an agreement offering them lower out-of-state tuition. Wyoming would compensate the schools for the difference. This arrangement, discussed at the Western Governors' Conference in 1949, laid the ground work for the creation of a western higher education compact. A conference committee proposed the expansion of professional education opportunities across the western states to include not only medical education but also dentistry, public health, and veterinary medicine. In 1952, WICHE held its first meeting. By 1953, eight western states legislatures approved its funding and their participation. The commission then selected William C. Jones, dean of administration at the Oregon's flagship university in Eugene, to be executive director. By June, the office opened at the University of Oregon. Eventually, 15 states, including the new states of Hawaii and Alaska, comprised the western compact. After a year, Harold L. Enarson, a political science professor at Eugene who had been involved in city government in Philadelphia and on a major federal board in Washington, DC, took over. Holding the executive director's position from 1954 to 1960, he expanded professional education opportunities. He also gained a large Carnegie Corporation grant in 1957 to facilitate data collection and policy development in anticipation of the major increases in college attendance during the 1960s. Importantly, a distinctive WICHE program, the Student Exchange Program, was formally launched in the late 1950s, providing interstate professional education opportunities in medicine, dentistry, and veterinary medicine across 11 WICHE states. In 1955, WICHE moved to the University of Colorado, Boulder, to better position itself within the western region (Abbott, 2004, pp. 1–75; www.wiche.edu/about /background). During the next 50 years, two other regional compacts began: the New England Board of Higher Education in 1955, representing 6 states, and the Midwestern Higher Education Compact in 1991, comprising 12 states. Among them, WICHE's Student Exchange Programs for professional education remained historically distinctive, with only the New England compact offering undergraduate and graduate discounted tuition programs being similar (www. nebhe.org). WICHE played important roles improving higher education within the compact's states, as will be noted in the following subregional history chapters. In 2012, still in the Boulder area, WICHE celebrated its sixtieth anniversary of providing interstate higher education coordination and services.

Western Higher Education Innovations

Provost Sally Johnstone of Western Governors University and Technology Director J. Ritchie Boyd of Montana State University offer a valuable chapter on technology and distance education in our companion volume, L F. Goodchild, R. W. Jonsen, P. Limerick, and D. A. Longanecker (eds.), *Public Policy Challenges Facing Higher Education in the American West*, which explores three distinctive higher education innovations that occurred in the WICHE West. They are the western WICHE telecommunications cooperative, western online nonprofit universities, and the beginnings of for-profit higher education in the country. Each is discussed generally here. First, the Western Cooperative for Educational Telecommunications (WCET) was created by WICHE in 1989. Its mission was to promote technology and distance education in the West. It assisted the University of Arizona in offering Master of Library Science to other states, especially New Mexico, and the University of North Dakota in providing four master's degrees, including one in space science, to other states. It has expanded to now include most states in the country, six other countries, and major technology companies, such as Adobe (www.wcet.info).

Second, the Western Governors University (WGU) based in Salt Lake City, Regis University in Denver, Colorado, and National University in San Diego advanced nonprofit online-degree-related higher education significantly in the West. Created in 1995 by 19 western governors, WGU has expanded beyond these states to now reach across the country with an enrollment of some 30,000 students. Most importantly, this total online university offers all of its credentials as well as bachelor's, master's degrees, and a professional master's (MBA) degree through competence-based curricular designs, which enable high-quality learning assessment. It is accredited by the Northwest Commission on Colleges and Universities in its home region. Dramatically, in February, 2003, all four regional accrediting agencies for higher education approved this institution. Further, it has gained accreditation from the rigorous National Council for Accreditation of Teacher Education, nursing and health care agencies, and won several national awards for its instruction and learning strategies (www.wgu.edu/about_WGU/WGUstory). Similarly, Regis University, the Roman Catholic Jesuit university in Denver, is the premier online distance education university among the 28 Jesuit institutions and 230 Catholic colleges and universities in the country. In 1997, the Regis College of Professional Studies began offering 13 bachelor of arts and sciences, 10 master of arts and master of science degrees, and 2 professional master's degrees (MEd and MBA). Some 350 courses provide instruction to 6,000 students across the country. Each of these institutions has become a significant online provider and reflects a regional distinctive characteristic of providing online education to adults who live in rural and remote places. Finally, National University began in 1971 in San Diego and has grown to 25 campuses in California and 2 in Nevada. This institution has both campus and online degree programs at the bachelor's and master's levels, with strong concentrations in business, education, engineering, and health sciences (www.nu.edu). These three universities specialize in offering distance education in the WICHE region.

Third, the significant rise of for-profit higher education in the American West and nationally has centered on three major players: University of Phoenix begun in 1989, all online Jones International University in Denver, and DeVry University whose main office is in Illinois but has a major presence in the region. By 2005, these types of institutions awarded

15 percent of the associate degrees, 4 percent of the bachelor's degrees, 8 percent of the master's degrees, 3 percent of the doctoral degrees, and 1 percent of the professional degrees in the United States (Hentsche, Lechuga, and Tierney, 2010, p. 3). According to fall 2009 enrollments, Arizona and Colorado were the only two WICHE states where these types of student enrollments went above 1 percent. In Arizona, 29 for-profit four-year institutions enrolled 457,515 students—with a majority coming from the University of Phoenix and its 86 campuses in 15 WICHE states alone—while the 14 for-profit two-year institutions attracted 12,267 students. Together they comprised 56 percent of the state's postsecondary enrollment of 828,631. Similarly, Jones International University in Colorado—with its bachelor's, master's, and doctoral online degrees—and 24 other four-year for-profits as well as 18 two-year for-profits had the second highest for-profit enrollment in the WICHE West of 64,372 students or 18 percent of the state's 352,034 total postsecondary enrollment. Nevertheless, California attracted a significant for-profit higher education presence, even though this type of education represented only 0.06 percent, or 174,491, of the state's some 2.7 million students. Here, University of Phoenix has 36 campuses, while DeVry University had 16 (www.devry.edu; www.jinu.edu; www.phoenix.edu). Sometimes, traditional universities also partner with for-profits to promote student access to higher-degree-related education as may be seen in Oregon State University's partnership with the international university, Navitas, or as in the University of California Irvine's "pathway program" with Capella University (Editors, "The States," *Chronicle of Higher Education*, Almanac Issue, 2011–2012, pp. 59–90; Hentsche, Lechuga, and Tierney, 2010, p. 37; Tierney and Hentschke, 2007).

LATTER-DAY EVOLUTION

Throughout the twentieth century, institutions in the West steadily lost their traditional distinctive characteristics, although they encouraged new distance education innovations. The public community colleges that experienced their earliest growth in the West spread into every state. Men and women attending college together became a nationwide phenomenon. Expanded research capability grew in the flagship public universities everywhere.

The organization and governance of higher education systems continued evolving, with universities and colleges attempting to maintain their autonomy in the face of trends toward statewide systems. The states that had lagged in establishing an extensive public sector, especially those in the Northeast, hastened to catch up. In the quarter century after World War II, the ratio of public to private institutions nationwide changed from 35 percent to 44 percent of the total and the public sector enrollment grew from 49 percent to 79 percent.

One of the more dramatic changes in higher education organization was seen as institutions maintained a steady drift toward offering higher-level degrees and a more comprehensive curriculum. In California, the state's six normal schools became teachers' colleges in the 1920s, and in the 1930s they dropped the word "teachers" from their titles and became state colleges. In the 1960s they added the word "university" to mark the comprehensive degree programs they were now offering. By the mid-1970s the group, now expanded to include 18 campuses, was organized into a statewide California State College and University System. Early in the twenty-first century, the system gained legislative authorization to offer the doctor of education degree.

The community colleges that had begun as institutions organized under the auspices of lower school districts in California, Florida, Kansas, and many other states drifted toward organization and finance within statewide systems. However, they maintained their greatest growth in the West. By the end of the twentieth century more than one-half of the postsecondary students in Arizona, California, Washington, and Wyoming were in community colleges.

The liberal arts colleges and the private junior colleges fared less well. Most liberal arts colleges throughout the country had difficulty maintaining themselves without expanding into the area of comprehensive or occupational programs. Many merged or otherwise left the category. More than 150 liberal arts colleges were modified during the 1970s alone. The private junior colleges, never strong in the West, had nearly disappeared by the end of the twentieth century.

The trend toward consolidating higher education governance under single boards accelerated after the passage of the Higher Education Act in 1965. State-level higher education coordinating boards became the norm. In 1967 California and Washington established state boards for community colleges. In the 1990s the trend toward centralization of governance found several Western states involved. Montana merged governance of their two-year and four-year colleges, and other centralizing reforms took place in North Dakota, Utah, and Colorado. On the other hand, Oregon began permitting higher education institutions to make purchases, enter into contracts, and manage their personnel outside the state government's central agencies. Hawaii similarly allowed its institutions to perform several functions that had been carried out by state bureaus (Cohen, 1998, p. 376).

The rivalry between the older state universities and new institutions that aspired to reach university status continued. These rivalries were most pronounced in Arizona, California, Montana, New Mexico, Oregon, and Washington. The universities that had been established originally as agricultural or teacher training schools aspired to full-research university status, including a range of professional schools. In 1960, the University of Washington and Washington State University reached a settlement, placing medicine, liberal arts and sciences, and commerce within the former, and veterinary medicine and technical training for agriculture and home management with the latter. But every time a new type of program appeared important to add, the rival universities each sought to be its home.

Rivalries in California were brought somewhat under control with the enactment of the Master Plan for Higher Education in 1960. Designed by President Clark Kerr, three cooperating systems of higher education arose in California to accommodate the massive influx of college students in the 1960s. The University of California was to do the doctoral training and to maintain schools for medicine and other venerable professions as well as admit the top 12.5 percent of the state's high school graduates to the undergraduate programs on its campuses. Teacher training and various occupation programs leading to the baccalaureate were to be emphasized in the California State College (CSU) system, where the top 33 percent of high school graduates were able to begin their four-year college education. All other secondary school graduates were able to attend the community colleges that were restricted to offering the associate degree as their highest degree and to emphasize prebaccalaureate and occupational training—with then the ability to transfer to the CSUs or other four-year institutions to complete their degrees. The plan offered a new governance model for higher education in the nation—one envied but not replicated elsewhere (Cohen and Kisker, 2010, p. 252; Douglass, 2000, pp. 265–298; see also Callan, this volume, p. 233).

Student access, given impetus everywhere by the Servicemen's Readjustment Act of 1944, was especially marked in the western states where population expansion was the greatest. Two million two hundred thousand G.I.s went to college or further education after the war, some 37 percent of all enlisted military persons. One interpretation contended that 20 percent of them could not have gone to college without the bill, while 80 percent of the others benefited from financial assistance (Olson, 1973, p. 609). Their overall effect on higher education regarding its structure and systems was considered more "marginal." They showed that adults could be good college students, and married students could function extremely well in their academic work, compared to the single college student. Most importantly, as their numbers swelled on college campuses, institutions accommodated them: larger campuses were possible, especially when graduate students carried a significant portion of the teaching load compared to before. In short, the G.I.s opened up higher education across the country, especially in the West, for the major expansion that would occur in the 1960s. Admittedly, students of color did not benefit proportionally. Critically, even Historically Black Colleges and Universities (HBCUs) were forced to merge or close when funding did not enable them to accommodate the growing numbers of African Americans who sought higher education there or when these students went to other colleges and universities after *Brown v. Board of Education* made attendance elsewhere more possible (Redd, 1998, pp. 35–36). Indeed, the student activism of the 1960s had its first major flowering in the University of California at Berkeley. It spread later to other areas as student protests against the Vietnam War and other social phenomena became widespread. Through these demands for access by historically more underrepresented students, campuses opened to them finally.

The University of California and the University of Washington (UW) were particularly affected by challenges to academic freedom. The faculty at the two institutions began with different modes of organization. Those in the University of California had a sense of coherence early on as the first meeting of the academic senate was held the year after UC was created. Those at the University of Washington were somewhat more under administration control, and well into the twentieth century, a high percentage of UW faculty employed were former students at the same institution. Those historical differences may have had an effect on the way the academic freedom cases developed at both institutions in the 1940s and the 1950s.

In 1946, some Washington legislators accused the UW faculty of having "probably not less than 150...who are communists or sympathizers with the Communist Party" (Gates, 1961, p. 197). The regents agreed that any such faculty member should be dismissed. A legislative committee found that eight professors were either members or previous members and the UW president brought charges against six of them. Eventually three were dismissed.

The regents of the University of California in 1946 similarly resolved that "any member of the faculty or student body seeking to alter our American government...on proof of such charge be subject to dismissal" (Stadtman, 1970, p. 321). The academic senate resisted when the regents determined in 1949 that all faculty members must sign an oath of loyalty and subsequently acted vigorously to defend the 31 faculty members who were dismissed for refusing to sign the oath.

Universities in the West have done well in maintaining funded research. The University of California research enterprise was given major impetus during World War II with federal contracts and grants for war-related research. Subsequently, when the Department of Defense began funding research on electronics, Stanford's programs grew. At the end of the century, when research expenditures were compared on a per capita basis, seven western states exceeded the national average. Five of the top eight American institutions ranked in terms of research expenditures were in the West: University of California Los Angeles; University of Washington; University of California, San Francisco; University of California, San Diego; and Stanford University. Internationally, various recent rankings also point to the strength of some 7–13 universities in the WICHE states. While being cautious about the sophistication or accuracy of any public ranking system, three international rankings—the Academic Ranking of World Universities, QS World University Rankings (and US News and World Report's World's Best Universities, which uses the same database), and the *Times* Higher Education World University

Table 2.4 WICHE research universities and the 2011 international rankings of the world's top 100 research universities

State	Institution	Rankings (1): Academic Ranking of World Universities	Rankings (2): QS World University Ranking and US News and World Report's World's Best Universities Ranking[a]	Rankings (3): Times Higher Education World University Ranking
CA	UC Berkeley	2	21	4
CA	Stanford U	3	11	5
CA	California Institute of Technology	6	12	10
CA	University of California	13	34	12
CA	University of California San Diego	14	77	30
WA	University of Washington	16	56	26
CA	University of California San Francisco	18		34
CA	University of California Santa Barbara	32		51–60
CO	University of Colorado	32		
CA	University of California Davis	46		38
CA	University of California Irvine	46		
AZ	University of Arizona	78		
AZ	Arizona State University	81		
UT	University of Utah	82		

Note: [a] US News and World Report's "World's Best Universities" uses the same data as QS World University Rankings.

Sources: www.arwu.org; http://www.topuniversities.com/university-rankings/world-university-rankings; www.timeshighereducation.co.uk/world-university-rankings; www.usnews.com/education/worlds-best-universities-rankings/top-400-universities-in-the-world?page=4. Retrieved on January 31, 2012.

Rankings—do seem to be indicators of research university stature globally. Generally, agreement of these rankings points to six research university leaders among the WICHE states: Stanford University; California Institute of Technology, University of California Berkeley, University of California Los Angeles, University of Washington, and University of California San Diego (see table 2.4). These institutional representatives reflect the strong university missions for research and professional education in the WICHE states, although the recent challenges to institutional operational funding provided by the states was dramatically exacerbated by the Great Recession.

Effects of the Great Recession

Nevertheless, the research funding and consequently the international recognition of these major research universities are threatened by the dramatic retrenchment of state funding for higher education in the WICHE West. During the Great Recession, only three western states, Alaska, North Dakota, and Wyoming, advanced their systems through increased state funding by 12.71 percent, 18.54 percent, and 15.46 percent respectively between FY2008 and FY2011. Contrarily, 12 of the 15 states pushed through dramatic declines in state funding during this period. The four top states to withdraw drastically from their annual commitments to higher education were:

1. Arizona at –28.27 percent from $1.3 billion to $1.02 billion or a $289.8 million decline;
2. Oregon at –25.71 percent from $725 million to $577 million or a $148 million decline;
3. New Mexico at –21 percent from $1.05 billion to $874 million or a $183.7 million decline; and
4. Idaho at –19.60 percent from $410 million to $343 million or a $67 million decline.

The average decline among these 12 retrenching WICHE states was a significant –14.4 percent—interestingly California retrenched less than one-half of 1 percent or some $56 million. However, the loss of operating funds at these institutions were offset somewhat by the dramatic rises in student tuition and fees, faculty and staff salary adjustments, personnel layoffs, program discontinuations, and the like.

Nationally, these western states were in the second hardest hit region in the country. Compared to other regions, they fared better than the states in the SREB region that experienced a dramatic and perhaps historic retreat from higher education funding. There, 10 of its 16 states retrenched at an average of –21.2 percent. Huge annual declines occurred in South Carolina with a –48.12 percent from $1.2 billion to $817 million, Louisiana with a –40.75 percent from $1.7 billion to $1.2 billion, and Alabama with a –34.8 percent from $1.9 billion to $1.5 billion, representing major operational funding retreats over these three fiscal years. Better support and still critical declines happened in the Midwest and in New England: 7 of 12 states in the Midwestern Higher Education Compact area fell off –11.6 percent, while 3 of the 6 states averaged –11.7 percent in the New England Board of Higher Education region. (See Zumeta and Kinne, 2001, who use data from the State Higher Education Executive Officers' January 2011, "Finance Survey.") More detailed western state analysis is conducted in the following chapter histories of the Middle Border, Southwest, Pacific West, and California as well as in our companion book, L. F. Goodchild, R. W. Jonsen, P. Limerick, and D. A. Longanecker (eds.),

Public Policy Challenges Facing Higher Education in the American West (2014).

Overall, then, the institutions in the West have taken their place in the fabric of American higher education. The eastern colleges and universities provided a template for their formation but western regional characteristics led to modifications and advances. Its distinctiveness can be seen in four areas. First, concerning traditional higher education, the 1960 Master Plan for California proposed the first three-tiered system of higher learning that provided community colleges, regional state universities, and research universities a new system model for state higher education. Its successes and failures led the western region as the largest provider of state higher education institutions and student populations served. Second, the broad western expanses required greater access for all persons through mission-driven institutions. These western universities were leaders in admitting women and the educationally disadvantaged and in types of democratic governance in the public sector. Contentions that higher education unfairly advantages students from high-income families have less credibility when they are addressed to the West, where concepts of equal opportunity have been more pronounced and where the public community college, especially in California, and relatively low-cost public universities first became widespread. Third, the expansions of tribal colleges and HSIs have brought greater distinctive vitality to the WICHE region, as these postsecondary institutions have responded to the postsecondary educational needs of these groups. Fourth, significant institutional distance education developments have led to new regional and national online universities to serve primarily adults in all degree levels in the form of nonprofit public, private, and for-profit corporations. Above all, these traditional, minority-serving, and innovative higher education institutions in the West have epitomized the concept of open access for the entire population. With the beginning of the twenty-first century, however, the Great Recession threatened these traditional and distinctive developments, as 12 of the 15 western states retrenched significantly their levels of operational funding for these colleges and universities. Similar to the other regions of the country, the future role of public higher education in the West has lessened and been threatened, awaiting the revival of state economies and the return of broader public support.

References

Abbott, F. C. *A History of the Western Interstate Commission for Higher Education: The First Forty Years.* Boulder, CO: Western Interstate Commission for Higher Education, 2004.

Blackmar, F. W. "The History of Federal and State Aid to Higher Education in the United States." *U.S. Bureau of Education Circular of Information,* no. 1. Washington, DC: Government Printing Office, 1890.

Boyer, P. *Native American Colleges: Progress and Prospects.* Princeton: Carnegie Foundation for the Advancement of Teaching, 1997.

Clifford, G. J. "No Shade in the Golden State: School and University in Nineteenth-Century California." Buffalo: SUNY Buffalo, 1992.

Cohen, A. M. *The Shaping of American Higher Education: Emergence and Growth of the Contemporary System.* San Francisco, CA: Jossey-Bass, 1998.

Cohen, A. M., and C. B. Kisker. *The Shaping of American Higher Education: Emergence and Growth of the Contemporary System*, 2nd ed. San Francisco, CA: Jossey-Bass, 2010.

Cohen, A. M., and F. B. Brawer. *The American Community College*, 5th ed. San Francisco, CA: Jossey-Bass, 2008.

Douglass, J. A. *The California Idea and American Higher Education: 1850 to 1960 Master Plan.* Palo Alto, CA: Stanford University Press, 2000.

Fisher, L. A. "The Role of Politics in the Organization and Development of Public Higher Education in Idaho and Washington." *History of Higher Education Annual*, 1985, 5: 111–132.

Gates, C. *The First Century at the University of Washington.* Seattle: University of Washington Press, 1961.

Goodchild, L. F., R. W. Jonsen, P. Limerick, and D. A. Longanecker (eds.). *Public Policy Challenges Facing Higher Education in the American West.* Higher Education and Society series. New York, NY: Palgrave Macmillan, 2014.

Gordon, L. D. *Gender and Higher Education in the Progressive Era.* New Haven, CT: Yale University Press, 1990.

Hentschke, G. C., V. M. Lechuga, and W. G. Tierney. "For-Profit Colleges and Universities in a Knowledge Economy." In G. C. Hentschke, V. M. Lechuga, and W. G. Tierney (eds.), *For-Profit Colleges and Universities: Their Markets, Regulation, Performance, and Place in Higher Education.* Sterling, VA: Stylus, 2010, pp. 1–22.

Hulse, J. W. *The University of Nevada: A Centennial History.* Reno: University of Nevada Press, 1974.

Olson, K. W. "The G. I. Bill and Higher Education: Success and Surprise." *American Quarterly*, 1973, 25 (5): 596–610.

Pfnister, A. O. "The Roles of Liberal Arts College: A Historical Overview of the Debates." *Journal of Higher Education*, 1984, 55 (2): 14–170.

Purdy, W. C. "The History of Higher Education in the Western States." Master of Arts in Education thesis. University of California Los Angeles, 2003.

Redd, K. E. "Historically Black Colleges and Universities: Making a Comeback." In J. P. Merisotis and C. T. O'Brien (eds.), *Minoriting Serving Institutions: Distinct Purposes, Common Goals*, New Directions for Higher Education, no. 102. San Francisco, CA: Jossey Bass, 1998, pp. 33–34.

Reyhner, J., and J. Eder. *American Indian Education: A History.* Norman: University of Oklahoma Press, 2003.

Rudolph, F. *The American College and University: A History.* New York: Vintage Press, 1962.

Serow, R. C. "Policy as Symbol: Title II of the 1944 G. I. Bill." *Review of Higher Education*, 2004, 27 (4): 481–499.

Sheldon, H. D. *History of University of Oregon.* Portland, OR: Binfords and Mort, 1940.

Stadtman, V. A. *The University of California 1868–1968.* New York: McGraw-Hill, 1970.

Tierney, W. G., and G. C. Hentschke. "Growth of the For-Profits." *New Players, Different Game: Understanding the Rise of For-Profit Colleges and Universities.* Baltimore, MD: Johns Hopkins University Press, 2007.

Torregrosa, C. H. (ed.). *The Hep 1991 Higher Education Directory.* Falls Church, VA: Higher Education, 1990.

Veal, D. L. *University of Wyoming.* New York: Newcomer Society, 1986.

Zumeta, W., and A. Kinne. "The Recession Is Not Over for Higher Education." *The NEA 2011 Almanac for Higher Education*, pp. 29–42. Washington, DC: National Education Association, 2011.

3

Forty-Five Years in the Academic Saddle: The American West, Higher Education, and the Invitation to Innovation

Patty Limerick

A Standing Invitation

The American West's pueblos and reservations, villages and cities, ranches and resorts, farms and federal facilities, in collaboration with the region's mountains, deserts, plains, canyons, mesas, valleys, rivers, lakes, and aquifers, along with a multitude of indigenous and transplanted plants and animals, request the honor of your presence at a celebration of the power of higher education to respond to, reckon with, and illuminate its setting and the lives of its complicated and engaging neighbors.

Please *RSVP* before the end of the twenty-first century

The distinctive landscapes of the American West and the great diversity of its human communities have delivered, to the leaders of higher education, an invitation to embrace innovation and to be selective in importing and relying on tradition. This invitation, a century and a half later, still awaits a positive *RSVP*.[1]

In chapter 2, Arthur Cohen writes about the rejection of this invitation. The participants in westward expansion, Cohen declares, "transported" their established institutions and practices "with only minor modifications." Whatever associations we have loaded onto the image of pioneers, "imitation" was their modus operandi. The seemingly distinctive aspects of western higher education—a greater receptivity to coeducation, and an expanded role and influence for the federal government—had their origins more in coincidences of timing than in any regional enthusiasm for innovation. A principal motive for founding colleges and universities was, after all, to prove that residents of the West had not skidded backward down the hill of civilization; on the contrary, the new communities of the West had quickly founded institutions that met the standards of the East. In truth, the stories of these foundings come well supplied with pluck and spirit and inspiration and commitment. And yet, assigned to write a chapter on the fresh and sparkling originality of higher education in the West, on the boldness and spirit with which westerners have broken from ill-fitting custom and followed a vision of education that celebrates and capitalizes on the distinctive natural and human challenges of their region, a realistic author would soon plead for an easier task.

Might the exercise of juxtaposing the history of the West with the history of American higher education encourage the region's educators to reconsider the 150-year-old invitation that has been awaiting response? It seems worth a try.

An Uncomfortable but Fortunate Kinship: The History of the West and the History of Higher Education

When providence, with the Western Interstate Commission for Higher Education (WICHE) as its voice, asks a western American historian to embark on an exploration of the history of higher education, the journey suddenly turns on itself and delivers the historian back to surprisingly familiar terrain.

Before embarking on that journey, the tour guide has a confession: an interlude of earnest effort did not transform me into an expert in the history of higher education. On the contrary, any claim I might have on authority comes from lived experience. I started college in 1968, and I wrote the first version of this chapter in 2008, and revised it in 2013. The genre of western American autobiography is awash in books with titles like *Fifty Years on the Old Frontier*, or *A Hundred Years at a Trading Post* (while the West is well known for its longevity-promoting healthful climate, that last title is not to be taken to heart). Though a little different in tone and mercifully short on autobiographical detail, this chapter takes its anomalous place in the genre of western reminiscence, a connection explicitly acknowledged by the title of the chapter.

In the late 1980s and 1990s, with an energetic movement to revitalize Western American history, a current of lively public discussions swept through our field. Even though there was much to enjoy in these discussions, it was hard to fend off sensations of tedium and dreariness when someone, often in a rather self-satisfied manner, would proclaim, "But how exactly do you define 'the West'?" That question may, in fact, be starting to percolate in the minds of readers of this chapter.

Really, who knows what that shape-shifting term means? In fact, it may well be the defiance of clear categorization and definition that makes the West so interesting to think about and explore. Name a variety of landscape, and the West can offer every possible variation on that theme: desert, canyonland, plains, foothills, mountain, forest, fertile valley, beach, rocky coast, sagebrush plateau. Name a continent, and people who originated from that continent are sure to have been influential figures in the West's past and present. A list of the West's tribal groups would be as long, if not longer, than the list of immigrant groups who traveled into the region. Human settlements range from villages, cities, suburbs, resort towns, and dispersed farms and ranches. Economic, ideological, and religious forms of diversity are as conspicuous and striking as the West's diversity of landforms, natural resources, aesthetic assets, and climates.

So, has the term "West" tottered and collapsed under the weight of such diversity and variability?

Nope.

For a term under such constant stress, the word "West" still goes through life with surprising robustness and resilience. Except for a few contrarian individuals conjuring up uncomfortable questions to ask Western American historians, the phrase "American West" delivers pretty clear meaning to people who encounter it. Asked to define the term, a good share of Americans might respond, "the part of the nation we learned about in Western movies." Others, mobilizing a little more knowledge, might offer something closer to "the part of the continent acquired by the United States and occupied by Americans in the nineteenth century, in a process that became a huge element in the nation's storytelling and in its identity." Beneficiaries of courses in Western American history might respond with particular authority, characterizing the West as "the part of the nation where water is usually in shorter supply, the reach of the horizon is less constrained, and there is a lot more land designated for federal ownership and management than in other parts of the country."

The definitions may vary, but it would be a rare soul who would be so stumped that she would have to ask, "The American What"?

A similar cultural agreement has been, and still is, at work in many parts of this region today. Nearly 20 years ago, two ambitious young historians undertook to pull the rug out from under the New Western History, a movement that sought to reinterpret and revitalize our understanding of the region's past. The term "West," one of their arguments asserted, was unavoidably ethnocentric, carrying meaning only for white Americans whose point of view originated in the Eastern United States. To clinch their case, the two scholars took to arguing that ethnic identity far outweighed regional identity. This led them to the claim that minorities—Indians, Mexican Americans, Asian Americans, and such others—were in the West, but not of the West. This assertion did not do much to unseat the New Western History, but it performed well enough at pulling the rug out from under the stance of these intellectual rebels. It really did not seem entirely sporting for two young white males to tell minorities that they were "in the West, but not of it." And, more to the point, this assertion flew in the face of the multicultural adoption of Western symbols like the cowboy hat, a form of adornment that sat comfortably on many American Indian, African

American, and Mexican American heads. It did not reckon with the nearly universal habit by which a minority person who has made a mark in a zone of endeavor is celebrated as a "pioneer" who has pushed back the "frontiers" of achievement. Westernness, in other words, has infiltrated individual and group consciousness in a wide spectrum of geographical, economic, ethnic, and political groupings. "Don't fence me in" has been the theme song and recruitment pitch of western identity.

And now, with both caution and eagerness, we approach the punch line: characteristic features of western life—diversity in particular—hold dual status as the greatest asset of our region's cultural heritage, and the most productive source of anxiety and discontent. Sometimes, for instance, the fact that Spanish is widely spoken among westerners provokes alarm, launching "official English" campaigns. A discussion of such campaigns will, reliably, provoke me to an educational lament. Multiple years of taking Spanish classes in California gave me a modest capacity to read in Spanish, and a pitiable, limping, halting approach to speaking in Spanish. Before acknowledging that my own cognitive deficiencies contributed to this outcome, I still demand one moment of lashing out at pedagogical malfunction. I went to school in Banning, California, surrounded by kids who were native Spanish speakers. And yet, to develop my capacity for conversational Spanish, I was placed in a chair, encased in earphones, and then instructed to chat with a recorded voice. "*Como está Pablo y Luisa?*" the voice on the tape would ask me. "*Pablo está bien, pero Luisa tiene catarro*," I would respond. Whoever had this endlessly remarked-upon cold, the counterparts of Pablo and Luisa were actually my neighbors in Banning. Fifty years later, I cannot let go of the conviction that I would be significantly better, at conversation in Spanish, if I had been instructed to chat—not with a tape recording—but with the living human beings in my proximity.

Thus the punchline, western American higher education could be the force that invites the western public to realize that we have a choice: we can see the human diversity of the region as a burden and a misfortune, or we can see that diversity as our asset and advantage. "*Patricia Nelson Limerick habla espanol como una niña de dos años*" offers one sad way of summarizing the failure of westerners to capitalize on our regional assets. But in innumerable ways, westerners could be invited to cut themselves off from lamenting and bemoaning the reality of their region's diversity, and to embrace, instead, the great enhancement of education waiting to be harvested from that diversity.

And now, back in the saddle and on to the next round-up of themes.

The history of the American West and the history of American higher education prove to be thematic twins, more fraternal than identical, but certainly carrying a striking set of shared characteristics. We begin with an inventory of these unexpectedly symmetric and matched heritages.

First, a variety of businessmen in the American West devised an arrangement that historian Richard White has described as a "dual or two-tiered labor system" (White, 1991, p. 282) that now also structures most of

American higher education (not—as far as I know—from intentional imitation). In western enterprises from mining to railroad construction, one set of workers got a higher rate of pay and a more elevated social status, while another set of workers received considerably less money and even less respect. The labor arrangements of contemporary higher education replicate the pattern: an elite cohort of tenured and tenure-track professors carry a limited teaching burden in order to pursue research, while the majority of courses, in many colleges and universities, are taught by instructors, adjuncts, and graduate students who receive far more limited compensation (and skimpy benefits, if they get any at all) and hold far less prestige. In historic western enterprises, the key factor of difference between the two classes of workers lay in race and ethnicity, with Mexican and Asian laborers occupying the lower level. Blessedly, higher education has not built this particular feature into its dual labor economy.

With its long-running experience with the dual labor system, western history offers a simple and clear lesson for higher education. Even if the system works for decades, and even though its beneficiaries come to take it for granted, eventually there is hell to pay. Anyone who cares about higher education should make the search for alternatives to the current unbalanced allocation of reward and prestige, between these two classes of higher education's workforce, into a top priority.

In our exploration of historical analogies, we appear to be off to a disturbing and depressing bummer of a start. This has no doubt put readers into the mood for a second, more spirit-lifting, though necessarily complicated, observation: the American West has benefited tremendously from federal support and subsidy, and so has American higher education, though neither the leaders of the West nor the leaders of higher education have made a full peace with this historical fact, nor has either group made much of a plan as to what to do when federal funding turns spotty and skimpy.

Western historians have written voluminously on this subject, tracking the impact of federal action in the acquisition of the western half of North America from France, Mexico, and Britain; in the conquest and relocation of Indian people; the distribution of land, minerals, timber, and water; in the construction of wagon roads, telegraphs, railroads, and highways; in the development of defense industries and nuclear-weapons production. The history of the region and the history of universities overlap explicitly in the theme of federal centrality, since the Morrill Land Grant Act of 1862 put the federal government squarely into the world of funding for higher education, just as western colleges and universities were coming into being. But it may well be that the extraordinary flow of federal money into higher education, during World War II and the Cold War, exceeds in scale and degree anything that western history records in the contribution of federal funds to regional well-being.

This similarity between the West and higher education in the area of federal dependence first zoomed into my field of attention 15 years ago, when a colleague in Western American Studies told me of a thought that came to him while returning to Boulder from field work with public lands ranchers. He was thinking about the way in which these ranchers graze their livestock on federal lands, paying fees considerably lower than they would pay for access to private lands, and yet resist regulation and accountability for their use of these lands. Is there any other group, my colleague asked himself, who depends upon public resources and who expresses comparable grievance and outrage when elected officials and taxpayers inquire into whether those resources are being used wisely and productively, or propose changes in the terms of their use? As he drove toward his university, his mind followed a similar direction: While they might be the last to realize it, ranchers on public lands and professors at public universities have a lot in common when it comes to their dependence on—and proportionate resentment of—government.

And the lesson from history? If they faced up to their heritage, residents of the West and beneficiaries of higher education might lead the nation in their expressions of gratitude for federal and state governments and for that redistribution of wealth that goes under the name of "taxation." At the very least, whenever big government and taxation come in for another round of demonizing, these ranchers and professors should be coauthoring op-ed pieces gently requesting the demonizers to cool it. Just as important, both the history of the West and the history of higher education offer stern warnings against taking federal money for granted, since the generosity of the public and its elected officials can be very changeable. Thinking of government funding as an entitlement proves to be an excellent way to land in a disordered heap when one of those episodes of changeability occurs.

The third similarity to be drawn between the history of the American West and the history of higher education, and following from the previous point, is that both have been shaped by the economic pattern of boom-and-bust. Episodes of stark scarcity punctuate both histories, though they often disappear from view during the recurrent episodes of amnesia brought on by periods of abundance. Both residents of the West and the personnel of universities and colleges are very susceptible to a habit of mind by which the periods of prosperity are assumed to be the norm and the standard, even though dynamic economic variations have regularly kicked that assumption around like a soccer ball in an intensely fought game.

This third similarity delivers one very large lesson: when a region or an institution is subject to swings from boom to bust and back again, it is the path of wisdom to cultivate adaptability, agility, and resilience, and to be alert and responsive to the earliest signs of change. In many western locales, industries that looked like they would be the centerpiece of the economy for ages to come have made sudden exits. The various eras of the region's history—the fur trade, mining, ranching, farming, logging, and land sales—have all followed lines of growth and decline that match, in gradient, the two long sides of an isosceles triangle with a very narrow base. In one widespread pattern of the last half of the twentieth century, industries dependent on the extraction of natural resources contracted (with the conspicuous exception of the ongoing boom in natural gas production), while the industries of tourism and recreation expanded. In these transitions, communities that have been able to navigate with flexibility and even opportunism have had greater success than communities that could only hold on to old economies and hope for their resurgence. The lesson here for higher education is not subtle. In the post–World War II boom, research turned into the professorial activity that earned the most money and esteem. In the busts, adaptability and goodwill in transferring the regalia of prestige and stature from research to teaching could harvest greater public appreciation (likely to turn into money when the economy recovers) and also, very likely, enhance personal gratification. And here is another happy thought: taking a break from the "publish or perish" mode of appraising professional performance would provide a useful opportunity to reappraise the now opaque and impenetrable reasons behind the designation of scholarly publishing as the primary measure of professorial achievement.

Another striking lesson, drawn from comparing the impacts of shifts from boom to bust on the history of the West and the history of higher education, lies in attitudes toward growth. For long phases in the West's past, growth was the operating synonym for progress, and the recruiting of more settlers was the driving hope and motive. Then, in a shift of opinion that still has the West off-balance, concern about the effects and prices of growth escalated, and westerners struggled to find a meaning for progress that did not require a steady increase in the use of resources, the development of land, and the recruitment of residents. Historian John Thelin described a similar pattern in higher education: "American colleges and universities have wandered into a state of continual expansion characterized by overextension of functions without clarity of purpose" (2004, p. 361). As Clark Kerr noted, thanks to free-flowing federal money, "the half century 1940–1990 was a largely golden age for the research university in the United States" (2001, p. 141).

After an era of astonishing growth in buildings, campuses, programs, positions, administration, and enrollments, higher education finds itself in a struggle for reorientation that very much resembles the struggle for reorientation in the American West. Leaders in the West and leaders in higher education spend their days and nights in an effort to find the answer to the riddle, "If 'better' can no longer mean 'more' and 'bigger,' what state of well-being should we pursue, and how should we measure our progress toward that goal?" For more than three decades, university and college leaders have struggled to deal with the interruption—and even reversal—of the trend of growth and expansion that many had come to take for granted. Perhaps the most important historical lesson is this: there are ways to deal with this shift, but they are certainly not going to make everyone happy. Academic leaders who wait to find a solution that will earn them universal applause are in for an unimaginably long wait.

A fourth point of convergence between the histories of the American West and higher education is that in both cases decision makers have yielded to the great temptation to postpone investment in the maintenance of infrastructure. In both arenas, construction—of railroads and highways, of new campus buildings—stood for progress and unleashed the enthusiasm that produced both funding and cheerful dedication ceremonies. But the sheer passage of time worked away at those material structures; the pressures of gravity, the intrusion of water, the stresses of temperature change, and the frictions of human use all took their toll. The need to repair and maintain physical structures is equally urgent, and equally demoralizing, in the American West and in higher education. Both arenas present evidence aplenty for the proposition that human beings find much more fun and satisfaction (which, in turn, unleash a corresponding willingness to pay) in the envisioning, planning, and anticipating of construction than they find in repairing and maintaining. In both domains, there is every reason to invest ingenuity in finding incentives and motivations to encourage Americans to see maintenance as exhilarating, sexy, and gratifying.

Our fifth point of similarity between the American West and higher education is the closest match of all. Very much like people who love the American West, people who love higher education are prone to nostalgia. Western nostalgiacs trace the region's descent from a romantic, colorful, and adventurous frontier past to a prosaic and dreary western present, while alumni who love their alma mater yearn for a golden age in the institution's past (which, not surprisingly, often coincides with the period during which the alumni were themselves young, vigorous, and untroubled by high cholesterol and the need for knee replacements), and faculty yearn for a period in the past when legislators and the public gave universities proper and deserved support. These acts of imagination are perfectly legitimate; yet, nostalgia has a way of gumming up the works in human enterprise. At its worst, it generates a fatalism and resignation that saps human energy and pulls the plug on the imagining of alternatives and solutions. For advocates and supporters of American higher education, nostalgia has its biggest and most lamentable impact in its power to tangle us up in an un-thought-out deference to tradition.

Living with a Chronic Condition: A Treatment Program for Tradition

"Sorting through fragments from the past, however, one is hard put to discover any true golden age."

Derek Bok, former president of Harvard University (2006, p. 21)

"Much of recent carping is based on nostalgia, an emotion which I do not share."

Henry Rosovsky, former dean of Harvard College (1990, p. 297)

No pharmacologist has ever designed a medication that equals the effectiveness of historical perspective as a nostalgia-blocker. Of the many therapeutic benefits of historical perspective, the most valuable lies in the capacity to immunize us against a view of the past that misleads us into exaggerating our own burdens and dilemmas. And, by reacquainting us with the not-always-enviable circumstances of our predecessors, historical perspective makes us wary of an unreasonable respect for, or even subservience to, that powerful form of nostalgia known as devotion to tradition. Historical perspective guides us in sorting through our heritage and deciding which traditions to preserve, which traditions to discard, and which traditions to revise and rehabilitate. Sharpening our ability to navigate between tradition and innovation, historical perspective provides us with a route of escape from resignation, fatalism, and a spirit-crushing sense of inevitability. It equips us to devise and make our peace with pragmatic and grounded, flexible and resilient strategies for supporting, sustaining, and maintaining universities and colleges in our own rough economic times.

So, let us quit praising historical perspective and let it get to work.

The University of Colorado's first president, Joseph Sewall, did not yield an inch to nostalgia. When he returned for a visit to Boulder, he said, "If you were to ask me, my friends, what ten years of my life were most filled with sadness, disappointment and sorrow, it is the years I have spent upon these grounds... I tried to be hopeful, but it was bitter work" (Davis, 1965, p. 57). In today's terms, we would say that President Sewall's troubles centered on undercapitalization and a lack of infrastructure, typical troubles of newly founded universities. A visitor once asked President Sewall if he could see the university's library. As William Davis recounted the story, "President Sewall allegedly replied, 'Haven't any library.'" The visitor asked to see the chemical laboratory. "Haven't any chemical laboratory." After several exchanges of this sort, the visitor exclaimed, "What in hell do you have?" To which Sewall bravely replied, "A University!" (p. 43)

In the early years of western higher education, President Sewall's struggles were far from unusual. In the creation of Colorado College, a Congregationalist minister named Thomas Haskell was appointed as "solicitor" for the college in 1874. The yield from his efforts proved unimpressive: Haskell "reported pledges of $14,050," but he "was able to collect only $375, barely enough to cover his personal expenses of $264.96" (Reid, 1979, p. 11). Even Stanford University, fabled for its financial well-being, got off to a rocky start. When founder Leland Stanford died in 1893, just as the third year of classes were set to begin, this California university's assets were frozen while his will struggled through probate and his estate fought (successfully) a federal lawsuit charging his company, the Central Pacific Railroad, with financial improprieties. A court ruling allowed his widow, Jane Stanford, to draw $10,000 each month from the estate for household expenses, and let her count the university's professors as household servants, a category that seems inherently in conflict with professorial pride (Mirrielees, 1959, pp. 82–95).

Worried over the precarious finances of Pacific Lutheran University in Tacoma, Washington, President Bjug Harstad saw opportunity in the Yukon Gold Rush of 1898. Seeking his prospects among the prospectors, President

Harstad lugged loads of provisions over Chilkoot Pass (150 pounds per sled) until he had amassed enough to head into the Yukon in search of a strike that would put the fledgling school on solid financial footing. "Everyone who can enjoy the happiness of home and need not consider such a trip as his duty should praise God," President Harstad wrote back to the school's supporters. Sadly, after a year of effort, he was forced to declare that "the school has not yet received any financial help from my trip" (Harstad, 1988, pp. 10 and 21).

Tales of the financial miseries of the founding presidents cannot help but raise our spirits. At the very least, we can be happy that we have buildings to struggle to repair and budgets to grieve for when they are cut. In the early years, presidents and boards of trustees enjoyed only the rarest moments of fiscal peace, a condition to which they have returned in the early twenty-first century. In contrast to the overwhelming task of creating colleges where none had been before, we drew an easier task by far. Unlike poor President Harstad, slogging through the Yukon, it is our considerably less strenuous task to reform, redeem, and find sustainability for a vast array of thoroughly founded—if not so thoroughly funded—institutions of higher education.

The most ardent commitment to nostalgia, the most stalwart effort to conjure up a college of the past where professors and students pursued knowledge under terms of the warmest mutual appreciation and agreeable material comfort, cannot put a dent in this historical reality: the difficulties of finding the money to start a college and maintain it in its early years were unending. Under those circumstances, when it came to judging the purity and propriety of contributions and donations, prissiness and persnickityness were luxuries that few academic leaders could afford.

In many cases, it was the philanthropy of holders of new fortunes, made from the Gilded Age extravaganza of capitalism, that saved the day and put universities and colleges on a workable financial footing. As historian Frederick Rudolph wrote, "The material promise of America...was now underwriting whole new ventures in higher education" (1962, pp. 353–354). Stanford University, of course, came into being thanks to the profits accumulated by the Central Pacific Railroad. Gifts from Phoebe Apperson Hearst, widow of mining magnate George Hearst, made an enormous difference for the well-being of the University of California at Berkeley. Mrs. Hearst began with scholarships for women, and then "built Hearst Hall, a social center for women, and the Hearst Memorial Mining Building; provided funds for the ethnological museum, to which she gave her own collections; supported funds for books and lectureships; built the Greek theater; and as a regent encouraged others to open their purses" (Curti and Nash, 1965, p. 163). As the Progressive movement kicked into high gear and faculty joined other Progressives in condemning the abuses of corporations, the tangle of sentiment and support became very dense. Thelin noted, "Ironically, the University of California and Stanford continued to attract generous support from the very families associated with the abuses [the Progressives] were trying to reform" (2004, p. 139).

Outside the West, John D. Rockefeller brought the University of Chicago into being; Coca Cola money made Emory University in Georgia into a great school; and similar examples could fill (and have filled) a big volume (Curti and Nash, 1965). These ironies do not come with a limited shelf life. I sometimes teach in the Guggenheim Building in the middle of the University of Colorado campus, with every entrance and exit making me think of the hundreds of academic liberals who have cheerfully and proudly listed Guggenheim Fellowships on their CVs without a footnote to acknowledge the troubles left behind by copper mines worldwide.

Adding another striking dimension to this tangle, historian Frederick Rudolph remarked on the ways in which the professionalization and institutionalization of higher education, with the formalizing of requirements for research performance, resembled the patterns of corporate America: "The same relationship between production and rewards was also being established in the great organizations that characterized American business life, not only in the giants like Standard Oil and U.S. Steel, but in the banks, the chain stores, the big department stores which were organizing on a complex impersonal scale" (1962, p. 404). The ties between higher education and industrial and commercial America, in other words, extended far beyond the entrepreneurial undertakings of major donors.

At the risk—or certainty—of being heavy-handed, here is a restatement: Most of the colleges and universities founded in the last half of the nineteenth century arose from the concentration of power and wealth in the hands of a new breed of financiers and industrialists. In the minds of many academics in the late twentieth and early twenty-first centuries, the acceptance of gifts from leading exploiters of labor and natural resources presents itself as a pact with the devil. But if that condemnation holds water, then the devil turns out to be the most significant supporter of higher education, standing—in a posture that seems the very opposite of diabolical—at the door of opportunity and holding it open to millions of young people. A great many people from humble circumstances have this devil to thank for the improvement of their lives, just as a great many professors enjoy tenured security at institutions brought into being by economic and social forces they abhor.

Consider, as one closing example of this persistent pattern, the mid-1940s origins of the prestigious and influential Creative Writing Program at Stanford University, under the leadership of the famed writer—and environmental activist—Wallace Stegner. The Stanford program would be, as Stegner biographer Philip Fradkin put it, "the second graduate writing program in the country, after Iowa's, and while under the direction of Stegner it was arguably the better one." But, as Fradkin noted, initially "there was the slight problem of money." Luckily the chairman of the English Department had a brother who was "a physician, Greek scholar, and Texas oilman." With funding from the Texas oilman, the Stegner Fellowships came into being, with an enormous impact on national literature: "Those who passed through the creative writing program at Stanford during Stegner's time," as Fradkin summed up the results of the Texas oilman's generosity, "published many hundreds of books and garnered every conceivable literary award except the Nobel Prize" (2008, pp. 112–113).

In the all-too-bright light of historical perspective, latter-day moral agonizing over funding from corporations and powerful private donors looks precious and naïve, a devotion to a brittle ideal of purity mocked by the origins of today's institutions of higher learning. We would not, after all, have universities and colleges to protect from contamination if our predecessors in the academic world had not risen above that concern. Maybe the people of the future will find a better way to redeem money that has been earned from injuries to nature and to humanity. But to this day, money acquired from practices that raise complicated moral questions still supplies crucial support for higher education.

When I taught at Harvard, I was treated to a moment of intense illumination when the dean of students undertook to make a more realistic person of me. He told me that every year a few principled and wealthy young people would come to report a crisis of conscience. They could no longer take money from families whose fortunes came from such reprehensible exploitation of labor and nature, so they would have to apply for financial aid. At that point in the conversation, the dean would say to the students: "And where do you think we got the money for financial aid at Harvard?"

For faculty members who have not had their naiveté treated with a conversation like that one, the current state of funding of higher education triggers an unhappiness that suspends reason, and certainly historical thinking. Quick to wither from inattention is this historical proposition: Eras of support for higher education have coincided with eras of national expansionism and support for military undertakings.

In the last half of the nineteenth century, the conquest of the West was the necessary context for the Morrill Land Grant Act and for federal support of higher education. More recently, in an unsettlingly similar way, the Cold War provided the necessary context for a remarkable phase of generous federal funding of universities. As historian John Thelin wrote, "academic scientists commanded respect and even deference for their expertise that might somehow help the United States surpass scholars in the Soviet Union and other Eastern bloc Communist countries" (2004, p. 280). Out of the hatred of communism arose a sense of national urgency that justified much greater public funding for higher education, with the primary beneficiaries being science and engineering, but with a spillover to the social sciences and humanities. "For a generation of new faculty members who enjoyed being hired under such conditions," Thelin noted, "it was not difficult to imagine that such conditions were the norm—and might even improve over time, given the American public's support for higher education" (p. 311).

When professors in our times lament the reduction of public funding for higher education, they are unlikely to take the next step in thinking historically: to acknowledge how much the episodes of free-flowing federal support for higher education came out of the context of arms races and brinksmanship, Korea and Vietnam, and frightening face-offs between the

Soviet Union and the United States. The eras of a broad social mandate for investing public resources in higher education coincided with a campaign for international dominance. That recognition alone can help us to keep our inclination to nostalgia within manageable proportions. Maybe there are less militaristic and nationalistic rationales that could open up the faucets of federal support for higher education, but it will take some creativity and ingenuity to bring them into being.

The readiness of students for college-level work offers another zone for prescribing historical perspective as an antidote to nostalgia and exaggerated dismay with our own circumstances. In their beginning years, many colleges and universities had to face the fact that a preparatory program (more or less a high school) had to be part of their operations. For institutions in newly settled territories, there was an obvious explanation for this situation: there were few, if any, high schools or even elementary schools already in operation. It was a natural assumption, then, that the inclusion of a preparatory program was a temporary expedient that a college or university would outgrow as public schools came into their own.

That pleasant optimism—the fantasy that the burden of precollegiate student preparation would soon be lifted from professorial shoulders—has proven to be a fruitful source of frustration. Every professor in the late twentieth and early twenty-first centuries has been flummoxed by the conundrum of pleasant, good-natured, fully enrolled college students, who cannot write an intelligible sentence and whose spoken expressions sometimes seem to hint at neurological troubles. What became of the delightful idea that preparatory education would cease to be the obligation of colleges and universities? To make a long story short, it belly-flopped. Rather than dwelling on the promise's failure to deliver, a better plan might be this: surrender the fantasy of students arriving at college with every skill brushed, polished, and perfected, and then get to work on projects to connect and engage professors with K-12 teachers in the fruitful cultivation of entry-level skills. As Thelin wrote, "the university-builders had certainly underestimated their dependence on a base of primary and secondary education" (2004, p. 134), and that underestimation continues to this day. Or, in historian Frederick Rudolph's words, "The first task before the state universities was to discover a bridge between the free public elementary school and the public university" (1962, p. 281). It is a "first task" that remains far from complete.

Historical perspective also helps in reckoning with the extraordinary rise of specialization and fragmentation of knowledge in research universities and in colleges that emulate them. Were we to undertake to craft the balance sheet of costs and benefits that came with academic specialization, reacquainting ourselves with the credibility-defying breadth and reach of our predecessors' minds might be a good place to start.

At the University of Wyoming in the 1890s, Professor C. B. Ridgway taught "physics, mathematics, astronomy, civil engineering, electrical engineering, physical soil analysis, and weather forecasting" (Hardy, 1986, p. 17). In the early 1880s at Colorado Agricultural College (later

Colorado State University), Professor Charles Davis taught "arithmetic, algebra, astronomy, ancient history, bookkeeping, geometry, mechanics, physics, and several classes in chemistry" (Hansen, 1977, p. 62). When the University of Southern California opened in 1880, President Marion M. Bovard, Professor Freeman D. Bovard, and full-time instructor Jennie Allen Bovard conducted a majority of all courses, covering a curriculum that included Latin, Greek, English composition and rhetoric, geometry, trigonometry, German, history, chemistry, calculus, logic, analytical mechanics, civil engineering, French, mental philosophy, political economy, astronomy, moral philosophy, history of civilization, international law, and geology (Servin and Wilson, 1969, pp. 15 and 20). When the State Normal School of Tempe (later Arizona State University) opened in the 1880s, Professor Bradford Farmer taught reading, writing, spelling, grammar, arithmetic, geography, US history, algebra, natural philosophy, Latin, literature, debate, US Constitution, "general" history, physiology, political economy, and the history and philosophy of education (Hopkins and Thomas, 1960, pp. 83–89).

Of course, we do not want to recreate those days of covering the waterfront intellectually, nor could we, given the explosion of knowledge in each of those fields. But the next time we struggle and strain to loosen the hold of departments on turf and resources, and to open up more space for interdisciplinary and multidisciplinary scholarship and teaching, these precedents are surely something to keep in our memories, simply as a reminder that the narrowness we take to be normal made a comparatively recent onset. When we think—as we must—about loosening the limits and constraints of our madly overspecialized academic practices, when we face up to the drastic underproduction of synthesis, when we struggle to find institutional mechanisms for building teams of researchers and teachers, we might find our spirits refreshed if we first saluted our forefathers and sometimes foremothers (not to mention our underrecognized contemporaries teaching in small departments) for their undaunted courage in teaching every topic under the sun.

The history of higher education has given us an inheritance of several thousand forms of belief and conduct that we are entitled to recognize and respect as our traditions. Just from this brief discussion, here are the central traditions of higher education, some of them more deserving of our respect and deference than others:

- The tradition of imitating and importing the mission of universities and colleges in the eastern United States or Europe, rather than responding to the opportunities presented by distinctive local conditions.
- The tradition of one professor teaching a range of subjects that would now be taught by dozens of professors.
- The tradition of a dual labor system in which an elite takes the lion's share of compensation and prestige.
- The tradition of faith in a golden age in higher education, to which we endlessly yearn to return.

- The tradition of depending on tides of federal and state money and feeling flummoxed and disoriented when those tides ebb.
- The tradition of swinging rapidly from periods of prosperity to periods of scarcity, and losing our bearings with every swing.
- The tradition of letting infrastructure decline without proper maintenance and then being surprised by the cost of catching up.
- The tradition of enshrining research and publication, aimed at a small audience of fellow specialists, as the first measure of merit in faculty.
- The tradition of getting so used to growth and expansion that no one can imagine an alternative form of well-being.
- The tradition of desperate presidents driven to their wits' end by precarious funding.
- The tradition of crucial support coming from philanthropists who did not go out of their way to earn posterity's admiration for their congenial relations with labor or their careful and respectful use of natural resources.
- The tradition of enrolling students not ready for college work.

This is not, it is hardly necessary to point out, a very coherent heritage. With such a hodgepodge to pick from, everyone has everything needed to identify and celebrate the traditions of their preference, and to marshal them in support of the practices of their choice. However, with such a mixed bag of traditions, everyone also has an obligation to be self-aware and thoughtful in making a claim for deference to any one of them.

At a session at the American Studies Association a decade ago, Ramón Gutiérrez, a distinguished scholar of colonial New Mexico and an experienced university administrator, made comments of considerable usefulness when it comes to appraising the stance of professors toward tradition. Characteristically, he used a manner both gracious and merciless to dissect the beliefs and behavior of our demographic cohort in the academic profession. Memorably, he used the uncomfortable term "gerontocracy" to characterize the regime of aging, tenured baby-boomers who work assiduously to police the boundaries of change and ensure that the customs they learned in graduate school remain in full force. Those remarks threw me into a state of some agitation. Could my Baby Boom generation, so full of oppositional pep and zing in the 1960s and 1970s, have evolved into department-turf-defending "gerontocrats" specializing in resistance to change? If the shoe fits, as the old aphorism goes, wear it. Though now with orthotics.

If we return to my colleague's unsettling observation of the match between the way ranchers and professors welcome and resent federal support and subsidy, this matter of conservatism proves to be another unexpected similarity. In both cases, participants have found it easy to read the pattern of events in their occupation as a decline: from the open-range days of adventure and opportunity in the western ranching world to today's uncertain livestock prices and constraints on land use; from the open-range days of generous funding and popular support for higher education to today's uncertain institutional funding and constraints on research support.

For both ranchers and academics, nostalgia triggers conservatism, which produces a somewhat more paradoxical situation in higher education than in ranching. Since ranchers have often been self-described political conservatives, it is not a particular surprise when they respond to unsettling change with an equally conservative stance of defensiveness and resistance to reform. But, with academics often positioned toward the left side of the political continuum, their conservative response to change in their profession seems, initially, a surprise. As Kerr phrased it, the faculty are "most conservative about their own affairs, never more so than when their own affairs are not going too well." Many of Kerr's experiences in the 1960s revealed to him "how radical some professors can be when they look at the external world and how conservative when they look inwardly at themselves" (2001, pp. vii and 118). The novelist Stephen King made the same point with a colorful analogy: Many instructors in universities, he observed, are "liberals in their politics but crustaceans in their chosen fields" (2000, p. 136). Derek Bok, meanwhile, contrasted the resistance to change in universities to the efforts in other organizations to "engage in an ongoing process of improvement by constantly evaluating their performance, identifying problems, trying various remedies, measuring their success, discarding those that do not work, and incorporating those that do." In any number of cases, university-based faculty play a part in the reappraisal of the operations of other organizations. Bok summed up the paradox: "In short, faculty seem inclined to use research and experimentation to understand and improve every institution, process, and human activity except their own" (2006, p. 317).

In the late twentieth and early twenty-first centuries, conservative, university-based gerontocrats have granted certain traditions (especially faculty governance and the guarantees of tenure), an exemption from the process of deliberate and thoughtful evaluation. Perhaps they needed that exemption because they are fairly recent developments in the higher education scene, and thereby lack the legitimizing power of antiquity, longevity, and duration. However, once we refuse the power of tradition to act as the force subtracting the adjective "free" from the word "free will," the pieces are in place for a thoughtful reconfiguring of our customs and assumptions.

When people receive actual, material inheritances from their ancestors, they sort through them, taking the toasters and ironing boards to Goodwill and retaining the necklaces and rings of lasting beauty. People in higher education have a very similar license for selectivity. Just like the possessions left to us by our parents, aunts, uncles, and grandparents, some traditions are past their time, antiquated, and ready for a respectful trip to eBay. Others of equal venerability are just ready to come into their own, manifesting a new relevance and value in changed times. And others, perhaps the most important traditions of all, were never possessions of our predecessors, and instead, await our invention and creation.

In other words, the invitation with which this chapter opened awaits our response.

The West to the Rescue: Giving Harvard a Helping Hand

"Higher education in America began with Harvard."

Historian Frederick Rudolph (1962, p. 3)

"Many of these problems have troubled the other great research universities as well, and if they are worse at Harvard, it is only because Harvard has most effectively pursued the wrong kind of success."

Harry Lewis, former dean of Harvard College (2006, p. 268)

"While pockets of innovation exist throughout American higher education, most professors teach as they traditionally have, confident that the ways that have worked well enough in the past will continue to serve in the future. Now is hardly the time for such complacency."

Derek Bok, former president of Harvard University (2006, p. 312)

The diagnosis of the ills of higher education, and the prescription of remedies for those ills, has long been a cottage industry. Of the many books in this genre, three are my favorites: Page Smith, *Killing the Spirit*, Derek Bok, *Our Underachieving Colleges*, and Harry Lewis, *Excellence Without a Soul*. These are my favorites because (1) I agree with their tone and with their conclusions and (2) I have known and liked the authors. It is a providential aspect that all three of the authors have some tie with Harvard; as a one-time assistant professor at Harvard on the revolving door plan, I have my own microtie with that institution. I call this providential, because Harvard is the point of reference for higher education everywhere on the planet. When the leaders of schools announce their aspirations and ambitions, they are very likely to say that they want to be the Harvard of the Rockies (or the Pacific Northwest or the Southwest or the Great Basin or Whatever Locale in Which They Have Found Themselves). They will very rarely say that they would like to be the Yale or Princeton or Cornell or Brown of the Rockies or whatever, even though those phrasings would convey sensible and appropriate ambitions. But Harvard is the lodestone, the point of reference, the mountaintop, the bellwether, the center of attention of American higher education, which, for my rhetorical purposes, turns out to be very lucky indeed. When people associated with Harvard express concern over the state of higher education, this is a concern that cannot be dismissed.

The principal worries of former Harvard history student Page Smith, Harvard Professor and former Harvard College Dean Harry Lewis, and former Harvard University President Derek Bok are also my principal worries. Adding resonance to the worries summarized in those books is a valuable text with a somewhat more tenuous connection to Cambridge, Massachusetts: former University of California President Clark Kerr's *The Uses of the University*, originally delivered as the Godkin Lectures at Harvard. If we focus on the dilemmas explored in these books, western universities turn out to be in the catbird's seat. They are positioned to come to the rescue of higher education. They could, in a very pleasant reversal of the usual configurations of superiority and inferiority, give Harvard a helping hand. In fact, former president Bok made an explicit case for the greater potential for self-assessment and productive change in universities of less exalted stature: "leaders of less affluent, less prestigious colleges have significant advantages over their counterparts in the upper echelons...They need not worry that any self-study that exposes educational weaknesses will appear in the pages of *The New York Times*." Thus many "teaching innovations," he notes, "do not begin in the best known universities but in colleges with less prominent reputations" (2006, pp. 337–338).

The inferiority complex of the American West, like the inferiority complex of colleges and universities that have not secured a place in the nation's top rankings, has been systemic and lasting. Of course, it is important to note that the western inferiority complex has been well-supported and maintained by a comparable and matching eastern superiority complex. Driven by both complexes, the imitative mode of the founders of the West's colleges and universities, striving to follow a model imported from the East and from Europe, has had lasting impacts. The idea that we are creatures exiled to the backward hinterlands, and thus forced to slog around in a state of second (or third or fourth) class citizenship, has been a hard one to shake. For better or worse, the destiny of the West and the destiny of higher education are linked and interdependent; the esteem in which the region is held will be a significant factor in increasing or lowering the esteem in which its institutions of higher education are held.

If we respond favorably to the invitation that opens this chapter, we take the route out of this legacy of perceived inferiority. The embrace, celebration, and critical investigation of our locale immunize us against the erosion of the soul that has come with that Sisyphean campaign to achieve the respect of the eastern establishment. Our location in the West is waiting to be recognized as our advantage. There are great rewards in accepting and expanding on the circumstances of a western location, rather than ignoring them, trying to transcend them, or even apologizing for them.[2]

Securing those rewards requires the negotiation of one small pact with the devil: namely, the embrace of the mythic image of the American West as a place of fresh starts, new beginnings, and bold and courageous innovations. The actual history of the American West does include some features that validate and support this image. But there are more features of imitation, replication, timidity, deference, and subservience to the models imported from the eastern United States. And the history of western higher education, as argued in chapter 2, has been a hotbed of this imitation, replication, timidity, deference, and subservience.

So this is the public-relations-driven pact with the devil that I am encouraging: Rather than continuing to debunk the less-than-historically-valid image of the American West as a place of bold innovation, let's take a more strategic approach. Let's say that it just took us a little while (a century or two, hardly a blink of an eye in geological time) to realize that this idea of a region of fresh starts and new beginnings could be more than a matter of rhetoric and self-deception. The West could be the place of bold innovation; it just took us a little while to get our courage up and to figure out how to put that mythic ideal to work on behalf of good causes.

We will take our marching orders from what the three Harvard-related authors consider to be the principal troubles and deficits of American higher education. We respond to those troubles and deficits by declaring this excellent news: Taking our location in the American West as our point of orientation turns out to provide remedies for most of those troubles and deficits. Harvard points out a problem; we show how to correct it! In taking up this chipper spirit, I draw my inspiration from yet another Harvard book, *The University: An Owner's Manual*, written by Henry Rosovsky. His conclusions are, as he says, "on the whole, joyful instead of jeremiads." His "benign attitude," he anticipated, would "make some people mad" because "to be positive is never popular in intellectual circles" (1990, pp. 295–296), a statement, which for a person with a certain attraction to controversy, makes the desire to join him in cheerful conclusions irresistible.

Let us match a few dilemmas with their place-based solutions.

The National Dilemma. Under the mandate to publish or perish, many professors squander their life energies in writing articles and books in obscure jargon, addressed to a tiny audience of fellow specialists. Not surprisingly, many of those professors find themselves subject to a sense of being unappreciated and underrewarded. "Many academic books and articles published today," Bok wrote, "seem uncomfortably narrow, bound too closely by the confines and conventions of their discipline to do full justice to the problems they address" (2006, p. 25). As Harry Lewis put it, "The pressure to publish a great deal in a short time makes academic writing duller, less adventurous, and more technical" (2006, p. 8). Smith made the same point, though with a notable increase in temperature and sharpness of language:

> The clearer it becomes that most research is carried on in a deadening and routine way, the louder become the exhortations to do more such work, as though salvation were to be achieved by mere volume. The last thing anyone wishes to do is to stop and try to think about the validity of what has become a kind of reflex. (1990, p. 21)

The Regional Solution. Professors bring their research findings to bear on local dilemmas, from political stalemates to environmental conflicts, from the challenges posed by the decline of one central industry and the rise of another to the need for poems to bring perspective to agitated public forums. Not surprisingly, the professors find unexpected joy in the experience of doing work that is meaningful and valued by people in need, and that joy is reaffirmed by institutional changes in the standards for promotion and raises. Of course, professors retain the right to publish versions of their research in the conventional academic outlets.

The National Dilemma. Teaching and research are locked in a hopeless tug-of-war. In this zero-sum game, time invested in undergraduates is time drained from career-advancing research. Smith, of course, made this point emphatically: Research "is dispiriting; it depresses the whole scholarly enterprise; and most important of all, it deprives the student of what he or she deserves—the thoughtful and considerate attention of a teacher deeply and unequivocally committed to teaching" (1990, p. 7). Or as Kerr put it, more mildly, "Teaching is less central than it once was for most faculty members; research has become more important" (2001, p. 32).

The Regional Solution. Professors cook up ways to direct course assignments to the illumination and resolution of local problems. A large and renewable energy source is thus tapped, while students can be much more effectively hounded to improve their writing when they know that what they write will land in the hands and minds of actual human beings who deserve texts characterized by accessibility and clarity.

The National Dilemma. Knowledge has been fragmented into disciplines and subdisciplines and resources have been divided among entrenched, border-guarding departments. Perhaps most troubling of all, science and humanities often operate like opposing armies, with social science caught sporadically in the crossfire. As Bok phrased it, "Professors and departments are not obligated to cooperate with other units or individuals even when it might be educationally desirable for them to do so" (2006, p. 39). As Kerr said in his original Godkin Lectures in 1963, "Another major task" facing higher education "is to create a more unified intellectual world" (2001, p. 89). Looking back in 2001 and noting the impact of post–World War II funding on the internal relations of campuses, Kerr offered this sharp diagnosis of one "pathology" or "disease" of the modern university: "Elevation of the sciences above the humanities and the social sciences, creating a widening gap between the 'hard' and 'soft' sides of intellectual life, and between the 'rich' and the 'not so rich' participants" (p. 199).

The Regional Solution. Since no single discipline can shed sufficient light on today's complex problems, members of departments simply must cross the borders and work with each other in order to come up with anything useful to offer to the university's or college's neighbors. In this cause, the sciences and humanities have to negotiate a lasting peace. Because so many regional dilemmas involve environmental matters, any understanding demands the full participation of humanists, natural and social scientists, and engineers.

The National Dilemma. Students want an education that will open the door to more satisfying and rewarding careers. Meanwhile, the majority of professors in the liberal arts believe that education's first (and second and third) priority is to exercise the soul and expand the mind, thereby casting the students' desire for employable skills as crassly commercial and narrowly utilitarian. "Students who have little money are especially concerned about jobs and careers," Harry Lewis wrote, "but Harvard portrays employability as antagonistic to the true purpose of a liberal education." More pointedly, Lewis explained with characteristic directness: "A liberal education in the sense Harvard now uses the term is simply an education not meant to make students employable" (2006, pp. 6 and 253). "Vocational courses," Bok wrote with an evocative Western flair, "have long been a burr under the saddle of those who teach the liberal arts. According to one survey, 60 percent of Arts and Sciences professors do not even think that preparing for a good job is a particularly important goal for undergraduates." And, Bok pointed out, "denying vocational concerns any place in the curriculum" carries the ironic outcome of diminishing "the chance to help undergraduates think about their careers in terms broader than simply making money" (2006, pp. 281–282).[3]

The Regional Solution. When we focus on connecting higher education to its surroundings, the question, "Shall we educate students for well-lived lives or for careers?" suddenly rewrites itself and becomes, "Shall we surrender to—or refuse—this unnecessary and false distinction?" After more than a century of squabbling over this choice, it is time to declare a place-based truce. The development of the mind and soul and the pursuit of a valuable career are interconnected projects, and social and moral calamities arise when careers are placed in a sphere quarantined and sequestered from wisdom, spirit, compassion, and virtue. Young people have enough burdens in life without having to deal with addled elders who have somehow or other cooked up a desire to keep the moral dimensions of earning a living separate from the moral dimensions of living a wise and reflective life.

The National Dilemma. The pursuit of prestige, the desire for the good opinion of peers and colleagues, and the effort to routinize channels of lateral and vertical faculty mobility have produced what Thelin called "homogenization and loss of institution distinction" (2004, p. 319). A one-size-fits-all mode of appraising faculty achievement became a powerful tool for squishing innovation.

The Regional Solution. The project of responding to the West's invitation to innovation holds, as its core, the restoration of respect for variation and the rejection of the dreary and spirit-squishing uniformity that (temporarily!) took over higher education's mode of selecting and retaining faculty. Of necessity, recognizing the wide range of skills, approaches, and temperaments needed for regional relevance shows the old one-size-fits-all standards to be antiquated and pointlessly restrictive. In the process, measures of institutional prestige, stature, and accomplishment acquire a refreshing flexibility.

Unexamined and unnecessarily constraining assumptions about the allocation of prestige are, after all, at the root of higher education's problems. Thus, we now address the two most popular faculty objections to accepting the opportunities of a regional orientation:

1. Will paying attention to western settings and constituencies make universities and colleges parochial and provincial? The answer is "No."
2. Will every faculty member have to drop their previous areas of expertise and study the West? The answer is also "No."

In response to the first question, in our own experience at the University of Colorado's Center of the American West, we have lost nothing in the way of national or international standing by declaring the study of our region to be our focus. The penalty, for my own turn toward "applied history," has been a frenzy among nominating committees and electorates of professional historical associations; having gone maverick in my professional practice, I have been elected vice president of the Teaching Division of the American Historical Association and president of both the Organization of American Historians and the Society of American Historians. Or we might consider the occasion when our Center of the American West was contacted by the French Embassy in Washington, DC. These sophisticated Europeans knew that if they wanted to know the nation where they were posted, they had to extend their attention beyond the East Coast and to learn about the West. Our center struck them as the obvious place to turn for help, guidance, and connection. Did we feel parochial and provincial when sought out by the French? On the contrary, we seemed to be at the mountaintop of savoir faire.

Now, we turn to the second concern, the fear that this approach will require everyone to drop their existing fields of expertise and retrain and retool as scholars focused on the American West.

Accepting the regional invitation to innovation, professors will not need to shift fields of expertise. On the contrary, all that faculty members will need to do is to engage in stimulating and thought-provoking conversations with their colleagues, exploring the relevance of their existing interests to the issues of their locale. Only in the rarest of circumstances will such conversations yield no projects worthy of action.

Let me give some examples of these unexpectedly fruitful collaborations. The Center of the American West once did a program for the National Park Service on sound and noise in the National Parks. And who gave one of the most stimulating and valuable presentations at that symposium? It was a medieval historian whose research explores rules of conduct at monasteries. The medievalist told us how, in creating rules of silence, monks drew a distinction between celestial sound (so the rule of silence did not prohibit speaking, chanting, and singing in ceremonies) and secular sound (the forms of chatter that fill our social worlds). Working its way into the minds of the audience, this distinction between celestial sound and secular sound made a very precise match to the distinctions made by people struggling over National Park Service policy between natural sounds (peeping frogs, chirping birds, bugling elk, quietly chatting hikers) and mechanical sounds (snowmobiles, ATVs, hikers bellowing into cell phones). The expertise of the medieval historian provided a fresh point of entry into a discussion otherwise at risk of staleness and repetition.

In another case, a classicist at the University of Colorado, Peter Knox, gave us a novel way of thinking about the complex attitudes of Whites toward American Indian people. Western American historians are well aware of the paradox by which some Army officers of the nineteenth century were not only sympathetic to the cause of the American Indian people they fought but also were sometimes outspoken and direct in their condemnations of the conduct of the federal government and white settlers. It had not occurred to me, however, to place this paradox in a broader context of the relationship between conquerors and the conquered long before the nineteenth century. When our colleague from classics gave a talk for the Center of the American West on the Roman poet Ovid and the time he spent on the frontier between Roman Empire and the barbarians, this broader context came soaring into my attention. From the classicist, we learned that Roman officers sometimes wrote down speeches, composed in perfect Latin, that had ostensibly been given by the barbarian leaders at the time of their defeats in battle. As he described this pattern, the fact that American military officers often did pretty much the same thing (Nez Perce Chief Joseph's "I will fight no more forever" speech might be the best known example) raised a flood of questions. Did US Army officers do this because many of them had studied Latin in their classical educations and thus knew that this was the expected thing for a military officer to do when fighting barbarians? Or were we observing something closer to a quality in human nature, by which the guilt of conquest was reduced by a ritualized expression of admiration for the nobility of the defeated barbarians, thereby affirming also the graciousness of the conquerors? While we still puzzle over those questions, we received the valuable lesson that our understanding of any dimension of Indian/White relations would be enhanced, freshened, and deepened if we listened closely to our colleagues who study comparable social relations in other parts of the world.[4]

The History Department at Montana State University offers another example. With an established strength in western American history, they decided to hire historians of other nations whose work connected directly to western topics. For instance, Brett Walker, a Japanese historian, found the history of the Yellowstone wolves to be an illuminating and useful comparison to his own case study of the elimination of wolves in Japan.

We return to the question: Does a regional approach mean that every member of the faculty must become an expert on the American West? The answer is an emphatic "No." But does a regional approach mean that every member of the faculty is invited into a conversation to discover and celebrate the relevance of their work to their surroundings? The answer is an equally emphatic "Yes."

And now, as we conclude this prolonged cheerleading session for place-based higher education, it is time to look directly at a mystery that has undoubtedly come to puzzle many readers: "Will this author ever notice, even for a moment, that digital technology is entirely transforming higher education in the twenty-first century?"

That moment has finally come.

Digital technology may have a disproportionately greater impact on Western higher education than its counterparts in other regions. The regional challenges of rugged terrain, high elevation, and vast geographic expanse have been made more manageable by an elaborate network of roads and highways along with a pattern of concentrating population in cities that characterizes the West. Nonetheless, remoteness still requires constant navigation and accommodation in the everyday transactions of many Westerners, and this unmistakably enhances the value that the educational institutions of cyberspace can offer the students of the region. "Distance learning" thus holds a great deal of promise for Westerners, offering a spectrum of advantages that the extent of geographic space could otherwise thwart.

I am not going to be of much value in the journey to that future. As an educator, I am, to the core of my soul, a proponent of proximity. I am happy to use electronic media to make an initial contact with students, and to stay in touch with them when we cannot meet in person. But everything I have loved about teaching has been made possible by the taken-for-granted, but still miraculous feature of everyday life at a college or university: Young people and their elders are in each other's immediate, material company. Thanks to this feature, I have had more than my share of intense and memorable experiences in classrooms. I have had even more than my share of one-on-one conversations that had equally lasting impacts on individual students, and on me. I have taken students with me on outings into our proximate "real world": to ranches undergoing natural gas development and to conferences where we dined with Westerners of note, from former secretaries of the Interior to the most accomplished Western writers. In line with the Harvard-centered section of this chapter, I have also taken a University of Colorado student with me to Cambridge, Massachusetts, where we visited with noted *New York Times* columnist Anthony Lewis in his home, and went (Mr. Lewis did not accompany us, though his presence would certainly have added to our success) on a "scavenger hunt" at the Harvard Law School, going to door-to-door seeking a professor I might know well enough to visit with (thank you, Professor Mark Tushnet, for helping us bring that scavenger hunt to a satisfying conclusion). If I list the great experiences I have had in the actual, material company of students, and I try to compile a comparable list of the exhilarating electronic exchanges I have had with students, the inventory presented in the two columns is strikingly unbalanced. I will not (as if I could!) block the road that will lead Westerners to an unforeseeable, but maybe very attractive, future in online education. But the very word "distance" in the term "distance learning" makes a person who is enchanted by the company of young people respond to the invitation to shift to digital communication with a decisive "No thanks."

More to the point, in the past century and a half, oddly matched teams of fundraisers and construction workers have brought into being a vast infrastructure: the enormous arrangement of buildings and grounds called "campuses." Even if online education proves to have so many advantages that the classrooms, dormitories, stadiums, athletic facilities, museums, cafeterias, and faculty offices are eventually converted into staging grounds for the production of Massive On-Line Open Courses, there will still be several decades, maybe even a century, in which anachronistic practitioners of material, place-based higher education will still be found puttering around those vestigial buildings. And there will be at least a few years when I can be trotted out, nursing home assistants trailing along beside me, to reminisce about the ancient days of yore when a professor could sit with a student and declare, "You can write better than this," and then lead the student in the very material actions required to make that declaration prophetic and productive. In these next years, place-based higher education will not instantly surrender all its relevance and value. On the contrary, it will—at the least—leave a foundation and legacy permitting students to bring experiences in their homes and surroundings into play in their digital discussions.

While some of the people who work in higher education have fallen into what we might call "institutional hypochondria," finding ills and ailments, aches and pains, in ordinary professional life, there is no denying that universities and colleges confront serious dilemmas in the early twenty-first century. A quotable remark from the clever George Norlin, president of the University of Colorado in the 1920s, retains some relevance today. When Norlin visited his home state of Wisconsin, a farm woman inquired into his party affiliation. Norlin replied that he was a Democrat. "But," she said in what she saw as a compliment, "you don't look like a Democrat." "No," President Norlin said to her, "I've been sick" (Davis, 1965, p. 264).

After my 40 years in the academic saddle, I seem to have joined President Norlin in feeling a little less than robust when I look around at the state of higher education in this region and in this country. But after any lamentation over current troubles, it is always useful to reach for our next dose of that prime antinostalgia blocker, historical perspective, and to remind ourselves, in Page Smith's words, that "the crisis of the university is...nothing new" (1990, p. 293). Still, the fact that crisis is nothing new does not mean that we are required to respond to the crisis of the hour with solutions that are also "nothing new."

Here is the crux: Can the universities and colleges of the twenty-first century claim anything in the way of a purpose or sense of direction? After World War II, "few universities had devoted much attention to the question of clarity of mission—or even missions," Thelin has explained. "About the only approximation of a mission that research universities could" offer "was a commitment to 'advance knowledge.'" This "vague, relativistic statement" left hard questions unaddressed: "Knowledge for what purpose, and for whom?" Thelin then delivered his body blow: "The problem was not that the center had failed, but rather that the modern American university had no center at all" (2004, pp. 314 and 316). Kerr's take on this problem of the "center" hit the target squarely: "I agree," he wrote, "that higher education is now adrift, but it may be at the vital center of a society adrift" (2001, p. 210). Harvard's Harry Lewis packed all this into an efficient sentence: "Universities are having a hard time making the case that the education they offer is about anything in particular" (2006, p. 24).

Western higher education could change that.

NOTES

1. Of all Western institutions of higher education, tribal colleges have probably been the most likely to respond favorably to this invitation. While the author of this chapter had much on her mind, they are discussed in chapters 4, 5, and 6.
2. The Center of the American West at the University of Colorado has fine allies and counterparts at the Udall Center at the University of Arizona, the Andrus Center at Boise State University, the Stegner Center at the University of Utah, the Center for the Rocky Mountain West at the University of Montana, and the Bill Lane Center for the American West at Stanford.
3. The study cited by Bok is Arthur Levine's, "Career Education: A Prospective, a Retrospective, and a Few Guesses." In M. A. Rehnke (ed.), *Career Programs in a Liberal Arts Context.* San Francisco, CA: Jossey-Bass, 1987, pp. 12 and 14.
4. The Center of the American West project that currently carries my greatest enthusiasm is another collaboration with the Classics Department, organized around the entirely convincing proposition that no one can understand the American West without closely reading the historical writing of Herodotus.

REFERENCES

Bok, D. *Our Underachieving Colleges: A Candid Look at How Much Students Learn and Why They Should Be Learning More.* Princeton: Princeton University Press, 2006.

Curti, M., and R. Nash. *Philanthropy and the Shaping of Higher Education.* New Brunswick, NJ: Rutgers University Press, 1965.

Davis, W. E. *Glory Colorado! A History of the University of Colorado, 1858–1963.* Boulder, CO: Pruett Press, 1965.

Fradkin, P. L. *Wallace Stegner and the American West.* New York: Alfred A. Knopf, 2008.

Hansen, II, J. *Democracy's College in the Centennial State.* Fort Collins: Colorado State University, 1977.

Hardy, D. *Wyoming University: The First 100 Years, 1886–1986.* Laramie: University of Wyoming, 1986.

Harstad, B. "A Trip into the Yukon Region, 1898–1899." *Concordia Historical Institute Quarterly*, Spring, 1988, 61 (1): 3–21.

Hopkins, E. J., and A. Thomas Jr. *The Arizona State University Story.* Tempe: Arizona State University, 1960.

Kerr, C. *The Uses of the University*, 5th ed. Cambridge, MA: Harvard University Press, 2001.

King, S. *On Writing: A Memoir of the Craft.* New York: Pocket Books, 2000.

Lewis, H. R. *Excellence without a Soul: How a Great University Forgot Education.* New York: Public Affairs, 2006.

Mirrielees, E. R. *Stanford: the Story of a University.* New York: G. P. Putnam's Sons, 1959.

Reid, J. J. *Colorado College: The First Century.* Colorado Springs: Colorado College, 1979.

Rosovsky, H. *The University: An Owner's Manual.* New York: W. W. Norton, 1990.

Rudolph, F. *The American College and University: A History.* New York: Random House, 1962.

Servin, M. P., and I. H. Wilson. *Southern California and Its University: A History of USC, 1880–1964.* Los Angeles: University of Southern California, 1969.

Smith, P. *Killing the Spirit: Higher Education in America.* New York: Viking, 1990.

Thelin, J. R. *A History of American Higher Education.* Baltimore, MD: Johns Hopkins University Press, 2004.

White, R. *It's Your Misfortune and None of My Own: A History of the American West.* Norman: University of Oklahoma Press, 1991.

Part II

State Development Perspectives and Federal Influences, 1945–2013

4

Middle Border States: Higher Education in Idaho, Montana, North Dakota, South Dakota, and Wyoming*

Jason E. Lane and Francis J. Kerins Sr.

Introduction

Idaho, Montana, North Dakota, South Dakota, and Wyoming comprise a land of great beauty, vast openness, intense independence, and great paradox. These states joined the union late in the nineteenth century and represent one of the last regions in the continental United States to develop educational institutions. They do not have the long histories of development like their fellow states in the East, nor the 400-year-old Spanish influences of the southwest states. The great American author Hamlin Garland (1917) referred to the land surrounding the Missouri River Valley region as the "Middle Border"—the place where the immigrants and homesteaders heading west encountered the prospectors and cattlemen making their way east from the Pacific coast. This Middle Border remains a subregion where seemingly disparate ideas, concepts, beliefs, and time periods continue to inhabit the same plane of existence, continually encountering and influencing each other.

The original inhabitants of the subregion date back thousands of years, but the current condition of these states was created by settlers who arrived less than 200 years ago, after the area was opened by Euro-American trappers and explorers in the late eighteenth century. The reservations of the area's American Indian tribes are now surrounded by the social mechanisms of settlers who began slowly establishing trading posts, forts, and towns in the middle of the 1800s. More massive development soon began with the building of railroads, which allowed people to move more easily across the vast wilderness and companies to transport the large wealth of natural resources to other parts of the nation (Lamar, 1956).

Following their dreams and aspirations, the settlers sought to create new societies and believed such was possible even in the harsh climates and rugged lands of the Middle Border. As James Bryce, the British historian, politician, and author of *The American Commonwealth*, observed during his visit to the Dakota Territory in 1883: "The confidence of these Westerners is superb...They see the country not merely as it is, but as it will be twenty, fifty, a hundred years hence" (Clough, 1937, p. 8). Indeed, the leaders of these western states fought early for the development of higher education, embedding in their laws during the 1890s such beliefs as "the stability of a republican form of government depend[s] mainly on the intelligence of the people" (Idaho Constitution, Art. X, §1) and "that none of the youth of the state who crave the benefits of higher education [will] be denied, and that all may be encouraged to avail themselves of the advantages offered by the University" (Compiled Statutes of Wyoming, §477).

However, the philosophical statements about education must be balanced against the real ruggedness of the land that produced many of the most storied names from the American West. The explorers led by Meriwether Lewis and William Clark and their guide Sacagawea provided some of the first English labeled maps of the land and conducted the first scientific exploration of the area. Later inhabitants include famed heroes and outlaws of the Wild West: President and Rough Rider Theodore Roosevelt maintained a ranch in the North Dakota Badlands; "Wild Bill" Hickock, Calamity Jane, and Wyatt Earp resided for a time in the town of Deadwood in the Black Hills of South Dakota; Butch Cassidy began his criminal career in Wyoming and later worked in Idaho; and Lakota Sioux holy man Sitting Bull led his nation to victory over George Armstrong Custer in the Battle of Little Big Horn in Montana.

In many ways, the subregion remains one of the least developed in the nation. Fewer people reside in the entire five-state subregion than in New York City (US Census Bureau, 2010). Broad expanses of public land, large farms and ranches, and vast mountain ranges make it possible to travel miles without seeing another person. The largest city is Boise, Idaho, with a few more than 205,000 inhabitants as of 2010. Further, none of the states has professional sports teams, making college athletics a prominent feature in each state's culture.

This chapter is divided into two primary parts. Part one provides an overview of the subregion, exploring the commonalities and differences in the development of the public, private, and tribal postsecondary education. The second part of the chapter presents a more detailed review of the development of the higher education sector in each state, focusing on the history since World War II.

Before proceeding, it is important to note that a broad review such as this does not allow for a full exploration of all elements of each state's higher education sector. Although we have attempted to be as inclusive as possible, there are some institutions, programs, and events in these states other than the ones identified in this chapter. No implications are made regarding the value, quality, or importance of those not mentioned; they are simply not included. A survey of this kind is, of necessity, selective and limited.

Middle Border and the Origins of WICHE[1]

The institutions in the Middle Border are joined not only through their geographic locations but also by their membership in the Western Interstate Commission for Higher Education (WICHE). WICHE originated soon after World War II and, some might say, was created in part due to the efforts of the president of the University of Wyoming and the Wyoming governor. This was a time of vast expansion for higher education sectors across the United States, as the G.I. Bill provided the opportunity for hundreds of thousands of new students to enter academe. However, it was not a tidal wave of impending undergraduate students that prompted the development of WICHE; rather the state and educational leaders of the western states were confronted with growing demands among veterans for access to graduate and advanced professional education.

The idea of an interstate compact regarding higher education was first put forward by George D. "Duke" Humphrey, the president of the University of Wyoming. In the years before WICHE, there were no professional schools for medicine, dentistry, or veterinary science in six of the eight Rocky Mountain States or the territories of Alaska and Hawaii. In 1945, on his way from Mississippi, where he had been president of Mississippi State University, to Wyoming, to assume the presidency of the University of Wyoming, Humphrey stopped in Colorado to meet the dean of the University of Colorado Medical School, Ward Darley. Humphrey had a son who wanted to attend medical school in the following year. Knowing how few medical schools existed in the subregion, Humphrey wanted to befriend Darley with the hope of improving his son's chances for admission. This initial discussion actually led to the first iteration of a higher education related interstate compact in the area, when in 1949 the University of Colorado Medical School reserved seats in their first-year class for students from Wyoming and New Mexico.

After assuming the presidency at the University of Wyoming, Humphrey began to realize that the shortage of medical education in the subregion was not just of personal concern for his son but also a significant public policy issue as well. The two states with medical schools were becoming less receptive to accepting students from other states, due to internal pressures from taxpayers not to exclude their children from these opportunities. Over time, it was becoming increasingly apparent that the shortage of medical education here was resulting in a shortage of medical professionals as well. With this rising concern as a backdrop, Humphrey and Darley met in 1946 and 1947 with the governors of Colorado and Wyoming to discuss the possibility of creating an interstate compact. In 1948, the governors of Colorado, New Mexico, Utah, and Wyoming gathered in Denver for the Mountain States Governors Conference on Education to discuss the possibility of facilitating greater access to professional education in the subregion. Consensus was that the way forward may be through the development of an interstate compact, and the four participating governors reached out to their peers in other states to see if it was possible to broaden the interest. All states of the current WICHE membership came to participate except for North Dakota and South Dakota, likely because both already had their own medical schools. During this time Humphrey and Darley continued to work on an agreement to allow students from New Mexico and Wyoming to attend the University of Colorado Medical School.

A few days after the inception of Colorado-based medical student exchange in 1949, the western governors met in Salt Lake City for their annual meeting to discuss the creation of a subregional compact and charged a small group of governors, including Charles Robbins of Idaho, to assess the need and bring recommendations to the next year's meeting. In response, the governors of the western states drafted the Western Regional Education Compact in 1950 and, when five states approved of the compact in 1951, WICHE was born. Montana was the only state in the Middle Border states among the initial five members to ratify the compact in 1951. Idaho and Wyoming both ratified the compact in 1953. The Dakotas, which were not among the original conveners, did not join until 1985 (North Dakota) and 1988 (South Dakota).

Overview of the Postsecondary Sectors

One of the defining characteristics of these states is the predominance of public higher education, even with the rapid expansion of private for-profit institutions nationally. Almost one-half of all institutions in each state are public (see table 4.1) and the percentage of students enrolled in public higher education in fall 2010 ranged from 76 percent in South Dakota and Idaho to 95 percent in Wyoming. In fact, Wyoming is a bit of a national anomaly, having only one four-year public institution and not having until 2005 a private, accredited four-year higher education institution.[2]

The responsibility for developing and expanding the higher education sector in each state mainly fell to the territorial and state governments. Each

Table 4.1 Total number of 133 institutions by type by state, 2010

	Idaho		Montana		North Dakota		South Dakota		Wyoming	
	4-year	2-year	4-year	2-year	4-year	2-year	4-year	2-year	4-year	2-year
Public	4	4	6	12	8	6	7	5	1	7
Private nonprofit	5	0	4	1	5	1	7	4	0	0
Private for-profit	3	16	0	6	2	7	5	3	2	2

Note: Total number of all institutions in the five border states equals 133. All tribal colleges are included except Wind River Tribal College (WY), a two-year college that does not report IPEDS data.
Source: IPEDS College Navigator, 2010.

state, while having some unique features, follows similar developmental patterns. With the exception of Wyoming, each state operates two doctoral-granting, research-oriented universities as well as regional, comprehensive institutions, which provide baccalaureate and some masters-level programs. Further, all of the state-supported two-year institutions—although South Dakota does not have any community colleges—and Native American tribes in four states—Idaho does not have any—recognize and collaborate with tribally controlled colleges, especially regarding student credit transfer for example. The private institutions, while educating a minority of college students, also provide additional access to underserved regions and groups.

Prior to statehood, the territorial governments worked to develop a university in their respective regions. The oldest of the public institutions in the Middle Border subregion is the University of South Dakota, which was founded in 1862 (although it did not start classes until 1882). The last state in this Middle Border states to establish its own university was Montana, which created the University of Montana in 1893, four years after Montana became a state.[3] The universities of North Dakota, Wyoming, and Idaho were established in 1883, 1886, and 1889, respectively. The oldest public institution in each state is patterned after the traditional university model, offering an array of undergraduate and graduate programs as well as professional degrees such as law and, in the cases of North Dakota and South Dakota, medicine.

Yet, we must note that many of the oldest institutions in this section of the country were founded by those settling the land and are most often affiliated with a religious group. In Montana, the first institution of higher learning to offer courses was not founded by either the territorial or state government. In 1878, Rocky Mountain College was created by the residents of Deer Creek, Montana (15 years before the University of Montana), making it the second oldest institution of higher learning founded in these Middle Border states.[4] Five years later (1883), the Dakota Collegiate Institute (now University of Sioux Falls) began formal instruction in South Dakota. In North Dakota, Presbyterian settlers founded Jamestown College and began instruction in 1884[5] (a year following the University of North Dakota) and, in 1890, the College of Idaho[6] in Caldwell (one year after the University of Idaho). In 1888, Mormons founded Bannock State Academy, a two-year institution in Rexburg, Idaho (now a four-year institution known as Brigham Young University-Idaho).

The other early significant institutional development occurred with the financial support allotted by the provisions of the Morrill Land Grant Acts of 1862 and 1890. Each state in the nation used their new resources to support the development of agriculture- and engineering-related fields in existing or new institutions (Williams, 1991). In Idaho and Wyoming, the money was used to support and expand the operations of the existing university. In Montana, North Dakota, and South Dakota, a separate agricultural college was created (see table 4.2 for a listing of the land-grant institutions in this subregion).

Table 4.2 Land-grant universities (not including tribal colleges)

State	Institution	Date Founded
Idaho	University of Idaho	1889
Montana	Montana State University—Bozeman	1893
North Dakota	North Dakota State University	1890
South Dakota	South Dakota State University	1881
Wyoming	University of Wyoming	1886

Even though these states have a high number of institutions in comparison to total state populations, the systems remain among the smallest in the nation. Total undergraduate enrollments range from 35,500 in Wyoming to 84,850 in Idaho—the other three states maintain enrollments hovering around 50,000 (IPEDS, 2010). Further, the Middle Border states have historically been host to many of the least expensive institutions in the nation, and these five states have contributed very limited funding to student aid, with each state ranking among the bottom seven in the total amount of state money allocated to student aid programs (NASSGAP, 2010). This is, in part, explained by the low number of total students; but none of the states has aggressive student aid programs.

Enrollment and institutional characteristics of the major state universities in this subregion are remarkably similar, yet differ from the national averages (private institution characteristics are discussed below). All of the major state universities are located in small cites, and all are medium-sized institutions in regards to enrollment, although they are small by national comparison in the category of major universities in the state. Enrollments of the nine state research-oriented, doctoral-granting universities[7] as of fall 2010 range from 10,151 at South Dakota State University to 15,642 at the University of Montana (IPEDS, 2010). According to fall 2009 data, all of these institutions serve fewer full-time students than the national average of 80 percent for all doctoral and research universities, except North Dakota State University (82%) and the University of Idaho (81%) (IPEDS, 2010). Interestingly, while women comprise 55 percent of total doctoral and research enrollments nationally during 2009–2010, only the proportion of women at Idaho State University and University of South Dakota exceeds this number, with men actually comprising the majority of enrollments at Montana State University-Bozeman, North Dakota State University, University of Idaho, and the University of North Dakota (IPEDS, 2010).

Other Public Four-Year Institutions

In addition to the major state universities mentioned above, there are other public institutions offering four-year degree programs that typically serve a specific geographic area of a state (the exception being Wyoming). These institutions tend to be small, fairly comprehensive institutions with enrollments under 4,700 students (IPEDS, 2010), and have a focus on professional education, such as business and teacher education (in part due to the origins of most of these institutions as normal schools in the past century). Of particular note, the most populated and second largest state in the subregion—Idaho—is home to the second fewest number of higher education institutions besides Wyoming. In addition to the two research universities, the only public four-year schools are Lewis-Clark State College in Lewiston and Boise State University in Boise. Boise State is unique among the institutions of the Middle Border in that it is the only urban university in the subregion and has a significantly larger student population, serving close to 20,000 undergraduate and graduate students. The institution began as a junior college affiliated with the Episcopal Church in 1932 (Barrett, 1984). Baccalaureate programs were first offered in 1965, and four years later the institution became a part of the state system of higher education (Chaffee, 1970). Boise State provides an array of curricular offerings ranging from associate to doctoral degrees primarily in the areas of education, business, and computer information systems as well as engineering, health sciences, and applied technology.

An area of public policy worthy of note is the long-standing concern in Montana, North Dakota, and South Dakota that the expansiveness of the public system is too much of a drain on limited state resources and that consolidation would improve efficiency within the public sector (see, e.g., Hill, 1934; Millett, 1984; Lane, 2008). Opponents of such consolidation state that the regional universities not only provide access to higher education in remote areas of the state but also serve as the major economic and cultural centers of the towns in which they reside. The specifics of the debates in each state are discussed in the separate state sections below.

Community Colleges and Technical Schools

Community colleges were a late addition to the WICHE consortium, not joining their four-year peers until the 1960s amid the rapid buildup of higher education across this subregion. Because of their association with public school systems in many of these states, there was a debate as to whether such institutions belonged to the higher education or K-12 sector (Abbott, 2004). After a meeting of WICHE commissioners in 1966 in which this issue was discussed, the commission's staff was directed to give greater attention to incorporating community and technical schools into their work.

Taken together, public two-year colleges serve approximately 69,000 students. Just over 20,000 students attend community colleges in Idaho and Wyoming, while about 7,000 students are enrolled in each of the Dakotas (IPEDS, 2010). Today, the subsector with the most differentiation between the states is that of the community colleges and technical schools. For example, while South Dakota does not have a community college system, Wyoming has an independent community college system, governed separately from the University of Wyoming. On the other hand, Idaho, North Dakota, and South Dakota operate community colleges that are governed as part of a coordinated statewide higher education system. (Tribally controlled colleges are treated in a separate section.)

Wyoming's community college system serves as a model for system planning. The Wyoming Community College Commission coordinates the state's seven community colleges, which are dispersed throughout the state to provide access to postsecondary education, job-training, workforce development, and lifelong learning. A coordinated course-numbering system and articulation agreements ensure that students can complete a significant portion of their bachelor's degree before transferring to the University of Wyoming.

The other Middle Border states have taken less coordinated approaches to providing educational opportunities at the two-year level. South Dakota, with no public community college system, does have four locally governed, public technical institutes that offer a range of vocational and technical programs, provide general education components, and award associate degrees. North Dakota's five two-year institutions developed along three different tracks; two (North Dakota State College of Science and Minot State University-Bottineau) were created by the state's constitution, two were created by local school districts (Bismarck State College and Lake Region State College), and Williston State College began as an extension of the University of North Dakota. Students in Idaho are served by three community colleges (one each in the north and south ends of the state and one in Boise) and a technical school in the eastern subregion. Montana has three community colleges as well as five vocational-technical institutes that now operate as colleges of technology connected to either the University of Montana or Montana State University.

THE PRIVATE, NONPROFIT SECTOR

Limited resources, small communities, rugged environments, and federal assistance prompted state and territorial governments to take the lead in providing access to higher education, resulting in a much smaller private sector than most other regions in the United States. The private colleges and universities are primarily liberal arts institutions, educating relatively small numbers of undergraduates. Only one private institution, Brigham Young University-Idaho, had enrollment exceeding 2,500 undergraduate students in 2010. A total of 21 private, nonprofit, regionally accredited four-year institutions operate in this subregion.[8] Eleven of the schools reported enrollments of fewer than a thousand students. Four of those institutions are located in North Dakota, three in South Dakota, two in Idaho and Montana, and no such institutions exist in Wyoming (IPEDS, 2010).

Almost all of the private colleges in this subregion have a Christian affiliation and offer experiences ranging from a liberal arts curriculum such as at Dakota Wesleyan University (Methodist, 1885) in South Dakota to focused training for a religious profession such as at Boise Bible College (Church of Christ, 1974) in Idaho. Catholics have been the most prodigious, currently operating five institutions: Mount Marty (1936) and Presentation College (1951) in South Dakota, Carroll College (1909) and the University of Great Falls (1932) in Montana, and the University of Mary (1955) in North Dakota. The Presbyterians founded Jamestown College (1884) in North Dakota and the College of Idaho (1891) in Idaho. The South Dakota Baptists supported the University of Sioux Falls (1883) and the Sioux Falls Seminary (1949). Other religiously affiliated institutions include Augustana College in South Dakota (Lutheran, 1884), Brigham Young University-Idaho (Mormon, 1888), Northwest Nazarene University in Idaho (Church of the Nazarene, 1931), and Trinity Bible College in North Dakota (Assemblies of God, 1948). Both Medcenter One College of Nursing in North Dakota (1909) and New Saint Andrews in Idaho (1994) have Evangelical ties and Rocky Mountain College in Montana (1878) is now affiliated with the Methodist, Presbyterian, and United Church of Christ ministries.

TRIBAL COLLEGES

The Middle Border states remain home to significant numbers of Native Americans, affiliated with approximately 20 reservations recognized by the state or federal governments. Even though some of the colonial colleges (Harvard, College of William and Mary, and Dartmouth) were founded with missions that included educating Native Americans, the deeds of their leaders never achieved the touted goals of their founders (Reyhner and Eder, 2000). In fact, for most of this country's history, the public US higher education sectors have provided a less than hospitable (if not hostile) environment for Native American students with attrition rates in mainstream colleges and universities reaching as high as 90 percent (Stein, 1988). Concern about the lack of educational opportunities led state and tribal governments, as well as the federal government's Bureau of Indian Affairs, to find new ways to support the educational pursuits of Native Americans.

Starting in the 1960s, interest grew among Native Americans to provide advanced learning opportunities for members of the several tribal nations located within the United States. In 1968, Navajo Community College (now Diné College) in Arizona became the first tribally controlled college, followed by the creation of several similar institutions on reservations throughout the United States.

In 1978, Congress passed the Tribally Controlled Community College Assistance Act, authorizing financial assistance for the creation of tribal colleges, and in 1994 the tribal colleges received land-grant recognition from the federal government. These institutions fill a unique niche within the higher education sector in the United States. Operating on reservations throughout the Midwest and West, they have the dual purpose of providing postsecondary education (primarily associate degrees) and preserving the culture of the affiliated tribe (Ortiz and Boyer, 2003).

Given the significant number of tribes in the Middle Border, it should be no surprise that more than one-half of the 28 tribal colleges in the WICHE region are located in these five states (see table 4.3). Even more remarkable, the relatively small number of institutions in this subregion makes the addition of 15 tribal colleges in Montana, North Dakota, and South Dakota, since the founding of Oglala Lakota College in South Dakota in 1970, one of the most significant developments since World War II. While the colleges target a specific group of individuals, they are mostly public, open-access institutions and have significantly increased the availability of postsecondary education opportunities throughout Montana, North Dakota, and South Dakota, more than doubling the number of public two-year institutions in each state.

Table 4.3 List of tribal colleges by state

State/Institutions	Locations	Year Founded
Idaho (no tribal colleges)	N/A	N/A
Montana (7 tribal colleges)		
Blackfeet Community College	Browning	1976
Chief Dull Knife College	Lame Deer	1975
Fort Belknap College	Harlem	1984
Fort Peck Community College	Poplar	1978
Little Big Horn College	Crow Agency	1980
Salish Kootenai College	Pablo	1977
Stone Child College	Box Elder	1984
North Dakota (5 tribal colleges)		
Cankdeska Cikana Community College (formerly Little Hoop)	Fort Totten	1974
Fort Berthold Community College	New Town	1973
Sitting Bull College	Fort Yates	1972
Turtle Mountain Community College	Belcourt	1972
United Tribes Technical College	Bismarck	1987[a]
South Dakota (3 tribal colleges)		
Oglala Lakota College	Kyle	1970
Sinte Gleska University	Rosebud	1971
Sisseton-Wahpeton Community College	Sisseton	1973
Wyoming (1 tribal college)		
Wind River Tribal College (Associate status)	Ethete	2005

Note: [a]The year the institution moved from a vocational center to a college.
Source: White House Initiative on Tribal Colleges and Universities. Retrieved from http://www.ed.gov/about/inits/list/whtc/edlite-index.html, on February 8, 2008.

PROFESSIONAL EDUCATION

Even though the student enrollments in each state remain small relative to most other states in the nation, the Middle Border states does need to provide a range of educational programs to maintain and support this area's economy and workforce infrastructure. This is no less true in the area of professional education. However, the limited number of students pursuing professional education makes it difficult for each state system to provide a large number of high-cost professional programs, such as dentistry, medicine, optometry, and veterinary medicine. This is the issue that led to the creation of WICHE. Now, many of the states participate in cooperative agreements, such as the Professional Student Exchange Program sponsored by WICHE, that allow students from their own state to pursue a professional degree at an out-of-state institution in the five state subregion. Concerning legal education, unlike the limited in-state options for most professional programs, each state in this subregion has a law school accredited by the American Bar Association. All of the law schools are public entities attached to one of the state universities. The University of North Dakota's law school is the oldest, founded in 1899, while the University of Wyoming's, the youngest, was founded a little more than 20 years later, in 1920. Each school accepts small annual classes of students relative to many of their peers in other states, but they do produce a very high proportion of the lawyers in the subregion. Here are the individual state law schools and their founding dates:

1. University of Idaho (1909),
2. University of Montana (1911),
3. University of North Dakota (1899),
4. University of South Dakota (1901), and
5. University of Wyoming (1920).

Another critical area of concern for these states is educating, attracting, and retaining medical doctors in the many rural communities throughout this subregion. Of the five states treated in this chapter, only North Dakota (University of North Dakota School of Medicine and Health Sciences) and South Dakota (Sanford School of Medicine at the University of South Dakota) operate medical schools. The other three states participate in WWAMI, a partnership between the University of Washington's School of Medicine and the states of Wyoming, Alaska, Montana, and Idaho.

HISTORY OF HIGHER EDUCATION IN THE STATES OF THE MIDDLE BORDER

The following sections provide specific information about the evolution of higher education in each of the states reviewed in this chapter. The sections

Table 4.4 General state facts

State	Idaho	Montana	North Dakota	South Dakota	Wyoming
Oldest public institution (founding)	University of Idaho (1889)	University of Montana (1893)	University of North Dakota (1883)	University of South Dakota (1862)	University of Wyoming (1886)
Oldest 4-year private institution (affiliation/ founding)	The College of Idaho[a] (Presbyterian/1890)	Rocky Mountain College (Christian/1878)	Jamestown College (Presbyterian/1883)	University of Sioux Falls (Baptist/1883)	Wyoming Catholic College (Catholic/2007)[b]
State Coordinating Body	Idaho State Board of Education	Montana University System	North Dakota University System	South Dakota Board of Regents	University of Wyoming Trustees/ Wyoming Community College Commission
State Budget Cycle	Annual	Biennial	Biennial	Annual	Biennial

Notes:
[a] Ricks College, a Mormon two-year institution, was founded in 1888.
[b] The first private, for-profit institution to develop a campus in Wyoming was the University of Phoenix in 2004.

are intended to provide the reader with a broad overview of the state and specific developments related to higher education since World War II.

IDAHO

Idaho, with its broad base in the south and narrowing landmass in the north of the state, is ten times the size of Massachusetts and the fourteenth largest state in the nation. Its population of more than 1.5 million residents makes it the most populous state in the subregion and the only one of the five states in the Middle Border with more than one member in the House of Representatives, although it is only the fortieth most populated state in the country. Idaho has the most diverse population of the Middle Border states; a significantly lower Native American population than the other states, but a Hispanic population that almost reaches 11.2 percent of the state's population (US Census Bureau, 2010). The land was officially organized as part of the Idaho Territory in 1863, divided into its current boundaries in 1864, and incorporated as a state in 1890.

During the early 2000s, the state realized significant benefit from creating a support structure for technology entrepreneurs. According to a 2004 report by the Idaho Economic Development Association, there were more patents per capita in Idaho than any other state. Further, employment in the science and technology field increased by 38 percent between 1991 and 2002, and in 2001 science and technology accounted for more than 25 percent ($9.3 billion) of Idaho's gross domestic product. In 2006, it had one of the highest rates of job growth in the nation. Major companies with operations in the state include Micron Technology, Hewlett-Packard, Dell, and AMI Semiconductor. However, as of this writing the state was just beginning to recover from the downturn resulting from the 2008 economic crash, which resulted in a loss of 60,000 jobs (Idaho Department of Labor, 2011).

The earliest private postsecondary institutions in the state were Ricks College (now BYU-Idaho) and the College of Idaho, founded in 1888 and 1890, respectively.[9] The first public institution was the University of Idaho, which was established by the state constitution in 1889 (see table 4.4). Beside the University of Idaho, the public sector expanded to include a metropolitan college (Boise State University), an additional doctoral-granting university (Idaho State University), a comprehensive college (Lewis-Clark State College), three community colleges (College of Southern Idaho, North Idaho College, and the College of Western Idaho), and a two-year technical school (Eastern Idaho Technical College). There are also five private, not-for-profit, accredited institutions providing educational opportunities (Boise Bible College, BYU-Idaho, New Saint Andrews College, Northwest Nazarene University, and the College of Idaho).

The two decades following World War II witnessed significant change in the landscape of Idaho's higher education sector. Before the war, the University of Idaho was the only public four-year institution in the state.

The state's two present-day largest institutions, Idaho State University (ISU) and Boise State University (BSU), started as junior colleges (Academy of Idaho in 1901 and Boise Junior College in 1932, respectively). However, a significant increase in enrollment following World War II led the state to approve four-year degree programs at ISU (1947) and BSU (1965). The rapid increases in enrollments, which resulted in more than doubling the student population in the ten years following the war, led to the hiring of new faculty and massive expansion in facilities, including classrooms, housing, and athletics. In fact, in the early 1970s, Idaho State University built Holt Arena, the first collegiate multipurpose, domed stadium and only the second such facility in the nation after the Houston Astrodome.

The postwar era was not without its setbacks for the state's higher education sector. In 1947, Albion State Normal School and Lewiston State Normal School were authorized by the state legislature to confer baccalaureate degrees and renamed Southern Idaho College of Education (SICE) and Northern Idaho College of Education (NICE), respectively. Yet, the expansion of four-year institutions was short-lived. In fact, as noted in the history of Lewis-Clark State College, "Concern over enrollments and Idaho finances following the outbreak of the Korean War, mixed with political maneuvering, led to the closure of NICE and [SICE] in 1951. The legislature reopened [NICE] in 1955 under the new name of Lewis-Clark Normal School," but SICE remained closed (Lewis-Clark State College, n.d., ¶11). Lewis-Clark received full institutional status in 1963 after operating for eight years as a branch campus of the University of Idaho and was renamed Lewis-Clark State College in 1971. It received accreditation as a four-year institution in 1973.

Constitutionally created in 1912, the Idaho State Board of Education (SBOE) oversees almost all aspects of public education in the state, including K-12 and postsecondary. Over the history of the SBOE, critics have raised concerns about the disparity in attention given to the different sectors; but we raise here only some specific issues about legal disparity within the system. In a nationwide review of state governance, Moos and Rourke (1959) noted Idaho as one of eight states at the time with a double standard within its higher education sector with, "the smaller colleges... created and governed by rigid statutes while the major university enjoys a wide degree of independence based on the constitution itself" (p. 188).[10] Further, while the SBOE governs all four-year institutions and the public schools, the two-year colleges are self-governed, only having to make legislative budget requests through the board. A legislative committee in 1995 did seek to eliminate some of the legal disparity within the higher education sector by granting the SBOE the authority to give institutions additional control over purchasing and capital expenses (Editors, *Chronicle of Higher Education*, 1996). However, in an interesting legal turn of events in 2005, the University of Idaho's inclusion in the constitution, which had provided it autonomy not enjoyed by other public institutions, restricted it from taking advantage of the legislature's willingness to allow most public four-year institutions to charge tuition. The University of Idaho was prohibited from doing so because the Constitution allows the university only to charge fees (Hebel, 2006).

In the decade and a half prior to the 2008 recession, all of higher education benefited from significant economic growth in Idaho. In the mid-1990s, the state worked to expand its economy beyond its traditional industries of mining, timber, and agriculture to include manufacturing, technology, and tourism. Most of the past decade, higher education saw significant increases in state appropriations, which were primarily used to increase low faculty salaries and improve access for the large number of high school graduates not pursuing a four-year degree.

In addition to increasing the funds for the system, the legislature also funded several programs designed to increase access for state residents, although the cost of education to the student has increased concomitantly. For example, in 1999 the legislature passed a bill to increase college-scholarship aid to children of firefighters or police officers disabled or killed in the line of duty. The next year, they created a college-savings program and the Idaho Promise Scholarship, a merit-based program (although it was not funded until the following legislative session). The following year saw the creation of a program to aid bilingual teaching assistants completing education degrees, an effort to accommodate the state's growing minority population.

In the midst of this period of growth in enrollments, state appropriations, and student fees, a 2001 tax cut and a significant drop in 2002 tax revenues resulted in the legislature cutting the higher education budget in the middle of the 2001–2002 fiscal year and then again in the following year. The legislature also reduced the awards from the Idaho Promise Scholarship and froze funds previously allocated for capital improvement projects. Despite such cuts, the legislature did authorize $136 million in bonds to build a higher education research complex in Boise, to be shared by the University of Idaho and Idaho State University (Editors, *Chronicle of Higher Education*, 2002, 2003). However, with the exception of the 2001–2003 period, Idaho higher education benefited significantly from a robust economy and increased interest in higher education by students and the general populace, at least until 2008.

The recession of 2008 hit Idaho worse than any other state in the Middle Border subregion. The state lost tens of thousands of jobs, total wages plunged about 6.4 percent, and there was a loss of more than 2,500 employers as of 2010 (Idaho Department of Labor, 2011). The recession fostered a number of changes for higher education, including cutting higher funding by 19.6 percent between FY2008 and FY2011, amending the state's constitution to allow the University of Idaho to charge tuition, reducing the bureaucratic oversight of purchasing, and the creation of the Higher Education Stabilization Fund (Association of Governing Boards, 2011; National Conference of State Legislatures, 2011; Zumeta and Kinne, 2011).

The fund, a "rainy day" account financed through the interest on tuition and fees, was intended to help public colleges and universities during state-funding shortfalls.

MONTANA

Montana is the largest state in this Middle Border states (fourth largest in the nation) and home to fewer than 1 million people (estimated 989,000 in 2010). The eastern part of the state is covered in prairie, while the west is defined by the Rocky Mountains. The largest minority group is Native Americans, representing 6.3 percent of the population (US Census Bureau, 2010). The economy remains primarily based on agriculture, producing a wide range of crops including wheat, barley, sugar beets, and honey, as well as raising cattle and sheep. The state also possesses a wide range of natural resources, including timber, gold, and coal.

Except for the far western edge of the state, the land was obtained by the US government as part of the Louisiana Purchase. The Lewis and Clark Expedition passed over the land in 1805. The discovery of gold and copper in the 1850s brought people to the area, leading to the creation of the Montana Territory in 1864 and eventually Montana's admission to the union as the forty-first state in 1889. Further, like Wyoming, women have long been allowed to participate in the governance of Montana, which was one of the first states to give women the right to vote and, in 1917, the first to elect a woman to Congress (Toole, 1959).

The oldest institution in the state is Rocky Mountain College, founded by the residents of Deer Creek in 1878. Fifteen years later (1893), the state legislature authorized the establishment of the University of Montana at Missoula, Montana State University at Bozeman, Montana Tech (formerly the State School of Mines at Butte), and the University of Montana-Western (formerly State Normal School at Billings). Presently, the Montana University System comprises two segments: The University of Montana, which has campuses in Missoula, Helena, and Dillon; and Montana State University, which has campuses in Bozeman, Billings, Great Falls, and Havre.[11] Further, there are three community colleges (Dawson, Flathead Valley, and Miles Community Colleges),[12] seven tribal colleges (see table 4.3), and three private colleges (Carroll College, University of Great Falls, and Rocky Mountain College).

As progressive as the state was in some arenas, it was the last state in the subregion to create a state-supported higher education sector. According to Malone, Roeder, and Lang (1991), the delay was caused by "intense jockeying among cities over which would become the capital" (p. 362). The adoption of the state constitution in 1893 created a multisite higher education system with four institutions: a university, agricultural college, school of mines, and a normal school. The legislature argued that such a system would provide all families with an educational institution within easy travel distance. Almost from the very beginning, however, critics of the multisite system, concerned about waste and undue competition, lobbied for closure of the smaller campuses. Such efforts, though, have proven politically unfeasible as citizens from areas with smaller institutions fear the loss of educational access, cultural opportunities, and economic development (Hill, 1934; Malone, Roeder, and Lang, 1991; Merriam, 1970).

As with the entire nation, enrollments following World War II increased through the 1950s and mushroomed in the 1960s, resulting in increases in the number of faculty and campus buildings (Malone, Roeder, and Lang, 1991). Toward the end of this era, the state opened five technical centers and began providing state funding for the three locally controlled community colleges making the Board of Regents responsible for their governance.

The boom in the 1960s led to additional concerns about duplication and coordination, which the state attempted to rectify as part of its new constitution in 1972 (Malone, Roeder, and Lang, 1991; Millett, 1984). With help from the Academy for Educational Development, the revised constitution created a strong Board of Regents and a commissioner, placing control of the public primary and secondary schools under a separate board of public education (Millett, 1984), whereas the original State Board of Education had been responsible for the entire public education sector since 1889. This new arrangement granted full authority over the higher education system, but preserved the right of the legislature to appropriate and audit funds (McClure, 1999). In 1976, the board created a set of duties for the commissioner and "declared that the commissioner outranked the presidents and the presidents should report to the board only through the commissioner" (Millett, 1984, p. 131). The board and commissioner worked to create a more coordinated system of higher education, finally centralizing all public postsecondary institutions in the state under the authority of the Board of Regents in 1987, creating a system of six four-year institutions, three community colleges, and five technical schools. In 1994, the system was reorganized with all campuses (except for the three community colleges, which receive significant local funding) affiliating with either the University of Montana or the Montana State University. A proposed constitutional amendment in 1996 that would have replaced the Board of Regents with a Department of Education headed by a gubernatorial appointee was defeated.

In the midst of the centralization efforts in the 1980s, the system received significant cuts in funding, placing the state's financial support of its two public universities near the lowest in the nation and more than 25 percent below regional peers (Malone, Roeder, and Lang, 1991). Further, all four-year institutions faced significant deferred maintenance, underfunded libraries, rising tuition, shrinking state support, and large out-migration of high school graduates seeking postsecondary education elsewhere. "It spelled the increasingly real threat of both lost opportunity for Montanans and declining economic, social, and cultural competitiveness for the state" (p. 366).

In the late 1990s, the fortunes of the state's public higher education sector began to change. The state appropriated more substantial support, including increases in operating, financial aid, and capital improvement budgets as well as new monies for construction and matching funds for federal grants. The voters approved the extension of a state property tax used to fund higher education, and the state Supreme Court nullified a new constitutional amendment mandating that all future tax increases need voter approval (some higher education leaders feared the amendment would restrict their ability to raise tuition and fees). In 2000, the Board of Regents eliminated a policy that allowed private colleges to prevent a public institution from offering an undergraduate program that duplicated offerings of the private college in the same city.

Unfortunately, the good fortunes did not last long. In the midst of 2001–2003 biennium, university officials, who were expecting funding increases, experienced significant cuts to their budgets as state tax revenues fell more than $150 million short of projections. A slow economy and sagging tax revenue resulted in almost no increases for the next several years, leading to double-digit tuition increases. Such funding patterns placed the state system in a deleterious situation, particularly given that a decreased population of high school students feeding into the state higher education system, growing competition from other states, and the general lack of state-supported incentives to stay in the state were negatively affecting enrollments. After several lean years, a projected state revenue surplus beginning in 2005 led to the much-needed infusion of cash to the Montana University System during the 2005, 2007, and 2009 biennial legislative sessions. During this time, students benefited from a mandated tuition freeze and increased appropriations for student aid programs.

Montana is usually one of the last states to be affected by a recession and this was no less true following the Great Recession. Fortunately, for FY2010, the state was able to tap into the funds provided by the American Recovery and Reinvestment Act (ARRA) of 2009. While the state appropriated 14 percent less funding to higher education than in the previous year, the use of the ARRA funds resulted in a net increase in funding for Montana's higher education institutions. In 2010, the state focused primarily on issues of access, increased money for community colleges, providing a special fund for distance learning activities, and allocated money to help offset tuition increases (National Conference of State Legislatures, 2011).

NORTH DAKOTA

North Dakota ranks nineteenth in total landmass; but its population of approximately 673,000 makes it the forty-eighth most populous state. North Dakota and South Dakota were both admitted to the Union on November 2, 1989. North Dakota comprises mostly vast plains, rolling hills, and river valleys. The rural nature of the state is enhanced with the population mostly concentrated in four cities: Bismarck (the capital), Fargo, Grand Forks, and Minot. The dominant minority group is Native Americans (5.4%), located primarily on the five reservations in the state and comprise the Arikara,

Chippewa, Hidatsa, Mandan, Metis, and Sioux tribes (US Census Bureau, 2010). The state's major industries include agriculture, tourism, manufacturing, and extraction and refinement of fossil fuels, such as crude oil and lignite coal.

The origins of higher education in the state can be traced back to the founding of the University of North Dakota in 1883, followed shortly by the opening of Jamestown College (a private, Presbyterian-oriented college) in 1884. The adoption of North Dakota's constitution in 1889 greatly expanded the public postsecondary sector. In order to appease cities across the newly created state, the legislature placed institutions in various population centers (Kelly, 1933). In fact, with the exception of the three locally founded community colleges, all public postsecondary institutions are directly referenced in the state constitution.

Largely, the state's higher education sector remains the same as when it was created, with the North Dakota University System now comprising 11 public institutions. This is in addition to four nonprofit, private institutions and five tribal colleges. The two largest institutions in the state are the University of North Dakota and North Dakota State University. The other public four-year institutions in the state are Mayville State University, Dickinson State University (added to the constitution in 1916), Minot State University (added to the constitution in 1912), and Valley City State University.[13] The School of Forestry in Bottineau became a branch campus of North Dakota State University in 1968 and in 1996 was renamed Minot State University-Bottineau. The Scientific School in Wahpeton is now the North Dakota State College of Science (NDSCS) and, along with Bismarck State College, Lake Region State College, and Williston State College provide two-year degree programs and other academic offerings. Of particular note, NDSCS was created in 1903 and is one of the oldest public two-year colleges in the nation, only two years younger than the first such institution, Joliet Junior College in Illinois. The public school in Ellendale no longer operates; however, the campus was bought in 1968 by Trinity Bible College, a four-year private institution. The other four-year religiously affiliated institutions include Jamestown College, University of Mary, and Medcenter One College of Nursing.[14]

The onset of World War II proved to be a significant negative influence on the enrollments of the higher education sector (Geiger, 1958; Robinson, 1966). During the 1939–1940 academic year, total statewide enrollment in higher education reached an all-time high of 7,000 students. However, by 1943–1944, the need for young recruits to aid the war effort caused enrollments to plummet to fewer than 1,900. Fortunately, the diminished enrollments were short-lived; the return of the veterans propelled enrollments to new heights, reaching 7,800 students by the fall of 1950 and increasing to 14,000 by 1961. Bolstered by the postwar prosperity and greatly enhanced budgets, state higher education leaders began demanding that the legislature invest more significantly in the state's colleges and universities (Robinson, 1966). Between 1947 and 1957, the state legislature appropriated funds to build more than 20 major buildings on campuses throughout the state.

The State Board of Higher Education (SBHE) was created in 1938 because of a broad-based desire to limit the role of politics in the governance of the higher education system; yet politics and politicians continued to dominate major debates and decision-making processes. Constitutional provisions charged the eight-member SBHE (the eighth position, reserved for a student from a North Dakota college or university, was added in the late 1970s) with authority over all state-owned higher education institutions in the state; however, the legislature's power of the purse ensured ongoing tensions.

Some of the political tension is due to cultural importance of education and a firm belief in citizen oversight of all aspects of state government, evidenced in part by much public commentary and a consistent desire to study the various educational sectors.[15] In the past four decades, studies have raised concerns about tuition becoming too expensive, institutions numbering too many, out-of-state students burdening North Dakota taxpayers, and that the institutions were poorly managed and an overall drain on limited state resources. However, studies also found the public higher education sector to be a critical component of the state's economic development, needed increased appropriations and flexibility (i.e., decreased state regulation), did not have competitive faculty salaries, and faced a deteriorating infrastructure. This constant give-and-take between higher education and the state government led John Richardson (1985), the Commissioner of Higher Education, to issue a 1985 white paper wherein he stated:

> We have come to recognize this very basic fact: North Dakota's past ways of tossing around higher education problems and solutions have not worked. For example, what typically happens when higher education complains, as we often do, about the problem of underfunding? Our critics cry, "Waste, inefficiency, too-high salaries," and other charges. We shout back about overwork, national markets for faculty and staff, deteriorating facilities, rising costs of equipment and books, and so on. What progress have we made?
>
> The pattern of complaining, blaming, criticizing, denying, proposing, and defending have not made you, me, or our supporting publics much more comfortable with our higher education system... It is time for a new kind of conversation and action." (Richardson, 1985, p. 4)

However, not until five years later was any significant change realized.

Several reports during the 1980s calling for increased coordination and the closure of campuses along with concerns about the loss of revenue due to voters repealing two tax measures and rejecting a third in 1989 resulted in the SBHE looking for ways to create new efficiencies in the state (Blumenstyk and Cage, 1990). With the support of the governor and the legislature, the members of the state board voted to create the North Dakota University System in 1990. In addition, the "commissioner" was elevated to "chancellor," but "the board still delegate[d] full authority to the institution presidents to administer their individual campuses" (Legislative Study Council, 1991). The lack of clear lines of authority between the presidents, chancellor, and board created new questions about the governance system and confusion and frustration for system leaders (Lane, 2008). The situation eventually led to Chancellor Robert Potts leaving his post in 2006 when the board did not support his attempts to exert authority over one of the university presidents (see Dalrymple, 2006).

The discussion about closing a campus predates even the creation of the SBHE. A 1929 study of the higher education sector in North Dakota by Professor Peik from the University of Minnesota, prompted by concerns about lack of funding, found that Maine was the only state in the nation with more teachers colleges per person than North Dakota. As a result, the report predicted that the state could not afford to offer anything more than an "average" education (Robinson, 1966). Debates about institutional closure would rage in the capital and throughout the state for many decades following. While agreement was occasionally reached on the need for closure, consensus about which institution was almost never found (except that the system did close the University of North Dakota's branch campus in Ellendale in the late 1960s after a fire destroyed much of the campus). Finally, in 1998 the legislature put forward to the voters an amendment to remove specific reference to institutions and locations from the constitution. In November 1998, 64 percent of the voters rejected the amendment.

After the resounding defeat of the referendum (removing any chance of closing one of the smaller schools as a cost-saving measure), the state called for a study to "address the expectations of the North Dakota University System in meeting the state's needs in the twenty-first century" (Roundtable for the North Dakota Legislature, 2000, p. i.). The call for the study resulted in the creation of the North Dakota Higher Education Roundtable, a 61-member group comprising leaders from the state government, higher education sector, and business industry. The roundtable issued a report in June 2000 that called for several substantive changes in how the university system operated and eventually resulted in a radical shift in how the state funds the system. In response to calls for more flexibility, the state legislature agreed to start allocating appropriations as a block budget (instead of line items) and to allow institutions to keep and decide how to allocate tuition revenues. Previously, the state collected the tuition revenue and decided how it should be allocated.

The Roundtable did not just lead to the change in administrative policy, it also created a mind shift in the general populace wherein voters, politicians, and the press began to regard higher education as a critical component for the future economic vitality of the state. The Roundtable eventually led to additional investments, including the Centers of Excellence program, which created a several million dollar fund to help universities attract external funding to the state and increasing the state's economic production (see Lane, 2008, for an extensive review of the development of the North Dakota Roundtable). Though as with many politically created entities, there does continue to be debate about the appropriate role and the overall effectiveness of the program.

During the past decade, the state also benefited economically from: increasing prices for agricultural commodities; the strengthening of the Canadian dollar, which brought more shoppers down from their northern neighbor; and an oil boom occurring in the western half of the state. In fact, as the 2008 recession washed across the United States, sweeping away tax revenues and rainy day funds, North Dakota continued to thrive. With a growing economy and low unemployment, the state became a poster child for success and evidenced the benefits of the state's longtime frugality and cautious nature when it came to spending public funds. Unlike most other states in the nation, North Dakota's higher education system continued to grow during this recession, with new buildings being erected and faculty salaries continuing to increase (Carlson, 2010; Fuller, 2010).

South Dakota

The second smallest state in the Middle Border states (seventeenth largest in the nation—South Dakota's landmass is larger than all of New England and New Jersey combined), the state has the largest number of accredited institutions (26) in the subregion. As of 2010, the population primarily resided in the eastern part of the state (forty-seventh largest state in terms of population) with just under 20 percent of the state's 814,000 people living in Sioux Falls near the southeast corner of the state (US Census Bureau, 2010). In comparison, Pierre, the state capital located in the middle of the state, has a population of 13,600. The western part of the state tends to be more rural and conservative with a focus on tourism and ranching. The eastern side is more densely populated and politically moderate with an economy based on service and farming. While most of the state is prairie land, the river bluffs of the Missouri River rise up in the east and the Black Hills define the western horizon, including Mount Rushmore and the Crazy Horse Memorial, the yet-to-be-completed mountain monument to the leader of the Oglala tribe. Agriculture, tourism, and service are the largest components of the state's economy.

The South Dakota Board of Regents was one of the first, constitutionally created, centralized governing board in the nation (Kelly, 1933). In fact, Moos and Rourke (1959) proffer that it was South Dakota that began the trend in the past century toward more centralized governance structures in each state (even though New York [1784] and Georgia [1785] had preexisting centralized structures). The creation of the South Dakota Board of Regents (SDBOR), however, was not the beginning of higher education in the state. The University of South Dakota predates the creation of the SDBOR. The institution was charted by the territorial legislature in 1862 and officially opened in 1882. The territorial legislature also created the South Dakota School of Mines in 1885. The adoption of the amended state constitution in 1896 centralized the governance of the public system under the SDBOR.

As of 2012, the regents govern six postsecondary institutions: Black Hills State University, Dakota State University, Northern State University, South Dakota School of Mines and Technology, South Dakota State University, and the University of South Dakota. In addition, there were four public locally governed, two-year technical institutes located in Watertown, Mitchell, Sioux Falls, and Rapid City, although the State Board of Education does have to approve bonds, tuition rates, and new programs (P. Gough, personal communication, February 11, 2008). There were four tribal colleges (see table 4.3), five private, not-for-profit institutions (Augustana College, Dakota Wesleyan University, Killian Community College, Mount Marty College, Presentation College), and three not-for-profit medical schools (Avera McKennan Hospital School of Radiologic Technology, Avera Sacred Heart Hospital, and Sanford Medical Center).

While the board's creation was a drastic deviation from how states at the time governed postsecondary educational institutions, the public higher education sector in South Dakota has remained remarkably stable since its onset, while the private sector has been struck by a number of mergers, closings, and degree changes. A study by the Carnegie Foundation for Teaching in 1933 found that there were seven public and nine private institutions operating in the state at that time (Kelly, 1933). As of 2007, six of the seven public institutions were still open; however, there were only seven private, nonprofit institutions (excluding medical centers) in operation (only three of these private institutions were a part of the 1933 cohort).

Almost since the creation of the state, the public postsecondary sector has been a much studied, but little changed, component of the political arena. According to a review by the South Dakota Legislative Research Council (2000; hereafter SDLRC), the state's higher education system had been studied 20 times by interim legislative committees since 1972—not to mention the numerous prior studies dating back to 1918. These studies have raised a variety of concerns, including there being too many state-supported institutions, not enough institutions in the western part of the state, and the Board of Regents not having a professional staff (Martorana and Hollis, 1960; SDLRC, 2000).

In response to the growing enrollments experienced by most institutions after World War II, the state hired external evaluators to assist with state planning. Early in the 1950s, the state hired the national consulting firm Griffenhagen and Associates (1953) to study the public sector. Based on the recommendation of their report, the 1955 legislature authorized the Board of Regents to hire its first professional staff, an executive director and necessary support staff, which grew into an expansive office now coordinating the governance and administration of the system and carrying out the work of the regents.

Nearly every study of higher education in the state since 1918 has suggested the closure or consolidation of programs and institutions (e.g., Schuurmans, 1994; Martorana and Hollis, 1960; Millett, 1984; SDLRC, 2000). For example, a 1974 visit by the Academy for Educational Development resulted in a report suggesting that six state college campuses were too many for a state of less than 700,000 people and recommended two to three consolidations (Millett, 1984, p. 103). For the most part, neither the legislature nor the board had the will to confront such a political battle. In fact, a member of the Board of Regents recalled that a former higher education commissioner, Richard Gibb, was almost run out of the state for suggesting closing an institution in a report issued in 1970 (Schuurmans, 1994). However, Southern State Normal School in Springfield, which became a branch campus of the University of South Dakota in 1971, was eventually closed in 1984 due to low enrollments and the efforts of a strong governor.

In contrast, Sioux Falls—the largest population center and, historically, an almost exclusive enclave of the private institutions—has been the location of much debate over the expansion of the public sector. In the middle of the 1990s, the SDBOR helped create the South Dakota Public Universities and Research Center (University Center) in Sioux Falls to centralize the efforts of the state's public universities to serve the city's populace. In 2006, the legislature authorized the board to purchase 263 acres and build a classroom building that could be used by the public colleges and universities to offer courses in Sioux Falls. As of 2012, the University of South Dakota, South Dakota State University, Dakota State University, Northern State University, and Black Hills State University were offering more than 50 degree programs at the associate, bachelor's, master's, and doctoral levels.

Substantial concern arose from several sectors in 2002–2003 when South Dakota became the only state in the nation not to provide any financial assistance to students. When the legislature eliminated its sole merit-based financial aid program in 2002–2003, it was already one of two states not providing any need-based aid (Arnone, 2004). However, the state had found other ways to assist with college funding such as adopting a college saving plan in 2001 and covering tuition for 200 students in critical technology degree programs. Further, in a response to declining enrollments, initiatives such as discounting out-of-state tuition for students from neighboring states and students of out-of-state alumni were adopted to bring people back to the state. In fall 2004, the legislature began funding the South Dakota Opportunity Scholarship, a merit-based program geared to encourage South Dakota high schools students to attend either a public or a private institution in state (Hebel, 2004). In FY2011, the state allocated nearly $2 million for the Opportunity Scholarship (South Dakota Board of Regents, 2011).

The mid-2000s witnessed other important changes to the higher education sector. For example, in 2005, the board reached an agreement with three of the technical institutes on articulation regulating the transfer of credits to six public colleges and universities. Further, like the other states in the subregion, the legislature recognized the importance of higher education for economic development and funded a number of programs to support the creation and development of graduate studies and research in areas of advanced technology and others likely to have commercial viability.

The Great Recession hit South Dakota's higher education system pretty hard, with the Board of Regents taking a 15.6 percent cut between fiscal years 2009 and 2012. For example, in 2011, the state support of public colleges and universities was reduced by $6.5 million and the board increased tuition by 4.6 percent and cut $4 million from university programs (Johnson, Oliff, and Williams, 2011). During this time period, the state system underwent an extensive review of academic programs, which resulted in many smaller programs being eliminated (Glenn and Schmidt, 2010). However, public higher education in South Dakota, which had lost some ground in terms of state funding during the years after the recession (about 5.7 percent decrease from FY2008 to FY2011), appears to be showing signs of turnaround (Zumeta and Kinne, 2011). Indeed, despite the loss of funding, enrollments continued to increase with total headcount increasing almost 8 percent between 2009 and 2010 and 28 percent between 2001 and 2010. As the economy begins to rebound and state funding returns, the state's higher education system may prove a bit more nimble to handle the challenges of the coming decade.

WYOMING

The least populated state in the nation, Wyoming comprises high plains in the east and the Rocky Mountains in the west that cover an area larger than the combined territory of New York, New Jersey, and Ohio. Of the 563,600 people residing in the state in 2010, about 11 percent lived in Cheyenne, the capital and largest city. In the same year, there were approximately 35,000 undergraduate students in the state, making it the smallest system in the subregion and the second smallest in the nation behind Alaska. The population is about 1 percent Native American, while just over 14 percent claim Hispanic heritage (US Census Bureau, 2010). Approximately 50 percent of the land is owned by the federal government, and the primary areas of economic production are mineral extraction and tourism, with visitors coming to such sites as the Grand Teton and Yellowstone National Parks.

The origins of the state date back to 1868, when a large block of land was carved out of the Dakota, Idaho, and Nebraska territories to create the Wyoming Territory. It received official statehood on July 10, 1890, making it the last state in this subregion to join the Union. However, excavations have revealed evidence of prehistoric human life dating back more than 10,000 years, and many important dinosaur fossils have been discovered in the state (and housed at the Tate Museum at Casper College).

Like all the states in Middle Border subregion, higher education predates statehood with the founding of the University of Wyoming in 1886. The university remained the only institution of higher learning in the state until 1945. In that year, after a hard-fought legislative battle and against the desire of the university board of trustees and its president, a junior college system was approved. The enabling legislation allows "any school district with an accredited four-year high school program to vote a special levy" to support the work of a junior college (Taft, 1978). Casper College (Casper in 1945) was the first junior college to be created, followed by: Sheridan Community College (Sheridan in 1948); Northwest Community College (Powell in 1946); Eastern Community College (Torrington in 1948); Western Wyoming Community College (Rock Springs in 1959); Central Wyoming College (Riverton in 1966); Laramie County Community College (Cheyenne in 1968); and Gillette College (Gillette in 2003). Gillette, along with Sheridan College, comprise the Northern Wyoming Community College District.

Early in the territory's history, much debate was waged over the need for a university, and eventually the territorial legislature began to see the benefits of offering advanced education: "The objects of such a university shall be to provide an efficient means of imparting to young men and young women, on equal terms, a liberal education and thorough knowledge of the different branches of literature, the arts and sciences, with their varied applications" (Revised statutes of Wyoming, 1887, title 42). Further, the authorizing bill "vigorously prohibited any religious qualifications or tests for anyone connected with the institution, or any instruction in sectarian tenets or principles" (Clough, 1937, p. 19). Such conditions evidence the efforts of the state's founders to promote equitable access in public activities—not surprising given the hard-won battles of the women of Wyoming to earn the right to vote 20 years before it became a state (Brown, 1981).

Because of the uniquely centralized system of higher education in the state, it should be noted that many early arguments centered on the organization of the higher education sector. An early historian of the state observed in 1914 that "while there have been prolonged contests to divide the higher educational institutions and parcel them out to different parts of the state, among the trustees there has always been a united effort to have University, technical colleges, and normal schools all under one board of trustees and one faculty. The state now acquiesces in this principle and the division contest no longer tempts politicians" (Herbard, 1914, p. 832). And, like the folklore in many western states, "Wyoming legend has it that in the distribution of institutions, Cheyenne, Rawlins, Evanston, and Laramie made selections in that order and chose the capitol, penitentiary, insane asylum, and university." And, as in most states, "There is no truth in the legend . . . [in the case of Wyoming,] Laramie had more influence than Rawlins and Evanston" (Larson, 1978, p. 145).

Until the past decade, the higher education sector was one of the most unusual in the nation. There was no statewide coordination of the higher education system; no private, regionally accredited higher education institutions; and some of the most liberal laws pertaining to the operation of unaccredited educational institutions.

The lack of coordination between the University of Wyoming and the state's seven public community colleges, governed by the Wyoming Community College Commission (WCCC), has been a source of legislative debate for many decades. The commission was created as an advisory council in 1951 and given statutory responsibilities in 1967. Even though the legislature defunded the commission in 1978 (Millett, 1984, p. 99), funding has since been restored and it now serves as an active coordinating commission. While discussions on the need for increased coordination continue to permeate the legislature, no state entity actively engages in this role. According to James Rose, executive director of the WCCC, the Wyoming Postsecondary Education Planning and Coordinating Council (WEPCC) exists in statute to provide a forum for discussion among the state's educational sectors but meets infrequently. As of this writing, the nonprofit, nongovernmental P-16 Education Council (http://www.wp-16.org/index.asp), created in 2006 by the efforts of education and business leaders in Wyoming and funded by a grant from WICHE, facilitates communication among various educational organizations in the state. The P-16 Council has been asked to provide the WEPCC with a set of specific recommendations as to how to better coordinate the system (J. Rose, personal communication, March 4, 2008).

The limited engagement by a state agency in the coordination of the sector does not mean that some coordination does not occur. In 1994, a coordinated course numbering system was created, allowing students at all public universities to choose among 3,000 courses with consistent names and numbers. In 2001, the institutions adopted an agreement that allows a student who graduates with an associate degree from one of the Wyoming community colleges to receive credit at the University of Wyoming for their lower-level general education requirements.

The lack of statewide coordination and governmental intervention had facilitated Wyoming's being one of the more favorable environments for the operation of unaccredited postsecondary institutions. Prior to 2004, the state allowed unaccredited institutions with a religious exemption to operate within the state. In 2004, out of concern for the proliferation of diploma mills, the state legislature passed a law that limited the religious exemption to institutions designated as religious nonprofit by the federal government and award degrees only in their religious or theological focus (Barron, 2004). As of 2012, the only regionally accredited, four-year private institution in the state was the University of Phoenix.[16]

In the past decade, Wyoming experienced a significant turn of financial fate. In the early 1990s, public colleges had been forced to raise tuition by double-digit amounts (Editors, *Chronicle of Higher Education*, 1995). In the mid-1990s, faltering oil and coal prices, combined with the general lack of income tax on individuals and corporations, led Wyoming to further reduce funds to state agencies, including higher education. In the late 1990s, although community colleges had to continue to raise tuition, the University of Wyoming received better news with the state legislature appropriating $2 million for deferred maintenance, $500,000 to bolster library acquisitions, and a specific allocation to raise faculty and staff salaries.

The rising price of oil and minerals continued to benefit the higher education sector throughout the late 1990s and early and mid-2000s by allowing the legislature to invest in a range of new initiatives. In addition to investing significantly in the operating and capital budgets of the university and community colleges, the legislature used monies from federal mineral royalties to create three permanent endowments (two are now authorized in the state's constitution) to support various academic initiatives. In 2005, $400 million was set aside for an endowment to provide financial assistance to high school graduates who take courses at a public institution in the state; and the other endowment provided $70 million to the university and $35 million to the community colleges targeted at recruiting and retaining faculty members. Earlier state surpluses allowed the legislature to set aside $30 million in 2001 (supplemented with additional funding during later biennium budgets) to match donations of $50,000 or more to the University of Wyoming's endowment (see, e.g., Hebel, 2004, 2007).

Toward the end of the decade, the financial picture did not look quite as rosy, but, similar to nearby North Dakota, Wyoming's support of higher education continued relatively unabated, with a 15.4 percent increase in funding from FY2008 to FY2011 (Zumeta and Kinne, 2011). While funding did not stall as it did in some states, Wyoming did look to make some administrative changes. For example, the state instituted a new policy that required students who participated in a WICHE medical student exchange program and sponsored by the state of Wyoming to spend at least three years as a medical professional in the state or reimburse the state for the amount of money expended on behalf of the student. This was in response to increasing concerns about the lack of medical professionals in the state, an issue that has plagued Wyoming since the creation of WICHE. In 2009, there was also a legislative proposal to increase the centralization of the administration of the state's community college system; the proposal was vetoed by the governor. In sum, higher education in the state continues to have a healthy outlook.

THE FUTURE OF THE MIDDLE BORDER STATES: DIRE DIRECTIONS OR AN EMERGING GOLDEN AGE?

The states of the Middle Border states are facing a very ambiguous future. The natural beauty of the Great Plains, the meandering grass lands, and the Rocky Mountains continue to attract a wide range of tourists and hunters during all months of the year. The more slow-paced lifestyle, almost nonexistent traffic problems, and friendly people are attracting more people to cities, such as Fargo, North Dakota and Sioux Falls, South Dakota. Yet, many policy analysts are painting dire predictions for this subregion (and have been doing so for decades). Most notably, compared to the rest of the nation, there is a disproportionately high number of institutions per person, making it difficult to maintain enrollments. This situation will only be exacerbated if current predictions about the number of high school graduates hold true. All of the states except Idaho are predicted to see a significant decrease in the number of high school graduates in the next 15 years (WICHE, 2008). Such predictions can be disconcerting for a subregion that faces difficulty attracting new residents, losing a significant portion of its youth to other

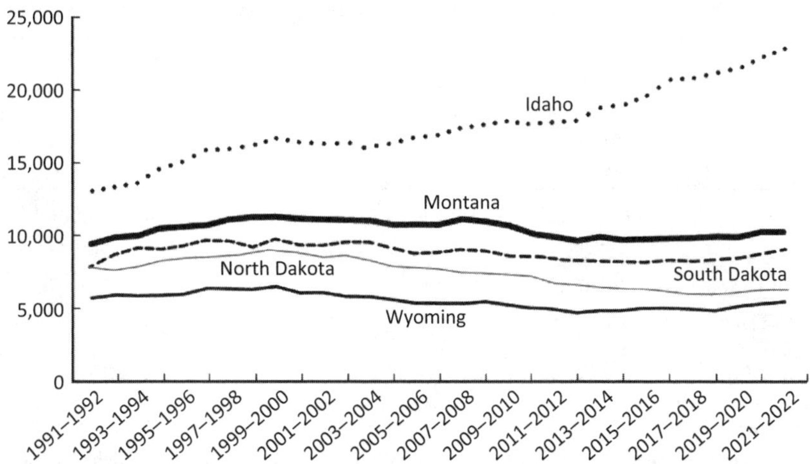

Figure 4.1 High school graduates 1991–1992 through 2004–2005 (actual); 2005–2006 through 2021–2022 (projected).

Source: WICHE, 2009. Calculations: Author's

states with better job opportunities and has historically not been an importer of college students from other states. Yet, the future may not be as dire as some of these indicators suggest (see figure 4.1).

As Joel Kotkin (2006) pointed out in an editorial in the *Wall Street Journal* about the resurgence of the Great Plains, "Alexis de Tocqueville observed, the rural American was never a pliant peasant. Rather he was an entrepreneur whose restless 'industrial pursuits' demanded he improve his land, or sell his farm and move on." Certainly, the citizens of this subregion are not giving up on the future of their states, nor should they. At the time of this writing, the five state area continues to demonstrate very strong economic indicators: the unemployment rate is negligible, energy is a major export, per capita income grows, and the Canadians are flocking over the border to take advantage of the very strong looney (Canadian currency). Moreover, as discussed above, the Middle Border states recognize the importance of higher education to their future and are beginning to create new initiatives to invest in the sector. Take, for example, Wyoming's creation of endowments and North Dakota's Center of Excellence program.

A recent examination of the budgets in these states reveals that, with the exception of Idaho, they are among the healthiest in the nation. During FY2010, North Dakota and Montana were the only two states in the nation without a budget gap and Wyoming and South Dakota have the smallest budget gaps in the nation (Fuller, 2010). Indeed, the five states covered in this chapter have provided very different levels of support for higher education throughout their history. During the FY2008–FY2011 recession, these states reflected this mixed support. Institutions in North Dakota and Wyoming received additional state budgetary funding. North Dakota's state

Table 4.5 Middle border state and federal support, FY2008–FY2011

State	FY2008 State Support ($)	FY2011 State Support ($)	Change in State Support FY2008–FY2011 (%)*	FY2011 Federal Stimulus Support ($)	FY2011 Total State and Federal Support ($)
Idaho	410,595,600	343,297,000	-19.60	4,766,900	348,063,900
Montana	196,547,880	176,375,276	-14.02	33,166,593	209,541,869
North Dakota	253,901,000	311,678,000	18.54	0	311,678,000
South Dakota	196,133,172	185,250,977	-5.87	11,365,508	196,616,485
Wyoming	290,504,588	343,389,743	15.4	40,500,000	383,889,743

Note: *(Additional factors—see article—were calculated in these state support changes; therefore, percentages do not foot.)

Sources: Zumeta and Kinne, 2011; Zumeta, W., and A. Kinne. "State Fiscal Support for Higher Education, by State, Fiscal Years 2006–07, 2009–10, 2010–11, and 2011–12," *Grapevine* from Illinois State University, and the State Higher Education Executive Officers' "Financial Survey," January 2011 (www.grapevine.illinoisstate.edu/tab).

contribution rose dramatically by 18.54 percent, going from $253.9 million in 2008 to $311.6 million in 2011. North Dakota also received federal stimulus funds for higher education, resulting in an additional $11.3 million. Wyoming advanced its funding greatly by 15.4 percent, going from $290.5 million in 2008 to $343.3 million in 2011. The other three states, however, experienced retrenchments in their state funding: Idaho dropped by 19.6 percent, going from $410 million in 2008 to $343.2 million in 2011. Montana reduced its funding some 14.02 percent, declining from $196.5 million in 2008 to $176.3 million in 2011. Finally, South Dakota's reduction was relatively minor at 5.87 percent, moving from $196.1 million in 2008 to $185.2 million in 2011. Loss of these funds affected institutional operating costs, personnel salaries, layoffs, and other cost-cutting measures. This subregion fared relatively well in the WICHE West, which saw 12 of its 15 states experiencing dramatic declines with the worst being Arizona at –28.27 percent, Oregon at –25.71 percent, and New Mexico at –21 percent (see table 4.5). The average decline in state funding across the subregion was –14.4 percent. The WICHE West was the second hardest hit in the country with the greatest loss of state funding occurring in the South (see Cohen's chapter, p. 39 for a more specific discussion).

After several decades of higher education being viewed as a drain on state budgets and politicians calling for more efficiencies in the system as well as increased regulation, in the 1990s and the 2000s there began a general shift toward viewing education as a foundation for the economic and cultural development of these states. During an interview on National Public Radio, Larry Swanson (2008), director of the O'Connor Center for the Rocky Mountain West at the University of Montana in Missoula, summarized the phenomenon this way:

> In our part of the country, [we] have a very tight labor market. And there is increasing focus on workforce development and education. So, we're almost entering a golden age for education out here. That is a complete change from the past. In this part of the world, most politicians used to talk about... education as a cost that needed to be minimized. In the kind of economy that has emerged in our region, more and more business people are understanding that investing in education is investing in our economic prosperities. So, that's changing a very important political dimension where you had one party running against spending on education and one party running for more spending on education. Increasingly, you are not going to find a candidate running in this part of the country who is not for spending more on education.

This change has resulted in states providing increasing support for higher education via increases in operating budgets, faculty salaries, student aid programs, and research support. Some states shifted their philosophical focus sooner than others and some have provided more support than others. However, the work of the state governments evidence a belief in the value of higher education. Support did temper a bit following the Great Recession, but the recognition of higher education being an important driver of economic recovery remained evident.

NOTES

*The authors would like to thank Taya Owens for her research support with this chapter. Whatever errors or omissions may exist remain ours alone.

1. This section is drawn from Abbott (2004).
2. The University of Phoenix and College America, for-profit institutions, opened campuses in 2005. As of the writing of this chapter, no private, accredited, non-profit institution operated in Wyoming, although Wyoming Catholic College was founded in 2007 and was granted preaccreditation status by the American Academy for Liberal Education (AALE) in 2010.
3. The founding of the University of Montana is popularly noted as 1893, because of the passage of an act by the state legislature authorizing the first four institutions of higher education in the state, including the University of Montana. However, Merriam (1970) suggests that the university actually began operation in Bozeman in 1885 and was formally recognized by the state only in 1893.
4. The University of South Dakota was created in 1862 and was the first institution founded in the Middle Border states. Both Augustana College and Sioux Falls Seminary have earlier founding dates than both University of South Dakota and Rocky Mountain College, but they were founded in other states and did not relocate in the subregion until after Rocky Mountain College was founded. In addition, Rocky Mountain College originated as Montana College Institute and became Rocky Mountain College after it passed into the control of the Presbyterian Church a few years after its founding (Malone, Roeder, and Lang, 1991).
5. While the petition to create a university was filed in 1883, the official charter was not issued until 1884.

6. The College of Idaho was renamed Albertson College in 1991 in honor of the Albertson family, who had generously supported the institution for many years. The institution was renamed as the original "College of Idaho" in 2007.
7. The nine doctoral universities are: Idaho State University; Montana State University; North Dakota State University-Main Campus; South Dakota State University; University of Montana; University of Idaho; University of North Dakota; University of South Dakota; and University of Wyoming.
8. For the purposes of the section, tribally controlled colleges are not included.
9. Ricks College, a Mormon two-year institution, was founded in 1888 (see Crowder, n.d.).
10. Indeed, they cited a state supreme court case indicating the University of Idaho to be one of six institutions in the nation "granted constitutional status as virtually a fourth branch of government" (p. 22). In *State v. State Board of Education, 33 Idaho 415, 196 Pac. 201 (1921),* the state court ruled that the State Board of Examiners could not ask the university to clear all expenses through them because control over money was central to control over policy and the state fiscal agency could not interfere with one without interfering with the other.
11. In 1939, the Office of Public Instruction designated the location of five training centers in the state (Billings, Butte, Great Falls, Helena, and Missoula), which operated in conjunction with local school districts. In 1989, the Montana Legislature authorized the transfer of governance from the school districts to the Montana Board of Regents, which reorganized the university system in 1994 and affiliated the centers with either Montana State University or the University of Montana (Montana State University—Great Falls College of Technology, 2005).
12. More than six decades ago, local communities founded Miles Community College (1939) and Dawson Community College (1940) to serve their local areas; these institutions continue to serve approximately 500 students each (IPEDS, 2008; Miles Community College, 2006; Dawson Community College, 2008). Flathead Community College was created in 1967 following the passage of the Montana Community College act in 1965 and serves approximately 1,800 students (Flathead Community College, 2008; IPEDS, 2008).
13. Unless otherwise noted, all four-year public institutions, the NDSCS, and the School of Forestry in Bottineau were included in the original state constitution.
14. Founded in 1909 as Bismarck Evangelical Hospital School of Nursing, it assumed its current name in 1988 (Medcenter One, 2007).
15. These publications include ND Legislative Council, Minutes of the Higher Education Committee, November 18–19 (Valley City, ND: Legislature, 2003); ND State Board of Higher Education, 1987; ND University System, *Partners for Quality: Plans and Priorities* (Valley City, ND: University System, 1990); ND University System, *Partners for Progress: Plan for 1990–1997* (Bismarck, ND: ND University System, February 25, 1996); ND University System, *Partners for Quality: What's Next?: A Proposal to the Bush Foundation from the ND SBHE* (Bismarck, ND: ND University System, n.d.); Report of the North Dakota Legislative Council, Fiftieth Legislative Assembly, 1987; Higher Education System Review Committee, Report of the North Dakota Legislative Council, Fifty Second Legislative Assembly, 1991; Report of the North Dakota Legislative Council, Fifty Third Legislative Assembly, 1993; Report of the North Dakota Legislative Council, Fifty Third Legislative Assembly, 1993; Budget

"A", Committee Report of the North Dakota Legislative Council, Forty Eighth Legislative Assembly, 1983; J. A. Richardson, "Preparing for the Next Century: A White Paper," State Board of Higher Education (Bismarck, ND: Legislature, 1985); J. A. Richardson, Testimony to LSC about *Partners for Progress: A Plan for North Dakota's Future* (Bismarck, ND: Legislature, August 4, 1989).

16. The first private, for-profit institution to develop a campus in Wyoming was the University of Phoenix in 2004.

References

Abbott, F. C. *A History of the Western Interstate Commission for Higher Education: The First Forty Years.* Boulder, CO: WICHE, 2004.

Arnone, M. "States Continued to Increase Spending on Student Aid in 2002–3, Survey Finds." *Chronicle of Higher Education*, May 28, 2004, A21.

Association of Governing Boards. *State Governance Action Report.* Washington, DC: Author, 2011.

Barrett, G. *Boise State University: Searching for Excellence, 1932–1984.* Boise, ND: Boise State University, 1984.

Barron, J. "New Law Targets Diploma Mills." *Casper Star Tribune*, July 28, 2004. Retrieved February 6, 2008, from http://www.casperstartribue.com.

Blumenstyk, G., and M. C. Cage. "Outlook for Higher Education in 50 States This Year." *Chronicle of Higher Education*, January 3, 1990. Retrieved from http://chronicle.com/che-data/articles.dir/articles-36.dir/issue-16.dir/16a02101.htm, on February 6, 2008.

Brown, D. *The Gentle Tamers: Women of the Old Wild West.* Lincoln, NE: Bison Books, 1981.

Carlson, S. "Promise on the Plains: Flush with Cash, North Dakota Weighs Its Commitment to Colleges." *Chronicle of Higher Education*, September 12, 2010. Retrieved from http:// chronicle.com/article/article-content/124362/, on January 13, 2012.

Chaffee, E. B. *Boise College: An Idea Grows.* Boise, ID: SYMS-YORK, 1970.

Clough, W. O. *A History of the University of Wyoming, 1887–1937.* Laramie, WY: Laramie, 1937.

College of Southern Idaho. *History & Mission*, n.d. Retrieved from http://www.csi.edu/welcome_/historyMission.html, on February 12, 2008.

Crowder, D. L. *The Spirit of Ricks: A History of Ricks College*, n.d. Retrieved from http://www.byui.edu/pr/thespiritofricks/default.htm, on February 11, 2008.

Dalrymple, A. "Minot State-Bottineau Looks at Name Change." Fargo Forum, n.d. Retrieved from http://www.in-forum.com/News/articles/191541, on February 12, 2008.

———. "Potts Steps Down." Fargo Forum, July 1, 2006. Retrieved from http://www.in-forum.com/articles/index.cfm?id=131681, on February 12, 2008.

Dawson Community College. *Dawson Community College Catalog.* Glendive, MT: Dawson Community College, 2008.

Editors. The Chronicle of Higher Education Almanac. *Chronicle of Higher Education*, 1997.

———. The Chronicle of Higher Education Almanac. *Chronicle of Higher Education*, 1996.

———. The Chronicle of Higher Education Almanac. *Chronicle of Higher Education*, 1995.

Editors. The Chronicle of Higher Education Almanac. *Chronicle of Higher Education*, 2000.

———. The Chronicle of Higher Education Almanac. *Chronicle of Higher Education*, 2002.

Flathead Community College. *History*, n.d. Retrieved from http://www.fvcc.edu/about_fvcc/history_mission.shtml, on February 5, 2008.

Fowle, M. M. "A Governing Board's Evolution to Effectiveness: A South Dakota Board of Regents Case Study." Unpublished dissertation. Philadelphia: University of Pennsylvania, 2005.

Fuller, A. "Led by North Dakota, Some States Shield Higher Education from Cutbacks." *Chronicle of Higher Education*, March 21, 2010. Retrieved from http://chronicle.com/article/Ledby-North-Dakota-Some/64760/, on January 13, 2012.

Garland, H. *A Son of the Middle Border.* New York: Macmillan, 1917/1962.

Geiger, L.G. *University of the Northern Plains: A History of the University of North Dakota 1883–1958.* Grand Forks: University of North Dakota Press, 1958.

Glenn, D., and P. Schmidt. "Disappearing Disciplines: Degree Programs Fight for Their Lives." *Chronicle of Higher Education*, 2010. Retrieved from http://chronicle.com/article/DisappearingDisciplines-/64850/, on January 13, 2012.

Healy, P. "Idaho Settles Lawsuit Over Rejected Grant for Gay Study." *Chronicle of Higher Education*, May 1, 1998. Retrieved from http://chronicle.com, on February 6, 2008.

Hebard, G. R. "The University of Wyoming, Laramie, Wyoming." In P. Monroe (ed.), *Cyclopedia of Education.* New York: Macmillan, 1914.

Hebel, S. "Prospecting for Intellectual Gold." *Chronicle of Higher Education*, March 9, 2007, 53 (27): A28.

———. "Chronicle of Higher Education Almanac: Idaho." *Chronicle of Higher Education*, 2006, 52 (1): 52.

———. "Flush with Mineral Money: Wyoming weighs Higher-Education Endowment." *Chronicle of Higher Education*, December 3, 2004, 51 (15): A22.

———. "South Dakota Looks West, and Within, to Draw Students." *Chronicle of Higher Education*, July 2, 2004, 50 (43): A21.

Hill, D. S. *Control of Tax-Supported Higher Education in the United States.* New York: Carnegie Foundation for the Advancement of Teaching, 1934.

Idaho Department of Labor. "Idaho's Job Recovery to Remain Slow in 2011," 2011. Retrieved from http://ieda.biz/white.html, on January 13, 2012.

Idaho Economic Development Association. *The Power of Idaho White Paper*, 2004. Retrieved from http://labor.idaho.gov/publications/Economic_Outlook_2011.pdf, on February 10, 2008.

Idaho State Board of Education. *Strategic Plan FY 2008–2012*, 2008. Retrieved from http://www.boardofed.idaho.gov/overview/OSBE-StratPlan2008–2012.pdf, on February 4, 2008.

Idaho State University. *History of Idaho State University*, n.d. Retrieved from http://www.isu.edu/departments/urelate/longhistory.html, on February 9, 2008.

Integrated Postsecondary Education System (IPEDS). *College Navigator*, 2010. Retrieved from http://nces.ed.gov/collegenavigator/, on January 12, 2012.

Jaschik, S. "Idaho High Court Blocks New Governance Plan for Education." *Chronicle of Higher Education*, July 7, 1993. Retrieved from http://chronicle.com, on February 6, 2008.

Johnson, N., P. Oliff, and E. Williams. "An Update on State Budget Cuts: At Least 46 States Have Imposed Cuts That Hurt Vulnerable Residents and the Economy."

Center on Budget and Policy Priorities, 2011. Retrieved from http://www.cbpp.org/cms/index.cfm?fa=view&id=1214., on March 28, 2012.

Kelly, F. J. *The State and Higher Education: Phases of their Relationship*. New York: Carnegie Foundation for the Advancement of Teaching, 1933.

Kotkin, J. "The Great Plains." *Wall Street Journal*, August 31, 2006.

Lamar, H. R. *Dakota Territory, 1861–1889: A Study of Frontier Politics*. New Haven, CT: Yale University Press, 1956.

Lane, J. E. *Sustaining a Public Agenda for Higher Education: A Case Study of the North Dakota Higher Education Roundtable*. Boulder, CO: Western Interstate Commission for Higher Education, 2008. Retrieved from http://www.wiche.edu/policy/ford/ND_Roundtable.pdf.

Larson, T. A. *History of Wyoming*. 2nd ed. Lincoln: University of Nebraska Press, 1978.

Lewis-Clark State College. "Lewis-Clark State College…Historical Review," n.d. Retrieved from http://www.lcsc.edu/welcome/history.htm, on February 5, 2008.

Malone, M. P., R. P. Roeder, and W. L. Lang. *Montana: A History of Two Centuries*, revised ed. Seattle: University of Washington Press, 1991.

Martorana, S. V., and E. V. Hollis. *Higher Education in South Dakota: A Report of a Survey*. Washington, DC: US Office of Education, 1960.

McClure, E. *The Structure of Higher Education in Montana: Meandering Murky Lines*. Helena: Montana Legislative Services Division, 1999.

Medcenter One. *Chronicle: Our History, Celebrating 100 Years*, 2007. Retrieved from http://www.medcenterone.com/PDF/100yrchronicle.pdf, on February 15, 2008.

Merriam, H. G. *The University of Montana: A History*. Missoula: University of Montana Press, 1970.

Miles Community College. *Miles Community College Course Catalog*. Miles City, MT: Miles Community College, 2006.

Millett, J. D. *Conflict in Higher Education: State Coordination versus Institutional Independence*. San Francisco, CA: Jossey-Bass, 1984.

Milton, J. R. *South Dakota: A Bicentennial History*. New York: W. W. Norton, 1977.

Montana Education Commission for the Nineties and Beyond. *Crossroads—Montana Higher Education in the Nineties*. Helena: Montana University System, 1990.

Montana State University—Great Falls College of Technology. *Self-study Report*. Great Falls: Montana State University, 2005.

Moos, M., and F. E. Rourke. *The Campus and the State*. Baltimore, MD: Johns Hopkins University Press, 1959.

National Association of State Student Grant and Aid Programs (NASSGAP). "41st Annual Survey Report on State-Sponsored Student Financial Aid 2009–2010 Academic Year." Olympia, WA: National Association of State Student Grant and Aid Programs, 2010.

National Conference of State Legislatures. "State Funding for Higher Education in FY 2009 and FY 2010," 2011. Retrieved from http://www.ncsl.org/documents/fiscal/HigherEdFundingFINAL.pdf, on January 13, 2012.

North Idaho College. *History & Tradition*, 2008. Retrieved from http://www.nic.edu/history/, on February 12, 2008.

North Dakota Legislative Council. "Report of the North Dakota Legislative Council." *Higher Education System Review Committee*. Bismarck: Fifty Second Legislative Assembly, 1991.

North Dakota State Board of Higher Education. *Partners for Quality: Plans and Priorities.* Bismarck: North Dakota State Board of Higher Education, 1987.

Ortiz, A., and P. Boyer. "Student Assessment in Tribal Colleges." In M. C. Brown and J. E. Lane (eds.), *Studying Diverse Students and Institutions: Challenges and Considerations*, New Directions for Institutional Research, no. 118. San Francisco, CA: Jossey-Bass, 2003.

Powers, W. H. *A History of South Dakota State College.* Brookings: South Dakota State College Printing Laboratory, 1931.

Reyhner, J., and J. Eder. *American Indian Education: A History.* Norman: University of Oklahoma Press, 2000.

Richardson, J. A. *Testimony to LSC about Partners for Progress: A Plan for North Dakota's Future.* Bismarck: North Dakota University System, 1989.

———. *Preparing for the Next Century: A White Paper.* Bismarck, ND: State Board of Higher Education, 1985.

Robinson, E. B. *History of North Dakota.* Lincoln: University of Nebraska Press, 1966.

Roundtable for the North Dakota Legislative Council Interim Committee on Higher Education. *A North Dakota University System for the 21st Century.* Bismarck: North Dakota University System, 2000.

Schmidt, P. "Violence, Corruption, and a Slowing Economy Left Many Colleges on Shaky Ground." *Chronicle of Higher Education* (Almanac 2007–2008), 2007, 54 (1): 3.

Schuurmans, M. "Springfield Normal School." In H. T. Hoover, C. G. Hoover, and E. Simmons (eds.), *Bon Homme County History.* Tyndale, SD: Bon Homme County Historical Society, 1994.

SKC Office of Institutional Research. *Salish Kootenai College Facts*, 2008. Retrieved from http://oir.skc.edu/, on March 12, 2008.

Smith, D. A. *Rocky Mountain West: Colorado, Wyoming, and Montana, 1958–1915.* Albuquerque: University of New Mexico Press, 1992.

South Dakota Board of Regents. *Fact Book: Fiscal Year 2011, 2011.* Retrieved from http://www.sdbor.edu/mediapubs/factbook/documents/FY11Factbook.pdf, on January 13, 2012.

South Dakota Legislative Research Council (SD LRC). "A Review of Legislative Studies of Higher Education." Issue Memorandum 97–20, August 7, 2000.

Stein, W. J. "A History of the Tribally Controlled Community Colleges: 1968–1978." Unpublished doctoral dissertation. Pullman: Washington State University, 1988.

Swanson, L. "U.S. West No Longer Bastion of Republican Politics." Weekend Edition, Sunday, January 13. Washington, DC: National Public Radio, 2008.

Taft, L. A. *History of Wyoming*, 2nd ed. Lincoln: University of Nebraska Press, 1978.

Toole, K. R. *Montana: An Uncommon Land.* Norman: University of Oklahoma Press, 1959.

University of Sioux Falls. *History of USF, 2008.* Retrieved from http://www. usiouxfalls.edu/, on February 10, 2008.

University of Washington. WWAMI, 2008. Retrieved from http://www. uwmedicine. org/Education/WWAMI/, on February 8, 2008.

US Census Bureau. *Census for 2010.* See www.census.gov.

———. *North Dakota: Selected Social Characteristics in the United States*, 2005.

Western Interstate Commission for Higher Education (WICHE). *Knocking at the College Door: Projections of High School Graduates by State and Race/Ethnicity, 1992 to 2022*. Boulder, CO: WICHE, 2008.

———. *Western Policy Exchanges*. Boulder, CO: WICHE, 1999.

Williams, R. L. *The Origins of Federal Support for Higher Education: George W. Atherton and the Land-Grant Movement*. University Park: Penn State University Press, 1991.

Zumeta, W., and A. Kinne. "The Recession Is Not Over for Higher Education." In *NEA 2011 Almanac of Higher Education*. Washington, DC: National Education Association, 2011, pp. 29–42.

5

History of Higher Education in the Southwest since World War II: Arizona, Colorado, Nevada, New Mexico, and Utah

William E. ("Bud") Davis

One hundred and sixty years ago, in the 1850s, the American Southwest was both an ecological and an educational desert. What would become the five southwestern states—Arizona, Colorado, Nevada, New Mexico, and Utah—had no colleges or universities. Moreover, the Southwest had no public school systems, let alone any students prepared for college. What population was there were Native Americans, who had been there for centuries, plus those Hispanics who had arrived in the 1500s, intermarried with the natives, and evolved into Mexicans and Chicanos. There were almost no white Anglo women, and what white men there were consisted of mostly hunters, trappers, traders, and explorers, later augmented by soldiers, railroaders, and missionaries. Sometimes they were called gringos by the Mexicans—not a term of endearment. By whatever name, they constituted a minority—a menacing minority hell-bent on gobbling up the land, killing the game, and harassing the natives.

It was a hostile, harsh country that often lived up to the adage that there was no law west of the Pecos—and *all* of this country was west of the Pecos River. However, despite its dire reputation, hordes of American emigrants crossed the prairies in increasing numbers and brought with them their dreams of towns and cities and territories and states—and, ultimately, churches, schools, and colleges.

This chapter takes a more cultural approach to exploring higher education in this subregion, as it befits its lands and peoples. One of the amazing occurrences in the development of education in the Southwest was the fact that, with the exception of Nevada, territorial and state universities were founded before the establishment of public education. Thus, most of these early colleges and universities literally had to prepare their students before they could undertake collegiate courses. An additional problem arose over what these students on a raw frontier should study. Should it be the Latin and Greek of the prestigious universities in New England, the South, and the Midwest, or should the courses prepare them for positions of leadership in the economic and cultural development of these territories yearning to become states? Historically, the institutions tried and are still trying to do both.

The Morrill Act of 1862

The Morrill Act of 1862, also known as the Land Grant College Act, was introduced by Justin Smith Morrill, a congressman from Vermont. First passed by Congress in 1859, it was vetoed by President James Buchanan. Resubmitted by Morrill in 1861, the act proposed the establishment of institutions in each state that would teach military tactics as well as engineering and agriculture. The bill gave each state 30,000 acres of public land for each senator and representative. The land was then to be sold and the money placed in an endowment fund to provide support for the public colleges in each of the states. With the secession of the South, the bill passed and was signed by President Abraham Lincoln on July 2, 1862.

This Land Grant College Act changed the course of higher education from a classical curriculum to more applied studies with a focus on agricultural, mining, and manufacturing that would prepare students for the world they would face once leaving the classroom. Further, the act seemed to reflect a commitment that there would always be money to finance educational facilities and that there would be continued government support of these public institutions.

In the five southwest states, only in Nevada, which entered the Union in 1864, was a land-grant institution approved after statehood. Not until 1887 were the doors opened at the University of Nevada in Reno. What would become Colorado State University was designated as a land-grant college in 1870. It was not until 1877, however, a year after statehood, that it began offering classes. The Thirteenth Arizona Territorial Legislature approved the University of Arizona as the land-grant institution in 1885. Twenty-seven years later, in 1912, Arizona became a state. Likewise, the

Table 5.1 Land-grant universities

State	Institution	Date Founded
Arizona	University of Arizona	1885
Colorado	Colorado State University	1870
Nevada	University of Nevada-Reno	1874
New Mexico	New Mexico State University	1888
Utah	Utah State University	1888

New Mexico Territorial Legislature designated New Mexico State University in Las Cruces as the land-grant institution in 1888; statehood did not come until 1912. And, finally, Utah designated Utah State University as its land-grant college in 1888, but the territory did not become a state until 1896 (table 5.1; Lightcap, 2007).

These public universities anchored a new focus of higher education in the West with studies directly affecting the land. As institutions on the frontier, they became a major part of the new state governments. How would the political leaders of these states select or appoint their representatives at these institutions? In regard to the selection of members of boards of regents in the southwestern states, Colorado and Nevada elected members of the governing board. (In only four other states are board members elected: California, Illinois, Nebraska, and Michigan.) In the remaining three southwestern states—Arizona, New Mexico, and Utah—the members of the governing board are appointed by their respective governors (Kerr and Gade, 1989, p. 56).

The End of the War and the Beginning of the Atomic Age

Years passed, and as World War II ended, there was great tension and stress, especially in that summer of 1945. The war in Europe had ended with the surrender of Nazi Germany in April of that year. However, the campaign in Okinawa against the Japanese had resulted in staggering casualties for the American forces; military and political strategists envisaged even more dead and wounded with the planned assault on the Japanese mainland. Meanwhile, on a pine-clad shelf of the Pajarito Plateau 35 miles northwest of Santa Fe, New Mexico, a hush-hush mission was nearing completion. For most of the early 1940s, the US government had been spiriting away the nation's leading physicists, chemists, mathematicians, and engineers from academic and scientific centers. They were assembled and put to work at remote Los Alamos to develop the world's first atomic bomb. New Mexicans were curious about the mysterious doings at Los Alamos, but they had no idea of the nature or magnitude of the endeavor. The secrecy surrounding the project prompted much humorous speculation, such as the Army was operating a nudist colony, a home for pregnant women in the Women's Army Corps (WAC), an internment camp for Republicans, or a factory to produce windshield wipers for submarines.

Further south in New Mexico, down around Alamogordo, a gunnery and bombing range had been selected as the testing grounds for the first atomic explosion. This was known as the Trinity Site. The vast quantity of materials needed for the project were shipped through Albuquerque and addressed to the University of New Mexico. These materials, however, never reached the campus, but were diverted to a railroad siding on the outskirts of the city. They were collected by the Army engineers and transported by truck to the Trinity Site. On the evening of July 15, 1945, all air traffic was barred between Albuquerque and El Paso, Texas. At 5:30 a.m. the following morning, the bomb was detonated. Historian Marc Simmons described the moment:

> A shock wave boom shook New Mexico and parts of Texas and Arizona. In Gallup, 235 miles from the Trinity Site, houses rattled and windows blew out. Guests in Albuquerque's Hilton Hotel tumbled from their beds in alarm and peering outside saw an awesome red glow filling the southern sky. The pyrotechnic display, visible for hundreds of miles, resembled nothing less than the fires of hell. The world's first atomic explosion...marked with a mushroom-shaped exclamation point, the commencement of a new age. (1982, pp. 367–368)

Perhaps it was fitting that New Mexico, an ancient, barren land in the heart of the Southwest still bearing the influence of Indians and Spaniards, should be the locale for the event that would launch the world into the atomic age. That mushroom cloud indeed marked a pivotal point in the history of mankind. Within a month of the Trinity blast, atomic bombs were dropped on Hiroshima and Nagasaki, the Japanese surrendered, and World War II came to an end.

The fallout from World War II was widespread, and in many ways profoundly affected higher education in the United States, especially at the collegiate institutions of the Southwest. The Selective Service Act of 1940, commonly referred to as "the draft," took a heavy toll on college-age male students. Within a short time after the outbreak of the war, women provided the bulk of enrollment in the nation's collegiate institutions. President Franklin D. Roosevelt and the Congress soon inaugurated programs through the Army and the Navy wherein male students were placed on college campuses to complete their degrees and prepare to become officers in the armed forces. Further, schools were established at many institutions for specialized military training in such areas as languages or communications technology. The Navy called its schools the V-5 or V-12 programs. The students jokingly defined the latter as "Victory in 12 years or we fight." These government-sponsored military programs not only helped keep the colleges open but also brought students from all over the country to previously semi-remote campuses in the Southwest. Young men who had only read about the "Wild West" saw it now, and, after the war, returned in unanticipated large numbers.

Further, in a fireside chat to the nation on July 28, 1943, President Roosevelt advocated government-financed education as part of veterans' benefits. Congress responded quickly and enthusiastically, passing Public Law 346, the Servicemen's Readjustment Act of 1944. This soon became known as "the G.I. Bill," slang for "Government Issue." The passage of this act was a stroke of genius, because, for the first time in the history of this nation, the doors of higher education were opened to those Americans who had the intellectual acumen and motivation for a college education. Too often in the past, many of these young people lacked either the finances or opportunity (sometimes both) to pursue their dreams of earning a college degree. Before the war, with the exception of those who worked their way through college, higher education was the purview of the economic elite.

In addition to the veterans, women and minorities (many of whom also were veterans) were attracted to the groves of academe in unprecedented numbers. Further, the whole status of women and minorities changed as more of them earned degrees in professional fields, such as law, medicine, business, and engineering. (Also, there was some speculation that the change was due to the fact that Rosie the Riveter was forced out of her job by the returning soldiers. She had to obtain a degree or other credential to compete with often less qualified men, or to find another avenue of employment.) The impact on minorities also changed the profile of American life as Hispanics, Native Americans, and African Americans attended colleges in increasing numbers and moved upward into positions of leadership and responsibility in society. Higher education for these formerly disenfranchised citizens, to be sure, was not the solution for every social problem; but it marked a prodigious beginning.

As might be expected, with increased enrollments and continuing federal research funds, small, backwater campuses began to emerge as full-fledged, comprehensive research universities. At places like the University of New Mexico, which had an enrollment of 1,600 before World War II, the student body mushroomed to 24,000 after the war. Arizona State University, which was a small teacher's college, became a prestigious national research university. And the University of Nevada Las Vegas, which did not even exist at the time of the war, was founded and became a full-fledged university.

Nationwide, most universities were totally unprepared for the deluge of veterans, women, and minorities who flocked to campuses in the postwar era. Early speculation was that few would take advantage of the G.I. Bill. Some myopic educators believed that the ex-servicemen were either too old to return to the classrooms, or, if they did, they would not make very good students. How wrong they were! By 1946, more than 2 million students were enrolled in the nation's universities. One-half were veterans taking advantage of the G.I. Bill. But the massive influx of college students also included 60,000 women and 70,000 African American men and women (as noted earlier, many of whom also were veterans).

With the exception of this tidal wave of students, there was a shortage of everything on most campuses—classrooms, laboratories, housing, and faculty to teach the classes. To address the shortage of facilities, collegiate institutions began to scramble for surplus military buildings released by the government—mostly barracks and Quonset huts that all too often became permanent fixtures on many campuses. But they helped span the gap until planning and funding for more permanent structures came along—and come along they did as the physical plants on campuses underwent unprecedented growth. It was boom time in higher education.

Best of all, the institutions of higher learning in the Southwest had finally been discovered. This formerly remote part of the country became a place of destination. It became a place of choice not only for those seeking higher education but also for those searching for locales for scientific research, corporate headquarters, major manufacturing and industrial sites, senior citizen and healthcare centers, entertainment and gambling casinos, outdoor recreation and winter homes for "snow birds," or permanent villages for retirees. In short, the Southwest became a Mecca for almost any kind of human endeavor where climate and scenery and livability were factors involved in the choice of a place to work, or live, and/or grow old gracefully.

THE WORK OF THE WESTERN INTERSTATE COMMISSION FOR HIGHER EDUCATION

With the conclusion of the war, state governments began to assess their higher education needs. Leading the efforts to improve professional education in the western states in 1946 and 1947, the new president of the University of Wyoming, George "Duke" Humphrey, and the dean of the Medical School at the University of Colorado, Ward Darley, approached their governors about furthering professional medical education in their states. These efforts led to the beginnings of the Western Interstate Commission for Higher Education (WICHE) in 1953 in Salt Lake City under the leadership of Meredith Wilson at the University of Utah, the chair, and Tom Popejoy at the University of New Mexico, the vice chair of its governing commission. Two early initiatives affected the southwestern states—and provide a perspective on WICHE's role in the region. First, Humphrey and Darley built upon earlier efforts in 1949 when the University of Colorado's Medical School agreed to hold a few positions open for students from both New Mexico and Wyoming. This effort encouraged them to seek a broader interstate agreement leading to the founding of WICHE and then the expansion of medical education interstate opportunities, especially for students from Arizona and New Mexico. This new compact brought together medical practitioners and educators as well as state executives and legislators for a "Western Forum on Medical Education" and subsequent symposia in the 1960s. WICHE's work assisted in the regional expansion of medical education already in Colorado and Utah with the addition of a new medical school at the University of Nevada-Reno in the early 1970s. Nevada later became the central medical school for continuing medical education through the Mountain States Regional Medical Program for Idaho, Montana, and Wyoming (Abbott, 2004, pp. 1–13, 99–111).

The second initiative involved expanding undergraduate mineral engineering education—a pressing need in western states. In the 1950s, eight WICHE states offered this type of education, with one of the regional leaders being the Colorado School of Mines that enrolled more students than all the others combined. Yet these five-year undergraduate programs suffered from a chronic lack of students, severely so in Alaska, Idaho, and Nevada and somewhat less so in Arizona, Montana, New Mexico, Utah, and Wyoming. WICHE sought to broker an interstate agreement for resident tuition among the other WICHE states, that is, California, Hawaii, and Oregon, that lacked such programs as well as to conduct some marketing and advertising efforts to promote these programs so that more students might enter these programs (Abbott, 2004, pp. 128–130). Such examples of WICHE's work in this subregion thus point to its mission to create interstate educational "contractual agreements" to promote graduate study and professional education, as well as undertake studies to encourage expansion of the related facilities for these types of studies.

WHERE EDGES MEET

Culturally, Author Tony Hillerman described the Southwest as a place "where edges meet—where the cold winds off the towering peaks in Nevada, Utah, and Colorado meet the hot air of the deserts of Arizona and New Mexico" (Hillerman and Meunch, 1974, p. 31). It is renowned for outdoor recreation and resorts abound in all five states. It is a land of artists. Famous painters like Georgia O'Keefe and R. C. Gorman or photographers like Ansel Adams are from here. Locales, like Taos, Santa Fe, Scottsdale, and Sonora were colonized by admirers of western art. Loveland, Colorado, with two foundries hosts an annual summer show that features some of the best sculptors in the nation. In these states, it is easy to find beauty and talent.

As for writers, the Southwest has a full roster of great authors. D. H. Lawrence (who hung out at a ranch halfway between Taos and Questa) once wrote that New Mexico was the greatest experience from the outside world he ever had and changed him forever: "But the moment I saw the brilliant, proud morning shine high up over the deserts of Santa Fé, something stood still in my soul, and I started to attend" (1936, p. 142). Willa Cather also fell in love with New Mexico, and used it as the setting for her western classic, *Death Comes for the Archbishop.* Conrad Richter wrote *Sea of Grass* and other novels with a southwestern setting, while living in New Mexico. And one feels the pain of the conflict between cultures in reading *The Man Who Killed the Deer* by Frank Waters. Oliver LaFarge, the Navajo author, won the Pulitzer Prize with *Laughing Boy*, and Scott Momaday, also a Native American, penned *The House Made of Dawn* and *The Way to Rainy Mountain.* Paul Horgan, a librarian at New Mexico Military Institute, garnered the Pulitzer Prize for his nonfiction narrative of the history of the Rio Grande, *Great River.* However, he also became a first-class western novelist with his *Distant Trumpet*, the story of the surrender of Geronimo, set in Arizona. Wallace Stegner covered the booming mining West with his novels, including his renowned *Angle of Repose.* Rudolfo Anaya, a member of the University of New Mexico faculty and dubbed the dean of Chicano literature, gained well-deserved recognition for his *Bless Me, Ultima*, and was honored by receiving the Presidential Medal in 2001. Tony Hillerman, also a retired University of New Mexico professor, set the Indian culture as an integral part of his mystery novels—and passed Arthur Conan Doyle as the world's all-time bestselling mystery writer. And humorist Max Evans captures the portrayal of the West's good "ole" boys in his *Rounders* and *Hi-Lo Country* and blue-feather Falini stories. Other evidence of the Southwest's claim to fame as a haven for writers would include: Jon Nichols for his *Milagro Beanfield War*, or Richard Bradford for *Red Sky at Morning*, or Norman Van Tilberg Clark for *The Ox-Bow Incident*. Natives in the region think all this is as it should be in this land of cloudless skies and *poco tiempo* (slow time).

History of Higher Education in the Southwest States

Indeed, creativity in the fine arts and literature is a hallmark of these five states and occupies a place of honor on the campuses of their colleges and universities. Students and faculty who seek to learn and master the new sciences and technologies are also dedicated to preserving the grandeur and beauty and cultural heritage of a proud, but often harsh past. Thus, the campuses are more than citadels of learning. They serve as the gathering and meeting places of creative people seeking a cultural identity as they strive to transmit knowledge from one generation to another and from one peoples to another. And, this is their story.

Arizona

Arizona, like New Mexico, borders Mexico. New Mexico's early history was heavily influenced by an indigenous Native American population and the northward migration of Mexicans. Typical of this southwestern subregion, Arizona also suffered from many problems that stifled its early growth—isolation, Indian wars, and vast unpopulated areas of mountains and desert. Further, to say it was arid would be an understatement. It was hot and dry, dry, dry. Trees did not just wilt and die—they petrified.

As World War II concluded, scientists and engineers found ways to tap the Colorado River to harness power, which led to air conditioning, which, in turn, made places like Phoenix livable. Residents of the great and sometimes grimy cities of the Midwest migrated by the hundreds of thousands, even millions, to live in the land of no winter—a place where they could play golf and bask in the sun. Consequently, Arizonans do not think or live like Mexicans, Indians, miners, or cowboys. They think and live like midwestern or eastern bankers and lawyers and entrepreneurs. And as for their attitude toward Hispanics, they passed laws mandating that those who are "illegal migrants" should pay nonresident tuition to attend the state's collegiate institutions in Arizona. Further, to qualify for in-state tuition status, they have to show proof that they have attended and graduated from Arizona high schools. It should be noted, however, that even with this law, Arizona has a college enrollment of 31 percent minorities, roughly one-half of whom are Hispanic.

In 1912, Arizona, along with its eastern neighbor, New Mexico, was granted statehood. Years earlier, however, in 1885 the thirteenth Arizona Territorial Legislature named Tucson as the site of the public university, much to the disappointment of the residents who would have preferred the capital, state prison, or insane asylum. It was not until 1891 with a faculty of 6 and a student body of 31 that classes met for the first time in Old Main. In 1887, the territorial legislature established a teacher's college in Tempe, the core of which was a 20-acre cow pasture donated by leading citizens who sought an institution to train public school teachers and provide instruction to their sons and daughters in agriculture and the mechanical arts. After three name changes, this teacher's college eventually became Arizona State University. The third public four-year institution was created as a normal school in Flagstaff and evolved as Northern Arizona University. The school opened its doors for students in September 1899 ("UA History," 2003).

From the very beginning of higher education in Arizona, the governors and legislators held fast to a commitment to three public four-year institutions of higher learning. Over time, these three universities have been supplemented by an excellent system of community colleges, each governed by its own board. The Arizona Board of Regents is a single governing board appointed by the governor for the four-year institutions, with the campus presidents and the board's executive director hired and reporting directly to the board. However, the board's executive director has no line authority over the campus presidents. Coordination between the community colleges and four-year universities was managed through a Joint Conference Committee that communicates with an informal Arizona Community College Association (Wickenden to Davis, personal communication).

Until World War II, the University of Arizona was the dominant institution, but big changes followed the cessation of hostilities. Engineers found ways to get water and power to Phoenix, and advances in refrigeration technology made it feasible and practical to aircondition homes and businesses. Phoenix became known as a place where in the winter Heaven had no appeal while in summer Hell had no terror.

The reputation of the state's climate spread, and recreation centers, luxury hotels, and health spas began to pop up across the state. Particularly attractive to affluent and previously snowbound natives of the East and upper Midwest were the retirement villages that offered senior citizens a full menu of activities for the aging. The lure of abundant sunshine and clear skies also drew the attention of corporate executives looking for sites to locate the ballooning technological industry, or military strategists looking for sites where the weather was clear and the earth dry and nothing ever rusted. People migrated to Arizona by the hundreds of thousands. While Tucson's population soon exceeded 500,000, Phoenix and its environs counted more than 3 million people by 2007. Some 29.5 percent of its people were Hispanic, with more than 19 percent of them speaking Spanish in their homes.

The surrounding Maricopa County was a breeding ground for what has been hailed by many as the greatest community college system in the world. It began in 1920 when the Phoenix Union High School District established Phoenix Junior College (now Phoenix College) as the first community college in Arizona. In 1960, the Arizona Legislature provided for junior college districts, and in 1962, the Maricopa County Junior College District was established by the approval of county voters, with the new system acquiring Phoenix Junior College. Soon, the system established branch campuses of Phoenix Junior College in Glendale and Mesa. These became independent campuses by the end of the decade. The Maricopa Skill Center in 1964 and the Maricopa Technical College in 1968 became Gateway Community College. Scottsdale Community College was added in 1968. Others followed: Rio Salado Community College in 1978; South Mountain Community College in 1980; Northeast Valley Education Center (now Paradise Valley Community College) in 1985; the Chandler-Gilbert Education Center (now Chandler-Gilbert Community College) in 1985; Estrella Mountain Community College in 1990; and the Red Mountain campus of Mesa Community College in 2001. (In 1971, the names of these institutions were changed from "junior college" to "community college"; "Maricopa County Community College District," 2007)

Building on a foundation of these healthy and viable community colleges, what emerged was a single, coordinated community college system. Its goal was to provide affordable and handy access to courses that would lead to associate degrees locally and smooth the way for students to move on to four-year institutions offering baccalaureate and graduate degrees. It also provided entry-level training for specified vocational courses, which in turn led to jobs. It could offer instruction to place-bound and job-bound students at times that fit their work schedules and at prices they could afford. These programs stimulated the economy, kept brains and talent in the county, and offered high-quality instruction and training. Its reputation for excellence and economy were well-deserved. The State Board of Directors for Community Colleges of Arizona presided over the entire statewide system until June 2002, when the Arizona Legislature reduced its powers and duties and transferred most oversight to individual community college districts. Further, the Maricopa County Community College District (MCCCD, for short) was simplified to Maricopa Community Colleges. Its governing board consisted of five elected members. Over the years, the ten-campus Maricopa system has become the model for community involvement—launching programs to aid everything from literacy to small business start-ups, and developing customized employee-training programs for local businesses and government ("Maricopa County Community College District," 2007).

Meanwhile, it was no small wonder that the online campus of the University of Phoenix grew to be recognized as the nation's largest proprietary university and credited in the *2012 Almanac of the Chronicle of Higher Education* as having the nation's largest enrollment with 307,965 students. Founded in 1976, the University of Phoenix is dedicated to meeting the needs of working students through day and evening classes offered at convenient campus locations or by studying entirely online. Its massive selection of courses led to degrees on the associate, bachelor's, master's, and doctoral levels. Certified by the Higher Learning Commission, the University of Phoenix was the first to provide fully accredited online degrees. Further, the university proclaims that whether a student attends classes on campus or takes courses online, it enables that student to earn a college degree without having to put his/her life on hold (*2012 Almanac of the Chronicle of Higher Education*, p. 22; University of Phoenix).

Further, Arizona State University with four campuses in the Phoenix area (including a recently constructed medical school) had enrolled 70,440 students and ranks first in the country as having the largest enrollment for a public university campus and having grown among the fastest universities in the country during the past decade (*2012 Almanac of the Chronicle of Higher Education*, pp. 22–23).

As Phoenix literally arose from the desert, newcomers arriving from other states reinforced the aspiration of native Arizonans to place high demands on education. With the addition of graduate programs involving advanced research in engineering and the sciences, Arizona State University became a Carnegie Foundation Doctoral/Research I University in 1994. Innovative changes in the 1990s at Arizona State University initiated by its president, Michael Crow, included a plan to become a model for the New American University—namely, one research university with multiple campuses. A decommissioned Air Force base in Gilbert, the site of the East Campus, was scheduled to become a polytechnic institute that would focus on professional programs. The West Campus in Peoria was to emphasize metropolitan issues and social policy. Meanwhile, the Main Campus in Tempe would stress traditional research programs. And a new campus in downtown Phoenix was added to feature the clinical biosciences and a medical school.

The third state university, Northern Arizona, also grew rapidly, with its enrollment passing 25,000 students by 2012. As the youngest member of the university triumvirate, it benefited from its association with its elder brethren. When their state appropriations went up, so did Northern Arizona's. It also became a major player in the higher education field with its distributed education and on-site and electronic learning at centers throughout the state. Among the innovative programs at Northern Arizona was its emphasis on Native American Student Services, a commitment to offering culturally sensitive programs that provided students assistance with the transition from their reservations to the university community. These Native American students represented more than 50 tribal affiliations through the United States.

Greater offerings for Native American students can be found at their tribal colleges within the state. Founded in 1968, Diné College became the central tribal college for the Navajo Nation, applying Native American principles (i.e., thinking, planning, living, and assuring) within the context of Navajo language, history, and culture to postsecondary associate degrees and one baccalaureate degree in teacher education. Since its important founding,

Navajo leaders have added six branch campuses to its main campus at Tsaile across the state and in New Mexico. Specific distinctive studies center on Navajo language and tribal culture, as well as tribal policy and environmental education (www.dinecollege.edu). Another tribal community college in Sells, founded in 1998, offers associate degrees in liberal arts, science, business, and social sciences as well as more occupational education in applied trades, serving the needs of the Tohono O'odham Himdag Nation (www.tocc.edu). These institutions and three others in New Mexico join part of the larger number of some 32 land-grant tribal colleges in the West (see table 5.2).

Meanwhile, the oldest institution of higher learning, the University of Arizona, saw its enrollment grow steadily, surpassing 39,000 students in 2010—a total second only to Arizona State University in the five-state southwest subregion and ranked twenty-first nationally. Among its major accomplishments in the last half of the twentieth century was the development of its medical school. Further, the 471 doctoral degrees awarded in the 2009–2010 academic year by its prestigious and wide-ranging graduate programs, enable the institution to be ranked twenty-ninth in the nation and ahead of both Arizona State University and the University of Colorado at Boulder in the five-state subregion in 2011 (http://www.nsf.gov/statistics/sed/2011/pdf/tab3.pdf). In addition, the Arizona Regents oversaw the Arizona Universities Network, a systemwide effort to expand and coordinate university education opportunities that would benefit time-bound and place-bound workers.

For the second half of the twentieth century, it appeared that the Arizona public institutions were well on their way to joining the ranks of the elite public universities in the country. All systems were GO! However, a funny thing happened on the way to the top of the academic pyramid, as the legislature slashed $746.9 million from the higher education appropriation of 2002–2003. These cutbacks came on top of a 5.4 percent budget cut that the university system had sustained in November 2001. In an effort to avoid total disaster, the Board of Regents authorized substantial increases in tuition for undergraduates at the three universities. Newly elected governor Janet Napolitano promised to spare colleges from further budget cuts, but no new dollars for higher education were provided by lawmakers in the 2003–2004 budget. The legislature, however, did approve $34.6 million for the three state universities to build new research facilities (Editors of the *Chronicle of Higher Education*, 2003–2004, p. 34).

State funding for the four-year institutions improved substantially in 2006–2007 with an increase of 12 percent, and again in 2007–2008 with another increase of 14.6 percent or from $1.1 billion to $1.3 billion. Additionally, the state created a new medical campus in downtown Phoenix and allocated $100 million over four years to Science Foundation Arizona, a nonprofit organization that supports medical and biotechnology research. Arizona's 10 community colleges, however, fared less well in the 2006–2007 session, with a meager 1.8 percent increase (Editors of the *Chronicle of Higher Education*, 2006–2007, pp. 39–40; Zumeta, 2008, p. 89).

Along with these increases in appropriations, however, in-state students from families with incomes below $25,000 a year could attend Arizona State University and pay no tuition. A hot topic in 2006, however, was passage of a ballot measure to prevent students who were not legal residents of the United States from paying in-state tuition, receiving state financial aid, participating in adult education classes offered by the state (Editors of the *Chronicle of Higher Education*, 2006–2007, pp. 39–40).

However, the dramatic effects of the Great Recession forced severe retrenchment among the Arizona public institutions of higher learning, leading to a –36 percent state funding decline between FY2008 and FY2012, while maintaining a state operating funding of public institutions at a significantly less amount of $814 million in FY2011 (http://www.sheeo. org/sites/default/files/publications/SHEF%20FY%2012-20130322rev.pdf, p. 62; Editors of the *Chronicle of Higher Education*, 2012–2013, p. 67). This is discussed further across the subregion later in the chapter.

With huge inward migrations in the past two decades, Arizona became a place with few longtime residents: millions who grew up somewhere else began to people it. Native Arizona proponents of increased standards and status for its universities were reinforced by newcomers who also sought and demanded prestigious state universities with large enrollments and extensive graduate research programs.

Not to be overlooked, both the University of Arizona and Arizona State University successfully sought and received admission to the nationally renowned athletic conference that includes the great universities in California, Oregon, and Washington—the powerful Pacific Coast Conference. The move reinforced and emphasized the state's desire to compete nationally in both the academic and athletic arenas.

NEVADA

Although sparse in population, Nevada may lead the nation with its endeavors to take education to its people. In 1864, Nevada was the first territory in the subregion to become a state. President Abraham Lincoln and the Union needed the vote of another nonslavery state. Another factor was the tremendous gold and silver production of Nevada's Comstock Lode, discovered in 1859 just in time to help the Union finance the Civil War.

Nevada's legislature approved a state university, which began as a prep school in Elko in 1874. The legislature closed the school in 1885, after it served only 30 students in a dozen years. Legislators then put the state university where the action was at the time—bustling, booming Reno, the political and financial hotbed of a sparsely populated subregion. Classes began in 1887.

Being located in Reno and near the state capital, Carson City, the fledgling university had the benefit of being the "only" child in the higher education family for nearly six decades and enjoyed the undivided support of the state through World War II. Expansion was slow, as the institution lacked the resources and enrollment to aspire to the ranks of the major research universities. In truth, it played only a small part in the academic life of the nation. The student body did not exceed 1,000 until 1927, and it was not until 1958 that the enrollment reached 2,000 students (Hulse, 2002, p. 164).

Before World War II there was almost a total commitment of public funds to support the university at Reno, to the neglect of the southern part of the state. This smacked more of political power than intellectual vision. With the end of the war and the population surge in southern Nevada, state leaders began to note that many of Nevada's young people were place-bound and job-bound and had to work part-time or full-time while going to college. With its burgeoning population, Las Vegas was starved for educational programs to meet the demands of these newcomers. Hence the state created a second major university and established a superb community college system.

The initial college-level classes in southern Nevada began on an extension basis in 1951 in a spare room at Las Vegas High School with one full-time faculty member and 12 students. Six years later, in 1957, by the action of the Nevada Board of Regents, the Las Vegas institution was founded officially as a southern regional division of the University of Nevada and opened its first classroom on its present campus site.

Twenty-nine students were awarded degrees at the university's first commencement in 1964. The following year, the Nevada legislature renamed the school the Nevada Southern University and the regents appointed its first president. It became the University of Nevada, Las Vegas (UNLV) in 1969. From this modest start, programs and facilities expanded at a rapid rate until by 2002, some 22,000 students were attending classes on the 337-acre campus in Las Vegas. Included in the curriculum were graduate programs and a law school (Hulse, 2002, pp. 79–80).

Meanwhile, the University of Nevada in Reno (UNR), the land-grant school and for almost three quarters of a century the only state-supported university, experienced an era of rapid growth. Its 1960 enrollment of 2,500 students jumped more than 9,000 by 1980; 20 years later, Reno's enrollment exceeded 13,000 students and had added a medical school to its offerings. Starting as a two-year program in 1971, the medical school's curriculum was expanded to four years in 1977. Because the school had no on-site teaching hospital, Nevada had to make use of in-state facilities for training and research. Few public dollars were involved in its initial stages, but the fledgling school received strong support via generous gifts from Howard Hughes, the New York Commonwealth Fund, H. Edward Manville, and other private donors (Hulse, 2002, pp. 48–49).

As UNLV grew and expanded much more rapidly than UNR, there was more political pressure on the legislators charged with allocating appropriations for higher education. To Las Vegas advocates, it seemed reasonable—what with the people in Clark County (Las Vegas) outnumbering those in Washoe County (Reno) by more than a million constituents—that UNLV should receive a larger proportional piece of the legislative pie.

If this were not complicated enough, a third faction entered the fray as the proponents of community colleges began to voice their demands in both urban centers and rural communities. In 1965, Nevada, along with South Dakota, was one of two states without a community or junior college. Grassroots support led to a pilot community college project being pushed through both houses of the legislature in 1970, authorizing Elko County school trustees to accept gifts for a community college and mandating a statewide survey of need. The issue of governance became a major bone of contention. The community colleges wanted their own board, while the regents wanted to control all of higher education. The elected Board of Regents prevailed, and in a volatile meeting in 1977, its members voted to appoint separate presidents for each community college to report directly to the board. Over the years, the community colleges became an integral part of the state's higher education superstructure, serving more than 50,000 students. They attracted strong support across the state, in the legislature, and from the regents.

Another major milestone in higher education's development in Nevada was the establishment of the Desert Research Institute in 1959. This was to become a unique organization that combined the classic academic tradition of high-quality basic research with the productive focus of applied multidisciplinary research. Through its studies, the institute sought to interpret the basic environmental processes related to the management and understanding of Nevada's arid land resources. The institute began as a research division on the campus in Reno, but in 1969 it became an autonomous division of the University of Nevada system (Hulse, 2002, p. 143).

A third four-year institution was added to the Nevada system in 1999 with the creation of Nevada State College in Henderson about 10 miles southeast of Las Vegas. Housed in a former vitamin factory, its first year was filled with controversy created by the hiring and firing of its first president. Further, the legislature initially was so divided on the virtues of the new college that it withheld operating funds for the first year. By 2002, however, a new president had been hired and 177 students enrolled for courses. In July 2003, the legislature included a line item in the state budget for 2003–2005. In addition, an anonymous donor gave $1 million to help the college build its first new building. In 2003, the US Bureau of Land Management allotted 550 acres of land in Henderson for a campus. And, in September of that year, Nevada State started its second year of operation with 531 students (Editors of the *Chronicle of Higher Education*, 2004–2005, p. 70).

In 2006, Nevada State College signed an agreement with three community colleges to begin offering baccalaureate degree programs on their campuses. This proved to be a popular move. By 2007, more than 1,900 students were enrolled, and the college was offering a wide selection of bachelor's degrees in high-demand academic fields, such as nursing, education, business, law enforcement, visual media, biology, psychology, and applied science (Editors of the *Chronicle of Higher Education*, 2006–2007, p. 71).

Meanwhile, the College of Southern Nevada emerged as the largest college in Nevada with three main campuses in the Las Vegas metropolitan area—the original campus in North Las Vegas, the newer campus in central Las Vegas, and a campus in Henderson. In addition, the College had 47 other locations across four counties in Southern Nevada. As part of the Nevada System of Higher Education, the College of Southern Nevada was founded in 1971 as Clark County Community College. It became Community College of Southern Nevada in 1978 and the College of Southern Nevada in 2007. Southern Nevada and Western Nevada Community Colleges received approval to drop "community" from their names in 2007, inasmuch as both colleges by that time were offering bachelor's degrees (Editors of the *Chronicle of Higher Education*, 2006–2007, p. 69).

Major changes occurred in 2004 when the former University and Community College System of Nevada (formed in 1968) became the Nevada System of Higher Education, governed by an elected Board of Regents. The two doctoral-granting research universities, one state college, four community colleges, and one research institute serving approximately 129,360 students on the degree-granting campuses comprised the system by AY 2010–2011. Nevada is known for a tumultuous brand of politics that often is unfathomable to nonnatives. This was evident in the first years of the twenty-first century as repeated political and legal battles erupted concerning higher education budgets and the conduct of the Board of Regents and the system's chancellor (Editors of the *Chronicle of Higher Education*, 2007–2008, p. 71).

State funding for Nevada's four-year institutions improved substantially in FY2002–2004, with an increase of 39.2 percent from $347 million to $483 million—a $136 million increase, and again in FY2007–2008, with a smaller increase of 7.3 percent, even with the Great Recession beginning to take hold in what would become one of the nation's most depressed states (Zumeta, 2006, p. 42, 2008, p. 89). As the dramatic effects of the Great Recession were felt, great retrenchment among Nevada's public institutions of higher learning occurred with a –23.8 percent state funding decline between FY2008 and FY2012, while maintaining a state operating funding of public institutions at some $473 million in FY2011 (http://www.sheeo.org/sites/default/ files/publications/ SHEF%20FY%2012–20130322rev.pdf, p. 62; Editors of the *Chronicle of Higher Education*, 2012–2013, p. 84). This is discussed further across the subregion later in the chapter.

Nevada has traditionally been characterized by its low-skill, high-wage gambling and mining industries. In its early years, the local culture did not put a lot of resources into higher education, and the state has had one of the lowest records of college attendance in the nation. Among the reasons often cited was that young people could get good-paying jobs parking cars or working at the casinos without a college education. Because revenues from gambling, mining, and oil operations supported most of the state's services, Nevadans were not used to paying a lot in state taxes.

Nevada has attracted a diverse population from all over the world—people who may have come to play and be entertained, but decided to stay and take advantage of the opportunities made possible by higher learning. The truly impressive change in higher education in recent years has been the development of campuses accessible to place-bound, job-bound students working part-time or full-time, while attending college. Also, the regents and the state have been quick to adapt four-year degree granting status to former "junior" colleges—something other states have been slow or even reluctant to do. To their credit, Nevadans seem willing to "take a gamble" by opening up access to higher education for place-bound and job-bound students.

UTAH

Like its regional neighbors, Utah is another state populated by immigrants. In the mid-nineteenth century, these doughty pioneers traversed plains, deserts, and mountains to get away from religious persecution and create a religious lifestyle free of caffeine, nicotine, and alcohol. They wanted that precious freedom to live according to their religious beliefs without harassment. However, as the years rolled by, the good people of Utah could not hide the state's growing reputation for the beauty of its scenery and the lifestyle of its people. Further, it was obvious that the state's reputation for its commitment to the premise that intelligence is the glory of God, motivated support for quality education on all levels. Populated chiefly by members of the Church of Jesus Christ of Latter-Day Saints (LDS) or Mormons, the first settlers in the Great Salt Lake valley were fleeing from persecution in Illinois and Missouri. These Mormons arrived by the thousands, afoot or on horseback, pulling hand-carts or riding in Conestoga wagons. These early Utah pioneers cherished the isolation of the area and organized their communities around tenets of their religion.

High on their agenda was the importance of schools and education. With pride, they can boast that the University of Utah, founded in Salt Lake City in 1850, was the first public university west of the Mississippi River. Shortly after congressional approval of the Morrill Act in 1862, Utah State College in Logan was designated as the official land-grant college. It opened its doors to its first classes in 1888 ("Higher Education in Utah," 2003). Meanwhile, in 1876, leaders of the LDS Church started a prep school and academy in Provo—the forerunner of Brigham Young University (BYU). The first collegiate work began in 1903. With an enrollment of more than 33,000 in 2012, BYU lays claim to being the largest religious-affiliated university in the world (http://yfacts. byu.edu/Article?id=104). About 98 percent of the students at BYU are Mormon, and two-thirds of its students come from outside Utah ("Brigham Young University," 2003).

One of the preeminent educators in the twentieth century was David O. McKay, the ninth president of the LDS church. McKay was an 1897 graduate of the University of Utah, where he was valedictorian and class president. He embarked upon a career in education and educational administration until called to a full-time church position in 1906. McKay served as president of the LDS church from 1951 until his death in 1970.

From 1918 to 1934, McKay was responsible for the construction of LDS seminary buildings near public high schools throughout Utah. These seminaries allowed students to take LDS religious courses along with their secular high school education. McKay also was responsible for transferring three LDS colleges to the State of Utah in the 1920s—Snow College, Weber State University, and Dixie College. Further, he guided Brigham Young University into becoming a full four-year university. Located in Provo, Utah, BYU today is the flagship educational institution of the Mormon Church. *The Princeton Review* ranked BYU as one of the best western colleges, and it holds the third best value college in the United States in 2005, and the best value for college in 2007. The university was also credited with having one of the finest libraries in the nation (McKay, 2003).

While the bulk of educational activity was taking place in the more densely populated north-central part of the state, down in the southwestern corner, what eventually became the University of Southern Utah opened in 1897 in Cedar City. Allegedly, the main attraction of the small town was that it had neither a saloon nor a pool hall!

Most of the higher education battles in post–World War II Utah have been related to the governance of the public collegiate institutions and the issue of decentralized control versus centralized control. Before 1967, the nine universities and colleges were governed by four different boards. In 1957, however, the legislature established the Coordinating Board of Higher Education, which gave way in 1959 to the Utah Coordinating Council of Higher Education. Under this Coordinating Council, each of the then-existing institutional governing boards continued to function with the institutions retaining considerable operational autonomy. The boards and the institutions fought vigorously to maintain direct access to the legislature.

In 1961, Weber State was removed from the State Board of Education and governed by a separate board of trustees. It was authorized to become a four-year college; in 1963, its name was changed to Weber State College. Two years later, what is now Southern Utah University was authorized, evolving from what had been a branch campus under the control of Utah State University.

The move to stronger centralization of the governance of higher education continued in 1969 when the legislature established a single board—the Utah State Board of Higher Education. It also provided for a commissioner of higher education plus nine institutional presidents to report directly to the board. The legislature also created formal advisory boards associated with each institution. In 1974, the name of the governing body was changed to the State Board of Regents. Weber State and Southern Utah both were designated as universities in 1990; two years later, Utah Valley State College was authorized to offer selected baccalaureate degree programs ("Higher Education in Utah," 2003).

Meanwhile, in 1970, 320 acres of the Fort Douglas military reservation on the east side of Salt Lake City were set aside specifically for the creation of a research park for the University of Utah to attract new high-tech industries. In 1973, David Pierpont Gardner became the president of the University of Utah and began to expand the research role. That same year, the University of Utah ranked twenty-sixth in the nation in the amount of federal funds received for research, which meant that the university was beginning to arrive as a major research institution. During Gardner's ten years as president, the University of Utah Hospital became a world leader in treatment of burns and other trauma. By the time Chase Peterson of the University of Utah Medical Center replaced Gardner in 1983, income from patents and commercial licenses on inventions from the university's faculty amounted to millions of dollars. Thus, by the end of the first decade in the twenty-first century, Utah had 12 public collegiate institutions, which included 5 community colleges and a technical school, as well as 7 four-year colleges and universities.

Gardner, who left Utah in 1983 to head up the prestigious ten-campus system of the University of California, later chaired the US Department of Education's Commission on Excellence and helped spark a national effort to improve and reform US schools through its influential report, *A Nation at Risk*. Gardner was widely hailed as an educator of uncommon leadership and courage during the second half of the twentieth century as the University of Utah played a prominent role in higher education research ("Becoming a Research Center," 2007).

During David McKay's tenure as president of the Church of Latter-Day Saints, he repeatedly proclaimed that the glory of God was intelligence. This revelation strengthened the resolve of the Mormons to support excellence in education on all levels and had a profound impact on all schools, including those higher education institutions supported by the state. The end result was Utah developing excellent public and church-related universities, supplemented by outstanding community colleges and vocational programs. Utah is also recognized as having one of the premier public school systems in the country.

Of the five southwestern states, Utah has been the most homogeneous—being mostly white and mostly Mormon. However, with a rapidly growing Hispanic population, the state is becoming more diverse. The roughly 30,000 Native Americans in Utah tend to reside in the southeastern part of the state. Utah has shown little inclination to make special provisions for the education of its Native Americans. However, members of the LDS Church have adopted Native American children and raised and educated them as members of their families, including their religious training.

In regard to Utah's Hispanic population, contrary to a policy of making it tough on what are sometimes described as "illegal migrants," state legislators three times have turned back proposals to charge these students nonresident tuition. Some Utahans believe that the cost to the state is puny while the rewards for the enterprising Hispanic student are stupendous. The people argue that it is better to build bridges than walls (Editors of the *Chronicles of Higher Education*, 2007–2008, p. 89). Although conservative in politics, Utah citizens have been very liberal in their support of education and have sought to provide the best of opportunities for their sons and daughters. Over 90 percent of the high school graduates who go on to college remain in the state for their education.

Like its brethren in adjacent states, Utah's aspirations for quality higher education often exceeded its ability to pay. Annually, it has seemed to struggle with limited funds for education despite its good intentions. State funding for Utah's public institutions declined in FY2002–2004, with a decrease of –4 percent from $628 million to $603 million (Zumeta, 2006, p. 42). However, somehow, even as the Great Recession was taking hold, there seemed to be a way to pull through. Surprisingly, in the 2007–2008 budget year, the legislature appropriated more money to higher education than the Board of Regents had requested. An increase of 14.3 percent over the previous year or $798 million, which was an increase of $93 million, broke all former records. In addition, lawmakers approved almost $124 million for building projects and capital improvements. These actions bore out the finding expressed in a report by the National Center for Higher Education Management Systems that rated Utah as the most successful state system in higher education in terms of performance relative to state money received per student (Editors of the *Chronicles of Higher Education*, 2007–2008, p. 31). Nevertheless, as the dramatic effects of the Great Recession grew deeper within the state and among Utah's public institutions of higher learning, there occurred a –7.8 percent state funding decline between FY2008 and FY2012, while maintaining a state operating funding of public institutions at some less than $729 million in FY2011 (http://www.sheeo.org/sites/default/files/publications/SHEF%20FY%2012-20130322rev.pdf, p. 62; Editors of the *Chronicle of Higher Education*, 2012–2013, p. 92). This is discussed further across the subregion later in the chapter.

COLORADO

Colorado, like other parts of the Southwest, was populated by nineteenth-century immigrants seeking gold and silver and adventure. Often, they had to settle for sugar beets and cherry trees and feed lots and cattle. The surge of immigrants from the Midwest followed the river route up the Missouri River to the Platte River in Nebraska, then down the South Platte to Denver. Later, hard-working farmers came to claim and till the fertile fields of eastern Colorado, cultivating sugar beets and the rolling hills of wheat and fruit orchards. A lot of these people had come to America from Sweden and Norway and Germany and Russia to join the great migration of easterners and midwesterners who crossed the plains to a beautiful, romantic land that combined the grandeur of the mountains with the bounty of the plains.

In 1859, Henry Ward Beecher, although not referring specifically to immigrants to Colorado, picturesquely described these western pioneers, saying, "they drive schools along with them as shepherds drive flocks. They have herds of churches, academies, lyceums, and the religious and educational institutions go lowing along the western plains as Jacob's herds lowed along the Syrian Hills" (1963, p. 655). Along with their quest for gold and silver, the Colorado pioneers also aspired to the higher attributes of culture—religion and learning. Thus, missionary zeal has been credited as the driving force that led to the founding of the Methodist-related Colorado Seminary in 1864. The fledgling school was closed in 1867, but reopened in 1880 as the University of Denver, which flourished on advanced programs in business, law, and the liberal arts (McGiffert, 1964, pp. x–xi). Another private school founded in this period (1874) was Colorado College in Colorado Springs. By 2007, *US News & World Report* ranked it twenty-sixth among the nation's best liberal arts colleges (2008, p. 86).

Public higher education in the state began shortly thereafter. The first public collegiate school was the Colorado School of Mines, which opened in 1874 in Golden. This small but elite institution established a national and international reputation for its expertise in the fields of mining and engineering. In Fort Collins, the Agricultural College of Colorado (eventually Colorado State University after six name changes) was established as the land-grant college in 1870, but classes were not held until 1877. Over the years, its main strengths have been agriculture, engineering, and, more recently, veterinary medicine. Meanwhile, the University of Colorado at Boulder was authorized by the Territorial Legislature in 1861, but did not open its doors until 1877. Because there was no secondary school system in the state, the university operated a "prep" school to prepare students for the classical college curriculum. With the red-tiled roofs of its native flag-stone buildings profiled against a backdrop of the front range of the Rockies, the Boulder campus gained international renown for its architecture and the beauty of its setting. The institution also garnered prestige and respect on the national scene as its academic and research programs matured, and its medical center flourished in Denver.

Three normal schools for the training of teachers were also founded: Colorado State College at Greeley, 1889, now the University of Northern Colorado; Western State College at Gunnison, 1901; and Adams State College in Alamosa, 1921.

Meanwhile, Mesa College in Grand Junction, founded as a junior college in 1925 and becoming Colorado Mesa University in 2011, was authorized to grant baccalaureate degrees in 1974 and master's degrees in 1996. Metropolitan State College of Denver was added to the ranks of the higher education baccalaureate institutions in 1965 and has grown to become one of the largest four-year public urban colleges in the nation. The state legislation renamed it Metropolitan State University of Denver in 2012.

Concerning state governance of higher education, Fort Lewis School of Agriculture (founded in 1933 in Durango) became a campus of the Colorado

State University System after World War II, as did the University of Southern Colorado (formerly Pueblo Community College). These institutions, along with the parent Colorado State University, are governed by the Board of Governors of the Colorado State System. The Colorado School of Mines is governed by its own seven member Board of Trustees with elected faculty and student members. The other three institutions, Western State, Adams State, and Mesa State, along with Metropolitan State College in Denver, are governed by the Trustees of the State Colleges of Colorado. Thus there were four governing boards, besides the one for the University of Colorado, in the state. Six regents elected for six-year terms govern the University of Colorado system, which includes the University of Colorado Boulder, the University of Colorado Colorado Springs, the University of Colorado Denver, and the University of Colorado Health Sciences Center—later renamed the Anshutz Medical Campus. (The latter two were merged in June 2004 as a single university, but retain separate facilities in Denver and suburban Aurora on a former military base.)

World War II provided unexpected blessings to all Colorado colleges and universities. Military programs brought students to Colorado campuses from all over the nation and postwar enrollments zoomed. The University of Colorado became a major player in space science and advanced mathematics, physics, and biological science. And, after the national service academies, it also became the largest producer of astronauts (Colorado Commission on Higher Education, 2007).

Colorado Springs was selected as the site for the Air Force Academy. Founded in 1954, it opened at Lowry Field in Denver and moved to Colorado Springs in 1958. Modeled after the federal military academies at West Point and Annapolis, its main mission has been to train officers for positions of leadership in the Air Force (United States Air Force Academy, 2007).

During the late 1950s, Quigg Newton (president of the University of Colorado and former mayor of Denver) and Governor Steve McNichols were the prime movers in developing what became known as the Research Corridor. Patterned after cooperative high-tech research conducted by clusters of universities in North Carolina, Chicago, and San Francisco, the universities along the front range of the Rockies, stretching from Fort Collins to Colorado Springs, worked in close cooperation with the expanding high-tech activity in the state. This research corridor attracted several government and private scientific research corporations, including IBM, Hewlett-Packard, Beech Aircraft, Ball Brothers Research, the US Bureau of Standards, Martin Marietta, Lockheed, the Air Force, and others. The forthcoming liaisons between institutions of higher learning and leaders in the high technology private sector established Colorado as one of the major scientific centers in the world (Davis, *Glory*, 2007, pp. 1–3).

In addition, to meet the demands for increased access to higher education, there was a surge in developing and/or expanding the programs of community colleges throughout the state. The State Board of Community Colleges and Occupational Education became responsible for the governance of: the Community College of Denver; Arapahoe Community College; Pikes Peak Community College; Pueblo Community College; Red Rocks Community College; Aurora Community College; Morgan Community College; Northeastern Junior College; Northwestern Junior College; Trinidad Community College; Colorado Electronic Community College; and the Higher Education Advanced Technology center in Denver. This board also oversees the Auraria Higher Education Center, which operates the single campus in Denver that provides common services to the Community College of Denver, Metropolitan State College of Denver, and the University of Colorado, Denver. Two local district junior colleges—Aims Community College and Colorado Mountain College—have independent governing boards. Both receive some general fund support in addition to local property tax support. Because of the independent and disparate nature of these respective boards, there has been little formal coordination of their activities or clarification of their respective roles and missions. This has led to what some legislators have considered to be an unnecessary duplication of effort and expenditures.

The Colorado Commission on Higher Education (CCHE) was created in 1965 to bring some semblance of coordination to the scope of higher education in the state. The commission received increased authority and directives from the legislature in 1985. Specifically, it was given the responsibility for long-range planning and approval of institutional roles and missions plus the recommending authority for capital construction and funding requests to the legislature.

However, one of the major obstacles to implementing a strong centralized system has been the historical fact that the University of Colorado, since its inception, enjoyed the independence of its constitutional status and its elected Board of Regents. On several occasions, the university has maintained that it is not subject to the authority of either the governor or the legislature. While the legislature has some control in that it can determine the level of state funding for the university, it cannot tell the regents what to do. This has led to some major conflicts, most of which have been resolved peacefully. However, the nagging image of that constitutional status still arouses apprehension and, sometimes, confrontation. CCHE is in a position to persuade, but has only limited power when it comes to command (Colorado Commission on Higher Education, 2007).

As the twentieth century wound down, John Buechner, as president of the University of Colorado, oversaw a dramatic expansion of the scientific productivity on the Boulder campus, leading to Nobel Prize–winning faculty, more astronauts in space, and worldwide renown for the university's many scientific research activities. He also provided the leadership and vision for the massive relocation of the university's Health Science Center from Denver to a former US Army hospital in the suburb of Aurora. This multibillion-dollar move and expansion established the University of Colorado as one of the nation's premier medical centers for teaching, research, and patient care.

With the dawn of the twenty-first century, the new university president, Elizabeth Hoffman, continued the institution's campaign to raise money from the private sector. One of the capstones to her endeavors was the receipt of the largest single gift in the history of the university—a $250 million grant for an institute on cognitive disabilities (Davis, *Glory*, 2007, pp. 877–887).

Outside support from the private sector assumed greater significance as state funding for higher education in Colorado dwindled. For example, in August 2003, the University of Colorado system was faced with a $44.8 million drop in state support. To meet this cut, it was necessary for the system to eliminate 500 staff and faculty positions, consolidate degree programs in journalism and engineering, cut programs in selected areas, and freeze salaries. A tuition increase of 15 percent was necessary to mitigate some of the damage, but it could not entirely make up for the cuts in state spending (Editors of the *Chronicle of Higher Education*, 2003–2004, pp. 39–40).

Thus, at the dawn of a new century, funding problems continued to plague Colorado with all public institutions of higher learning impacted by tax limitations, which, in turn, led to budget cuts. The old belief that state collegiate institutions should be relatively free for a qualified resident student has become a part of folklore and ancient history. What the legislature took away, the schools sought to restore by raising tuition; but even this did not alleviate the necessity to cut back on faculty and programs.

In many ways the colleges and universities of Colorado reflected the retrenchments in education nationwide. According to a study released by the College Board in October 2003, over the previous decade, the cost for higher education had risen more than 40 percent. Average tuition and fees at four-year, state-funded colleges jumped 47 percent in this ten-year period, with the sharpest hikes averaging 14.1 percent in 2002 (Editors of the *Chronicle of Higher Education*, 2003–2004, pp. 39–40).

While institutions of higher learning in Colorado reflected growth in students and stature with accompanying excellence in the sciences and medical arts, these advances were threatened by budget cuts, limits on capital construction, and higher costs to individual students and their families. Between 2002 and 2004, public higher education funding in Colorado declined some –21.8 percent from some $757 million to a significantly less $591 million (Zumeta, 2006, p. 42). In 2006, however, higher education advocates cheered, as Colorado voters rolled back the nation's most restrictive limits on state spending adopted in earlier years. The vote suspended a constitutionally imposed spending cap. College leaders pointed out that the stringent limitations had contributed still to a more than 20 percent reduction in the state's financial support for higher education since 2000. Supporters of higher education had stated that had the colleges and universities not received some relief, some public institutions would have been forced to close, while others would have had to rely almost solely on tuition increases or private fund-raising. The legislature approved a 16.5 percent increase in funding for the 2005–2006 appropriation. With the increase in revenue and state support, tuition increases were held to 2.5 percent (Editors of the *Chronicle of Higher*

Education, 2006–2007, pp. 43–44). Even with an increase of 8.6 percent in appropriations, however, tuitions continued to rise. By 2007–2008, tuition at the University of Colorado Boulder was $5,643 for residents and $22,989 for nonresidents. Also causing dismay was a constitutional amendment establishing stringent ethics rules, which according to the state attorney general would keep children of public employees from receiving certain college scholarships and bar professors at public universities from accepting Nobel Prize money or similar awards (Editors of the *Chronicle of Higher Education*, 2007–2008, p. 44).

Colorado's position as a leader in higher education in western states has been a casualty of tight fiscal policies. As the end of the first decade of the twenty-first century closed, CU no longer was included among the top 50 research universities in the country. Even within Colorado, the Colorado School of Mines (thirty-third) is ranked ahead of CU (thirty-fifth) as a public national research university. This is a big comedown for what once was hailed as the state's flagship institution (Editors of *US News & World Report*, 2008, pp. 81–85). Further, the University of Colorado's image was badly damaged when two women claimed to having been gang raped by football players and recruits at a party in 2001. This resulted in a scandal that cost several top university officials their jobs, including the head football coach, the athletics director, and even the president (Sander, 2007, p. A20).

With the leadership of a new president, Hank Brown, the university's eroded prestige began to be restored. CU-Boulder in 2007 set a school record for sponsored research funding, $266.2 million, which was sixth in the nation among public universities in federal research funding. Enrollment on the Boulder campus in 2007 was 29,000 and applications for admission had increased by 16 percent in two years. Further, the CU Foundation, the university's development arm, ranked ahead of 99 percent of its peers for the year ending June 30, 2007 (Sander, 2007, p. A20). For Coloradans, these were good signs that the state's flagship university was not dead in the water.

However, the dramatic effects of the Great Recession forced significant retrenchment among the Colorado public institutions of higher learning leading to a –14.3 percent state funding decline between FY2008 and FY2012, while maintaining a state operating funding of public institutions at somewhat higher $647 million in FY2011 (http://www.sheeo.org/ sites/ default files/publications/ SHEF%20FY%2012-20130322rev.pdf, p. 62; Editors of the *Chronicle of Higher Education*, 2012–2013, p. 70). This is discussed further across the subregion later in the chapter.

NEW MEXICO

Almost five centuries ago, around 1539, Spanish Conquistadores under the command of Coronado set up camp across the Rio Grande River from present-day Albuquerque. Using this as their base, they sent exploring parties in all directions seeking legendary cities of gold, which they never found.

Wherever they went, however, the Spanish and Indian cultures began to merge and create a rich and colorful pageantry that has forever touched and enriched the lives of New Mexicans.

Along the way, by the 1800s, the religious influence of the Catholics from Spain and Mexico began to be challenged by the Protestants from this nation's eastern seaboard, as they vied to save the souls of converts and the native population. These mostly white missionaries of various faiths were joined by hunters, traders, and trappers. Tracks for railroads led to the founding of towns and cities, and, eventually, opened the state to formal learning, including schools for these people on this rugged frontier who hungered for education.

New Mexico, along with its western neighbor Arizona, was granted statehood in 1912. It was the last of the five southwestern states to establish a four-year public university. The first New Mexico territorial collegiate institution was what is now New Mexico State University, founded in Las Cruces in 1888 as the agricultural and engineering land-grant school. A year later, in 1889, the Territorial Legislature authorized the founding of the University of New Mexico in Albuquerque and the New Mexico Institute of Mining and Technology in Socorro. Four years later, in 1893, two state normal schools were approved: New Mexico Highlands in Las Vegas and Western New Mexico in Silver City. A sixth institution was added in 1933 as Eastern New Mexico University was created, another normal school.

Each of the six four-year collegiate institutions has constitutional status and is governed by its own Board of Regents. Among the two-year collegiate institutions, New Mexico Military Institute and Northern New Mexico Community College (formerly El Rito) have constitutional standing. The other educational institutions are either branches of four-year universities or governed by local elected boards.

After New Mexico was granted statehood in 1912, various studies recommended that the number of higher education institutions in the state should be reduced and that the individual boards of regents should be replaced by a single, statewide consolidated governing board. However, each of these studies and proposals was rejected by the legislature or the people of the state (Davis, *Miracle,* 2007, pp. 1–87).

A study by the noted higher education fiscal scholar John Dale Russell led to the creation of the Board of Educational Finance (BEF) in 1951. The legislature established the BEF to serve as a buffer between the institutions and itself and to reduce the confusion in funding higher education. Initially, the BEF was a mixed, legislative-executive agency, with legislators regularly appointed as members. After 1959, it operated as an executive agency to coordinate public higher education. One of the major responsibilities of the BEF was to make recommendations to the legislature pertaining to appropriations for operational budgets and capital outlay for the respective state institutions. In 1986, the BEF was disbanded and replaced by the New Mexico Commission on Higher Education.

In 1977 the governor's Committee on Technical Excellence recommended that the legislature fund upgrades to the scientific research at the academic institutions, resources to increase library holdings, and several million dollars for science and engineering buildings. Essentially, this strong support prepared these institutions to compete with other universities in the country for federal and private technical and scientific research (Davis, *Miracle,* 2007, p. 238).

Over the past 50 years, New Mexico's universities have earned special distinction in their programs for educating members of minority groups. The University of New Mexico in the 1970s and 1980s, for example, became the Mecca for Hispanic and Native American authors of the contemporary Southwest under the leadership of Rudolfo Anaya, the acknowledged dean of Hispanic writers. Playing a major role in the development of Native American and Hispanic students, professors, and lecturers was the University of New Mexico Press, which published numerous books by these authors. Further, the American Indian and Hispanic law programs at the University of New Mexico have served as models for other collegiate institutions. Summer session courses taught in Spanish for school administrators from Latin American countries have forged strong bonds throughout the Western Hemisphere. Excellent museums and strong collections of books relating to the Hispanic and Native American cultures characterize the holdings on the campuses of the state institutions. Cooperative programs on increasing the number of bilingual teachers in the public schools and native speaking teachers on the reservations have been highly successful. And in the health sciences, great strides have been made in educating Native American physicians and healthcare specialists, supplemented by nationally recognized residencies in family practice in isolated and remote areas.

One of the significant developments in higher education in the state was the creation of a medical school at the University of New Mexico in 1964. The original two-year curriculum was expanded to a four-year program in 1966 (Davis, *Miracle,* 2007, pp. 199–203).

The state's other four-year colleges and universities and the community colleges also have made educating minority students a high priority. New Mexico Highlands University, Western New Mexico University, and New Mexico State University have had outstanding success in increasing opportunities for all minority students, particularly Hispanics.

Another of the great success stories in New Mexico has been the emergence of the New Mexico Institute of Mining and Technology in the field of federal sponsored grants. Under the leadership of its president, Dan Lopez, New Mexico Tech led the nation in 2003 with $56.1 million from the federal government for antiterrorist programs. From 1999 to 2003, the school received over $103 million in "nonshared earmarks" from the federal government. National kudos continued to pour in for what natives refer to as New Mexico Tech. *Newsweek* in its August 20–27, 2007 edition named it as one of the nation's hottest 25 schools. The magazine praised New Mexico Tech for being the "hottest in the war on terror." It reported:

> New Mexico Tech, in a friendly desert town (Socorro) an hour south of Albuquerque, has reduced admissions red tape while quietly building, with a flood of federal dollars, one of the prime research centers for fighting the War on Terror. It is in some ways the Los Alamos of a new age, this time focusing on searching suitcases and disabling roadside explosives rather than building the A-bomb. (Editors of *Newsweek*, 2007, p. 53)

Three sets of demographics have been significant factors in the development of higher education in New Mexico. In 2003, the state led the nation in the percentage of people living in poverty—17 percent. It was forty-sixth in the country in per capita income—$23,941 versus a national average of $30,941. And New Mexico had the second highest percentage of minorities in its total population—54.6 percent. The state's largest percentage of minorities is Hispanic with 42.1 percent, followed by Native Americans with 9.5 percent. Obviously, Anglos are outnumbered by the collective minorities (Editors of the *Chronicle of Higher Education*, 2003–2004, p. 67).

Meanwhile, the New Mexico Education Assistance Foundation (NMEAF), which helps administer the state's Student Loan program, has a number of financial aid programs that assist struggling students in financing their college educations. There are "up-front" loan forgiveness programs for students majoring in the teaching and healthcare professions. Other special incentives reward borrowers, including programs that charge no interest to borrowers who make timely scheduled repayments. These measures have led in part to New Mexico having one of the lowest default rates in the country. In addition, in 2006 and 2007, the NMEAF forgave $6.5 million worth of outstanding loans. As reported in the *Chronicle of Higher Education*, in 2003, New Mexico was one of the leaders in the nation in receiving increased legislative appropriations for higher education. The legislature approved a dramatic 51 percent increase in scholarship funds for outstanding students, increased appropriations for loan forgiveness programs for school teachers by 34.5 percent, and increased state funds for a similar program for nurses by 14.6 percent. A separate legislative appropriation allocated $2 million to statewide nursing education programs (Editors of the *Chronicle of Higher Education*, 2003–2004, p. 67).

Among the outstanding features of higher education in New Mexico have been those special programs designed to meet the needs of minority students and students from Central and South America. Five Hispanics were among the first students when the University of New Mexico first opened its doors in the summer of 1892. Further, from the time Mariano Otero first served as president of the first Board of Regents, one or more Hispanics have served on the university's governing board.

At the turn of the twentieth century, the "pueblo style" of the Pueblo Indians was selected as campus architecture with the first buildings in adobe. The Native American influence was further emphasized during the presidency of James Fulton Zimmerman, who included representatives of the area tribes in his inaugural ceremony. Repeatedly, throughout those beginning years,

Table 5.2 List of tribal colleges by state

State/Institutions	Locations	Year Founded
Arizona (2 tribal colleges) Diné College (main campus and 7 branch campuses)	Tsaile (main); (Branches): Tuba City Chinle Window Rock Kayinta Crownpoint, NM Shiprock, NM	1968
Tohono O'odham Community College	Sells	1998
New Mexico (3 tribal colleges)		
Institute of American Indian Arts	Santa Fe	1962
Navajo Technical College	Crownpoint	1979
Southwest Indian Polytechnic Institute	Albuquerque	1971

Source: http://www.aihec.org/colleges/TCUmap.cfm; www.indiancountrytodaymedia network.com; see White House Initiative on Tribal Colleges and Universities. Retrieved from http://www.ed.gov/about/inits/list/whtc/edlite-index.html, on February 25, 2012.

presidents and board members and faculty of the respective collegiate institutions made profound statements as they sought to capitalize on the Hispanic (and to a lesser extent, the Native American) presence in the state through recruitment of students and faculty and emphasis on academic courses and research. But these efforts had limited success, and the Hispanic and Native American presence at UNM both blossomed and waned during the first half of the twentieth century. Joining them have been three Native American colleges within the state: the Institute for American Indian Arts (IAIA) in Santa Fe in 1962, the Southwest Indian Polytechnic Institute in Albuquerque in 1971, and the Navajo Technical College in Crownpoint in 1979 (table 5.2). IAIA clearly has created a distinctive four-year college mission with its educational focus on advancing Native American tribal art in "Studio Arts, New Media Arts, Creative Writing, Museum Studies and Indigenous Liberal Studies" as the center of its academic studies—unlike any other Native American college—yet so appropriate for the art culture of Santa Fe (www.iaia.edu).

It was not until after World War II that Hispanics at UNM were initiated into fraternities and sororities. There was lip service to multiculturalism, but little perceivable progress. For all practical purposes, UNM and its sister state institutions (with the exception of Highlands University and Western New Mexico) remained mostly Anglo in their upper administration, faculty, and student body.

World War II changed all that. Returning veterans had seen enough of racial bigotry and intolerance and set a fresh tone with new attitudes toward Hispanics and Native Americans. It did not happen all at once, but over time these groups became a more integral part of the campuses. There were ugly incidents, but, for the most part, the student body and faculty and administration of the state's colleges and universities strongly supported the elimination of all signs of discrimination and intolerance and sought ways to embrace and expand the state's legacy of multiculturalism.

By far the highest priority relating to minority students in New Mexico, however, is to increase their numbers in earning degrees on both the undergraduate and graduate levels in order that they might prepare themselves for positions of leadership in all professional areas of our society (Davis, *Miracle*, 2007, p. 50). That the University of New Mexico is succeeding in achieving many of its goals for minority students was reflected in its high ranking by *Hispanic Business Magazine* in 2007. UNM ranked first in law schools and in the top ten programs nationally in engineering (fifth) and medical schools (sixth). The high ratings were attributed to a proven record of recruiting and graduating Hispanics and other minority lawyers, doctors, and engineers, reflecting the cultures of the people of New Mexico ("Hispanic Mag Ranks UNM High," 2007, p. C1).

More recently, new partnerships have been developed between the University of New Mexico and Central New Mexico Community College (CNM). The two institutions agreed to work on a dual enrollment program, making it easier for students to attend CNM for two years and then transfer to UNM. Planning was started for "gateway" programs to help students who were not adequately prepared for university work ("UNM, CNM Sign Deal on Facility," 2007, p. A10).

State funding for the public institutions of higher learning began in the past decade in a good way as FY2002–2004 saw 6.5 percent budgetary increase from $605 million to $644 million, which was an indicator of state support for higher education. However, the dramatic effects of the Great Recession forced severe retrenchment among New Mexico public higher education institutions leading to a –21.3 percent state funding decline between FY2008 and FY2012, while maintaining a state operating funding of public institutions at only some $423 million in FY2011, compared to earlier years (http://www.sheeo.org/sites/default/ files/publications/ SHEF%20FY%20 12-20130322rev.pdf, p. 62; Editors of the *Chronicle of Higher Education*, 2012–2013, p. 86). This is discussed further across the subregion later in the chapter.

While colleges and universities in New Mexico do not claim to have all the answers to all the problems in public and higher education, they are at least seeking ways to collaborate on helping people to live in harmony with themselves and with each other in the awesome beauty that surrounds them. Their dreams and aspirations are reflected in the Navajo salutation: "Hoshongo, neek a doolee." Or, as the Anglos might say: "May you walk in beauty."

SUMMARY

Across these five states, 227 public four-year institutions, public two-year community colleges, private universities, a growing number of for-profit

Table 5.3 Number of institutions in the subregion by type by state, 2010

	Arizona		Colorado		Nevada		New Mexico		Utah	
	4-year	2-year	4-year	2-year	4-year	2-year	4-year	2-year	4-year	2-year
Public	4	20	12	15	6	1	8	20	7	6
Private nonprofit	11	0	11	1	2	0	3	0	3	1
Private for-profit	29	14	25	18	7	5	8	2	17	6
Totals	**44**	**34**	**48**	**34**	**15**	**6**	**19**	**22**	**27**	**13**
State Totals	**78**		**82**		**21**		**41**		**40**	
Public Four-Year and Two-Year Total	99	38%								
Private Four-Year and Two-Year Total	32	12%								
For-Profit Total	131	50%								
Subregional Grand Total	**262**									

Source: US Department of Education for AY2009–2010 postsecondary enrollments, "Colleges and Universities" (http://nces.ed.gov) as cited by Editors, "Almanac of Higher Education, 2011–12," *Chronicle of Higher Education,* August 26, 2011, 58 (1). p. 24.

institutions, and tribal colleges comprise the subregional landscape of higher education. Specifically, 99 public universities, colleges, tribal, and community colleges, or some 38 percent of postsecondary education in these states, provide the bulk of baccalaureate, graduate, and professional studies. Another 32 private colleges and universities (or 12 percent), many reflecting religious-related or church-sponsored higher education, fill unique educational missions in these states, whether from older mainline Protestant denominations and the Catholic Church or from the Mormons. Some 131 for-profit institutions of higher learning (or some 50%) are offering new applied business, technical, medical, and vocational studies in the subregion (table 5.3).

Within the WICHE West, these southwest institutions provide considerable opportunity for students of color to earn their bachelor's and advanced degrees. Superseded by California's postsecondary system having a 45.2 percent minority student population or the Pacific Western states of Alaska, Hawaii, Oregon, and Washington (as is discussed in another chapter) with their 32.6 percent diverse student population, these five southwestern states have an overall 26.7 percent diverse student population. New Mexico leads the subregion with respect to the number of minority students with a state average of 44.9 percent, with Arizona, Nevada, and Colorado clustered

Table 5.4 Southwest WICHE states and minority postsecondary student enrollments Fall 2009

Southwest States	Public 4-Year Institutions (%)	Public 2-Year Institutions (%)	Private 4-Year Institutions (%)	For-Profit Institutions (%)	State Total Average (%)
Arizona	27.7	34.6	16.3	26.4	26.2
Colorado	18.3	26.3	16.2	35.7	24.1
Nevada	38.1	28	33.1	40.1	25.8
New Mexico	49.2	55.1	26.2	49.1	44.9
Utah	9.3	16.8	11.5	13.3	12.7
Regional Institutional Type Average %	20	32.1	20.6	32.9	
Subregional Total Average %					26.7

Source: US Department of Education for Fall 2009 postsecondary enrollments, "Access and Equity" (http://nces.ed.gov) as cited by Editors, "Almanac of Higher Education, 2011–12," *Chronicle of Higher Education*, August 26, 2011, 58 (1), pp. 31–36.

somewhere between 26 and 24 percent, while Utah reflects the least diversity among its student populations at 12.7 percent. As the subregional leader, New Mexico educates these students at minority-serving universities and colleges as well as community colleges, where their diverse student bodies are at 49.2 percent and 55.1 percent, respectively. In the five-state subregion, public and private four-year colleges and universities hold large minority student populations, with approximately 20 percent in each group. However, more attractive to these ethnic and racial groups have been the community colleges and for-profit institutions with 32.1 percent and 32.9 percent, respectively. Significant growing Latino, Native American, and Asian communities throughout the southwestern states are seeking postsecondary education, which has made this subregion a national leader in minority education (table 5.4).

These advancing five state systems, however, enacted dramatic retrenchments in their state operating budgets with the Great Recession between FY2008 and 2011. Much was lost. The hardest decline in state funding was in Arizona where the state budget for higher education dropped –22.0 percent, going from $1.3 billion in 2008 to $1.02 billion in 2011—a loss of some $289 million in operating funds. New Mexico fared little better with a significant drop of –21 percent from $1.05 billion to $874 million or a loss of some $183.7 million. These unfortunate state leaders were followed by major losses in Utah and Colorado where public institutions of higher learning endured declines of –13.65 percent and –10.52 percent, respectively. Only Nevada came out relatively unscathed with a –.47 percent loss over the three years or a $21.07 million gap from the last prerecession budget. These

Table 5.5 Southwest state and federal support, FY2008–FY2011

State	FY2008 State Support ($)	FY2011 State Support ($)	Change in State Support FY2008–2011 (%)*	FY2011 Federal Stimulus Support ($)	FY2011 Total State and Federal Support ($)
Arizona	1,315,406,400	1,025,534,200	–22.00	0	1,025,534,200
Colorado	747,481,054	675,318,216	–10.52	89,194,099	765,512,315
Nevada	675,011,774	653,935,362	–0.47	0	653,935,362
New Mexico	1,058,394,058	874,736,332	–21.00	11,887,500	886,623,832
Utah	812,337,500	714,802,000	–13.65	19,837,800	734,639,800

Note: *(Additional factors—see article—were calculated in these state support changes; therefore, percentages do not foot.)

Source: W. Zumeta and A. Kinne, "The Recession Is Not Over for Higher Education." *The NEA 2011 Almanac for Higher Education*. Washington, DC: National Education Association, 2011, pp. 29–42; "State Fiscal Support for Higher Education, by State, Fiscal Years 2006–07, 2009–10, 2010–11, and 2011–12," *Grapevine* from Illinois State University, and the State Higher Education Executive Officers' "Financial Survey," January 2011, www.grapevine.illinoisstate.edu.

budget declines were offset by federal stimulus funding of $120.9 million due to the recession in Colorado, New Mexico, and Utah. In the WICHE western region, where 12 of the 15 states endured budgetary retrenchments, Arizona experienced the second worst state funding decline, superseded only by Oregon with its –25.71 percent loss (as noted in chapter 6). Reflecting the national trend of lower state funding of higher education, the southwest states await an economic recovery and reengaged political support for all types of higher education so that they might regain their critical educational role in offering new opportunities for occupational, humanistic, scientific, artistic, and professional careers (see table 5.5).

CONCLUSION AND GENERAL OBSERVATIONS

The Southwest is a vast geographic area of mountains and desolate plains with a sprinkling of oases of culture and learning in deserts of this subregion. For centuries, it was the setting for the turmoil of almost continuous warfare between Spaniards and Indians and white adventurers—a place where men and a few bold and hardy women struggled for survival in a hostile environment. The Southwest began to be discovered in the late nineteenth century. Building on the development of the pueblo culture and cliff dwellings of the early natives and later the northward migration and culture of the Hispanics and Indians of Mexico, the immigrants from the East and Midwest added yet another dimension to the history and lifestyle of the subregion. Following the ideas of our western historian Patty Limerick in chapter 3, conquest and conflict often characterized those early years of this region as well as later acculturation—and, sometimes, accommodation.

Economic development of the subregion accelerated in the latter part of the nineteenth century, as the Old Spanish Trail brought new settlers to this subregion. Rails were then laid, roads were paved, airports were built, and communication systems began to link this once remote area to the larger world. Within this area, the pueblos were augmented by towns and cities with their houses, businesses, churches, and, eventually, elementary and secondary schools, junior and then community colleges, tribal colleges, as well as colleges and universities.

While a few of the universities sought to adopt the academic standards of their eastern brethren, most remained sensitive to the educational needs of their region—particularly the Hispanics and Native Americans among the minority groups. Over time, the blending of the cultures superseded the centuries of conflict, and the area became a mosaic of people—sometimes a quarrelsome, hostile mosaic—but still a mosaic. This blending brought forth great creativity in the arts, literature, and the lives of those in the Southwest. Rather than a road to somewhere else, the subregion became an attractive destination for all ethnic and racial groups to work and to live together—and to study and to learn.

WICHE also played a role in expanding professional and undergraduate education in the subregion. Unfortunately, recent economic struggles have caused state retrenchments in public higher education budgets, which may be reversed as the national recovery gains more momentum and affects these southwestern states.

A number of critical policy and administrative issues confront high education in the Southwest, these are discussed with implications for all of the subregional chapters.

College Costs Are Going Up. The annual report, "Trends in College Pricing," released by the College Board in October 2003 states that the cost of education over the previous ten years increased more than 40 percent, and that tuition over that period jumped 47 percent. In the previous year alone, tuition increased 14.1 percent. An Associated Press article by Justin Pope written four years later reported even more bad news: the average tuition and fees at four-year public colleges rose 6.6 percent in 2006–2007. According to Pope's source, the nonprofit College Board's annual survey of costs revealed that in-state students at four-year institutions were paying tuition of $6,185, up $381 from the previous year, while undergraduates at private colleges paid an average tuition of $23,712. The net cost for a full-time student (including on-campus room and board) was $13,589 at a public four-year college and $32,307 at a private four-year college. George Washington University in Washington, DC, became the first major university with a published price of more than $50,000, including room and board.

State Support Is Going Down. This increase in the cost to the student and his/her family is attributed to declines in state funding, leading one observer (Gaston Caperton, president of the College Board) to comment in 2003: "In a troubled economy, colleges are faced with holding down prices without sacrificing education quality." Some educators attribute the disenchantment of state legislators to a dwindling lack of confidence in the direction our public universities are going. In many states, they are viewed as islands of liberalism in seas of conservatism. More negatively, the faculty sometimes views their campuses as oases of enlightenment in a desert of ignorance. State higher education budget declines from 2008 to 2013 greatly affected the vitality of the subregion's institutions of higher learning, especially in Arizona with a –36.6 percent drop, Nevada with a –23.8 percent decline, and New Mexico with a –21.3 percent change.

Lower division undergraduates balance the budget at some universities. Some of the disenchantment of legislators might be attributed to the allegation that in certain graduate research universities, graduate assistants are teaching the bulk of the lower division undergraduate classes. Usually, the rationale is that this practice frees up the older, more experienced full-time faculty for research and publishing. What seldom is mentioned is that utilizing graduate students to teach lower division courses has significant impacts on operating budgets. The graduate assistants are less expensive than full-time faculty.

Should every faculty member be a researcher? Reduced teaching loads for faculty deeply involved in research are both desirable and justifiable. However, studies have shown that a high percentage of the PhDs never publish anything after their dissertation. A lot of faculty getting release time for research are not researching. Further, one of the truly sad fallouts of the mania for research is the number of tenure-track teachers who never publish anything and never get tenure. Because of the panic to publish or perish, some outstanding student-centered, learned faculty bite the dust, often to the chagrin of students, colleagues, and department chairs.

Identity Crisis and Classifications. The emphasis on research has led to an identity crisis for many collegiate institutions. The Carnegie Foundation in 1996 came up with the classification of Doctoral/Research I universities, which was very satisfying to those universities receiving the classification. For some other institutions, however, chiefly those who were something other than Doctoral/Research I universities, it was a put-down; they looked upon themselves as second-class citizens in the academic pyramid. The Carnegie Foundation quickly learned it had made a huge mistake, and in 2000 changed its classifications to Doctoral/Research-Extensive and Doctoral/Research-Intensive. This meant that for those who wanted to be research universities, most of them could attempt to expand their institution's mission.

Colleges and Normal Schools—Gone with the Wind. As we move into the twenty-first century, very few institutions are satisfied with being "colleges." Many want to call themselves "universities," which they consider to be a more prestigious term. A university used to be generally defined as "a collection of colleges and an institution which offered doctoral degrees." But no more. Another term that has gone with the wind is "normal" school. Those used to be the colleges emphasizing the training of teachers and education administrators. Fifty years ago, for example, students who wanted to become professionals in the field of education often chose schools such as Colorado State Teachers College, which in the 1950s was reputed to be one of the three best schools for education in the country along with Stanford and

Teachers College of Columbia. But no more. Today, the venerable former normal school college in Colorado is the University of Northern Colorado.

State-Assisted Universities. A new term that perturbs legislators is "state-assisted," which is used to replace the old term of "state-supported." Really, it is just a new way of bookkeeping. In days gone by, many activities that allegedly were self-supporting and generated both revenue and expenditures (such as residence halls, food services, athletics, book stores, interest on endowed funds, grants and gifts, state and government contracts, university presses, and others) were classified as "auxiliary services." The "general operating budget" was usually used in reference to funds that were generated from tuition and fees plus legislative appropriations. Someone, somewhere, came up with a new way to crunch the numbers, one in which all of an institution's revenues and expenditures were lumped together. In this way, an institution could show that it generated more funds than the legislature appropriated; thus it could claim to be "state-assisted," rather than "state-supported." Legislators know that if any public institution adds up all of its revenue and expenditures, the legislative appropriation most likely will be less than 20 percent of the total. So, when these institutions refer to themselves as "state-assisted," legislators sometimes feel unappreciated.

Rankings. At least one national magazine has uncovered a bonanza by annually devoting an issue to selecting and ranking the nation's best colleges and universities. The readers and observers in the rural parts of the country, however, are really not surprised that the "rating game" seems to be heavily stacked in favor of the elite institutions in the East, the Midwest, and California, meaning the criteria give brownie points for the number of students turned away, or the emphasis on graduation and retention rates. Most penalized are those colleges and universities in urban areas with large numbers of minority students, or students working full-time or half time—namely, the lower-income, often disenfranchised, second-chance students who may not have taken all the courses in middle school or high school to prepare them for college. Sometime, some magazine is going to get around to ranking the "people's" colleges on how well they serve their communities, or all of the people of a state.

Governance. In some states, where each institution or system has its own governing board, it continues to be open season on the legislature. These public officials are hounded by more lobbyists than those representing the National Rifle Association or the tobacco industry as universities and colleges compete for the public dollars. From time to time, while one or more institutions seem to forge ahead, quite often this competition results in an overall watering down wherein all institutions are treated the same—badly. Some legislators are delighted to have good reasons to say no. Thus, changes in the governing structure have been of great interest in the past 50 years. In the Southwest, for example, both Utah and Nevada have put their intramural squabbles behind them and organized strong centralized governing boards with jurisdiction over all postsecondary education. Like Solomon, Arizona split the baby, creating a central board for its three universities, but leaving the community, technical, and junior colleges with boards of their own. Colorado and New Mexico have taken tiny steps in creating coordinating councils with limited power, leaving the institutions and systems with their own governing boards as well as direct access to the legislature and permitting the community and junior colleges to retain their individual governing boards. There is no doubt that administrative overhead is reduced and administering a state's universities and colleges and two-year institutions is more cost effective with a strong central board. However, the big universities, which usually are the power brokers in a state, have been known to fight to the death to retain their own boards.

Intercollegiate Athletics. Even the purists in academe have to admit that sometimes a great athletic program can attract favorable national attention for a university. Notre Dame's prowess and national reputation on the football field preceded its academic reputation. It is no accident that Stanford University, one of the truly elite national universities, also ranks number one in the support and scope of its intercollegiate athletic program. Arizona State University's rapid growth was not damaged by its outstanding football and baseball programs in its rise both academically and athletically.

Almost every year, some small college or university (such as Appalachian State) knocks off a major big-time university in a football or basketball game. Yet when graduation rates are published and university presidents are quoted, there is much hand-wringing and wailing about an overemphasis on college athletics, particularly football and basketball. The remedy is so simple it boggles the mind! Most of the problems could be resolved by going back to the rules when athletes had to complete one year of solid academic work before they were eligible for varsity competition. Today, a freshman sometimes participates in as many as three football games before ever darkening the door of a classroom.

Free Tuition. Some states already have started going back to a practice that at one time was the glory, as well as the intent, of state universities—free tuition for those prepared for the rigors of the college curriculum. Several southern states—Alabama, Florida, Georgia, and Louisiana—have great programs for entering freshmen. Louisiana, perhaps, has the best. Any high school graduate (public or private) who has completed the 13 required solid academic subjects with a 2.5 average (halfway between a C and a B), and an ACT score of 20 (one point below the national average), receives a tuition scholarship to any public or private university in the state (tuition for a private institution is equal to the higher tuition of a public institution), renewable through completion of a degree or five years, contingent upon the student's maintaining a B average. The scholarships are funded by the legislature and presented by legislators at high school commencements. New Mexico has a program for outstanding scholars, funded through proceeds from its state lottery.

Faculty Salaries. Studies repeatedly have shown that where there is great education, there are great teachers. Lock-step salary schedules have been the bane of public schools, and, too often, for universities. One way to recognize and reward great teaching is through endowed chairs and professorships with the interest on endowments utilized as salary supplements. Matching funds from the state legislature often provide attractive lures for support from the private sector for endowed chairs and professorships. The Louisiana Legislature, for example, provides a 40–60 match—$40,000 for an endowed professorship against a $60,000 donation; $400,000 for an endowed chair to match a $600,000 gift. (Starting from scratch, Louisiana State University raised 477 endowed professorships in three years.) In a very short time, this can have a tremendous impact on retaining valued professors, as well as recruiting nationally for new professors.

Minorities. Educators and politicians often pay a lot of lip service to increasing the number of minorities in the student bodies and faculties of our institutions. Too often, however, they do nothing tangible to make a difference. In an effort specifically to increase the number of African American PhD recipients prepared to teach on the collegiate level, the Louisiana legislature appropriated $600,000 per year for doctoral fellowships for African American graduate students ($17,000 each) at Louisiana State University (LSU). The university utilized these funds to hire Isaiah Warner away from the National Science Foundation to accept an endowed chair and head up the Chemistry Department. By 1999, there were 32 African American doctoral candidates in chemistry at LSU, numbering more than the rest of the nation put together. *Newsweek* magazine in 2003 cited LSU for its diversity and specifically mentioned the chemistry program. If universities and colleges elsewhere are to make a breakthrough in the education of minorities, their states have to invest, and invest wisely, and find ways to recognize and support these students as models and future teachers. In this regard, Native American nations are pursuing the expansion of associate and undergraduate education in their tribal colleges.

Teaching Academies. There is an old tradition that when Europeans meet a distinguished teacher or professor on the street, they tip their hats. In the United States, they would tap their foreheads. Of all the professions in the United States that require a college education, the lowest on the economic totem pole is teaching. The really smart young people prepare for careers as doctors, lawyers, or merchant chiefs—not to mention industrial, media tycoons, or rocket scientists, football, or basketball coaches. "Show me the money" may not be the credo of today's youth, but it would be foolish to ignore its impact on career decisions for those unwilling to take the vows of semipoverty that sometimes accompany the choice of teaching as a profession.

Scholars, would-be teachers, and those concerned with upgrading our schools and colleges might take a page from the Chinese in Taiwan. Seeking to attract their best and brightest young people into teaching, the government provides board, room, tuition, and fees to college students, preparing them to take up teaching as a career. In exchange, upon completion of their training, the government reserves the right to assign them to specific schools for the first four years of their professional careers.

Sounds familiar? It seems to be similar to quid pro quo offered to graduates of our three military academies—the Air Force Academy, Annapolis, and West Point. For four years of the finest education for careers as leaders in our nation's armed forces, the federal government pays all the expenses, including board, room, tuition, fees, books, uniforms, equipment, top-of-the-line classrooms, drill fields, playing fields, and laboratories, and salaries for faculty, staff, and cadets. The package even includes travel expenses to and from home and the academies.

Applicants are carefully screened, examined, and interviewed, and each must be recommended by a member of the US Senate or Congress from his/her home state. The program spares no expense to recruit and educate the best and brightest of the potential leaders for our national defense. Should we accept less for those who educate our children? Can we not do the same for our best and brightest potential teachers?

Why not establish federal "Teaching Academies" that are designed to attract and select and educate our future teachers and professors? Certainly, we could screen, examine, and interview potential candidates. Further, we could require that they be nominated by members of Congress. Fully committed, we could do as much for our leaders in education as we do for our leaders in national defense. For example, what would prevent our federal government from utilizing existing campuses and programs as teacher training centers much as we have done for our land-grant institutions since 1862? Is teacher preparation less important than agriculture and engineering?

At one time our states did identify and partially subsidize what once were called "normal schools" and later "teachers colleges." These modest institutions specialized in preparing teachers and administrators for our public schools. However, following the money trail, few of these exist today in their original, pure form. They have become diversified, shadow imitations of the elite research universities that emphasize high technology and industrial development and prepare students for law and medicine and business and high technology and a whole lot of other things. Many of these "national research" institutions, however, have severed their relationships with public education and teacher training—opting for the more fiscally lucrative positions in the sciences and selected professional fields. If our nation is serious about excellence in all levels of education, it might see fit to devise teaching academies and provide the ways and means to attract our best and brightest into the education field. Then, in the United States as in Europe, when a truly great educator and teacher goes to his/her "other world" rewards, perhaps on the tombstone might be inscribed: "Master Teacher or Professor." And when meeting live teachers or professors on the street, people would tip their hats rather than tap their foreheads.

Higher education in the Southwest has developed in a unique cultural and historically diverse subregion in the West. Arizona, Colorado, Nevada, New Mexico, and Utah have provided various types of higher education institutions to meet the growing needs of their religious communities, citizens, and new tribal nations. The continued growth and vitality of higher education there will depend on its central role in the cultural, economic, and scientific development of these states. The subregion's future holds the promises of extraordinary opportunities and the challenges of demanding difficulties—only its political, higher education, and campus leaders as well as faculties, students, and local constituencies will find the way to further its development.

REFERENCES

Abbott, F. C. *A History of the Western Interstate Commission for Higher Education: The First Forty Years.* Boulder, CO: Western Interstate Commission for Higher Education, 2004.

"Becoming a Research Center, 1973–1990." Retrieved from www.lib.utah.edu/150/07/index.html, on October 14, 2007.

Beecher, H. W., quoted in Robert E. Spiller (et al., eds.), *Literary History of the United States,* 3rd ed. London and Toronto: Macmillan, 1963.

"Brigham Young University." Retrieved from www.en.wikepidia.org/wiki/BrighamYoungUniversity, on September 19, 2003.

Colorado Commission on Higher Education. Retrieved from www.weab.edu/blade/cfac/cche-masterplan.html, on September 4, 2007.

Davis, W. E. *Glory Colorado II.* Boulder: University of Colorado Press, 2007a.

———. *Miracle on the Mesa.* Albuquerque: University of New Mexico Press, 2007b.

Editors of the *Chronicle of Higher Education.* Almanac Issues from 2003–2004 through 2007–2008, *Chronicle of Higher Education*, published annually in August.

Editors of *Newsweek.* "25 Hottest Schools." *Newsweek,* August 10, 2007: 53.

Editors of *US News & World Report.* "America's Best Colleges, 2008 Edition." *US News & World Report,* 2008.

"Federal Government Land Holdings in the West." *Parade,* August 1, 2007.

"Higher Education in Utah—Highlights/Milestones." Utah State Board of Regents, October 2003.

Hillerman, T., and D. Meunch. *New Mexico.* Portland, OR: Portland Graphic Arts Center, 1974.

"Hispanic Mag Ranks UNM High." *Albuquerque Journal,* September, 6, 2007, p. Cl.

Hulse, J. W. *Reinventing the System, Higher Education in Nevada, 1968–2000.* Reno and Las Vegas: University of Nevada Press, 2002.

Kerr, C., and M. L. Gade. *The Guardians.* Washington, DC: Association of Governing Boards of Schools and Colleges, 1989.

Lawrence, D. H. "New Mexico." In E. D. McDonald (ed.), *Phoenix: The Posthumous Papers of D. H. Lawrence,* New York: Viking Press, 1936, p. 142.

Lightcap, B. The Morrill Act of 1862. Retrieved from www.nd.edu/~rbarger/www7/morrill.html, on October 14, 2007.

Maricopa County, Arizona. Retrieved from www.en.wikipedia.org./Maricopa County, Arizona, on October 23, 2007.

Maricopa County Community College District. Retrieved from www.en.wikipedia.org/wiki/Maricopa_County_Community_College-District, on October 23, 2007.

McGiffert, M. *The Higher Learning in Colorado: An Historical Study, 1860–1940.* Denver, CO: Sage Books, 1964.

McKay, D. O. Retrieved from www.en.wikipedia.org/wiki/David O. McKay, 2003, on September 19, 2003.

Sander, L. "University of Colorado Settles Lawsuit over Alleged Gang Rapes." *Chronicle of Higher Education*, December 14, 2007, p. A20.

Simmons, M. *Albuquerque: A Narrative History.* Albuquerque: University of New Mexico Press, 1982.

"UA History." Retrieved from www.arizona.edu./home/history.html, on September 19, 2003.

United States Air Force Academy. Retrieved from www.en.wikipedia.org /wikiUnitedStatesAirForceAcademy, on August 23, 2007.

University of Nevada, Reno. "History, Stats, & Highlights." Retrieved from www. unr.edu/content/history.html, on September 19, 2003.

University of Phoenix. Retrieved from www.uofphyx.info/cobrand.jsp:sessioid, on October 14, 2007.

"UNM, CNM Sign Deal on Facility." *Albuquerque Journal*, August 17, 2007: A10.

Wickenden, Thomas (Associate Executive Director, Arizona Board of Regents). Letter to William E. Davis, September 3, 2003, pp. 1–2, personal communication.

Zumeta, W. "Higher Education Funding: On the Way Up, But for How Long?" In H. S. Wechsler (ed.), *The NEA 2008 Almanac of Higher Education*, 2008, pp. 85–100.

———. "The New Finance of Public Higher Education." In H. S. Wechsler (ed.), *The NEA 2006 Almanac of Higher Education*, 2006, pp. 37–48.

6

Higher Education in the Pacific West: Developments in Washington, Oregon, Hawaii, and Alaska

*William E. ("Bud") Davis, Lester F. Goodchild, and David A. Tandberg**

Introduction

The states of the Pacific West provide four distinctive narratives on American higher education. The two northwestern continental states of Washington and Oregon, the mid-Pacific Hawaii islands, and the massive subarctic Alaska offer some subregional similarities, as their state cultures and postsecondary missions came into high alignment during their histories. Initially, they all had strong seaport commerce. Washington and Oregon quickly became major logging centers; gradually more manufacturing expanded in Washington, while federal and military developments predominated in Alaska and Hawaii. Each had significant claims to tourism and as travel destinations. The aftermath and effects of World War II brought a greater strategic regionalism, as their defense concerns linked them more because of their relative nearness to the Soviet Union. Following the war, certain state higher education system emphases developed with a focus on public research universities in Oregon and Washington, applied research and professional education in Hawaii's public higher education, as well as extensive community college developments in both Washington and Oregon.

At the University of Washington beginning in 1958, President Charles E. Odegaard, who took over the campus academic leadership, represented the best of northwestern presidential aspirations, management, and leadership for the region. His tenure until 1973 saw public higher education's extensive university expansion. Seeking excellence in all that he did, he proclaimed the mission charge for higher education in the region: "Western states must do their part in accepting and building the best" (Sanders, 1987, p. 7). Since World War II, these states have expanded public, private, and for-profit

Table 6.1 Number of institutions by type by state, 2010

	Alaska		Hawaii		Oregon		Washington	
	4-year	2-year	4-year	2-year	4-year	2-year	4-year	2-year
Public	3	2	4	6	9	17	16	27
Private nonprofit	1	0	5	0	24	0	19	0
Private for-profit	1	0	4	1	5	5	12	7
Totals	**5**	**2**	**13**	**7**	**38**	**22**	**47**	**34**
State Totals	**7**		**20**		**60**		**81**	
Public 4-year and 2-year total (%)	84	50						
Private 4-year total (%)	49	29						
For-profit total (%)	35	21						
Subregional Grand Total	**168**							

Source: US Department of Education for AY2009–2010 postsecondary enrollments, "Colleges and Universities" (http://nces.ed.gov) as cited by Editors, "Almanac of Higher Education, 2011–12," *Chronicle of Higher Education*, 2011, *58* (1), August 26.

higher education to serve their numerous clienteles. Public universities, colleges, and community colleges in the four states comprise 84 institutions or 50 percent of higher education in the subregion, while 49 private institutions of higher learning, some 29 percent, augment postsecondary education. Alternatively, 35 four- and two-year for-profit institutions, at 21 percent, offer other career, technical, and vocation studies to support the economic development in these states. Washington and Oregon reflect higher education powerhouses similar to other larger states in the subregion and country with 25 public universities and colleges combined with such major research universities as the University of Washington and the University of Oregon and significant land-grant institutions as Washington State University and Oregon State University. The strength of these state systems may also be seen in the high number of community colleges in each state with 27 and 17, respectively. Overall, 168 institutions of higher learning provide the continental and pacific arenas with extensive postsecondary opportunities (see table 6.1).

History of Higher Education in the Pacific West States

In this chapter the subsequent narratives of the individual four states (Washington, Oregon, Hawaii, and then Alaska) are divided into three major sections, each noting: (1) the development of state universities as a predominant focus, (2) the creation of state higher education governance systems, and (3) the recent conditions within the state's system of higher learning. Finally, there is discussion of how contemporary problems of persistent and dramatic state budget cuts, demographic changes, as well as evolving institutional missions are reshaping the intended role of public higher education in these states.

WASHINGTON

Initially, higher education began in Washington with the founding of the Christian interdenominational Whitman College in Walla Walla in 1859. Washington now has a diverse system of higher education, with 81 institutions of higher learning in the state. These include 16 public four-year colleges and universities, including 2 public research universities, 27 public community and technical colleges, 19 private not-for-profit four-year institutions, and 19 for-profit institutions (*Chronicle of Higher Education*, 2011). About 86 percent of students enrolled in degree-granting institutions in fall 2010 were attending a public rather than a private not-for-profit (12 percent) or private for-profit (2 percent) institution. The public universities and colleges enrolled 197,654 students in fall 2010, while 266,327 attended community colleges. Thirty-six private and for-profit institutions enabled 43,000 other students to access postsecondary studies (National Center for Education Statistics, 2011).

A notable aspect of higher education in Washington is its capacity to draw upon federal research and development (R&D) funding. Federal R&D funding at all institutions was approximately $727 million in 2009. This is almost entirely due to the University of Washington's (UW) continued success in this area. As figure 6.1 shows, UW's annual federal R&D expenditures ($619 million in 2009) far exceed the national average for universities receiving this type of funding. In fact, since 1993 or the past 17 years, UW has been ranked in the top three universities nationally for federal R&D expenditures (National Science Foundation, 2010).

As the data on federal R&D expenditure reveal, of the four major institutions of higher learning in the state, the University of Washington is the primary research university there and in the subregion, leading most other public postsecondary institutions with extensive undergraduate, graduate, and professional education. In the 1950s and 1960s, a major campus expansion began to accommodate the rising student demographics. Its new emphasis focused on research with an increasingly research-oriented faculty. President Odegaard's 1959 inaugural address set the university standard for the region: to make Washington "a great university . . . a leader among institutions, not a follower, a pioneer among pioneers as great universities must by definition ever strive to be" (Gates, 1961, p. 226). Its seal proclaimed in Latin: "*Lux sit*"—let there be light. The university built two additional branch campuses at Tacoma and Bothell to accommodate undergraduate students in 1990. Alternatively, Washington State University, as a land-

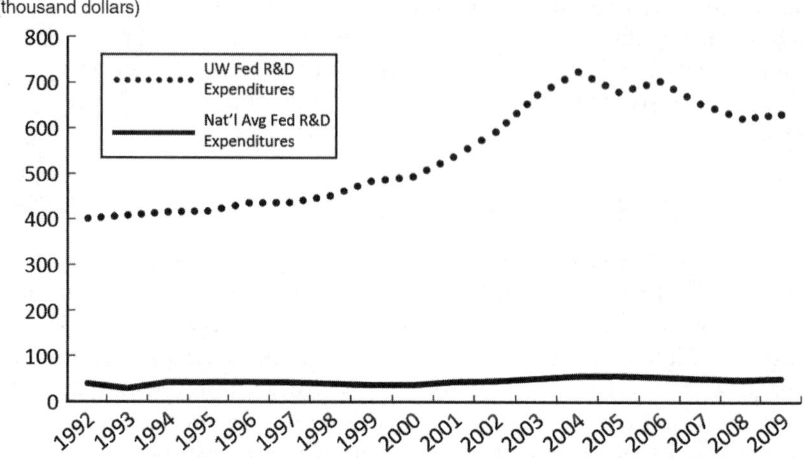

Figure 6.1 Real federal research and development expenditures.
Source: National Science Foundation. Calculations: Authors.

grant institution, focused on applied research through the professions. The state's largest private universities, Seattle University and Gonzaga University, are both Catholic and Jesuit. In 1969, the state formed the Council on Postsecondary Education to coordinate activities among the public institutions and certain activities with private colleges and universities. In 1973, the Northwest Indian College in Bellingham became one of the WICHE region's 23 tribal land-grant colleges, offering baccalaureate and associate degrees (www.nwic.edu). The largest public university profiles follow with commentary on the other major groups.

University of Washington Developments

Founded in 1861 as the Territorial University of Washington, the school with its single professor represented all the high boosterish hopes of its Seattle citizens, for the area had not even attained statehood. In 1917 the university's mission was clarified in relation to Washington State University. The legislature assigned *common* and *exclusive* major lines to these two institutions and established the pattern that would substantially define the programmatic structure of the public sector. This historic statute (RCW 28B.10.115) applied to fields in which both universities had "common major lines" and restrained other public institutions:

> The courses of instruction of both the University of Washington and Washington State University shall embrace as major lines, pharmacy, architecture, and forest management as distinguished from forest products and logging engineering which are exclusive to the University of Washington. These major lines shall be offered and taught at said institutions only.

A related statute (RCW 28B.20.060) assigned certain studies as "exclusive major lines" to the University of Washington: "law, medicine, forest products, logging engineering, library sciences, and fisheries." Major new roles awaited the institution.

With World War II, a new university era dawned with federal and state developments. First, the federal government's initial major funding created the Applied Physics Laboratory in 1943 to assist the Navy in antisubmarine warfare during the war. State leaders also were determined in 1945 to make the university the leader of professional medical and dental education in the region, when they authorized $4.2 million for buildings and operational expenses for a new combined School of Health Sciences (University of Washington, *Timeline*). In 1945, the university had 10,000 students and an $8 million budget. The G.I. Bill and returning veterans then expanded enrollments during the next four years. The campus grew to 16,500 students with a $29 million budget (Gates, 1961, p. 194).

Unfortunately, similar to other universities in the country, the 1950s saw government attacks on questionable faculty allegiances to and affiliation with the Communist Party. Already in 1931, the Washington legislature had developed a loyalty oath for teachers. In 1947 and 1948, it investigated "un-American activities" at Washington State University and the University of Washington, respectively. Washington's Canwell Committee found 150 Communist faculty members on campus. University regents and President Raymond B. Allen brought charges against six tenured faculty. After an investigation, three were dismissed in the "first important academic freedom case of the Cold War." In 1964, the US Supreme Court in *Baggett v. Bullitt* rejected the legitimacy of this state oath; none of the faculty members was ever given restitution (Gates, 1961, pp. 196–211; Sanders, 1979, 153–177; Schrecker, 1986, pp. 94–106, 320–324).

Nevertheless, the university became a member of the prestigious Association of American Universities in 1950. It signaled a dramatic transformation in its stature as national research policy directed its efforts. Because of the Soviet threat to the United States, the National Defense Education Act of 1958 and continual federal science funding brought extensive resources to the campus for doctoral students, residence halls, and research. During the 1950s, some 1,500 researchers were involved in more than 826 major funded research projects, and $21 million in new construction and renovations remade the campus for science, art, classrooms, libraries, administration, and student union buildings. Some $9.5 million was spent on expanding medical and dental education. These developments "reflected the recognition that in America generally that the research function was vital to the welfare, perhaps even the survival, of the nation" (Gates, 1961, pp. 213–219).

The next two decades greatly advanced these strides. The university now offered doctoral, masters, and baccalaureate degrees in all areas, except agriculture. By 1960 the "baby boom" generation of students further swelled the campus to 18,000 students, which almost doubled by

1973 to 34,000. The university's budget ballooned from $100 million to more than $400 million in response. Continued expansion of medical education with the construction of a 300-bed teaching hospital cost the state some $30 million in 1960. The National Institutes of Health assigned the University Hospital as one of its 12 Clinical Research Centers in that year (Sanders, 1987, p. 32). The expansion of the campus came from the extraordinary support of the state's two US senators, Henry M. Jackson and Warren G. Magnuson. Their tireless efforts at promoting the university led to its considerable federal gains (Gates, 1961, pp. 127, 212, 221; Sanders, 1987). Nevertheless, similar to other campuses in the country, student anti-Vietnam protests and the burning of its ROTC center highlighted an 18-month period of protests. By 1969, the university became one of the top five research universities in the country according to federal funding awarded. Overall, it was in the top 15 research universities in the United States with 2,000 faculty and 32,000 students by this time. The institution was also authorized to be one of the four Sea Grant Colleges in the country in 1971 (Sanders, 1987, pp. 4, 10, 18–20, 26). Finally, in 1972, the "Western Interstate Plan" for medical education among Washington, Alaska, Montana, and Idaho (WAMI) began. Under this new four-state medical education plan, students started their studies in their home states, completed medical education at the University of Washington, and then did clinical rotations in home state hospitals (Abbott, 2004, pp. 100–107).

Nevertheless, other developments in the latter part of the twentieth century brought significant diminutions to this "Golden Era." Retrenchment and recessions characterized the 1970s. State economic distress continued and signaled that higher education would be in for tough times. Critically, the share of the budget appropriated to higher education continued to decline. The legislature used $40 million of the university's revenues and $18 million from its land-trust funds to support the state's general fund in 1977 and 1979, respectively. The fiscal challenges continued, as the economy deteriorated more in the early 1980s. Reflecting the extreme difficulties of this era, the governor declared a state of emergency and asked the university for a 10.1 percent cut in 1981. Subsequently, the university declared a state of financial exigency with 30 academic programs, and tenured faculty were targeted for discontinuation. Ultimately, eight programs were dropped, eliminating mostly staff and nontenured faculty. Ten other programs suffered significant reductions (Sanders, 1987, pp. 38–42). Despite this, the university administration found funds to support other programs that demonstrated the continuing and important role that the university played in the region from launching its Pacific Rim Project by the School of Business Administration, to the Center for International Trade in Forest Products, or to the Law School's Institute for Marine Studies in Law (pp. 48–49).

The university is actually made up of three separate campuses. While nearly 90 percent of its students are enrolled at the main Seattle campus, the university's Bothell and Tacoma campuses retain fairly unique identities and together enroll nearly 8,000 students. Relatively young, the University of Washington Bothell and University of Washington Tacoma were both founded in 1990. Nestled in the Puget Sound area, UW Bothell shares a campus with Cascadia Community College. Bothell advertises itself as having "all the resources of the University of Washington but with the advantages of a small, progressive campus." There the faculty work toward having a "unique, interdisciplinary and entrepreneurial culture" (University of Washington Bothell, 2009). In 2008, UW Bothell implemented the "21st Century Campus Initiative" in an effort to become "a dynamic center for discovery and learning," calling for enhanced emphasis on the development of a diverse and inclusive learning environment that utilizes innovative teaching methods and addresses the challenges of the twenty-first century. On the other hand, UW Tacoma is nestled in Tacoma's historic Warehouse District in century-old brick buildings that have received architectural awards for their transformation into modern classrooms (University of Washington Tacoma, 2010). UW Tacoma's Chancellor Debra Friedman has called for looking for ways to diversify their financial portfolio without losing their public mission and retaining the attitude of "changing the world by changing one student at a time" (Friedman, 2011).

In 2000, Washington's leadership proclaimed its new strategic theme as "Discovery is at the heart of our university," for it had "received $1.02 billion in grants and contracts, 78 percent of which came from the federal government. The university receive[d] more federal research funding than any other public university in the country, and the second most federal research funding of all universities in the country" (University of Washington, *Vision and Values,* 2011; University of Washington, 2009). In addition, the university has maintained large enrollments throughout the fiscal downturn with 57,218 students enrolled in 2010, some 15,392 being graduate students. Its faculty now represented some of the most talented in the nation, with six having received Nobel Prizes, and ten others having won "genius grants" from the MacArthur Foundation. As noted in a 2009 Planning and Budgeting Brief, "the University has 86 faculty members who are members of the American Academy of Arts and Sciences, the Institute of Medicine, the National Academy of Sciences, or the National Academy of Engineering. This is the 4th highest total of academy members among public universities, and the 12th highest total of academy members among all universities in the nation." By 2007, Washington had achieved a $2 billion endowment—the highest within the state (*Chronicle of Higher Education, Almanac, 2008–2009,* p. 73). The University of Washington became one of the major public research universities in the region alongside the University of California Berkeley and the University of California Los Angeles, as well as ranked in the top 100 in the world (see Cohen, this volume, p. 63).

Washington State University (WSU) Developments

The citizens of Pullman convinced both the Oregon-Washington Railroad company and the Spokane and Palouse Railroad company to bring their lines through the town in 1885 and 1887, respectively, and then created the state's first agricultural college three years later on 160 acres. The State Agricultural College and School of Science was founded with a legislative bill in the spring of 1890 (Neill, 1977/1889, pp. 5–9), offering major programs in agriculture and mining. By 1893, the Department of Agriculture began, and ten years later a Department of Domestic Economy was launched for women. Importantly, veterinary science opened in 1895, while the School of Forestry started in 1906. Many other academic and professional programs were also offered at this key southeastern state institution. In 1917, President Ernest O. Holland reorganized university academic study into five colleges (sciences and art, agriculture, mechanical arts and engineering, veterinary, and home economics) with four schools (mines, education, pharmacy, as well as music and applied design). These changes resulted from the legislature's statutory assignment (RCW 28B.30.060) of "exclusive major lines" in "agriculture in all its branches and subdivisions, veterinary medicine, and economic science in its application to agriculture and rural life." Finally, the Graduate School was begun in 1922, and the doctorate awarded (Von Bargen, 2008; CAHNRS, *College History*).

By 1940, the campus had reached its highest enrollment in 20 years at approximately 5,100. It reflected an expanding campus with a new school of business administration, veterinary medicine classrooms and laboratory building, as well as the engineering laboratory building. With the end of World War II and the authorization of the G.I. Bill, returning vets swelled the campus by 2,800 students to reach a high of 7,900 in the fall of 1948. During the 1950s and 1960s, the campus added several important laboratories, one centered on the creation of a nuclear reactor and the other on radiocarbon dating. WSU subsequently established extension offices in each of the state's 39 counties, and research centers in all the areas of the state, including satellite campuses in Spokane, the Tri-Cities, and Vancouver (Washington State University, *History*).

In the 1970s and early 1980s, President Glenn Terrell's administration expanded applied arts and sciences on the campus. The Veterinary College became the major professional provider in the region with its tristate WOI (Washington, Oregon, and Idaho) veterinary medicine program and student exchange program. Facilitated by the Western Interstate Commission for Higher Education (WICHE), the Washington State University plan involved collaborations between Idaho State University and Oregon State University, where students completed initial professional studies in their own states and finished their clinical work at the universities in Idaho or in Washington. Along with the development at Colorado State University under a similar arrangement, the two programs doubled "the number of places available for students from Western states that had no veterinary programs of their own" (Abbott, 2004, pp. 190–192).

As the university approached its centennial in the late 1980s, major changes occurred on campus as the new presidency of Samuel H. Smith, former dean of the College of Agriculture, achieved its new role as a top research university. The Washington State Council on Postsecondary Education granted the institution the right to award doctoral degrees in engineering and agriculture and to launch a branch campus in Spokane and expand their Vancouver, Pullman, and Tri-Cities (in the city of Richland, WA) branch campuses (Washington State University, *History*).

The 1990s gave the university new state and national stature with major expansions in selected areas. Its telecommunications operations for distance education were expanded by the legislature, leading to its recognition as the most wired campus in the nation by the end of the decade. The regents approved $75 million for a series of new buildings to expand its pure and applied research efforts. Offering more educational opportunities along the state's southern border, the university expanded its branch campuses at Richmond, as well as at Vancouver. In the 2009–2010 academic year, the university enrolled approximately 25,000 students within its undergraduate programs and 5,000 students within its graduate programs. It was rated in the top 60 research universities in the country with $213 million in research, a $1.7 billion operational budget, and a $683 million endowment (Washington State University, *Quick Facts*; Washington State University, *History*).

Other Public Universities and Colleges

Three other public universities augment Washington higher education: Eastern Washington University, Central Washington University, and Western Washington University. Each served a different area in the state, beginning as normal schools with a focus on teacher training. By 1937 the institutions were redesignated as colleges of education, which they remained through World War II. Faced with unprecedented enrollment pressure from returning veterans under the G.I. Bill and in response to the Strayer Commission's statewide review of both K-12 and higher education, they became state colleges and granted various master's degrees (MA, MS, and MEd). For example, Western Washington University began as Northwest Normal School in 1886 as a teachers' school for women. It later began admitting men and changed its name to Western Washington College of Education in 1937. After World War II, the growth of enrollments required the university's mission to broaden and become a regional university. This followed the trend of many former normal schools, which adopted university stature across the country. This shift had fully occurred when the institution was renamed Western Washington State College in

1961 and later to Western Washington University in 1977. One of the developing goals of this institution centered on being a research university, yet maintaining a strong liberal arts college. Current President Bruce Shepard writes of the university's mission as enabling students to develop a "purposed life," in which striving to achieve individual goals centers one's activities. Reflecting the goals of a liberal arts university, its current motto proclaims: "active minds, changing lives" (Whatcom County Historical Society, 2011; www.wwu.edu/about/president; http://library.wwu.edu/specialcollections/sc_chronology).

To offset the enrollment expansion of UW campuses in the 1960s, the state also opened Evergreen State College in 1971 in Olympia. The same law that established the college also specified that the campus must be no smaller than 600 acres (Sanders, 1987, p. 8). The first president of Evergreen State College was Charles J. McCann, and much of Evergreen's unique administrative and curricular structures are directly attributable to his vision and leadership. Evergreen State College, which became an accredited institution in 1974, developed into an impressive institution, one that usually shows up on national lists of top public institutions in the country. This public nontraditional, experimental institution offers an interdisciplinary baccalaureate and master's curricula and narrative faculty grading (no grades). Evergreen aims to provide distinctively rigorous academics and an engaged campus community. Its curriculum focuses on solving practical problems with themes and experiences in the real world (Evergreen State College, 2010). Evergreen has its own organic farm, a nature preserve, and several outreach and public service centers serving a variety of missions. Evergreen currently has 4,500 undergraduate students and 340 graduate students enrolled at one of four campuses. In keeping with its mission, the college also enrolls a large number of low-income students (43%), first-generation students (29%), and students of color (20%) (Evergreen, 2010).

Community and Technical College Development

Early on, the state developed junior and community colleges to assist with transfer education and early vocational education. Many of what we now call two-year community colleges emerged from formerly autonomous junior colleges. Washington's first junior college was started in 1915 in Everett when 42 students began a one-year college program on the top floor of Everett High School. However, the college was closed in 1923 for lack of students. Ten years later, Centralia College, the state's oldest existing community college, was opened in 1925. Centralia was shortly followed by Skagit Valley College in 1926, Yakima Valley College in 1928, and Grays Harbor College in 1930. By 1941, eight junior colleges were operating in Washington, all locally administered and locally funded, with a combined enrollment of approximately 1,000. State support was provided for the first time in 1941; at the same time, however, the legislature also restricted the number and location of junior colleges, prohibiting their establishment in counties having either a public or a private four-year institution. In total, nine community colleges were established from 1925 to 1960. In 1941 a community college was again established in Everett. With an original enrollment of 128 students, the college started in a converted elementary school, and now has become a campus of 20,000 students at seven locations in the county and online. One of the unique elements of the institution is an early college academy for high school students called the Ocean Research College Academy (Everett Community College, 2010).

In 1961 the restrictions against expansion of community colleges were removed and junior colleges were designated as "community" colleges. The financing of community colleges was separated from local school districts in 1963. A separate, independent community college system was established in 1965. During the next two decades, the state founded another 18 community colleges to provide expanded contract, community, and developmental education. By 2006, 7 more were added, so that now 34 public institutions offer associate degrees around the state (Chance, Anet, and Pailthorp, 1976, p. 123; *Chronicle of Higher Education, Almanac, 2008–2009*, p. 73). Community colleges account for a considerably larger share of public enrollments in Washington than the national average (64 percent vs. 49 percent) (Delta Cost Project, 2010).

Recently, community colleges in Washington have been allowed to award a limited number of applied baccalaureate degree programs. After a five-year pilot program, the legislature granted this authority to the community colleges in 2010. Applied baccalaureate degrees are now being offered by 7 of the state's 34 community and technical colleges in such technical fields as interior design, behavioral science, applied management, hospitality management, radiation and imaging sciences, nursing, and applied design. Nevertheless, the demand for these programs so far has been modest with 57 degrees awarded in 2009 and 100 in 2010 (Washington State Board for Community and Technical Colleges, 2011).

Unlike many states, Washington's community and technical colleges have their own board and do not receive any local property tax support, since their public funding comes entirely from the state. The State Board for Community and Technical Colleges (SBCTC) governs the state's 34 community and technical colleges. In the 1991 Washington's Community and Technical College Act, the legislature shifted responsibility for technical colleges and adult basic education from the K-12 system to the SBCTC. It has been reported that both state and institutional leaders have noted the benefits of the structural change, arguing that it creates efficiencies as it consolidates all of postsecondary workforce education under the same structure; that it has brought increased attention and resources to adult basic education, and allowed them to more effectively advance statewide initiatives (Perna, Finney, and Callan, 2012). In addition, the act requires that the colleges "offer an open door to every citizen, regardless of his or her academic background or experiences, at a cost normally within his or her economic means" (RCW 28B.50.020(1)).

Private Higher Education

Within the state, there are 19 private not-for-profit four-year colleges and universities. The four largest institutions have enrollments ranging from approximately 4,400 to 9,000 mostly undergraduate students. Founded by the Roman Catholic Church's Society of Jesus, a religious community of priests and brothers, founded both Gonzaga University in 1887 in Spokane and Seattle University in 1892. They enrolled 8,735 students and 8,836, respectively, in the 2009–2010 academic year. In 1891, the Methodist Church established Seattle Pacific University, which had 4,448 students in the 2009–2010 academic year. The Lutheran Church opened Pacific Lutheran University in Tacoma in 1891 and had 4,413 students on its campus in 2009–2010. As a state, Washington puts high value on private higher education, and several of their institutions have been ranked highly in a variety of national and regional rankings. The 19 private not-for-profit institutions of higher learning typically enroll around 9 percent of the matriculated students in the state (including for-profit institutions). From a state perspective, private higher education thus "provide[d] particularly significant educational opportunities in the areas of the state in which access to public senior institutions is limited" (Chance, Anet, and Pailthorp, 1976, p. 142). In coordinating higher education across all institutions in the state, the current Washington Higher Education Coordinating Board has an advisory council where the private institutions have a representative to aid coordination across sectors. Nineteen for-profit institutions (12 four-year colleges and 7 two-year colleges) are also active in Washington serving close to 9,000 students.

Coordinating Higher Education in the State

The 1960s witnessed important state and campus activity, much of it driven by a concern over unprecedented population growth and resultant projected enrollment pressure. Under the leadership of Washington's President Odegaard, the Council of Presidents of the State Colleges and Universities collaborated on what probably was the first attempt at a strategic plan. In 1964, their report titled "A Plan for Public Higher Education in Washington" was released. Based on an assumption that the "open door" philosophy of opportunity should be maintained, the presidents stated that this should be through the provision of suitable opportunities among a number of institutions that would vary individually in types and levels of postsecondary education. The state colleges emphasized lower-division levels and upper-division and master's level (50/50 ratio), while the two research universities focused on upper-division, master's, and doctoral levels (40/60 ratio) (Chance, Anet, and Pailthorp, 1976, p. 127).

This plan segued into a more comprehensive examination the following year when the Temporary Advisory Committee on Public Higher Education (TACPHE) was established by the legislature to conduct a review and develop recommendations for a new public higher education institution—a state college—in southwestern Washington. The membership was composed of executive, legislative, and higher education representatives from both the public and private sectors. Most of its recommendations were accepted and among them was the establishment of a new four-year institution, Evergreen State College, as a result of a national clamor for reform and innovation in higher education.

Another important recommendation called for the establishment of a state-funded (no local levies) community college system under a State Board for Community College Education. The new system assumed responsibility for the junior college and vocational-technical institutes, most of which were operated by local school districts as part of the K-12 system. In this manner, a system initially composed of 27 comprehensive community colleges sprung forth virtually fully formed. Initially, six districts elected to retain their vocational-technical institutes, but were later reduced to five (Bellingham, Lake Washington, Renton, Clover Park, and Tacoma). All five were redesignated as technical colleges and brought into the now rebranded community and technical college system.

Among other TACPHE recommendations, a state need grant program was created, the first in Washington. This program was modestly funded at about half a million dollars in its beginning. By the 2007–2009 biennium, it had increased to $377 million in grants to about 71,000 students a year. It also recommended a state-level board to be responsible for coordinating and planning for the system. The Council on Higher Education (CHE) was created in 1969, becoming operational in 1970. The initial board was composed of citizen members, elected officials (including the governor) and other policymakers, institution presidents, and the head of the State Board for Community College Education.

The Federal Higher Education Amendments of 1972, particularly Section 1202 that spoke of single statewide planning agencies, caused the legislature to redesignate the CHE as the Council on Postsecondary Education (CPE) in 1975 and change the composition of the membership. However, over the next few years, the CPE structure proved to be increasingly unwieldy, as all members had an authoritative vote on federal matters. This more or less came to a head when all members would be allowed to vote on the selection of the agency director (a vote that previously had been limited to the citizen members). In 1982, the legislature decided to take another look at education, which would include both K-12 and higher education. A blue ribbon citizen-legislative task force was empanelled for the task, which later became known for the Senate Bill that created it (SB 3609) as the "3609

Committee." Charles Odegaard, now emeritus president of the University of Washington, was a member and was asked to chair the committee's higher education subcommittee, which among other things would address the matter of governance. The committee concluded that the structure of the CPE had indeed become unwieldy and recommended its reconstitution into a Higher Education Coordinating Board (HECB) that would have clearer lines of authority for exercising its assignment. This proposal was enacted during the 1985 legislative session. Much of the board's previous authority to "recommend" was changed to "approval," thereby granting it formal governing authority for new programs. Its statewide planning responsibilities also were clarified, and legislation linked the mandated statewide plans to state policy by requiring legislative action on them as a policy matter. If the legislature failed to act, the plan would become state policy by default. These and related changes became effective in 1987 when the membership of the CPE was changed and it became the HECB (Title 250, Washington Administrative Code). A burst of activity thus transpired during the 1980s with the formation of four research university branch campuses and the transfer of the five remaining vocational-technical institutes from the K-12 sector to the community college system where they were redesignated as technical colleges.

More recently state and institutional leaders have begun to perceive that HECB was playing a limited and ineffectual role in promoting the state's policy goals and priorities for higher education. Reflecting this dissatisfaction in spring 2011, the legislature abolished the HECB effective on July 1, 2012 (E2SSB 5182). The HECB is to be replaced by a new entity that oversees student financial aid and a new Council on Higher Education that has responsibility for policy functions. Implying this lack of perceived effectiveness in HECB's policy functions and reflecting a desire on the part of elected officials to grant increased authority to the institutions, the legislation stated:

> The legislature further intends to eliminate many of the policy and planning functions of the higher education coordinating board and rededicate those resources to the higher education institutions that provide the core, front-line services associated with instruction and research. Given the unprecedented budget crises the state is facing, the state must take the opportunity to build on the recommendations of the board and use the dollars where they can make the most direct impact. (E2SSB 5182, p. 3)

At this point it is too early to predict how these changes will be implemented and what effect they will have.

Recent Developments in Washington Higher Education

The HECB's 2005 strategic plan addressed typical state concerns for improving access to higher education, transfers, affordability, and degree program approval, as well as doing more to meet the regional postsecondary needs by reviewing the successes of the University of Washington's Bothell and Washington State University's Tri-Cities branch campuses (Washington Higher Education Coordinating Board, 2011). In 2006, the state expanded access to higher education by enabling Washington State University's Tri-Cities campus in Richland (a two-year college) to become a full-fledged four-year institution. The legislature also approved a plan for Everett Community College to contract with one of the state's four-year schools to provide access to upper-level courses north of Seattle (*Chronicle of Higher Education, Almanac, 2005*).

In its 2008 strategic plan, the board addressed increasing diversity, fostering greater K-12 pipeline facilitation, increasing baccalaureate completion rates, and improving affordability (Washington Higher Education Coordinating Board, 2007). In the 2007–2009 biennium allocations for higher education, the governor and legislature endorsed significant improvements with "a 15% increase or some $443 million," a "36% increase in need-based financial aid," and "a 14.6% increase in maintenance and construction projects" (*Chronicle of Higher Education, Almanac, 2007–2008*, p. 92).

State funding of higher education in Washington reached a high in 2009 when the state was "flush with money" (*Chronicle of Higher Education, Almanac, 2008–2009*, pp. 69; Illinois State University, 2011). However, this largesse did not last and in 2009, as a result of the national economic decline, significant cuts were made to the state's support of higher education. As figure 6.2 reveals, Washington cut funding far below the 2009 levels and even below the 2006 level, with the federal stimulus funds in 2010 only slightly making up the difference. From 2008 to 2011, Washington cut funding by 16 percent outpacing the national average by 9 percentage points. Despite significant reductions in state appropriations, Washington's

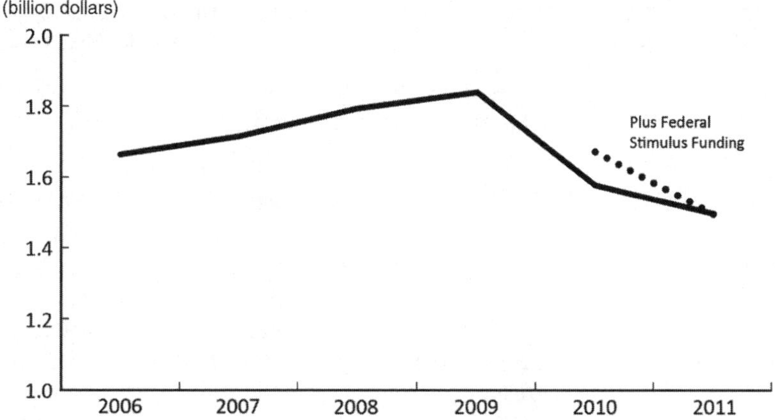

Figure 6.2 Real Washington state appropriations for higher education.

Source: Illinois State University's *Grapevine* Annual Survey. Calculations: Authors.

increase (5.8 percent) in tuition revenue per Full-Time Equivalent (FTE) student from 2005 to 2010 was well below the national average of 14.9 percent. The combined reduction in state support and smaller than average increase in tuition revenue led to a 4.9 percent decrease in total educational revenue per FTE from 2005 to 2010 (SHEEO, 2011). This fiscal reality led the State Board for Community and Technical Colleges for Washington to declare a state of financial emergency. The declaration of a financial emergency allows the Board to take drastic measures in order to "right the ship." These include, among other things, the possible dismissal of tenure-track faculty members more quickly and easily (Fain, 2011).

OREGON

This section of the chapter details the history, physical expansion, and development of the Oregon State University, University of Oregon, and community colleges with a focus on the coordination of the state's 60 institutions, of which 24 are private universities. Oregon state universities and colleges with their 310,000 students in 2010 focused their missions on the natural environment for educational and research programs and vocational studies for the industries in this state. Their missions may be described as "the enhancement of the economic growth of the State and Region" through teaching, research, and service (Castle, Holland, and Knudsen, 1970, p. xxiii). Yet, the shift of state funding and emphasis in the 1990s from its four-year institutions to now centering on 22 community colleges and distance education have reshaped higher education and its culture within the state. Unfortunately, the contemporary persistent problem in Oregon is funding with it being near the bottom of per-student spending on public higher education nationally (SHEEO, 2011). On the other hand, federal research dollars (approximately $440 million in 2009) represent a significant funding source for its universities and their contribution to developing the state's economy and culture (National Science Foundation, 2010).

Historical Introduction

This paradise on the northwest coast really bloomed and boomed in the nineteenth century. It was settled from the East and from the West—the latter representing the sea-going adventurers from New England. For example, Portland, Oregon, was named after Portland, Maine. Along the Willamette Valley, traces of New England still linger with neat little towns, while in the rural areas, rivers with covered bridges or ferries enabled those modern-day tillers of the soil to travel. The "Great Migration of 1843" began to populate this area. Initially, an estimated 700 to 1,000 emigrants left their homes and worldly possessions to travel cross-country to Oregon, opening up "The Oregon Trail." They arrived in the Willamette Valley by early October. These first pioneers were followed by tens of thousands of immigrants looking for adventure and a new life (Hine and Faragher, 2000, pp. 181–189; Limerick, Milner, and Rankin, 1991, pp. 171–175; Nugent, 1999, pp. 77–79). From May 1848 to August 1848, the Oregon country functioned as an independent government with a three-member executive office and small judicial and legislative branches. In 1848, it was annexed by the United States and a territorial government was created. In February, 1859, Oregon became the thirty-third state (Willamette University, *History of Willamette*).

Portland, the "City of Roses" incorporated in 1851, sits at the northern head of the Willamette Valley—the area in northwest Oregon that surrounds the Willamette River as it proceeds northward emerging from the mountains near Eugene to its confluence with the Columbia River at Portland. This beautiful valley became an agricultural area and choice for many immigrants on the Oregon Trail in the 1840s. It is estimated that between 70 and 75 percent of the people who live in Oregon reside in the Willamette Valley (Hine and Faragher, 2000, pp. 196–197, 421).

The cities of Eugene, Corvallis, Albany, and Salem are integral to the Willamette Valley. Five of the nine public higher education institutions are located in this subregion. This population density means the rest of the state is sparsely populated. The pioneers who settled in the Oregon Territory brought with them a hunger for civilization, including churches and schools. This hunger for learning and education prompted the establishment of elementary schools and soon extended to church-related colleges and universities.

Creating Institutions of Higher Learning in Oregon

In 1842, Oregon's first higher education institution was founded in what is now Salem. Missionary Jason Lee, who had arrived in the territory in 1834, served as the first president of the Board of Trustees of what originally was called the Oregon Institute. Its mission was to educate the children of the missionaries. In 1852, it became "Wallamet University." The following year the Oregon Territorial Legislature granted the school a charter. Then, in 1870, the current spelling was adopted (Willamette University, *History of Willamette*). Among the other significant "firsts" in the Northwest was Willamette's School of Medicine in 1866, which subsequently merged with the University of Oregon in 1913, and the Law School established in 1883.

The Oregon pioneers continued to establish institutions of higher learning. Pacific University, located in Forest Grove, was chartered by the Territorial Legislature in 1849 as Tualatin Academy and awarded the first baccalaureate degree in this subregion in 1863. Lewis and Clark College opened in Albany under the Presbyterian Church. It awarded its first bachelor's degree in 1905 and moved to Portland in 1942. Reed College, perhaps Oregon's most distinguished undergraduate liberal arts and science college, was founded in Portland in 1905. The Reeds, who founded it through pioneer wealth, stipulated that the college would have no limits other than insistence on equality and secularism. A unique aspect to the development of higher education in Oregon is the number of failed institutions scattered throughout its history. This trend began in the 1850s with McMinnville College being the first and continued into the 2000s with Cascade College closing its doors in 2008. Even discounting the numbers of merged institutions, the failed and current numbers far exceed that of Oregon's neighbor to the north by about three times (Pemberton, 1932; Brown, n.d.). In other words, a significant number of attempts to launch higher education occurred in Oregon.

Oregon State University

Incorporated by the Free Masons in Corvallis, the area's first community school for primary and preparatory education was founded in 1856 as Corvallis Academy. However, not until 1865 did the school offer its first college-level curriculum under the administration of the Methodist Episcopal Church. August 22, 1868, is a red-letter day in the history of this institution—the day that official Articles of Incorporation were filed and also the day that the Oregon Legislative Assembly designated Corvallis College as the Agricultural College of the State of Oregon, which made it the recipient of 1862 federal Morrill Land-Grant Act income. In 1870, the members of the first graduating class were awarded the bachelor of arts. Oregon State's early programs followed the land-grant university tradition, emphasizing agriculture, engineering, and the sciences. A shift occurred after World War II through the 1960s with the expansion of liberal arts and humanities undergraduate studies. The growing diversity in degree programs led to another name change when the college became Oregon State College in 1937. The current title, Oregon State University, was adopted on March 6, 1961.

With enrollment of nearly 27,000 students in the 2009–2010 academic year, Oregon State University is only one of two universities in the country designated as a land, sea, sun, and space-grant university by the federal government. It leads the state's general purpose universities in attracting financial support for research from outside agencies, securing a projected $250 million in 2010. As part of its land-grant mission, it established Extension Service offices throughout the state. Its research activities include Oregon Forest Research Laboratory, a major Marine Science Center located at Newport, and the Wave Research Laboratory. Named after its Nobel Prize–winning graduate and faculty member, the Linus Pauling Institute focuses on the sciences. The university is extending its mission by opening a branch campus in Bend at Central Oregon Community College (Oregon State University).

University of Oregon

The University of Oregon at Eugene became the second public university in the state as it opened its doors in 1876, graduating its first class two years later. It became the flagship university in the Oregon public university system with the expansion of professional education beginning in 1884 with law, followed by the schools of education, commerce, architecture, and journalism, as well as doctoral education by 1926. After World War II, the administration and faculty emphasized natural science programs in chemistry, physics, and biology. The national recognition resulted in its being selected in 1969 as one of the then 60 members of the prestigious Association of American Universities. Perceived as Oregon's public liberal arts university, it seeks distinctive undergraduate, professional, and graduate programs in its colleges of arts and science, professional colleges, and music school. Its 27,000 students comprise approximately 21,000 undergraduates and 6,000 graduates. The university awarded almost 5,000 degrees in the 2010 academic year. The 1989 construction of a new $45.6 million science center expanded research. This development led to an increase in science funding of $115 million in grants, of which $101 million came from the federal government in FY2007–2008. This focus on basic and applied research may further be noted by the university's two Nobel Laureates and nine Pulitzer Prize–winning faculty (Office of Institutional Research, University of Oregon, 2008; Office for Research, Innovation and Graduate Education, University of Oregon).

Undoubtedly, one of the most effective presidents in the history of the university was David B. Frohnmayer, a former state attorney general, who served the university from 1994 to 2009. As the only native son to be a president, he retired with a record unmatched by few (if any) university presidents in the history of Oregon's higher education or elsewhere. In January 2001, at a time when the financial support from the state had dwindled from 40 to 12 percent of the university's budget, President Frohnmayer set a goal to raise $600 million by December 2008. With such benefactors as Phil Knight (cofounder of the Nike Corporation) and Lorry I. Lokey (each of whom contributed more than $100 million), the campaign goal was exceeded by more than $253 million to total more than $850 million (University of Oregon, 2008 and 2009). Part of this success resulted in the groundbreaking construction of a $27 million living and learning residential complex, its first expansion since the 1960s, through state bonds. The University of Oregon has numerous respected and highly ranked academic programs. The university's Warsaw Sports Marketing Center was the country's first sports business program housed in a college of business, the Lundquist College of Business. Today, the center is recognized by *ESPN*, *Sports Illustrated*, *Sports Business Journal*, and others as the leading think tank and training ground for the sports business industry. The undergraduate architecture program is consistently ranked among the highest in the country and is currently ranked as the number one public program for "Sustainable Design Practice and Principles" by *DesignIntelligence* magazine. The university also continues to receive recognition from the *US News and World Report* rankings for programs within the university's College of Law and the College of Education (University of Oregon, 2011).

The Oregon Health and Science University

One of the leading health centers in the nation combining teaching, research, and treatment, the Oregon Health and Science University can trace its roots back to the 1860s when Willamette University School of Medicine was started in Salem. Willamette University and the University of Oregon merged their medical programs in 1913 and created the University of Oregon Schools of Medicine, Dentistry, and Nursing in Portland. Then, in 1974, the legislature combined those three schools and separated it from the University of Oregon. In 1995, the state authorized it as a public not-for-profit corporation with its own governing board. As part of the merger with the Oregon Graduate Institute of Science and Technology in 2001, it became the Oregon Health and Science University. Today, the university is organized into five schools: medicine, nursing, dentistry, pharmacy (in cooperation with the Oregon State University), and the nation's only academic health center with a school of science and engineering focusing on human and environmental health. For close to 20 years, its School of Nursing cooperated with Eastern Oregon and Southern Oregon universities as well as with Oregon Institute of Technology to extend four-year nursing degree programs to some of the state's more rural areas. In 2007, the university ranked forty-second among 100 American universities in federal funding for science and engineering. It is Portland's largest employer with 12,400 employees (Oregon Health and Science University).

Oregon's Three Regional Public Universities

Oregon's three regional state universities—Western, Southern, and Eastern—have all experienced title and mission changes over the years similar to patterns found in a number of states. Western Oregon University in Monmouth and Southern Oregon University in Ashland were initially established as private colleges in 1856 and 1872, respectively. They subsequently became state-supported and controlled institutions, and along with Eastern Oregon University, established in La Grande in 1929, were designated as normal schools. Over the years, the names of these three institutions changed to the geographic designation plus "College of Education," "College," or "State College," and to "University" in 1997. Concurrently, their missions also changed and expanded from preparing teachers for careers in elementary and secondary education to much broader degree programs in the liberal arts, humanities, sciences, as well as business, accounting, and computer science, for instance. The three universities also offer master's degrees in education.

Each university developed emphases that set them apart from other public and independent institutions in the state. Western Oregon University is the first and oldest public university in Oregon, founded by pioneers who had traversed the Oregon Trail. It began as a private college in Monmouth in 1856. After five name changes that responded to the institution's broader role as a comprehensive university, it was renamed Western Oregon University in 1997. It has been noted for excellence in teacher preparation, especially through its Teaching Research Institute. Its 70-member staff conducts research on informing and facilitating change in educational and human service system to improve the quality of life for individuals (Western Oregon University).

Eastern Oregon Normal School opened its doors in 1929 as the sole pubic, four-year general purpose institution east of the Cascade Mountains. In 1997, it became Eastern Oregon University. It partners with Oregon State University to offer baccalaureate level degrees in agriculture. It also joined with Oregon Health and Science University to offer a degree in nursing. Eastern's innovative approach is to establish educational centers in various communities providing video, Internet, and onsite faculty visits (Eastern Oregon University).

Southern Oregon University had nine name changes over the years until assuming its current name in 1997. Its community contribution is its national recognized theater and performance studies. The long-established Oregon Shakespeare Festival in Ashland provides the university with a recognized cultural resource with which it has bonded to benefit both institutions. For example, the university supports a Center for Shakespeare Studies along with degree programs in theater performance, production, and design (Southern Oregon University).

Portland State University (PSU)

This late-blooming city university is located in downtown Portland. Founded in 1946, it has the largest enrollment of any university in the state at 28,000 and is the only state university located in a major metropolitan city within the state of Oregon. It was established as the Vanport Extension Center in 1946 to satisfy the demand for higher education by veterans of World War II. The center moved to downtown Portland in 1952. Its name was changed to Portland State College in 1955 to commemorate its maturation into a four-year, degree-granting institution. Graduate programs were initiated in 1961 with a particular focus on community engagement that accounted for its establishing the School of Social Work, the Toulan School of Urban Studies and Planning, and the Institute of Metropolitan Studies. Doctoral programs were added in 1968. The Oregon State System of Higher Education granted the institution university status in 1969 and renamed it Portland State University (Portland State University, 2011).

In the 1990s, Portland State developed an innovative model for the comprehensive reform of its undergraduate education with the development of an interdisciplinary general education program known as "University Studies." This program was launched in 1994 and now frequently receives the recognition of *US News and World Report* as one of the "America's Best Colleges: Programs to Look For" and is well known for the positive impact it has had on the retention of first-year students (University Studies Program, Portland State University, 2011).

Within the Oregon University System, PSU is notable as not only the largest but also the fastest growing university (Oregon University System, 2004). In the 2012 edition of the *The Best 376 Colleges* by the *Princeton Review*, PSU is recognized among "the Best in the West" and as a "College with a Conscience." According to the PSU website, the university has continued to grow, moving from a liberal arts undergraduate college to become an "urban research university" expanding beyond bachelor degrees into more than 40 master's and doctoral level programs such as mathematics, biology, chemistry, applied physics, computer science, applied psychology, engineering and technology, and sociology. It has also integrated the idea of being an urban serving research university throughout its functions and curriculum. Accordingly, the institution adopted the motto of "let knowledge serve the city." In fact, in AY2007–2008 PSU student volunteers put in 1.44 million hours of service to the community at an estimated worth of $25 million. The university is one of 48 members of the Coalition of Urban Serving Universities that serves as "a national voice within public higher education to articulate and promote an urban agenda." In fall 2010, the university enrolled more than 29,818 students, 57.5 percent full-time students. In the 2010–2011 academic year, PSU awarded 5,620 degrees, including 3,825 bachelors, 1,735 master's, and 60 doctoral degrees (Portland State University, 2011). The largest grant awarded in the history of Portland State University was in September 2008 by the James F. and Marion L. Miller Foundation. The grant was a $25 million challenge grant to assist the university in becoming a regional and national leader in sustainability research and education. The grant funded the development of the Portland State Institute for Sustainable Solutions, which focuses its research on four areas: (1) the integration of human societies and the natural environment, (2) creating sustainable urban communities, (3) implementing sustainability and mechanisms of change, and (4) measuring sustainability (Institute for Sustainable Solutions, Portland State University, 2011).

Oregon Institute of Technology

This institution was founded as the Oregon Vocation School in 1947 to train and reeducate returning World War II veterans. The first classes were held in a deactivated Marine Corps hospital three miles northeast of Klamath Falls. The following year, the fledgling school's title was changed to the Oregon Technical Institute. Associate degree programs in Surveying and Structural Engineering Technologies were accredited by the Engineers Council for Professional Development. The campus began offering accredited bachelor's degrees in 1966. The name change to the Oregon Institute of Technology (OIT) was approved in 1973. At its Portland campus after 1988, it offered bachelor and master of science degrees in manufacturing technology, which was extended to Seattle, WA, in partnership with the Boeing Company in 1998. The institution became the only accredited, public polytechnic institution of higher learning in the Pacific Northwest and enrolled 4,000 students in fall 2010. Its program offerings span information technology, electrical and mechanical engineering, and operations management. The OIT has now become a regional leader in allied health education, offering bachelor's degrees in medical imaging, dental hygiene, clinical lab sciences, respiratory care, and biological health sciences (Oregon Institute of Technology, 2011).

Community Colleges in Oregon

Oregon's community college system and its 17 community colleges have played key roles as access points for many of the state's citizens. In fall 2009, there were 279,381 undergraduate students enrolled in Oregon's public higher education system, 66 percent (or 185,231) of those are enrolled in Oregon's community colleges (National Center for Education Statistics, 2011). In other words, the community colleges function as major transfer education institutions for the four-year public university system, similar to California and Pennsylvania. The system's history dates from the 1940s when school district leaders in some parts of the state developed post-high school programs. These adult "night school" programs launched a major higher education effort. In 1957, the legislature began funding these junior colleges along with district and federal monies. In the mid-1960s, legislative authority created a new class of community college districts. Initially called "Area Education Districts," the idea was to allow parts of Oregon not already in a community college district to establish by local vote non-campus-based programs for their citizens with instructional services contracted with accredited institutions. Four districts were organized under this authority, each with its own board of directors and taxing powers. By 1970 some 13 community colleges opened in the state, reflecting the national trend. In 1981, Area Education Districts were renamed Community College Service Districts by legislative action.

The next 30 years saw significant expansion, which was further heartened when Barbara Roberts, a former local board member of Mt. Hood Community College and longtime community college advocate, was elected governor in 1990. With the same ballot, however, voters approved Ballot Measure 5, a limitation on total property tax revenues. While school districts and community colleges were assured of replacement revenue for lost property tax revenues, the rest of the state government took the hit for making that happen. Further, this measure virtually ended local property tax elections, which was a regular and positive connection between the colleges and their voting communities. Nor could Governor Roberts keep the underlying state appropriation for community colleges from sharing in the cuts necessary to backfill lost property tax revenues. The effect of Measure 5 was even more draconian on the Oregon University System, which took cuts and did not receive any state refunding. During the next 15 years, both state appropriations and state-board-approved allocations to community colleges blurred the line between local support and state support, as the budget fortunes of individual districts shifted to the State Capitol.

From a governance perspective, state responsibility for Oregon community colleges was initially established in 1969, with the creation of the Division of Community Colleges and Vocational Education under the Oregon Board of Education and in the Department of Education, an agency headed by the elected State Superintendent of Public Instruction. In 1987, Michael Holland, a former Chemeketa Community College board member and Oregon Community College Association president, led a successful effort to separate the office from the state Superintendent of Public Instruction and to reestablish it as a stand-alone Office of Community College Services, reporting separately to the State Board of Education. With his success, Holland was selected to be the first Oregon Commissioner for Community College Services. In an effort to redress this problem, the Community College Service Districts allowed individual institutional development and accreditation in the late 1990s for four schools: Columbia Gorge Community College–Hood River, Tillamook Bay Community College–Tillamook, Oregon Coast Community College–Newport, and Klamath Community College–Klamath Falls. Upon his retirement from American Association of Community Colleges, Dale Parnell returned from Washington, DC, to serve as the second commissioner for the community colleges. He was followed by Roger Bassett, former executive secretary of the Oregon Community College Association. In the late 1990s, Bassett, who simultaneously served as an education policy advisor to three governors, negotiated a merger of two state offices for community college administration and the state's job-training programs. Camille Preus, who next served as commissioner, established state responsibility for community colleges and workforce programs under a new Oregon Department of Community Colleges and Workforce Development. The State Board of Education continues to be the policy board for this department. Maintaining historic ties to the school districts, new community college districts may still be formed only by a vote within the proposed boundaries of a district; and locally elected Boards of Education still have all responsibilities for college district decisions, including budget approval, setting tuition, and selection of college presidents.

Mid-Twentieth-Century Advances

Major growth in the OSU system came during the chancellorship of Roy E. Lieuallen, who served as chancellor of the Oregon State System of Higher Education from 1961 to 1982. He proclaimed the merits of a unified system and laid the groundwork for major changes in Oregon's public support for higher education. For example, as the system's enrollment grew from approximately 25,000 students in 1960 to 62,000 in 1981, Lieuallen increased the system's facilities to accommodate them after 1975. Following the direction that he set for the state system, a strategic plan was undertaken in 1982 to identify objectives. With this planning, the state and governing board projected how four-year public universities and colleges could fulfill these objectives. For example, regional committees were developed in specific geographic areas of the state consisting of faculty in academic areas (such as English, mathematics, social sciences, and sciences) from the four-year institutions, community colleges, and public secondary schools. These meetings led to adjustments in admission standards and greater mission differentiation between the community colleges and the four-year institutions. The problem of deteriorating physical plants also was a major issue on all state college and university campuses. Governor Victor Atiyeh, who held office from 1979 to 1987, organized bus tours for legislators to visit personally all of the state campuses and see the condition of the facilities. As a result, the legislature adopted plans for deferred maintenance and formulated a timetable to replace old structures with modern ones and to adjust to the ever-evolving expansion into high technology research and productivity. Special attention was given to increasing the number of minority students enrolled on the college campuses. Full, renewable waivers of tuition were granted to a percentage of incoming minority students for each campus. This led to aggressive recruiting of minorities on the part of the respective campuses to attract those with the potential to succeed. The goal of doubling the minority enrollment was achieved in its first year.

Oregon System Successes in the 1980s

The nine Oregon public colleges and universities in the state system raised admission requirements statewide, effective from fall 1985. These institutions also adopted a funding model that allocated money internally, based on the institution's academic disciplines, levels, and types of instruction. The results were dramatic; among other accomplishments, several highlights include:

1. Between 1983 and 1988, appropriations for the state system increased 72.4 percent and the system's share of the state general fund budget increased from 12.9 percent to 16.0 percent.
2. Tuition freezes were implemented for 1983–1984, 1984–1985, and 1986–1987. As a result, tuition at the state's institutions rose only 7 percent in six years, compared with an increase of 47 percent at state institutions nationally.
3. The state system institutions developed a plan in 1982 for awarding 440 privately financed $1,000 Presidential Scholarships annually to encourage top Oregon high school students to attend Oregon's state colleges and universities.
4. The 1985 legislature approved $30 million for capital construction, followed by $64.9 million in 1987. In addition, in 1985, the legislature appropriated funds specifically designated for deferred maintenance on all state system campuses.
5. Faculty salaries for state system institutions were increased by 19 percent in the 1985–1987 biennium. This was followed by another increase of $30 million in the 1987 biennial appropriation.

6. In 1985–1986, through private funds, the state system supplemented the legislative appropriation with $125 million in outside federal aid and private gifts, grants, and contracts. The following year outside funds rose another 47 percent.
7. Expanded offerings in Asian languages and a highly successful student exchange programs with Asian universities, especially mainland China, were initiated.
8. The Oregon four-year institutions worked with area community colleges on co-enrollment arrangements to provide remedial courses for students who were not prepared for admission to the baccalaureate programs.

In summary, the strategic plan and its implementation led to significant successes.

However, beginning in the late 1980s and accelerating through the 1990s, Oregon higher education lost political and financial support. Two factors brought about this shift: the election of governors who did not favor higher education and a worsening state economy. The latter development led to a tax revolt similar to California and Colorado. It signaled a major shift in state support and the need to adjust the governance system (Office of the Chancellor, *Oregon University System Fact Book, 2002, 2004, 2008, 2009*).

A Strategic Plan for 2007

In March 2007, the Oregon State Board of Higher Education published "An Investment in Oregonians for Our Future—A Plan to 2025 for the Oregon University System." It described how much had been lost during the past 20 years. The plan listed new strategic priorities:

1. Increase education attainment to assure competitive strength for Oregon and its citizens;
2. Invest in research that is globally competitive, building on existing excellence and Oregon's market advantages; and
3. Assure the long-term financial viability of and adequate support for OUS and its institutions through creation of effective governance, organizational, and financial models.

The Foreword emphasized that the plan was propelled by the need to prepare students for the global century, and went on to emphasize the consequences of 15 years of "disinvestment." Specifically, the planning section pointed out that "at a time when a strong higher education system is most needed, Oregon has pursued a policy of disinvesting in its public universities and colleges." The report concluded: "Financial instability and decline, as well as legal and state policy restrictions, have brought Oregon postsecondary education to a crisis point." It referred to the negative results of Ballot Measure 5 in 1990, which had a great similarity to a tax restriction previously passed and implemented in California. From 1991 onward, Oregon higher education took some of the deepest cuts of any of the large state budgets in the United States. Meanwhile, enrollments in the state's public universities grew significantly during that period.

By 2007, the year of the Board's Strategic Plan, Oregon ranked forty-fifth in the nation in state funding per student in postsecondary education. To meet the national average, Oregon higher education in that year needed an additional investment of $264 million. At the same time, Oregon students had to pay 55 percent of the cost of their education in public higher education institutions, while 10 years previously they paid about one-third of the cost with the state picking up the other two-thirds. The student-faculty ratio—a measure of faculty capacity to provide both classroom and out-of-class instructional support for students—worsened in 1992 and was one of the highest in the 50 states. Faculty salaries dropped to such a comparatively low level that the ability of OUS institutions to recruit and retain regular rank, full-time faculty was diminished, resulting in an increase in the use of part-time and adjunct faculty to meet teaching loads. This "divestiture era" had left a legacy of the state's withdrawal from its public colleges and universities. More recent efforts have not overcome this 1988 shift. The annual "Almanacs" published by *The Chronicle of Higher Education* provide a litany of bad news for Oregon public higher education. From 2003 to 2007, the publication reported annual disinvestments in higher education.

By 2007, the *Chronicle's Almanac* cheered the efforts of Governor Ted Kulongoski who proposed increasing the spending on higher education. The budget for the Oregon University System received a 23 percent increase for the biennium. It also provided $233 million for campus capital projects to deal with the maintenance backlog. Overall, the student's share of the state's educational budget was projected to drop to about 53 percent. As it turned out, according to the 2007 *Chronicle Almanac*, the 5 percent budget increase in 2005 provided little relief for public universities. Expenditures for employee health insurance, pension obligations, utilities, building materials, and insurance all had increased. As a result, Oregon universities enrolled 7,800 in-state students for whom they received no state funds. Six out of seven campuses made significant budget cuts, averaging about 6 percent for the 2006–2007 fiscal year. Faculty salaries lagged behind the national average by about 15 percent. And deferred maintenance reported a $600 million backlog. Tuition increases, however, were held to an average of 3 percent, down from a 10 percent increase in the previous two years.

The Oregon University System's Governance Structure and Recent Developments

The Oregon Legislative Assembly created the first Board of Regents through legislation passed in February 1885. It replaced the College's Board of Trustees, which had reported to the Columbia Conference of the Methodist Episcopal Church, South. The original Board of Regents consisted of nine members appointed by and reporting to the governor of Oregon. Ex-officio members of the board included a president; secretary, and treasurer, who were appointed to two-year terms of office. The board's by-laws were amended later to include a vice president. In March 1929, the legislature developed a new approach to public higher education that it hoped would be a national model, when it created the Oregon State Board of Higher Education (OSBHE) to oversee the established public institutions with one of its goals being the elimination of unnecessary duplication. By 1931, the board appointed the system's first chancellor and began to administer the legislature's vision of a unified state system of higher education (Oregon University System, 2010). In these early years, the board's power was highly centralized, with concomitant decrease in institutional autonomy. It would take 30 years from its inception for new developments to strengthen the board.

Today, the OSBHE is a 12-member board appointed by the governor to oversee the Oregon University System (OUS), which includes seven diverse baccalaureate and graduate-level institutions. It elects a president and vice president to oversee its work. The board now has statutory authority for OUS and is responsible for planning a comprehensive system, approving all degree programs, granting degrees, developing, and approving budget requests (both operating and capital construction), as well as controlling and managing property. The administrative arm of the board is the Department of Higher Education, which was established in 1929, that functions as a statutory cabinet department of state government. Its primary duties included administering the policies set by the OSBHE and the coordination of OUS. The chancellor, the chief administrative officer of the department, is hired by and serves at the board's pleasure.

However, recent developments have thrown state higher education governance in Oregon into a state of flux. In the 2011 legislative session, the legislature enacted Senate Bill 242 that granted OUS significantly increased procedural autonomy and established a new Higher Education Coordinating Council (HECC). Specifically, the bill:

1. Creates the HECC and grants the commission authority to coordinate higher education policy with the OUS and the community colleges;
2. Abolishes the Oregon Student Assistance Commission and transfers its functions to the HECC;
3. Redefines the OUS as the public university system with more authority and independence to manage affairs, operations, and obligations;
4. Creates a process for the OSBHE to enter into performance compacts with the state institutions in conjunction with funding requests; and
5. Grants the SBHE greater authority over the fiscal affairs of public higher education, including spending and tuition and fee rates (subject to limits set by the HECC).

At the same time, the legislature enacted the governor's proposal for an overarching Education Investment Board (Senate Bill 909). However, the two bills were not tightly linked or coordinated, and, therefore, it is far from clear where higher education governance in Oregon will evolve over the next two years. Specifically the higher education-related items in SB 909 included:

1. The establishment of the Oregon Education Investment Board (OEIB) that will oversee a unified public education system that begins with early childhood services and continues throughout public education from kindergarten to postsecondary education;
2. Direction to the OEIB to appoint a Chief Education Officer;
3. Direction to the OEIB to submit a report related to proposed changes in public education to the legislative committees on education by December 15, 2011.

The December 15, 2011, report to the legislature included several relevant proposals. Among these were the recommendations that Oregon:

1. Develop[s] an outcomes-based P-20 education system budget proposal for 2013–2015 that defines the core educational outcomes that matter for students, their families, and the state, which then drive the investment strategies;
2. Streamlin[es] governance of higher education, so that one board or commission offers direction and coordination for the Oregon University System and allows universities to establish independent boards for their institutions if they wish. (Education Investment Board, 2011)

The governor appears most interested in the outcomes of SB 909 and announced his intention to appoint a leader for the Education Investment Board. However, he also emphasized that the governance structure is still to evolve until 2013 (Hammond, 2011). At this point it is not clear how OUS, HECC, SBHE, and OEIB will all work together. Clearly, higher education governance in Oregon is an unsettled issue.

The 2008 *Chronicle Almanac* reported that Oregon, which had historically ranked near the bottom of all states in per-student spending for its public colleges, expanded its need-based student aid program and increased institutional appropriations modestly. Yet Oregon was far from a stable position before the disinvestments occurred (*Chronicle of Higher Education, Almanacs, 2003–2008*). Most recently, the national economic decline has resulted in increased fiscal difficulties for higher education in Oregon. The state's need-based financial aid program ran out of money in 2010. The double whammy of a reduction in state support and the dramatic increase in demand for financial aid doomed it. Officials in Oregon estimated that only 25 percent of eligible students would receive aid in AY2010–2011 (Keller, 2010). In addition, as figure 6.3 reveals, Oregon had to cut its higher education funding far below the 2008 level and even well below the 2006 level, with the federal stimulus funds only slightly making up the difference. The

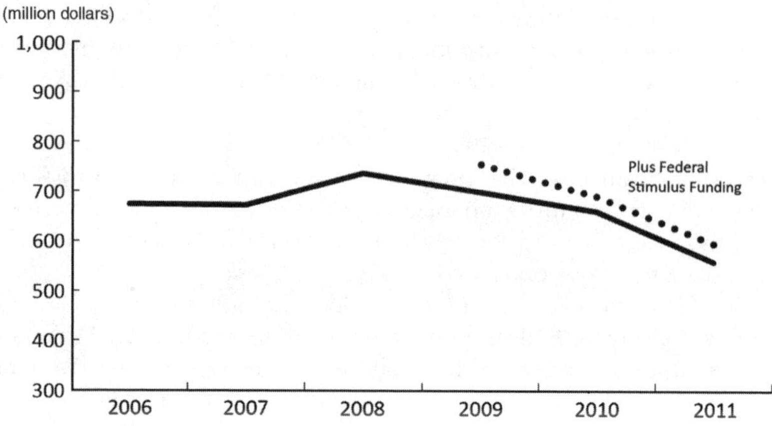

Figure 6.3 Real Oregon state appropriations for higher education.
Source: Illinois State University's *Grapevine* Annual Survey. Calculations: Authors.

decline in Oregon significantly outpaced the national average. Nationally, state appropriations for higher education experienced a 7 percent decline from 2008 to 2011, while Oregon experienced a 19 percent decline (Illinois State University, 2011). While it is often believed that as a result of cuts to state appropriations to higher education institutions, students will see commensurate (or thereabout) increases in tuition rates, this is not always the case. Despite significant reductions in state appropriations, Oregon's tuition revenue per Full-Time Equivalent (FTE) student actually declined from 2005 to 2010 (4.9 percent decrease). The decreases in state appropriations and tuition revenue have resulted in one of the largest reductions in total higher education revenue in the country (SHEEO, 2011).

HAWAII

Hawaii's College of Agriculture and Mechanic Arts was established in 1907 under terms of the 1890 Second Morrill Land-Grant, which included American territories. The institution was renamed the College of Hawaii in 1912 and its campus moved to its present location in Manoa Valley on the island of Oahu. After petitioning the legislature for university status, the University of Hawaii came into being in 1920 (University of Hawaii System, 2011). As the land-grant institution, this university has led the territory and then the state in higher education ever since. The legislature further expanded its mission to become a sea-grant and space-grant institution. However, the university also included other types of postsecondary education, such as community colleges and professional schools. During the 1960s, its initial expansion ultimately resulted in the growth of four community colleges with three others to follow. In effect, they became the branch campuses of the university with 72 percent of its undergraduates completing transfer general education at the seven community colleges by 1993 (Kamins and Potter, 1998, p. 270). On the other hand, the university found great support in the 1970s for major expansions to all four-year campuses at Hilo and then at West Oahu. In the 1980s and 1990s, university retrenchment occurred with the downturn in the island economy, leaving the institution in extreme fiscal crisis that was exacerbated by significant state funding losses and collective bargaining efforts of public employees who rejected the initial bargaining agent. As a result, the faculty lost salary increases when they attempted their own organizing and voted for a strike in November 1983. Many research faculty left the university because of these events (Yount, 1996, pp. 3–6).

Currently, there are 20 institutions of higher learning in the state, 10 of which are public (6 of these are community colleges). The university and its campuses enrolled 37,000 students in the 2009–2010 academic year, while 39,000 attended community colleges. Ten private and for-profit institutions enabled 24,000 students to undertake postsecondary studies (IPEDS, 2011). Federal research funding was approximately $211 million in 2009 (National Science Foundation, 2010).

University of Hawaii Developments

The College of Agriculture and Mechanic Arts in Honolulu was founded in this territory with a plantation economy in which the focus of study initially was "tropical agriculture and engineering related to sugar plantations" (Kamins and Potter, 1998, pp. 44–47). In 1912, it became the College of Hawaii and relocated to the Manoa Valley on the Island of Oahu. Eight years later it was raised to university stature with widespread citizen support. It then comprised two colleges: the College of Arts and Sciences and the College of Applied Sciences. It graduated its first PhD in education in 1931 after its merger with the island's Territorial Normal School, which was renamed the university's Teachers College (pp. 20, 34). Significantly, the Oriental Institute was founded in the mid-1930s and became the internationally famous East-West Center. As part of the University of Hawaii (UH), the institute made the university a center for "Asia-Pacific expertise" (University of Hawaii System, 2011). World War II then consumed the islands and its population, starting with the attack on Pearl Harbor on December 7, 1941. Not surprisingly, one-half of the student body of 3,500 was military personnel by 1945.

After the war, university growth was dramatic, especially in professional education. From the 1950s through to the 1970s, the University of Hawaii experienced nearly unabated growth with numerous new schools, colleges, and programs, as well as significant new construction. These additions included: nursing, public health, medicine, law, business, and education colleges; institutes for biomedical research and astronomy; as well as significant expansions in the number of science-related doctoral programs. Similar to other campuses in the United States, fear of communism after the war led to legislative investigations from the House Committee on Un-American

Activities in 1950. The State of Hawaii passed a loyalty oath for public employees with only two persons dismissed on the campus—a student employee and a visiting faculty member (Kamins and Potter, 1998, pp. 60–64). Expansion of the campus in the remainder of the decade focused on doctoral education and professional schools. Doctoral programs were begun in botany, chemistry, entomology, genetics, soil science, and marine biology between 1953 and 1955. By 1961, the university awarded doctorates in 16 areas. Academic reorganization under the presidency of Paul S. Bachman led to the establishment of the College of Education, the College of Business, the College of Engineering, and an independent School of Nursing (pp. 65–71).

The admittance of Hawaii as the fiftieth state in August 1959 brought new federal research and applied studies funding. Its new Institute of Geophysics reflected the need for greater study of geology suited to the islands' volcanic activities. Importantly, $10 million came to create the East-West Center for international education and training related to the US Department of State (Kamins and Potter, 1998, pp. 76–80).

The 1960s witnessed a huge expansion of the university due to student growth, development of professional schools, advances in graduate education, and increases in federal funding. By 1963, the university gained $3 million in geophysics federal grants from the National Science Foundation. Eight new centers for research in special science and medical areas also followed. Additional funding in many areas and new faculty recruitment with the addition of a Noble Prize winner in the sciences and a Pulitzer Prize winner in English moved the institution into the top 50 research universities in the United States (Yount, 1996, pp. 185–223). In the middle of this "Golden Era," the university experienced the rise of student protests over the denial of tenure to a faculty member and the beginning of anti–Vietnam War protests. These incidents forced the resignation of the president as student arrests ended the administrative building sit-ins. Nevertheless, in three years, enrollments reached 21,000, and it had garnered some $12 million in federal grant funding. The institution had achieved research university stature through these strategic efforts. Importantly, a new university system had been put in place to differentiate the need for higher education across the Hawaiian Islands, as described next (Kamins and Potter, 1998, pp. 82–90, 94–101, 320).

New campus leadership under President Harlan Cleveland continued the institution's dramatic growth during the next decade. In 1973, the two-year medical school was extended to offer four full years with internship training at community hospitals. The legislature augmented this expansion by doing the same for the law school. The following year, the College of Education further advanced doctoral education with the addition of PhD and EdD programs. Such boosterism came at a price, as a 14 percent fiscal retrenchment greeted the university for the 1973 fiscal year. Another president submitted his resignation, as complaints and difficulties arose (Kamins and Potter, 1998, pp. 102–116). Nevertheless, the institution advanced its research stature for the next 20 years until state finances brought a reassessment of public support for higher education.

Increasingly, political issues in the state capital influenced the university campus by the 1990s. A state economic downturn greeted the new president, Kenneth Mortimer, in 1995. He charged the university to refocus its energies on selective graduate programs rather than the exuberant plethora that had grown to 87 master's degree and 59 doctoral degree specializations for an institution of almost 20,000 students, 8,000 faculty, and 6,500 staff. Nevertheless, the flagship campus now has 20 collegiate units with significant specializations tied to the location, culture, and peoples of Hawaii. These include its School of Architecture, School of Hawaiian Knowledge, School of Ocean, Earth Science, and Technology, and School of Pacific and Asian Studies. In 2010, there were 37,000 students enrolled in the University of Hawaii system, with 25,000 of them at Manoa (Kamins and Potter, 1998, pp. 129, 321, 329; Yount, 1996, 106–110; University of Hawaii at Manoa, 2010).

The island geography of Hawaii presents challenges to the university system. The advent of information technologies has provided opportunities to transform the delivery of education throughout the state, including the use of public broadcasting, two-way video systems (known as the SkyBridge), public access television channels, and, later, the Hawaii Interactive Television System (HITS), which is a two-way, analog microwave video system using ITFS (Instructional Television Fixed Service) frequencies between all the campuses of the system. The advent of the World Wide Web and the development of learning management and collaboration tools increased access to students throughout the state. In January 2002, a new digital interactive video service, HITS2, replaced the older analog HITS and SkyBridge, to increase two-way video capabilities throughout the university system (Distance Learning at the University of Hawaii, 2011).

Technologies have provided opportunities for Hawaii's residents to access programs throughout the university system without the need for significant expansion of physical infrastructure. More than 50 credentials and degrees, in whole or in part, have been offered to residents using distance delivery technology (University of Hawaii, 2008). In fall 2008, 621 technology-assisted (excludes off-campus face-to-face) classes were delivered off-campus to students both in-state and out-of-state, a 29 percent increase from fall 2007. These classes accounted for 13,276 registrations. In particular, UH Manoa, as well as Hawaii, Kapiolani, and Leeward community colleges increased their technology-assisted offerings in all degrees.

As a result of its cultural and historic ties to the Pacific, the University of Hawaii has special responsibilities throughout this Pacific region that includes: American Samoa, Guam, the Commonwealth of the Northern Mariana Islands, the Compact Nations of Palau, the Federated States of Micronesia, and the Republic of the Marshall Islands. These obligations provide baccalaureate education in these more remote locations.

University of Hawaii Hilo and West Oahu Developments

After World War II, postsecondary instruction began on the Big Island at Hilo. Extension education enabled undergraduate education to begin there formally in 1947. The University of Hawaii Hilo branch campus grew during the 1950s, reaching approximately 250 students. In 1965, it functioned as an undergraduate center for the first two years due to expanding educational needs. By 1970, it became a full four-year university campus of 1,000 students with its own administrative chancellor and established its own Hawaii Community College. By 1985, Hilo offered a master's degree in Hawaiian language and literature. However, tension between the four-year and two-year institutions mounted and eventually led to a separation by July 1990, with the community college being governed by the University of Hawaii community college group. The growth of this 2,900-student campus was "tied to the scientific-technical programs," such as "astronomy to aquaculture, geophysics to scientific farming" with its new Research and Technology Park. During the following 15 years, the campus formed six collegiate units: the College of Agriculture, Forestry, and Natural Resource Management; the College of Arts and Sciences; the College of Business and Economics; the Ka Haka 'Ula O Ke'elikōlani (College of Hawaiian Language); the College of Continuing Education and Community Service; and the College of Pharmacy (University of Hawaii at Hilo, 2011). Finally, greater need for postsecondary education arose on the island's western side as the development of the new Kona Center campus demonstrated that it will become "a separate four-year college" in time (Inouye, 2001, pp. 243–250; Inouye and Kormondy, 2001, pp. 1–7, 30–31, 34–35; Kamins and Potter, 1998, pp. 249–250, 321).

The crowding at the University of Hawaii Manoa campus in 1973 led to the creation of another branch college for upper-division undergraduates on the leeward side of Oahu in 1976 by the legislature. Because of their similar missions, it was administered by the University of Hawaii Hilo campus chancellor. Problematic land deals stalled the development of an actual campus, which reached only approximately 750 students by 1995. Finally, the legislature passed and the governor approved a $100 million bond issue to build the campus (Boylan, 2001, pp. 252–258, 321; *Chronicle of Higher Education, Almanac, 2007–2008*, p. 51; Yount, 1996, pp. 181–184).

Private Higher Education

Within the state there are 5 four-year private colleges and universities and 5 for-profit institutions (4 four-year for-profit colleges and 1 two-year, for-profit college; see table 6.1). Enrollments at the three largest institutions range from approximately 2,000 to 9,000, mostly undergraduate students. Hawaii Pacific University, with its roots joined to the Christian Church, was established in 1965 and was enrolling approximately 10,184 bachelor's and master's students in 2010. Its seven collegiate units are: the colleges of liberal arts, natural sciences, business, international relations, communications, and professional studies, and school of nursing. It merged with Hawaii

Loa College, also an interdenominational postsecondary residential school on the western side of Oahu, in 1992 (Hawaii Pacific University). Founded by the Roman Catholic Church's Society of Mary, a religious community of priests and brothers, founded Chaminade University in 1955 in Honolulu. Chaminade enrolled 3,818 undergraduate and graduate students in the 2010 academic year. Finally, Brigham Young University-Hawaii, sponsored by the Mormon Church, began in 1955 in Honolulu and enrolled 3,494 undergraduate students in 2010. There is no relationship between these private institutions of higher learning and the state's public governance system.

Creating a State Governance System of Higher Education

At the University of Hawaii's founding, the legislature created a five-member Board of Regents to function as the governing board for the university, its later branch campuses, and the six community colleges. Such a governance structure was distinct in American higher education. Several stages led to this development. First, the legislature reorganized the Board of Regents in 1943, requiring "a member from each of the counties of Hawaii, Maui, and Kauai, plus eight others, including the UH president and superintendent of the territorial Department of Public Instruction" to offer representation from the major islands (Kamins and Potter, 1998, pp. 6, 50). In 1961, it studied the state's postsecondary needs beyond the university. The US Office of Education selected a higher education researcher from Pennsylvania State University's Center for the Study of Higher Education, S. V. "Marty" Martorana, a major researcher on community colleges, to conduct the study. His recommendation suggested that the university itself establish six community colleges. The creation of this system centered on raising public technical schools to community colleges and transferring their governance to the university. The preliminary report was augmented by the US Department of Health, Education, and Welfare, which recommended that the state develop a higher education system. The University of Hawaii at Manoa was to maintain upper division undergraduate studies and graduate education as the state's flagship institution but the system also retained University of Hawaii Hilo and community colleges. Such a structure enabled the state to deal with its postsecondary needs by creating a larger system administration (Kamins and Potter, 1998, p. 84). This process began in 1965 with legislative approval, was formalized in 1968, and was completed by 1972. Gradually, these community colleges functioned more as transfer branch campuses, as liberal arts general education grew proportionately greater than vocational education to the point that by the 1970s the majority of general education instruction occurred there (pp. 259–265, 270).

Recent Developments in Hawaiian Higher Education

Over the next two decades, the university's mission and governance structure were still directly welded to the 15-member Board of Regents, the state government, and the legislature. With the economic difficulties of the

1990s, the conditions worsened and state government intruded into university prerogatives. A referendum approved by voters in 2000 "supported constitutional autonomy for the University of Hawaii, ensuring the institution more control over its resources." It gave the administration more control over its internal structure, management, and operations. These developments led to a historic change in the executive administration of the university and the system as the flagship campus in Manoa installed its own campus chancellor. On the other hand, the ten-campus university now has a president with a Council of Chancellors of all the campuses and executive staff for the state higher education system reporting to this office (*Chronicle of Higher Education, Almanac, 2001–2002*, p. 51; Kamins and Potter, 1998, p. 85; Yount, 1996, pp. ix–xii, 111–145; University of Hawaii System, 2011). Subsequently, the return of significant state support to the University of Hawaii Oahu's campus from the legislature resulted in the building of "a new medical school and biomedical research facility" in Honolulu in 2003 (University of Hawaii System, 2011).

In November 2006, the citizens again sought to fix the governance structure of the university system by "depoliticiz[ing] how candidates for the University of Hawaii's Board of Regents are selected." They passed a constitutional amendment seeking to replace the traditional gubernatorial appointments process by creating an advisory board for these appointments, to create better representation of the islands, and to stipulate term limits. The legislature is to determine the new process (*Chronicle of Higher Education, Almanac, 2007–2008*, pp. 50–51).

Hawaii's higher education system has not been immune to the economic crisis felt by the rest of the United States. As seen in figure 6.4, Hawaii has had to make significant cuts to its state higher education budget even though it made good use of federal stimulus funds. Again, like the other

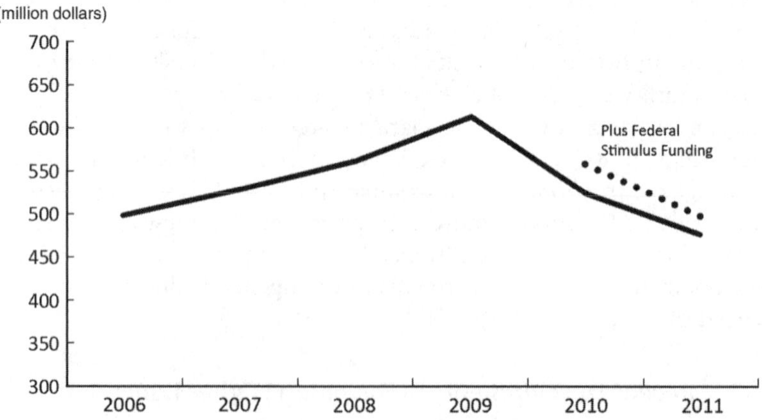

Figure 6.4 Real Hawaii state appropriations for higher education.

Source: Illinois State University's *Grapevine* Annual Survey. Calculations: Authors.

states discussed so far, the decline in Hawaii (11 percent from 2008 to 2011) outpaced the national average (7 percent) (Illinois State University, 2011). However, Hawaii experienced an unprecedented increase of 63.2 percent over 2005–2010 in tuition revenue per FTE student. This increase more than made up for the decline in state appropriations (SHEEO, 2010).

ALASKA

Alaska is a special place—a land of few people, profound cold, and vast distances. In Alaska's brief lifetime as a state, among those adventuresome spirits who called it home were pioneering educators who sought to bring to the people the knowledge and the rewards of learning. Alaskans, those born there and those who answered the call to relocate there, are a very special breed—tough, resilient, heroic. They confront the challenges of what might well be America's most harsh contemporary frontier.

High on the agenda of Alaskans is providing opportunities for learning to all people, including those in sparsely populated areas. At the forefront of decision making are the state legislators, who determine where and how the state's funds are spent. They approve funding for frontier education where teachers must have a burning desire to even commit some of their professional lives to teaching in "the bush." Juneau, the capital city, is located in lower southeast Alaska, where no highways link it to the rest of the state.

Alaska's overwhelming size and its majesty and grandeur are an open invitation to adventure. People in the "lower 48" think that Texas is big, but Alaska contains 586,412 square miles—a little more than two and one-third times the size of Texas. The state's geography is described by labeling its five regions. "Southcentral Alaska" is the southern coastal region and contains more than one-half of the state's population, including Anchorage and such towns as Wasilla, Eagle River, and Palmer. "The Alaska Panhandle," also known as "Southeast Alaska," is home to the state capital, Juneau—a landlocked town. "Southwest Alaska" is largely coastal, bordered by both the Pacific Ocean and Bering Sea. It is sparsely populated and is unconnected to the road system. The "Interior," the home of Fairbanks and the main campus of the University of Alaska, is renowned for large rivers, such as the Yukon and the Kuskokwim River, as well as Arctic tundra lands and shorelines. Finally, the "Northern/Arctic Region" is referred to in a variety of ways, including Northern Alaska or the Far North Region. Located above the Arctic Circle, it is the home of the Inupiat Eskimos. Herds of caribou inhabit the modern oil fields there. It also has the nation's northernmost community, Barrow, where from May to August the city sees 24 hours of daylight, and from November to January, a full 24 hours of twilight. Ilisagvik College is located in Barrow.

Following the American acquisition of Alaska, the land went through several administrative changes before becoming an organized territory on May 11, 1912. Forty-seven years later, on January 3, 1959, Alaska became the forty-ninth state. It has boroughs rather than counties. Its 16 boroughs do not include all land. Areas that are not part of any borough are referred to as the "Unorganized Boroughs."

Six years ago, Alaska had a population of more than 686,000 people. Some 89.7 percent speak English with 87 percent of its people being Caucasians, while the other 13 percent are natives like the pure Eskimos and Athapascans. Alaska has eight main Native groups: four Indian, two Eskimo, and two Aleut. Anchorage is the only city in Alaska with a population of 278,000. Three of the towns in the state have populations exceeding 10,000: College (the home of the University of Alaska located adjacent to Fairbanks), Fairbanks, and Juneau. Twenty-five other towns have populations between 1,000 and 10,000. Eighty-nine percent of the students who go on to pursue higher education come from within the state (*Chronicle of Higher Education, Almanac, 2008–2009*, p. 70).

Educational Challenges

In his novel *Alaska*, James Michener refers to an actual historical 1977 Molly Hootch trial before Alaska's Supreme Court. Because of this decision the state's remote areas have sufficient high schools with quality teachers (Michener, 1988, p. 744). The Molly Hootch case is second only to the Alaska Native Settlement Claims Act for its impact on the state. It dramatically changed how access to secondary education was provided to most of the state.

Sadly, because of the immense distance and sparse population, when the brightest native students from these remote villages finish the eighth grade and aspire to continue their education, they have to leave their families and go to a boarding school. To address the passion Alaskans have for education, the Alaska Department of Education and Early Development administers many school districts, including several boarding schools, such as Mt. Edgecumbe High School in Sitka, Nenana Student Living Center in Nenana, and Galena High School in Galena. Mt. Edgecumbe High School is often cited as an educational model for its success in developing educationally disadvantaged students from the "bush," 90 percent of whom go on to college. It was instituted on Japonski Island in 1947 in a deserted World War II airfield and administered by the US Bureau of Indian Affairs. Then, along with other state-administered boarding schools, it began to educate leaders from rural areas, many of whom went on to serve in the Alaska Legislature.

Alaskan Institutions of Higher Learning

In recording the beginning of higher education in the state, Neil Davis in *The College Hill Chronicles* (1992, p. 35) wrote: "Alaska has received an influx of persons who tend toward individualism. They like to think they are acting on their own." One of the great state leaders in education, James Wickersham, met in 1915 with three prominent Fairbanks citizens to pick a general location for a proposed college. Davis related:

> On the brow of a low hill overlooking the Tanana Valley, and with Mt. McKinley looming clearly on the southwest horizon, they found the place they were looking for. As they stood there in the sunshine and listened to a gentle breeze murmur through the open stands of aspen and birch, each knew this had to be the new school's location. (1992, p. 35)

Wickersham then steered the bill accepting the land grant through the Territorial Legislature. Governor J. F. A. Strong signed it on May 3, 1917, with deep reluctance. Many opponents shared his concern, believing that Alaska was too sparsely populated and too young to have a college and that Fairbanks was not a good location for the university. It became the founding date for the University of Alaska.

The new college was a reality, needing only the construction of a physical plant, students, and the hiring of the faculty and a president. The president turned out to be Charles E. Bunnell, a teacher, banker, lawyer, hotel manager, and the partner of a lumberyard and sheet metal works. Bunnell established a reputation for being a sound businessman with high principles and was strictly opposed to liquor, gambling, and prostitution. After entering politics and losing the election for the post of Alaska Territory Delegate to Congress in 1914, Bunnell became a federal judge.

Four years passed after the 1917 legislature accepted the land grant and Governor Strong had appointed the original Board of Trustees for the Alaska Agricultural College and School of Mines. In August 1921, the board finally appointed Bunnell as its first president, and the university opened to a half-dozen students. Bunnell served as the fledgling university's president for the next 27 years.

September 13, 1922, marked the dedication of the first classroom building on College Hill. A week later, on September 22, 1922, President Bunnell, six faculty members, and the six students walked the four miles from Fairbanks to College Hill to officially open the then Alaska Agricultural College and School of Mines. Bunnell taught classes and also performed other duties not normally associated with being a university president, including working in the boiler room shoveling ashes from the furnace.

The University of Alaska matured quickly after World War II. Because of Alaska's frontline position in relationship to the Soviet Union, the Cold War brought a continual flow of federal grants for research related to the university. However, as the university's first and only president entered his twenty-sixth year in office in 1948, the "Young Regents" spoke out against the "Old Guard." As reported by historian Davis,

> The Young Regents thought it was time for the university to improve its offerings enough to serve the entire territory, not just the Fairbanks area. By contrast, the Old Guard felt possessive of the university. They had been running the school for many years, quite successfully, they thought, and they saw no reason why anything should change. (1992, p. 217)

However, the Young Regents prevailed. In a stormy meeting in May 1948, Bunnell begrudgingly offered to resign. After much hostility and turmoil and delays in the search, Terris Moore assumed the presidency of the University of Alaska in July 1949. Bunnell was appointed president emeritus and refused to vacate his office or move from the home provided for the president and his family. Bunnell continued "on the job" until the day of his death on November 1, 1956, shortly before his seventy-eighth birthday. He and his many supporters believed that while governors come and go, when a good university president is found, people can expect him to serve the public for life (p. 217).

Much of the change in Alaska's higher education had been brought about by the advent of World War II. As early as 1935, far-sighted military leaders such as General Billy Mitchell proclaimed that Alaska could be of great strategic importance in a foreign war. This prophecy indeed fulfilled Alaska's role as a battlefield, a lend-lease transfer station, and a North Pacific stronghold that were keys to victory in the Pacific theater of war. The conflicts in the Aleutian Islands marked the only battles fought on American soil when the Japanese bombed Dutch Harbor six months after Pearl Harbor and occupied the islands of Attu and Kiska. Russian pilots trained in Fairbanks. Workers risked their lives building the Alaska Highway. After these few intensive war years, the lives of Alaskans changed forever, as the influx of workers and military came into the state's smallest communities. Further, new means of transportation and communication came in as US aircrafts were routed through Alaska and Siberia to Russia's battles with the Nazis.

Until 1942, passengers and freight arrived in Alaska by either boat or plane. However, the building of a 1,420-mile Alcan Highway through the Canadian and Alaskan wilderness plus a far-north construction boom that included telephone lines, oil pipelines, railways, and roughly 300 military bases opened up the continental northwest frontier.

Following World War II, Alaska gained the admiration of the other 49 states in that the state pays its citizens annual dividends from what is called the "Permanent Fund"—revenue derived from oil royalties and capital investment programs. Alaska is the *only* state in the union that has no income tax or sales tax.

University of Alaska Fairbanks

The University of Alaska Fairbanks (UAF) is considered to be the flagship campus of what has become the University of Alaska System. It is a land-grant, sea-grant, and space-grant institution. As a space-grant institution, it participates in 52 other programs nationally under the National Aeronautics and Space Administration (NASA) dedicated to furthering science and technology The university also participates in the sun-grant program, an association of five land-grant universities dedicated to furthering research on energy and agriculture (Washington NASA Space Grant Consortium,

2011). The university offers degrees in 16 PhD and 50 master's programs. Its doctoral programs are concentrated heavily in the sciences, for example, atmospheric sciences, environmental chemistry, geophysics, marine biology, oceanography, and space physics. UAF boasts seven major research units: the Agricultural and Forestry Experiment Station; the Geophysical Institute (which operates the Poker Flat Research Range); the international Arctic Research Centers; the Arctic Region Supercomputing Center; the Institute of Arctic Biology; the Institute of Marine Science; and the Institute of Northern Engineering. The Fairbanks campus, located 200 miles south of the Arctic Circle, is renowned for research in Arctic biology, Arctic engineering, geophysics, supercomputing, and aboriginal studies (University of Alaska-Fairbanks).

Student life in Fairbanks could be stressful. Harkening back to the 1950s, Davis again comments:

> Winter's cold and darkness depressed many (students), especially since the campus closed in on itself during those months. Few students had automobiles, and almost none of them ran in winter. The bus that rumbled into Fairbanks several times a day was the only way out of the conclave unless one wished to walk six miles to town or catch the rare train that ran past College Hill... More important was the unrelenting routine of classes, day after day, for eight months with only five days off (not including Sundays)—Thanksgiving Day, three days at Christmas, and New Year's Day... Registration for the second semester was the day after the first semester's final examinations, leaving no break between semesters at all. (1992, p. 297)

Nevertheless, University of Alaska Fairbanks' enrollment had reached approximately 16,000 students by 2010, 9 percent of whom were graduate students (IPEDS, 2011). Totally unique to higher education in the United States, the University of Alaska operates community college degree-granting programs within its institutional mission and structure. Each of main university campuses controls a number of internal community colleges. In addition, UAF also operated five rural and urban branch community college campuses: Chuchi, Kuskokwim, Northwest, Tanana Valley, and the UAF Community and Technical College in Fairbanks. The Fairbanks campus also is the home of the CUAF Center for Distance Education, an independent learning and distance delivery mechanism (University of Alaska-Fairbanks).

University of Alaska Anchorage

The city of Anchorage is 20 times larger than the cities of Fairbanks or Juneau. The University of Alaska Anchorage (UAA), with an enrollment of 28,000 students, has the largest student body in the University of Alaska System. UAA comprises eight colleges and schools: the College of Education, College of Health and Social Welfare, College of Arts and Sciences, College of Business and Public Policy, the Community and Technical College, School of Engineering, School of Nursing, and School of Social Work. Most popular undergraduate majors are elementary education, psychology, nursing, accounting, and business administration (University of Alaska Anchorage, *About UAA*, 2011). The university remains primarily a commuter campus without a significant research component. Its graduate programs are composed almost entirely of some 30 master's degrees. Two PhDs (biological sciences and clinical-community psychology) are offered in collaboration with University of Alaska Fairbanks; however, students must apply through the Fairbanks campus. Likewise, an MD is offered through the cooperative interstate WICHE Student Exchange Program, and the WWAMI (Washington, Wyoming, Alaska, Montana, and Idaho) medical education and internship program; however, students are admitted to the program through the University of Washington (University of Alaska-Anchorage, *Majors*, 2011). Internally, there are four community college campuses serving within the university, offering associate degrees that are affiliated with the University of Alaska Anchorage: Matanuska-Susitna College, Kenai Peninsula College, Kodiak College, and Chugiak-Eagle River College. In a more unusual higher education mission expansions, this institution has moved from being a community college to a small research university with several doctorates; yet these four community college degree-granting campuses were retained within the institution. What is now UAA opened in 1954 as Anchorage Community College (ACC) and began offering upper-division classes in 1969. It became the four-year University of Alaska Anchorage in 1976. The two-year, four-year, and rural extension units merged in 1987 to form the present institution (University of Alaska Anchorage, *University of Alaska Anchorage Campuses*, 2011).

University of Alaska Southeast

The third campus of the University of Alaska System is the University of Alaska Southeast (UAS). Established in Juneau, the state's capital, in 1972, UAS also has two community college campuses in Ketchikan and Sitka. With more than 6,000 students, it is organized with four colleges and/or schools: Arts and Sciences, Management, Career Education, and Education. It offers graduate degrees in business, education, and public administration (University of Alaska-Southeast, 2008).

Alaska's Higher Education Governance System

Reflecting the state's small population, the University of Alaska land-grant system is the second smallest in the country, surpassing only the state of Rhode Island. Over the years the University of Alaska expanded rapidly. The two community colleges were governed by the same Board of Regents as the four-year institutions, yet were administered separately under one or more chancellors until 1988.

Then, the issue went to a public vote at the instigation of the community college faculties and administrations who wanted to split away from the University of Alaska system and go under the jurisdiction of a separate governing board. There have been political differences as to how to deal with these governance problems and fiscal support for the institutions while providing equal educational opportunities to the citizens. One of Alaska's governors, for instance, proclaimed that being president of the University of Alaska was more important than being the governor. This confrontation, this internecine warfare, burst forth in the late 1980s when state leaders needed to decide if the community colleges would have their own board and local independence, or whether they would be part of the University of Alaska System as branches of the campuses in Fairbanks, Anchorage, and Juneau. The outcome was a Solomon-like decision—they ended up doing both.

In the fall of 1988 and spring of 1989, a series of town meetings were held around the state to discuss the very contentious proposal to reduce some of the autonomy of the local community colleges and move them administratively under one of the three regional University of Alaska campuses. The debate concluded with the legislature and the state coordinating board, formally urging the Board of Regents to consolidate the system. Subsequently, the board appointed three chancellors, one for each of the main campuses (namely, University of Alaska Fairbanks; University of Alaska Anchorage; and University of Alaska Southeast) and one for the community colleges. All of these chancellors reported to the statewide president at the Fairbanks campus. Thus, the state administers its system of higher education with two tiers of public colleges. One is the three universities in Fairbanks, Anchorage, and Juneau. The other is the community colleges, sometimes called junior colleges or technical institutes. These two-year community educational institutions provide postsecondary education and lower-level tertiary education.

In 2010, Alaska had seven colleges and universities. Accredited universities included the University of Alaska Anchorage, University of Alaska Fairbanks, and University of Alaska Southeast. There are two public independent community colleges, Prince William Sound Community College and Ilisagvik College, an Inupiaq tribal community college. Finally, there is one private university, the Alaska Pacific University in Fairbanks, and one for-profit postsecondary institution, Charter College, that operates in Wasilla, Alaska.

Recent Developments in Alaskan Higher Education

Alaskans have prided themselves in not paying state personal-income or sales taxes. The state derived most of its revenue from corporate income taxes and from taxes and royalties charged to oil and gas producers. When Alaska's energy industry was booming, the state always had plenty of money for the University of Alaska System and other public institutions. Over the past decade, however, a long-term decline in the state's oil industry has made it much harder to keep state government afloat.

In 2002, the University of Alaska System was credited with displaying a knack for survival. In a year when other states had difficulties with deficits, Alaska public universities secured both a modest budget increase and permission to expand. Even with the state facing a $1 billion budget gap, the universities were perceived to play a key role in revitalizing the state's economy; its legislators approved a 4 percent increase in the higher education budget. Further, in an effort to keep the best students at home, the legislature approved the student-loan programs for those who remained in the state to work after graduating.

In 2004, lawmakers unanimously voted to create a need-based aid program for students that would award about $450,000 annually to students entering fields with worker shortages, such as nursing and teaching. The awards were to be financed with a combination of federal funds and revenue taken in by the Alaska Student Loan Corporation. Anticipating increased future revenue because of a $1.4 billion surplus from oil prices, the legislature in 2006–2007 approved a $282.5 million (13.8%) increase in appropriations to the University of Alaska System. Another significant action that year was the approval of locating a community college in Barrow (Ilisagvik College). This institution in the northernmost city in the United States became Alaska's first federally recognized tribal college, entitling it to federal funds.

In 2007, with oil production on the decline and economists projecting long-term gaps in Alaska's budget, lawmakers in Juneau had major problems in addressing the University of Alaska System's budget request. It rejected pleas for a 9.3 percent increase and gave the system just 3.55 percent more than it had received the previous year. (While this was bad news for Alaska public higher education, in other states experiencing actual budget cuts, *any* increase would have seemed like a victory.)

Rising oil and natural-gas prices in 2008 led to an economic boom with public higher education receiving a 7 percent boost. Legislators also approved a fourfold increase ($48 million) in the university system's budget for deferred maintenance (*Chronicles of Higher Education, Almanac*, 2008). State support of higher education in Alaska has been relatively immune to the economic turmoil ravaging the rest of the nation for the past four years. In fact, from 2006 to 2011, higher education in Alaska received a 22 percent increase in state appropriations (see figure 6.5; Illinois State University, 2011). Two primary reasons for Alaska's ability to continue to increase support of higher education despite the national economic decline are its exceptionally high tax rate on the revenue generated by its oil wealth. Despite Alaska's continued state support of higher education in the form of increased state appropriations, the state also increased tuition revenue per FTE by 25.4 percent from 2005 to 2010 (SHEEO, 2011).

Higher education thus holds a special place in the minds of Alaskans, as evidenced by the fact that 43 percent of the population attends, or has attended, college. One high point in the development of Alaska's higher education in the 1970s was when the legislature approved an education loan

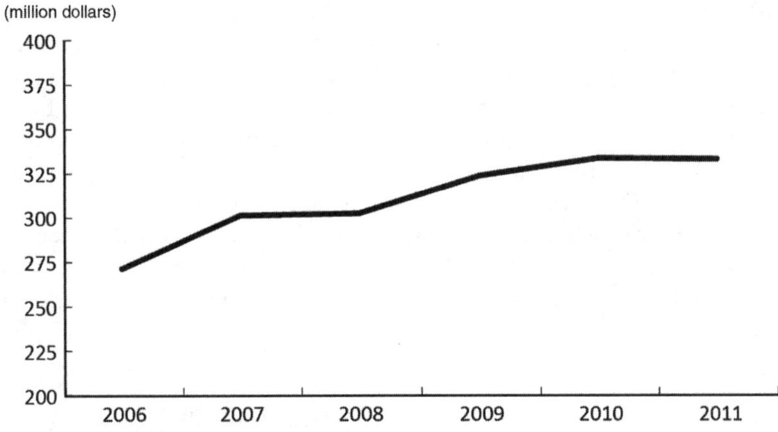

Figure 6.5 Real Alaska state appropriations for higher education.
Source: Illinois State University's *Grapevine* Annual Survey. Calculations: Authors.

forgiveness program for graduates of any institution who continued to work in Alaska. Another milestone occurred when the state offset its limited ability to offer a wide range of programs by becoming involved in the WICHE and WAMI (subsequently WWAMI) western regional programs, as noted earlier in this chapter (University of Alaska).

The first decade of the twenty-first century reflected Alaska's commitment to funding higher education on a level that would acknowledge and proclaim its pride and confidence in the university system's many contributions to the advancement and well-being of the state. While Alaskans supported quality education on all levels, they still worry about "brain drain." Many of its best students leave the state after high school graduation and fail to return. The University of Alaska tried to combat this through an "Alaska Scholars Program," in which the university offers four-year scholarships to the top 10 percent of the state's high school graduates if they enroll as freshmen in an Alaska university. Truly, Alaska is a place of hope and adventure, where people believe that learning is a wise investment for the student and for the state.

Comparative State and Contemporary Issues

Like much of the rest of the country, Washington, Oregon, Hawaii, and Alaska have experienced recently a slowdown in the annual growth rate of high school graduates. While higher education institutions have long experienced heavy enrollment demands, this is no longer the case now and for the foreseeable future as figures 6.6 and 6.7 reveal. The projected change in the number of high school graduates in each of the states is dramatic. However, it is most pronounced in Washington and Alaska, where the difference between the percent changes from 1992 to 2007 compared to 2008 to 2022 is 49.4 and 65.9 percent, respectively. In Alaska, if the projections hold true, the situation will quickly become dire, as the state continues to face difficulties in attracting and retaining younger families and working professionals. In each state, colleges and universities are going to have to adjust to lower demand among high school graduates and a different age profile among the students.

In the face of statistics predicting significantly reduced high school graduates, the "education pipeline" as a whole needs to be examined. When comparing the Pacific West states to the rest of the nation, it becomes clear that in moving further down the educational pipeline these states do relatively worse

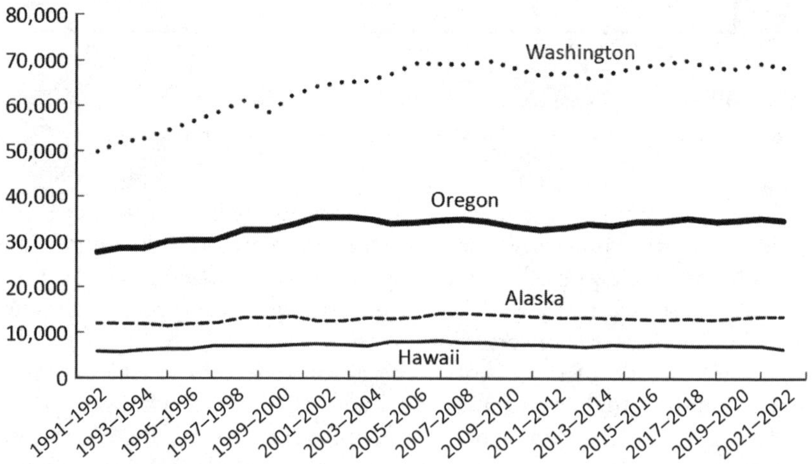

Figure 6.6 High school graduates, 1991–1992 through 2004–2005 (actual); 2005–2006 through 2021–2022 (projected).

Source: WICHE, 2009. Calculations: Authors.

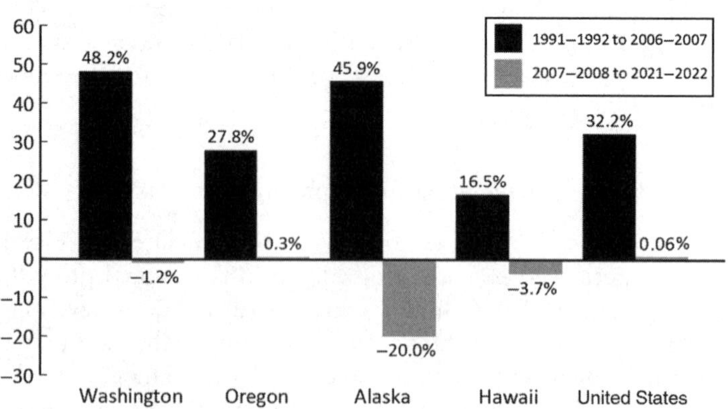

Figure 6.7 High school graduates (real and projected); percent change from 1991–1992 to 2006–2007 and from 2007–2008 to 2021–2022.

Source: WICHE, 2009. Calculations: Authors.

(see figures 6.8 and 6.9). These statistics compound the issues presented by a significant reduction in high school graduates. The situation worsens again for Alaska, which is not only faced with dramatic reductions in high school graduates but also confronted by a significant number of students, some

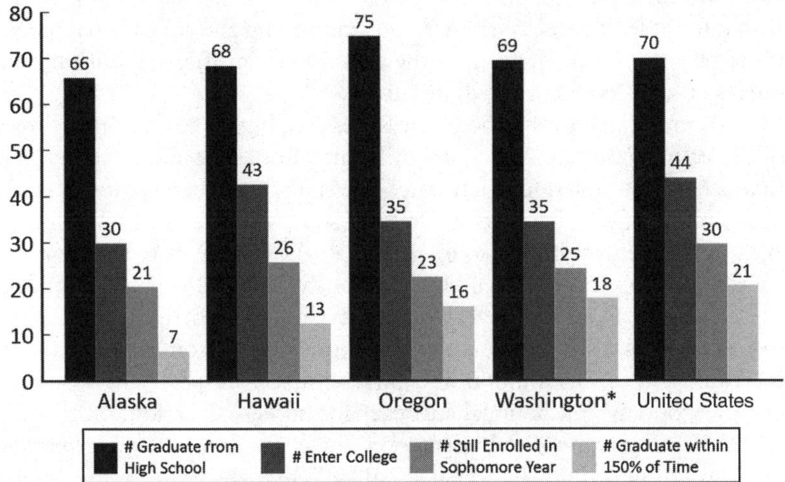

Figure 6.8 For every 100 ninth grade students the number who graduate high school directly enter college, are still enrolled in their sophomore year, and graduate within 150 percent of program time.

Note: *Washington reports their data on entering first-time students differently from the rest of the nation. While the US Department of Education instructs institutions and states to report all first-time students including dually admitted and other early entrant and fast-track students, Washington does not include these students and, therefore, their numbers for students who go directly to college are artificially low in comparison to the other states.

Source: NCHEMS. Calculations: Authors.

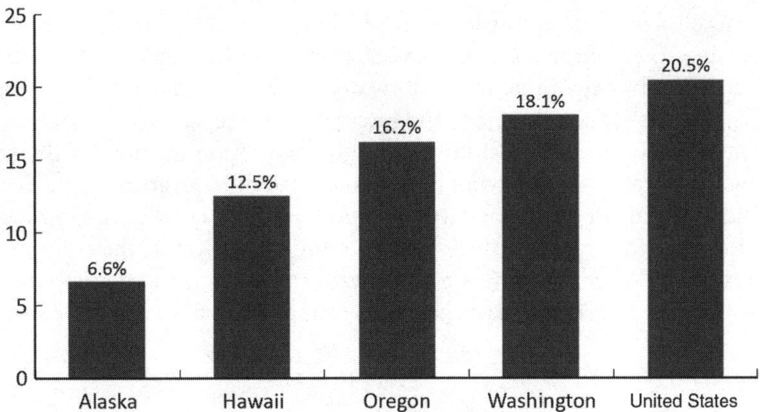

Figure 6.9 Percentage of ninth graders who graduate from high school on time, go directly to college, return for their second year, and graduate within 150 percent of program time.

Source: NCHEMS. Calculations: Authors.

66 percent, not graduating from their colleges and universities in a timely manner, if at all—resulting in only 6.6 percent of the state's high school graduates actually finishing college. If the Pacific West States are going to succeed in the future, their leaders must think creatively and develop ways to attract, retain, and graduate larger numbers of students, many of whom represent nontraditional students and those from underserved populations. In addition, for at least three of these states, improving the educational pipeline needs to be accomplished, without the promise of significant additional state resources at least for the immediate future.

Most dramatically during the Great Recession, higher education in three of the four Pacific West states suffered significantly from state budgetary retrenchments, as has been noted for each state. The state comparisons show a marked decline overall of –19 percent in Oregon, somewhat less so in Washington with its –16 percent, and least so in Hawaii at –11 percent state funding drops (Illinois State University, 2011). Only Arizona with its –28.27 percent decline fared worse in the 15-state WICHE region (as Cohen notes, this volume, p. 64). Fortunately, federal stimulus monies eased this decline somewhat in Oregon and Hawaii with $38.9 million and $22.1 million, respectively. Because of its energy economy and political advocacy for higher education, on the other hand, Alaska augmented its budget over these fiscal years by a remarkable 22 percent (Illinois State University, 2011). While the State of Washington has a significant political culture and history for supporting higher education and may return to its more supportive funding for its public universities and colleges, difficulties undoubtedly will continue in Oregon and Hawaii, as difficulties remain structurally endemic to these states' economies.

CONCLUSION

Higher education in the Pacific West dramatically demonstrates the determination to offer high-quality undergraduate, graduate, and professional education wherever there is adequate need. State universities and colleges, seeking to enlarge their research mission stature, along with community colleges and private and for-profit institutions have responded to demands for postsecondary education by expanding to meet greater teaching needs of its populations, the betterment of the subregion, and research and defense needs of the nation. Recent downturns in state funding of higher education in three of the states during the Great Recession point to a possible major reassessment of public support and funding of postsecondary education. Future higher education success is possible if the citizens of these states continue to invest in the colleges and universities of Washington, Oregon, Hawaii, and Alaska, and develop innovative solutions to the significant challenges facing them now and in the future.

NOTE

*The authors would like to thank Bill Chance, John Richardson, and Kerry Romeburg as well as Paul Stonecipher, a doctoral student in higher education at Florida State University, for his invaluable research and editorial assistance.

REFERENCES

Abbott, F. C. *A History of the Western Interstate Commission for Higher Education: The First Forty Years.* Boulder, CO: Western Interstate Commission for Higher Education, 2004.

Boylan, D. B. "The University of Hawai'i—West O'ahu." In F. T. Inouye and E. J. Kormody (Eds.), *The University of Hawai'i-Hilo: A College in the Making.* Honolulu: University of Hawaii Press, 2001.

Brown, R. List of Colleges and Universities that Have Closed, Merged, or Changed Their Names. Retrieved from http://www2.westminster-mo.edu/wc_users/homepages/staff/brownr/closedcollegeindex.htm, n.d., on November 2, 2011.

Castle, E. N., C.W. Howland, and J. G. Knudsen, *Report to the President of Oregon State University from the Commission on University Goals.* Corvallis: Oregon State University, 1970.

Chance, W., P. M. Anet, and K. Pailthorp. *Planning and Policy Recommendations for Washington Postsecondary Education, 1976–1982.* Olympia, WA: Council for Postsecondary Education, 1976.

Chronicle of Higher Education. *Almanacs,* 2001, 2002, 2003, 2004, 2005, 2006, 2007, 2008, 2011.

College of Agricultural, Human and Natural Resource Sciences, Washington State University. *College History—Focusing on History of Graduate Education.* Retrieved from cahnrs.wsu.edu/overview/cahnrs-history.pdf, n.d., on November 2, 2011.

Davis, N. *The College Hill Chronicles.* Fairbanks: University of Alaska Foundation, 1992.

Delta Cost Project. Data, 2010. Retrieved from http://deltacostproject.org/data/index. asp., on December 10, 2011.

Distance Learning at the University of Hawaii. *What Is Distance Learning?* Retrieved from http://www.hawaii.edu/dl/general/, 2011, on November 2, 2011.

Eastern Oregon State University. *EOU Regional Centers.* Retrieved from http://www. eou.edu/advising/regional.html, n.d., on November 2, 2011.

Everett Community College. Fact Book. 2010. Retrieved from www.everettcc.edu., on November 2, 2011.

Evergreen State College. *Our National Reputation and Praise.* Retrieved from http://www.evergreen.edu/about/praise.htm, 2010, on November 2, 2011.

Fain, P. Faculty Fears in Washington, October 17, 2011. Inside Higher Ed. Retrieved from http://www.insidehighered.com/news/2011/10/17/financial_emergency_in_washington_state_ could_lead_to_layoffs_of_tenured_faculty. on December 10, 2011.

Friedman, D. "Chancellor Debra Friedman Talks with Staff and Students." Video file. Retrieved August, 31, 2011, from http://www.youtube.com/watch?v=lJySShllsWw.

Gates, C. M. *The First Century at the University of Washington, 1861–1961.* Seattle: University of Washington Press, 1961.

Hammond, B. "Oregon to Seek Powerful 'Chief Education Officer' to Revamp Preschool, Public Schools, College." *Oregonian.* December 1, 2011.

Hawaii Pacific University. Retrieved from http://www.hpu.edu/, n.d., on November 2, 2011.

Hine, R. V., and J. M. Faragher. *The American West: A New Interpretive History.* Yale, CT: Yale University Press, 2000.

Illinois State University. *Grapevine Reports*, 2011. Retrieved from http://grapevine.illinoisstate.edu/, on December 10, 2011.

Inouye, F. T. "The University of Hawai'i at Hilo." In F. T. Inouye and E. J. Kormody (eds.), *The University of Hawai'i-Hilo: A College in the Making*. Honolulu: University of Hawaii Press, 2001.

Inouye, F. T., and E. J. Kormody. *The University of Hawai'i-Hilo: A College in the Making*. Honolulu: University of Hawaii Press, 2001.

Institute for Sustainable Solutions, Portland State University. *Institute for Sustainable Solutions at Portland State University*. Retrieved from http://www.pdx.edu/sustainability/sustainabilityresearch, 2011, on November 2, 2011.

Integrated Postsecondary Education Data System (IPEDS). *Peer Analysis System*. Retrieved from http://nces.ed.gov/ipeds/datacenter/, 2011, on December 10, 2011.

Jones, J. P. *The History of the Development of the Present Campus Plan for the University of Washington*. Published privately, 1940 [n.p.].

Kamins, R. M., R. E. Potter, and Associates. *Malamalama: A History of the University of Hawai'i*. Honolulu: University of Hawaii Press, 1998.

Keller, J. "Public Colleges, a Historic Strength of the Pacific West, Are Weakened." *Chronicle of Higher Education*, August 22, 2010.

Limerick, P. N., C. A. Milner II, and C. E. Rankin (eds.). *Trails: Toward a New Western History*. Lawrence: University of Kansas Press, 1991.

Michener, J. *Alaska*. New York: Random House, 1988.

National Center for Education Statistics. Retrieved from http://nces.ed.gov, 2011, on December 10, 2011.

National Oceanic and Atmospheric Administration. *Sea Grant Overview: Science Serving America's Coasts*. Retrieved from http://www.seagrant.noaa.gov/aboutsg/index.html, 2011, on November 2, 2011.

National Science Foundation. Academic R&D Expenditures. Retrieved from http: // www.nsf.gov/statistics/rdexpenditures/,2011, on December 10, 2011.

Neill, T. *Incidents in the Early History of Pullman and the State College of Washington*. Fairfield, WA: Ye Galleon Press, 1977. (Originally published in 1889)

Nugent, W. *Into the West: The Story of Its Peoples*. New York: Knopf, 1999.

Odegaard, C. E. *The University of Washington: Pioneering in Its First and Second Century*. New York: Newcomen Society in North America, 1964.

Office for Research, Innovation and Graduate Education, University of Oregon. *Fast Facts*. Retrieved from http://research.uoregon.edu/content/fast-facts#GraduateSchool, n.d., on November 2, 2011.

Office of Institutional Research, University of Oregon. *University Profile*. Retrieved from http://ir.uoregon.edu/profile, 2010, on November 2, 2011.

Office of the Chancellor. *Oregon University System Fact Book, 2002, 2004, 2008, 2009*. Oregon State System of Higher Education.

Oregon Health and Science University. *About*. Retrieved from http://www.ohsu.edu/xd/about/facts/index.cfm, n.d., on November 2, 2011.

Oregon Institute of Technology. Retrieved from http://www.oit.edu/, 2011, on November 2, 2011.

Oregon State University. *About*. Retrieved from http://oregonstate.edu/main/about, n.d., on November 2, 2011.

Oregon University System. *Fall Headcount, Actual and Projected, 1994–2013*. Retrieved from http://www.ous.edu/sites/default/files/factreport/enroll/files/enrdmnd.pdf, 2004, on November 2, 2011.

Oregon University System. *OUS History.* Retrieved from http://www.ous.edu/about/ chanoff/ous-history, 2010, on November 2, 2011.

Oregon University System and Global Business Network. "A Plan to 2025 for the Oregon University System." Office of the Chancellor Emeritus, Oregon State System of Higher Education. March, 2007.

Pemberton, H. E. "Early Colleges in Oregon." *Oregon Historical Quarterly*, 1932, *33* (3), 230–242.

Perna, L., J. Finney, and P. Callan. State Policy Leadership Vacuum: Performance and Policy in Washington Higher Education. Philadelphia, Institute for Research on Higher Education, 2012 Portland State University. Retrieved from www.pdx.edu, 2011, on November 2, 2011.

Portland State University. *Profile.* Retrieved from http://www.pdx.edu/profile/snapshot-portland-state, 2011, on November 2, 2011.

Princeton Review. *The 376 Best Colleges.* Retrieved from http://www.princetonreview.com/college-rankings.aspx, 2011, on November 2, 2011.

Sanders, J. *Cold War on the Campus: Academic Freedom at the University of Washington, 1946–64.* Seattle: University of Washington Press, 1979.

———. *Into the Second Century: The University of Washington, 1961–1986.* Seattle: University of Washington Press, 1987.

School of Social Work, University of Hawai'i System. *SSW Historical Background.* Retrieved from http://hawaii.edu/sswork/history.html, 2010, on November 2, 2011.

Schrecker, E. W. *No Ivory Tower: McCarthyism and the Universities.* New York: Oxford University Press, 1986.

Southern Oregon University. *Ashland Center for Theatre Studies.* Retrieved from http://www.sou.edu/acts/, n.d., on November 2, 2011.

State Higher Education Executive Officers (SHEEO). *State Higher Education Finance Report, 2011.* Retrieved from http://www.sheeo.org/finance/shef-home.htm, on December 2011.

University of Alaska. Retrieved from www.alaska.edu, n.d., on November 2, 2011.

University of Alaska-Anchorage. *About UAA.* Retrieved from http://www.uaa.alaska.edu/futurestudents/about_uaa.cfm, 2011, on November 2, 2011.

———. *Majors.* Retrieved from http://curric.uaa.alaska.edu/admreg/Majors.htm, 2011, on November 2, 2011.

———. *University of Alaska Anchorage Campuses.* Retrieved from http://www.uaa.alaska.edu/campuses/index.cfm, 2011, on November 2, 2011.

University of Alaska-Fairbanks. Retrieved from http://www.uaf.edu/, n.d., on November 2, 2011.

University of Alaska-Southeast. *Academic Programs.* Retrieved from http://www.uas.alaska.edu/future/graduate/learn/index.html, 2008, on November 2, 2011.

University of Hawaii. *Measuring Our Progress Report 2008.* Retrieved from http://www.hawaii.edu/ovppp/mop/mop08_webaccesible.html, 2008, on November 2, 2011.

University of Hawaii at Hilo. *Academics.* Retrieved from http://hilo.hawaii.edu/academics/, 2011, on November 2, 2011.

University of Hawaii at Manoa. *Academics.* Retrieved from http://www.uhm.hawaii.edu/academics/, 2010, on November 2, 2011.

University of Hawaii System. *History of the University of Hawai'i System.* Retrieved from http://hawaii.edu/about/history.html, 2011, on November 2, 2011.

University of Oregon. *University of Oregon Raises Record $853 Million in Campaign Oregon.* Retrieved from http://uonews.uoregon.edu/archive/news-release/2009/2/university-oregonraises-record-853-million-campaign-oregon, January 30, 2008, on November 2, 2011.

———. *UO-Eclips, Jan. 30.* Retrieved from http://uonews.uoregon.edu/archive/uo-news/2009/january/uo-e-clips-jan-30, January 30, 2009, on November 2, 2011.

University of Oregon. Retrieved from http://www.uoregon.edu/, on December 1, 2011.

University of Washington. *Board of Regents.* Retrieved from http://www.washington.edu/regents/, 2011, on November 2, 2011.

———. *Efficiency and Effectiveness 2003–2008.* Retrieved from http://www.washington.edu/staterelations/?staterelations=UW_Efficiency_Effectiveness.pdf, 2009, on November 2, 2011.

———. *Planning and Budgeting Brief.* Retrieved from http://www. washington.edu/admin/pb/home/pdf/briefs/archive/UW-Academically-Elite-Not-Economically-Selective. pdf, 2009, on November 2, 2011.

———. *Timeline.* Retrieved from http://www.washington.edu/150/timeline/. n.d., on November 2, 2011.

———. *Vision and Values.* Retrieved from http://www. washington.edu/discover/visionvalues. 2011, on November 2, 2011.

University of Washington Bothell. History. Retrieved from http://www.bothell.washington.edu/ about/history, on December 21, 2011.

University of Washington Tacoma. About UW Tacoma. Retrieved from http://www.tacoma. uw.edu/about-uw-tacoma, on December 21, 2011.

University Studies Program, Portland State University. *UNST Introduction.* Retrieved from http://www.pdx.edu/unst/unst-introduction, 2011, on November 2, 2011.

Von Bargen, M. "College of Agricultural, Human and Natural Resource Sciences: College History, Focusing on History of Graduate Education, 1893–2002," Washington State University, 2008. Retrieved from http://cahnrs.wsu.edu/overivew/cahnrs-history.pdf, on May 23, 2009.

Washington Higher Education Coordinating Board. *2008 Strategic Master Plan for Higher Education in Washington.* Retrieved from http://www.hecb.wa.gov/publicationslibrary/master-plans, 2007, on May 23, 2009.

Washington Higher Education Coordinating Board. Retrieved from http://www.hecb.wa.gov/, 2011, on November 2, 2011.

Washington NASA Space Grant Consortium. *About WSGC.* Retrieved from http:// www.waspacegrant.org/about_wsgc/, 2011, on November 2, 2011.

Washington State Board for Community and Technical Colleges. Research and Data, 2011. Retrieved from http://www.sbctc.edu/college/d_index.aspx, on December 21, 2011.

Washington State University. *History.* Retrieved from http://about.wsu.edu/about/ history.aspx, 2011, on November 2, 2011.

———. *Quick Facts.* Retrieved from http://about.wsu.edu/ about/facts.aspx, 2011, on November 2, 2011.

Western Oregon State University. *Teaching Research Institute.* Retrieved from http:// www.wou.edu/tri/, n.d., on November 2, 2011.

Whatcom County Historical Society. The History of Western Washington University. Retrieved from http://whatcomhistory.wordpress.com/2011/03/10/the-history-of-western-washington-university/, 2011, on November 2, 2011.

Willamette University. *History of Willamette.* Retrieved from http://www.willamette.edu/about/history/index.html, n.d., on November 2, 2011.

Yount, D. *Who Runs the University: The Politics of Higher Education in Hawaii, 1985–1992*. Honolulu: University of Hawaii Press, 1996.

7

Higher Education in California: Rise and Fall

Patrick M. Callan

Introduction

Higher education in California was one of America's great public policy and educational success stories in the second half of the twentieth century. The post–World War II era introduced several decades of robust population expansion, and California led the nation—and indeed the world—as it achieved almost phenomenal growth of college opportunity. Sharp increases in student enrollments and campuses were paralleled by the rising quality and reputation of the state's public and private colleges and universities, of its advanced research, and of higher education's support of a vibrant state economy.

California's private colleges and universities have made vital contributions to the state throughout its history and they continue to do so. The principal story of the postwar era, however, derives from the growth of the nation's largest array of public colleges and universities of all kinds—research universities, regional state colleges and universities, and community colleges. This expansion reflected national trends at the time, but California was unique in its commitment to access and in the influence and continuity of a core public policy framework that was articulated in the 1960 *A Master Plan for Higher Education, in California, 1960–1975* (California State Department of Education, 1960). The Master Plan's early successes in expanding college access created momentum that was sustained for decades. Yet despite the remarkable durability of this venerable framework, the Master Plan's relevance and utility have become problematic as California confronts the impact of educational, economic, and demographic change.

Two convergent themes are central to the modern history of California higher education: the public policy framework that enabled and supported broad college opportunity for most of the post–World War II era and the expansion of access through a massive and diverse array of colleges and universities. In the following pages, I will describe these themes and then turn to three changing conditions facing higher education that have emerged over the past three decades:

1. unstable, constrained public finance combined with political volatility;
2. demographic shifts; and
3. a decline in the effectiveness of public schooling.

A concluding section draws these themes and conditions together, while presenting several challenges confronting California in the first decade of this century.

THE STRUGGLE FOR POLICY-DRIVEN GROWTH

In virtually all states, veterans benefiting from the G.I. Bill after World War II created public pressure to expand the enrollment capacity of colleges and universities.[1] This pressure intensified in California in the late 1950s as population growth accelerated, and the first "tidal wave" of baby boomers approached college age. In 1960, the state responded by creating a 15-year Master Plan for Higher Education. The plan, the values and policies it reflected, and the growth that it envisioned are the context for the questions and challenges that confront higher education in California 50 years later.

During the three decades after World War II, California did not differ from most other large states in seeking to plan and support enrollment growth of higher education. In fact, these issues became the dominant public policy themes for higher education in this era. California distinguished itself, however, through its path-breaking commitment to higher education opportunity, through the size and scale of its higher education systems, and through its development of the Master Plan, the state's comprehensive policy framework to expand capacity and manage growth.

Whether higher education in California would expand was never at issue during this period. What was perceived as problematic, however, was the extent to which conflicts among local, institutional, and political interests would impede realization of an overarching policy goal: universal educational opportunity through planned and coordinated growth. Efforts to address these conflicts trace back at least to the Depression Era. In 1932, a legislatively commissioned study conducted by the Carnegie Foundation for the Advancement of Teaching found that problems of policy and organization in higher education had resulted in overlapping functions, waste, and inefficiency; lack of unified policy; and inequitable distribution of state funds. In addition, the study found: "There is a lack of articulation among the various units of the educational system. This has resulted in vigorous controversies over admission requirements, transfer regulations, and curricula. These controversies are aggravated by regional rivalries and local ambitions" (Carnegie Foundation for the Advancement of Teaching, 1932, p. 16).

The problems identified by the Carnegie report persisted despite the legislature's creation of an advisory and ineffectual State Council for

Educational Planning and Coordination. In 1945, a joint committee called the Liaison Committee was formed by the State Board of Education (SBOE) (which at that time had statewide jurisdiction over junior colleges and state colleges) and by the University of California (the University). The Liaison Committee was a voluntary effort to manage campus growth and program expansion and to deter legislatively imposed coordination. The principal policy vehicles of the Liaison Committee were ad hoc studies commissioned by it and the legislature, studies that addressed such issues as the degree-granting authority of junior colleges, state colleges, and the University; admissions standards; the needs and locations for new campuses; and the necessity and requisites of a state scholarship program (Douglass, 2000, pp. 170–197).

In the absence of an overarching policy framework, the legislature could implement, ignore, or even augment the smorgasbord of recommendations presented by these studies—and it did all of these. For example, at the urging, principally, of the Santa Barbara Chamber of Commerce and despite initial opposition by the University, the state college at Santa Barbara was transferred to the University in 1943. (In 1946, a state ballot proposition was enacted prohibiting such transfers in the future.) New state college campuses were authorized in 1946 at Los Angeles and Sacramento, in 1948 at Long Beach, and in the late 1950s at Fullerton, Hayward, Northridge, and Stanislaus County. The University of California added medical and engineering schools at its Los Angeles campus and colleges of letters and sciences at its Davis and Riverside campuses. In 1955, the legislature established the first state scholarship program.

By the late 1950s, the lack of what the Carnegie report had termed "unified policy" had created a planning vacuum in which initiatives and aspirations for growth and change were scattered widely across communities and institutions, and ultimately were controlled by the legislature and the governor. The "problems of policy and organization" found in the 1932 report had not only persisted but had also been exacerbated by the G.I. Bill, the increase in birth rates after World War II, and in-migration. In the 1957 legislative session, the scramble for new campuses intensified: bills authorizing 17 new state colleges were considered and four bills were approved; none of the four had been on the list of priorities recommended in the Liaison Committee's 1957 planning report. Several were placed in sparsely populated areas represented by powerful state legislators.

Academics and politicians alike recognized that reform was needed to bring order to chaos and uncertainty. Clark Kerr, who had assumed the presidency of the University of California in 1957, took the initiative. In 1959, Assemblywoman Dorothy Donahoe, at his encouragement, introduced a resolution calling on the Liaison Committee to prepare a master plan for higher education and to present it to the legislature at the beginning of the 1960 session. It also called for a two-year moratorium on legislation affecting higher education. The resolution was adopted by both the Assembly and the Senate.

The major concerns of the educational leaders who initiated and then wrote the Master Plan were immediate ones. In his memoir of this period, Clark Kerr reflected:

> The plan looked to us who participated in its development more like a desperate attempt to prepare for a tidal wave of students, to escape state legislative domination, and to contain escalating warfare among its separate segments...And the preparation, the escape and the containment in each case was barely on time and barely succeeded. The Master Plan was a product of stark necessity, of political calculations, and of pragmatic transactions. (2001, p. 12)

Eight months after the adoption of the resolution, a proposed Master Plan was presented to the legislature, and its major provisions were enacted into statute. It became the state policy structure that resolved the immediate challenges to higher education. Reaffirmed many times, the Master Plan remained in place long after the emergency described by Kerr had passed. Each sector of California higher education gained immediate benefits:

- The junior colleges (subsequently designated "community colleges") gained acceptance as an integral part of higher education and were given the largest mandate for expansion.
- The state colleges, which ultimately became the California State University (the State University), were removed from the public school system and were given degree-granting authority through the master's level as well as an independent governing board.
- The organization of the University of California was not affected, but its monopoly on state-funded, advanced graduate and professional programs and research was confirmed.
- The legislature was relieved of the increasingly controversial political pressures for new campuses by delegating initial approval of these decisions to a new coordinating council.

Rarely do all parties to a negotiated plan achieve not only their own individual goals, but, in so doing, benefit the overarching public interest—as reflected in this case in greater college opportunity and controlled institutional competition. The Master Plan framers were able to accomplish this feat because they advanced institutional aspirations in the context of a common policy goal: the commitment that every California high school graduate who was able to benefit from college could attend a college or university. California became the first state or, indeed, governmental entity to establish this principle of universal access as public policy (Condren, 2007, p. 261; Rothblatt, 2007, p. 261). It was this principle that made the Master Plan a major innovation in social as well as educational policy. Its specific provisions established an organizational and policy framework for meeting the state's commitment to access and for balancing what Kerr later characterized as the egalitarian and meritocratic imperatives (Kerr, 1992, pp. 55–57).

The organizational provisions of the Master Plan were straightforward. College opportunity would be provided by grouping public colleges into three statewide "systems" organized according to their missions, each with designated enrollment pools. The junior colleges would offer instruction up to the fourteenth grade level and would include courses for transfer to baccalaureate-granting institutions as well as vocational and technical programs. These colleges would be open to all Californians who were capable of benefiting from attendance. The state colleges, now the California State University, would offer undergraduate education and graduate programs through the master's degree and could participate in joint doctoral degree programs with the University of California. Students were to be admitted from the top one-third of high school graduates. The University was to draw its students from the top one-eighth of California high school graduates. Within public higher education, the University was to have sole authority to offer doctoral degrees (except for joint doctoral programs offered with the state colleges), as well as professional degrees in medicine, law, dentistry, and veterinary medicine. The University was also designated the state's primary agency for state-supported academic research. Selective admissions at the state colleges and the University restricted the growth of four-year institutions, and this meant that most students would enroll, at least initially, in junior colleges. Californians who enrolled in junior colleges for academic or financial reasons could qualify for transfer to a state college or University campus after two years, and all qualified students were to be accepted. These provisions for transfer, along with the promise of college access to all who could benefit from it, connected and balanced the egalitarian and meritocratic dimensions of the plan.

The Master Plan recommended and the legislature established a governing board for state colleges, separating those institutions from the State Board of Education. To replace the Liaison Committee, a state board to coordinate higher education was created by statute. This new board was made up of representatives of the public systems of higher education and the private non-profit colleges and universities. The legislature expressed in statute its intention to establish new campuses only upon recommendation from this board. The state scholarship program for eligible undergraduates in public and private institutions was expanded. This program served the dual function of providing students with the option of attending private colleges and universities and enabling the private institutions to absorb a portion of the projected enrollment growth. Public higher education was to be low-priced, and California residents were not to be charged tuition, reflecting the state's commitment to access.

The Master Plan pioneered the concept of universal access to education and training beyond high school. It was also unique in establishing mission differentiation as the basis of organization and governance for all of the state's public colleges and universities, including the explicit delineation of eligibility criteria for admission to each of the three public systems. The plan sought to recognize, balance, and institutionalize the values of competitive excellence and egalitarianism, selectivity and open admissions, and growth and efficiency. Costs were controlled through constraints on the mission and enrollment in each of the three public sectors and through concentration of growth in the community colleges. In short, the plan constituted the policy and organizational framework for both the expansion of college opportunity and for the University's high national and international ranking.

Since the Master Plan's adoption in 1960, formal revisions to its framework have included the creation of a statewide Board of Governors for community colleges in 1967; the transformation of the statewide coordinating board into the California Postsecondary Education Commission (CPEC) in 1973 and its elimination in 2011; the imposition of student charges (still not called "tuition") in all three public sectors; and the legislative authorization for the State University to offer its own doctoral degree, the EdD, in 2005.

Growth: Students, Campuses, and Dollars

After World War II, California's dramatic growth and the state's response to its population increases provided the context and the impetus for higher education policy. In the early 1960s, California became the nation's most populous state: the population in 1960 was 15.7 million residents and by 2010 that number had more than doubled. Expansion of higher education in California was inevitable because of the pressure of its rapidly growing population compounded by public demand for college access. As in other states, public demand for higher education rose to political saliency as local communities pressed their legislators for action. California responded to this pressure by increasing college enrollment at a rate that exceeded the state's rapid population growth (see table 7.1).

In purely quantitative terms, the transformations of higher education in the past half-century have been staggering, even after considering population growth. Total enrollment of undergraduate and graduate students in public and private non-profit higher education increased from about 163,000 in 1950 to 250,000 in 1960 and to about 2 million in 2010 (see table 7.2).[2] Public higher education accounted for most of this enrollment growth:

- Community colleges absorbed the greatest share of growth, from about 56,000 students enrolled in 1948 to 98,000 in 1960, to more than over 1.1 million in 2010.
- Enrollment in the State University grew from just under 23,000 in 1948 to 61,000 in 1960 and to almost 360,000 in 2010.
- The University enrolled about 43,000 students in 1948, some 44,000 in 1960, and 232,000 in 2010.
- Private colleges and universities accounted for approximately 41,000 students in 1950, 47,000 in 1960, and 203,000 in 2009. Even with this substantial growth, however, the independent institutions' share of all California college enrollments dropped from about 25 percent in 1950 to about 10 percent in 2009.

Table 7.1 Growth of population and public higher education enrollment

Year	California Population (in thousands)	Population Growth (%)	Total Growth in PublicHigher Education Enrollment* (%)
1960	15,727	49	67
1970	20,038	27	300
1980	23,780	19	36
1990	29,828	25	12
2000	34,099	14	16
2005	36,154	6	14
2010	37,254	3	6

Note: * Enrollment data is for Fall full-time equivalent students.
Sources: Population: US Census Bureau, *Statistical Abstract*, "Bicentennial Edition: Historical Statistics of the United States, Colonial Times to 1970," and *Statistical Abstract* yearly editions. Retrieved from http://www.census.gov/compendia/statab/past_years.html on April 10, 2008; 1970–2008 data from California Department of Finance, Demographic Research Unit, E-3 Race/Ethnic Population Estimates with Age and Sex Detail (1970–1989, 1980–1999, and 2000–2008 editions). Retrieved from http://www.dof.ca.gov/HTML/DEMOGRAP/Data/DRUdatafiles.php, on August 8, 2011; 2010 data from California State Data Center, Census 2010. Retrieved from http://www.dof.ca.gov/research/demographic/state_census_data_center/census_2010/view.php, on August 8, 2011; Enrollment: 1960 from California Higher Education Policy Center, "Financing the California Master Plan: A Data Base of Public Finance for Higher Education in California 1958/59 to 1996/97" (San Jose, CA: June 1997); 1970–2010 from California Postsecondary Education Commission, "Fiscal Profiles, 2010" (Commission Report 10–22, December 2010).

Table 7.2 Enrollment in California higher education, 1948–2010

Year	CCC	CSU	UC	Independent*	Total
1948	55,933	22,787	43,469	N/A	N/A
1950	56,624	25,369	39,492	41,036	162,521
1960	97,858	61,330	43,748	47,000	249,936
1970	526,584	186,749	98,508	N/A	N/A
1980	752,278	232,935	122,761	133,313	1,241,287
1990**	818,755	272,637	152,863	145,375	1,389,630
2000	999,652	279,403	165,900	173,341	1,618,296
2005	1,121,681	324,120	201,403	202,035	1,849,239
2010**	1,161,807	358,063	232,613	203,068	1,955,551

Note: Enrollment data is for Fall full-time equivalent students.
N/A: Data not available.
*Independent enrollment numbers include all students at institutions that are members of Association of Independent Colleges and Universities.
**Independent data are for 1991 instead of 1990 and 2009 instead of 2010.
Sources: Figures for 1948 and 1950 from California State Department of Education, *A Master Plan for Higher Education in California: 1960–1975* (Sacramento, California, 1960); CCC, CSU and UC data for 1960 from California Higher Education Policy Center, "Financing the California Master Plan: A Data Base of Public Finance for Higher Education in California 1958/59 to 1996/97" (San Jose, CA: June 1997); Independent data for 1960 from the Association of Independent California Colleges and Universities, "1960 Guidebook;" UC, CSU, and CCC data for 1970–2010 and Independent data from 1980, 1991, 2000, 2005, and 2009 from California Postsecondary Education Commission, "Fiscal Profiles, 2010" (Commission Report 10–22, December 2010).

Public and private four-year baccalaureate-granting institutions enrolled two-thirds of California's college students in 1950 and 39 percent in 2010 (see table 7.2). In terms of numbers of students served, the community colleges became the predominant sector of California higher education, enrolling substantially more students than the other sectors combined. This distribution followed from public policy decisions concerning access, institutional mission, capacity, and student eligibility in the 1960 Master Plan.

The framers of the Master Plan encouraged access by prohibiting tuition for California residents at any public campus, but this provision, which eroded as the institutions increasingly levied "fees," was finally abandoned. Even though tuition remains relatively modest at the community colleges and the State University, college attendance is expensive in California because of the state's high cost of living (Zumeta and Frankle, 2007).

The initial state scholarship program was created in the mid-1950s primarily to enable academically high-achieving students to attend in-state private colleges and universities. As the public institutions raised tuition and fees, the original program was modified and grew into a constellation of Cal Grant programs. In 2008, these grants were awarded to about 297,000 students at a cost of almost $1.2 billion (see table 7.3). In addition, each of the public systems of higher education administers its own financial aid programs. In the University and the State University, set-asides from student fees are the principal source of support for these programs.

Increases in college participation in California were made possible by massive increases in capacity as existing campuses were expanded and new campuses were built (see table 7.4). The number of California Community College campuses, where the largest growth was concentrated, increased from 43 in 1945 to 64 in 1960, and to 112 in 2011; the State University added 14 campuses from 1945 to 2011, amounting to a total of 23; and the University had 10 campuses by 2011. Thus, the number of public college and university campuses totaled 145 in 2011.

Table 7.3 Cal Grant awards, 2008

Institution	Total Number of Awards	Total Award Amount (in millions of dollars)*
UC	53,090	350
CSU	74,825	253
CCC	124,931	168
Independent	23,970	224
Private Career Colleges/Other	19,702	202
Total	**296,518**	**1,196**

Note: *Amounts represent awards offered and not reconciled payments.
Source: California Student Aid Commission, Preliminary Grant Statistics Report 2007–2008.

Table 7.4 Campuses by sector, 1945–2011

Year	CCC	CSU	UC	Independent*
1945	43	9	2	69
1950	55	12	2	74
1960	64	16	6	78
1970	92	20	9	100
1980	105	20	9	115
1990	106	21	9	120
2000	107	22	9	126
2005	108	23	10	N/A
2011	112	23	10	119

Notes: N/A = Data are not available.
*Independent includes WASC Accredited nonpublic institutions.
Sources: California Postsecondary Education Commission, California Colleges Mailing List. Retrieved from http://www.cpec.ca.gov/OnLineData/AddressOptions.asp, on August 10, 2011; University of California History Digital Archives. Retrieved from http://sunsite.berkeley.edu/uchistory/general_history/overview/maintimeline.html, on March 11, 2008.

Table 7.5 State and local operating support for public higher education, 1960–2010 (in millions of dollars)

Year	CCC	CSU	UC	Total
1960	58	55	99	169
1970	366	285	330	741
1980	1,276	814	902	2,749
1990	2,489	1,632	2,077	5,498
2000	3,986	2,175	2,716	7,293
2005	4,806	2,476	2,699	8,225
2010	5,764	2,346	2,591	10,701
Inflation-Adjusted State and Local Operating Support for Public Higher Education, 1960–2010				
1960	384	363	653	1,115
1970	1,843	1,435	1,661	3,730
1980	3,025	1,929	2,138	6,513
1990	3,719	2,439	3,104	8,217
2000	4,520	2,467	3,080	8,271
2005	4,806	2,476	2,699	8,225
2010	5,764	2,346	2,591	10,701

Note: CCC data is for State General Fund and Local Property Taxes. CSU and UC data is for State General Fund. Inflation Adjustments based on US Bureau of Labor Statistics.
Sources: Data for years 1960–1990 from California Higher Education Policy Center, "Financing the California Master Plan: A Data Base of Public Finance for Higher Education in California 1958/59 to 1996/97" (San Jose, CA: June 1997); 2000, 2005, and 2010 data from California Postsecondary Education Commission, "Fiscal Profiles, 2010" (Commission Report 10–22, December 2010).

The 15 years from 1945 through 1960 reflect the uncoordinated building of new campuses that led to the enactment of the Master Plan. In the 1960s and 1970s, growth followed the Master Plan's guidelines: New community colleges brought higher education within commuting distance of students; and for the four-year systems, new campuses recommended in the plan were built. As described in the next section, however, institutional and community pressures in the 1990s began to replace planning based on population and projected regional needs, as decision making about the placement of new campuses reverted to the politicized approach that had dominated the decades prior to the Master Plan.

The spectacular growth of California higher education cannot be explained simply by population increases or market forces. Rather, the growth of colleges and universities in the state is directly attributable to public policies and state financial support of those policies over more than half a century. The operating revenues from state and local sources for public higher education from 1960 through 2010 are summarized in table 7.5.

Altered State Realities: Constrained Public Finance and Political Volatility, Demographic Shifts, and the Public Schools

The Master Plan for Higher Education was developed to meet the challenges that California faced in the second half of the twentieth century. In the twenty-first century, California and its colleges and universities must adapt to new economic, political, demographic, and educational changes that have reshaped the state and its public sector. This section identifies and explores these altered state realities.

Unstable, Constrained Public Finance Combined with Political Volatility

The 1960 Master Plan was the product of the optimism of the post–World War II era, an era characterized by massive expansion of public services to meet the needs of a growing population. In addition to its support of higher education, California made and implemented major commitments to public schools, highways, parks, and extensive water and irrigation projects. This expansion took off in the mid-1940s and early 1950s under the gubernatorial administrations of Earl Warren and Goodwin Knight, peaked during the administration of Edmund G. Brown from 1958 to 1966, and was sustained under his successor, Ronald Reagan.

In 1978, however, the California electorate brought an abrupt end to the era of public sector expansiveness by overwhelmingly adopting Proposition 13, an initiative that reduced property taxes by about 60 percent and severely constrained future tax increases. In addition to inaugurating an era of reduced public spending, Proposition 13 ushered in an era of "government by plebiscite," in which the initiative, sparsely used before 1978, was increasingly commandeered to "legislate" on a broad spectrum of issues. Such issues included but were not limited to: minimum spending on public schools (1988), legislative term limits (1990), mandated prison terms (1994), affirmative action (1996), and Native American casinos (1998). One effect of the extensive use of initiatives has been directly or indirectly to mandate specific expenditures, even as Proposition 13 and other tax-cutting measures constrained revenue growth. The consequence has been a reduction of the discretionary funds available for appropriation—that is, funds that support higher education and other expenditures that are not legal mandates or entitlements (Schrag, 1999, 2006).

Higher education has not escaped the harsh realities of the diminished public sector in the 30 years since 1978. Another effect of Proposition 13 has been the state's increasing dependence on income, capital gains, and sales taxes—the revenue streams most sensitive to economic conditions. As a result, during periods of recession and state revenue shortfall, higher education has faced harsh fiscal restraints. On the other hand, the economic dynamism of California has also enabled several years of generous state support when the economy has been flourishing. It was fortuitous that Proposition 13 and the reversal of public sector fortunes did not begin until after the baby boomer college enrollments had peaked and after most of the new campuses and campus expansions envisioned by the 1960 Master Plan were completed or well underway.

The most significant, and apparently permanent, departure from the Master Plan has been the abrogation of its foundational public policy commitment to college opportunity—that is, its commitment to make higher education available for every Californian who can benefit from college. This historic obligation undergirded the differentiated missions and admissions policies of the three public sectors. There has never been a formal retraction or revision of the commitment, and it continues to enjoy the rhetorical support of most political and higher education leaders. However, it is a promise that the state honors only in the best of economic times, and sacrifices subtly during years of budget problems. Between 1960 and 1980, the Master Plan commitment to access was California's most fundamental public policy. But since the 1980s, this commitment has eroded steadily, often without public discussion or deliberation.

Recessions bring state financial stringency and in California they have brought severe restrictions in college access, principally at the broad-access institutions—the community colleges and the State University:

- Community college enrollments were reduced by more than 250,000 students in the recession of the early 1980s.
- In the recession of the early 1990s, enrollments decreased by over 170,000 in the community colleges and 50,000 in the State University.

- The recession of the early 2000s brought enrollment reductions of nearly 150,000 in the community colleges. (California Higher Education Policy Center, 1997; California Department of Finance, 1999–2007; California Postsecondary Education Commission, 2006)

State and institutional responses to the recession that began in 2007 and its aftermath have to date followed the pattern of earlier recessions but with greater severity: deep budget cuts, steep tuition increases in the four-year sectors, and limitations and reductions of enrollments (California Postsecondary Education Commission, 2010).

What is particularly noteworthy in the context of the Master Plan's commitment to college opportunity is that the broad-access institutions—the State University and the community colleges—have been the locus of enrollment reductions. In each recession, the community colleges have responded to state budget cuts with reductions in faculty, courses, and class sections, and tuition has been increased.

The broad-access institutions of California higher education, particularly the community colleges, enroll most of the low-income, first-generation, and Latino college students. Many of these students work and support families, attend part-time, and depend on evening and weekend classes. Scheduling changes and the elimination or reduction of part-time faculty, courses, and class sections reduce capacity, and this reduced capacity, along with tuition increases, results in lower enrollments. This subtle form of rationing of higher education opportunity has occurred without formal changes in policy or state priorities. Despite the Master Plan's commitment to access, the suppression of enrollments at the broad-access institutions for more than three decades is de facto state policy in difficult budgetary times.

An analysis of the impact of the 2004–2005 community college budget reductions and enrollment losses by the Institute for Higher Education Leadership and Policy observed:

> The greatest impact has been felt by the less well-prepared students who are not as savvy to deadlines, fees, financial aid, and ways to navigate the system...Many of the colleges we studied primarily serve first-generation students who have limited understanding of the educational system. Students who are somewhat uncertain about attending in the first place or about their ability to succeed are those most likely to be discouraged by the reduced access to classes and services, according to campus officials. Some respondents were very concerned that this will shut down the pipeline to the diverse clientele that the community colleges aim to serve. (Shulock, 2004, p. 47)

After enrollments in broad-access institutions are reduced, the enrollments do not recover immediately when economic conditions and state appropriations improve, instructional capacity is restored, or even when tuition is frozen and financial aid is increased. These experiences from the 1990s are illustrative:

- The State University experienced budget cuts and raised tuition substantially in 1991, 1992, and 1993. Student fees increased by 103 percent during this period. Enrollments decreased each year from 1992 and 1995 and did not recover to the 1990 level until 2001, even though state funding was fully restored (and more) by 1997 and a multiyear tuition freeze was instituted.
- At the community colleges, state and local funding was cut in 1993 and 1994 and was restored to its prerecession level in 1996. But enrollments were depressed for the remainder of the decade; they reached and surpassed the 1991 level in 2000. (California Higher Education Policy Center, 1997; California Department of Finance, 1999–2007; California Postsecondary Education Commission, 2006)

It is reasonable to conclude that the college aspirations of students or potential students may have been dampened when they were confronted with precipitous fee increases or denied access to college courses or services such as counseling and childcare.

The state's failure to plan for predictable enrollment growth has been at least as problematic as its response to financial downturns. By the early 1990s, it was widely expected that the number of high school graduates in California would increase substantially during the first decade of the twenty-first century. Projections in 1995, based on the continuation of established trends, set the impact on college enrollments at an additional 450,000 students by 2005 (Breneman, Estrada, and Hayward, 2005). In the late 1950s, it had been these types of projections that had evoked the planning and policy response embodied in the Master Plan. In contrast to the foresight of that era's leaders, more recently, California did not develop a state plan to accommodate its growing numbers of high school graduates. Political pressure for such a plan was lacking. The influential Legislative Analyst's Office argued for an incremental rather than a comprehensive approach; and no higher education leader stepped forward to press the case for planning, as Clark Kerr had done in 1959. In 1994, Kerr, by then in his eighties, urged that the state adopt a comprehensive approach, arguing that "the course of facing-the-future-all-at-once" in 1960 had helped California create the best system of higher education in the nation in terms of both access and quality (Kerr, 1994).

Compounding the failure to plan, state and higher education leaders regressed, in effect, to the practices of the 1950s that the Master Plan was designed to remedy. In the 1990s, each sector, with the support of communities, local boosters, and their legislators, put forward its own aspirations for new campuses. Policy leaders gave in to local and regional political pressures and ignored demographics in the placement of new institutions. New campuses were established by the University at Merced and by the State University at Monterey, both in sparsely populated locations and far from the areas where projected growth of high school graduates was concentrated.

For the first time since the enactment of the Master Plan, pork-barrel politics dominated decision-making processes for campus placement. California's capacity for comprehensive higher education planning was nonexistent and the vacuum created by the absence of a statewide plan helped open the door for the politicized approach to increasing higher education capacity.

It is impossible to ascertain precisely the importance of the Master Plan in the successful expansion of California higher education in the 1960s and 1970s. Assuredly, a robust economy, along with dedicated state and higher education leaders, contributed to the success. By the same token, it is impossible to pinpoint the effect of the lack of statewide planning on recent history. However, by 2006 the community colleges—the point of college access for most Californians—enrolled 120,000 fewer students than had been projected in the mid-1990s.[3] In addition, smaller proportions of high school graduates were enrolling in college, and the likelihood that a California high school student would enroll in college by age 19 was 36 percent, compared to 57 percent in the leading states on this measure (National Center for Public Policy and Higher Education, 2008, pp. 3–6).

DEMOGRAPHIC SHIFTS

The rate of growth and the sheer size of California's population is only one-half of the demographic story. The other half is the transformation of an overwhelmingly white populace—more than 90 percent at the time of the Master Plan's adoption—to a "majority minority" state in which no population group constitutes a majority (see table 7.6). By 2000, about 47 percent of Californians were white; 33 percent were Hispanic; 11 percent were Asian/Pacific Islander; and 7 percent were black. In contrast to the first 25 years after World War II when the state's growth was fueled primarily by westward in-migration of Americans from other states, the immigrants of the past four decades have been overwhelmingly Asian/Pacific Islander and Hispanic. By the turn of the century, more than 1 in 4 of the 34 million Californians was foreign born. Between 2000 and 2010, Hispanics and Asian/Pacific Islanders have continued to grow as a share of the population, while the percentage of whites has continued to decline.

Not surprisingly, these demographic shifts are more pronounced in the state's young population (see table 7.7). Hispanics accounted for 43 percent of California's high school graduating class of 2010, followed closely by whites at 33 percent, with Asians, Filipinos, and Pacific Islanders at 14 percent, and African Americans at 7 percent. Public school enrollment reflects the depth and permanence of this profound transformation.

In short, California's higher education pipeline in the early twenty-first century bears little resemblance to the homogeneous, preponderantly white baby boomer generation of the 1960s and 1970s. Many of the "new Californians"—Chinese Americans and Japanese Americans in particular—enroll in California's most selective colleges and universities (see table 7.8). Many others, however, are hampered by barriers of poverty, language,

Table 7.6 California population by ethnic group, 1960–2010

Year	White	Hispanic	Asian/Pacific Islander	Black	American Indian	Total Population
1960	14,465,000	N/A	N/A	884,000	N/A	15,727,000
1970	15,480,723	2,423,085	671,077	1,379,563	83,838	20,038,286
1980	15,949,865	4,615,231	1,257,019	1,793,663	164,290	23,780,068
1990	17,023,502	7,760,598	2,748,810	2,106,060	189,503	29,828,473
2000	16,098,880	11,085,437	3,872,800	2,220,712	184,754	34,098,744
2004	16,287,111	12,707,737	4,374,758	2,193,043	213,316	36,505,743
2008	15,568,737	14,197,927	4,868,770	2,229,045	211,619	38,134,523
2010	14,956,253	14,013,719	4,903,647	2,163,804	162,250	37,253,956
Percent of Total Population, 1960–2010						
1960	92	N/A	N/A	6	N/A	100
1970	77	12	3	7	0.40	100
1980	67	19	5	8	0.70	100
1990	57	26	9	7	0.60	100
2000	47	33	11	7	0.50	100
2004	45	35	12	6	0.60	100
2008	41	37	13	6	0.60	100
2010	40	38	13	6	0.40	100

Note: The Total for 1960 includes those who selected "other" and totals for 2000 and 2004 include individuals who selected multiple races. The Hispanic category for 1970–1990 equals a sum of Hispanic White, Hispanic Asian/Pacific, Hispanic Black, and Hispanic Indian.
N/A = Data are not available.
Sources: Data for 1960 are from US Bureau of the Census Statistical Abstract, "Bicentennial Edition: Historical Statistics of the United States, Colonial Times to 1970." Retrieved from http://www.census.gov/compendia/statab/past_years.html, on April 10, 2008; 1970–2010 data from California Department of Finance, Demographic Research Unit, E-3 Race/Ethnic Population Estimates with Age and Sex Detail, (1970–1989, 1980–1999, and 2000–2008 editions). Retrieved from http://www.dof.ca.gov/HTML/DEMOGRAP/Data/DRUdatafiles.php, on August 8, 2011; and table 3A Total Population by Race (1) and Hispanic or Latino: April 1, 2010. Retrieved from, http://www.dof.ca.gov/research/demographic/state_census_data_center/census_2010/view.php#PL94, on August 19, 2011.

weak public schools, and poor high school completion rates. These barriers adversely impact enrollment rates of Latinos, even as they approach majority status in the public schools.

PUBLIC SCHOOLS

The effectiveness of California's public schools was not an issue for the framers of the Master Plan. The limited indicators available in 1960 offered no reason for fundamental concerns about the health of public education. For example, the state's public schools, though not without their critics, consistently ranked high among the leading 10 states and above the national average in expenditures per pupil; and its school teachers ranked among the

Table 7.7 Distribution of California public school enrollment and graduates by ethnicity, 2010 (in percentage)

	White (Not Hispanic)	Hispanic or Latino	Asian/ Filipino/ Pacific Islander	African American	American Indian/Alaska Native
Kindergarten	25	54	11	6	0.60
Grade 1	25	53	11	6	0.60
Grade 2	25	52	11	6	0.70
Grade 3	25	52	11	6	0.70
Grade 4	26	51	12	7	0.70
Grade 5	27	51	11	7	0.70
Grade 6	27	51	11	7	0.70
Grade 7	27	50	12	7	0.70
Grade 8	28	50	12	7	0.80
Grade 9	27	50	11	7	0.80
Grade 10	28	49	12	8	0.80
Grade 11	30	47	12	7	0.80
Grade 12	31	45	13	8	0.80
Total	**27**	**50**	**12**	7	**0.70**
High School Graduates	**33**	**43**	**14**	7	**0.80**

Note: The rows of percentages do not add to 100 because individuals who selected multiple ethnic groups or none at all are not reflected. Students who are not associated with a specific grade are also not included.
Sources: K-12 data from California Department of Education, DataQuest, Enrollment by Gender, Grade and Ethnic Designation. Retrieved from http://dq.cde.ca.gov/dataquest/, on August 19, 2011.

Table 7.8 Distribution of higher education enrollment by ethnicity, 2009 (in percentage)

	White	Latino	Asian/ Pacific Islander	Filipino	Black	Native American	Unknown	Total
UC	38	16	33	4	4	0.60	5	100
CSU	38	27	14	4	6	0.60	9	100
CCC	32	30	11	3	7	0.70	18	100
Total Public	**33**	**28**	**13**	**3**	**6**	**0.70**	**15**	**100**

Source: CPEC, Ethnicity Snapshots. Retrieved from http://www.cpec.ca.gov/StudentData/EthSnapshotMenu.asp, on August 19, 2011.

best educated in the nation. At the time, it was reasonable to assume that graduates of California high schools would be able to benefit from the college opportunities that implementation of the Master Plan would create, and its architects made that assumption.

In 1978, the burden of Proposition 13 fell particularly heavily on public schools. Combined with legislative implementation of a court-mandated equalization of district funding, the passage of Proposition 13 set school finance into a downward spiral, one that was marked with only brief spurts of recovery in peak state revenue years. In 2010, California ranked forty-second in spending per pupil. California's spending per pupil was $1,740 below the national average and well below that of major industrial states ($8,076 below New York, $5,920 below Massachusetts, $3,882 below Pennsylvania, and $2,749 below Michigan). In 2009, California ranked near last among states in staff to student ratios, and last in the ratio of guidance counselors and librarians to students. These declines occurred at the same time that the schools needed more resources to address increasing ethnic and language diversity and the poverty that afflicted almost one in five of California's children (National Education Association, 2007; EdSource, 2008).

From the 1990s, the National Assessment of Educational Progress has assessed the performance of fourth and eighth grade students in math, reading, and science by state. In 2009, 23 percent of California's eighth graders scored at levels of proficient or above in math, compared with 44 percent in the best-performing states; 22 percent of California's eighth graders scored at levels of proficient or above in reading compared to 42 percent in leading states, low-income California eighth graders scored very poorly in math (12 percent were proficient compared to 27 percent in leading states); and in science, 18 percent were proficient compared with 41 percent in leading states in 2005. The poor performance of eighth graders suggests that they are not well prepared for challenging high school coursework in these basic disciplines.

One consequence for higher education is that only 25 percent of high school graduates are academically prepared for college-level work (California State Department of Education, 2008; Governor's Committee on Educational Excellence, 2007; National Center for Public Policy and Higher Education, 2006). In 2007, the University reported that more than 28 percent of its entering freshmen, drawn from California's highest-achieving high school graduates, did not perform at the required level as measured by its analytic writing placement exam. In 2010, 35 percent of regularly admitted freshmen in the State University needed remediation in mathematics and 49 percent needed remediation in English; 27 percent of students lacked proficiency in both reading and mathematics (California State University Analytic Studies, 2011). Although statewide standards for college readiness or placement examinations are lacking, a survey by the community colleges indicates that approximately one-half of community college students require basic skills instruction (Academic Senate for California Community Colleges, 2004, p. 9; Brown and Neimi, 2007; California State University Analytic Studies, 2008; University of California Office of the President, 2008).

CONCLUSION

The 1960 Master Plan and the expansion of California higher education were not without flaws or critics. By real-world standards, however, they served Californians well in an era of rapid population growth.

Importantly, the Master Plan was cost-effective in managing growth—including a 300 percent enrollment increase in the first decade after its passage. The Master Plan enabled the state to meet its commitments to college opportunity by efficient distribution of campuses and programs. Campuses were situated in population centers, and decisions as to where to locate new campuses were removed from the pork-barrel politics of earlier eras.

By resolving the issues of institutional mission and program allocation and by encouraging each sector, as the Master Plan legislation articulated, "to strive for excellence in its sphere," California developed a diverse array of colleges and universities to meet the needs of a growing population that had a broad range of abilities, motivations, and educational aspirations. By sparing the legislature and public the battles over turf that dominated the higher education landscape in other states, the Master Plan contributed to public confidence, which in turn brought state financial support to higher education. The affirmation of the University of California's franchise in doctoral education and state-supported research positioned the University to maintain and enhance its standing among leading research universities.

The Master Plan and California's higher education system achieved almost iconic status in California, but California faces a very different set of challenges than in 1960. The performance of California education has declined substantially, and core provisions of the Master Plan have succumbed to political and budgetary pressures. Although citizens' commissions and special legislative committees in every decade since the 1960s have consistently reaffirmed the core provisions of the Master Plan, the letter and spirit of these provisions have been set aside when expedient. Reducing opportunity at the community colleges, and, at times, at the State University, has become a standard state response to financial difficulty. In contrast to the first decade of the Master Plan when enrollments exceeded expectations, the community colleges now enroll considerably fewer students than were projected by conservative forecasts less than a decade ago.

Despite these enrollment shortfalls, the community colleges have grown exponentially as their roles in serving local labor markets—and most Californians who aspire to a baccalaureate degree—have solidified. The community colleges enroll the overwhelming majority of college students in California. Relatively few students, however, actually benefit from the transfer opportunities within public higher education that were central to the Master Plan—fewer than 70,000 transferred in 2007 (13,923 to the University and 54,379 to the State University) (California Postsecondary Education Commission, 2008). One consequence is that California consistently ranks in the bottom one-third among states in baccalaureate degree production (National Center for Higher Education Management Systems,

2008). In short, the egalitarian provisions of the Master Plan commitment—access and transfer—are in serious disrepair.

The diminished college opportunity that exists today in California casts a shadow on the state's economic future. A 2007 report from the Public Policy Institute of California warned that the state's workforce would likely fall far short of the level of education and skills needed in the future. The report's authors estimated that 39 percent of the jobs in the state's increasingly knowledge-based economy would require college degrees by 2020, but only 33 percent of working-age adults were projected to have acquired them by that time. The report warned that it is unlikely that the gap would be filled by in-migration of college-educated and trained workers because of California's high costs of living, particularly housing. The authors recommended higher rates of college participation and graduation among Californians (Johnson and Reed, 2007). A separate analysis projected a decline in the educational attainment of California's adult population and in personal income by 2020, "unless the state can increase the number of Hispanics/Latinos going to college and getting degrees" (National Center for Public Policy and Higher Education, 2005, p. 1).

As the indicators of a growing educational deficit accumulate, the state's financial condition offers little prospect of sustained infusions of new public dollars. Sporadic increases in state appropriations when the economy is growing rapidly can be generous, as in the "dot com" boom of the late 1990s and again as the state economy recovered from the recession of the early 2000s. However, the state budget faces a chronic structural deficit and, in years of weak state budgets, cuts to higher education are likely to continue to be severe (Jones, 2006; Martinez and Nodine, 1997).

The adaptability of California higher education and the Master Plan to a radically transformed demographic, fiscal, and educational environment is limited. California has little capacity to set and adjust priorities *across* its higher education systems and programs in response to changing circumstances, particularly at a time when the state has reneged on its basic commitments to college opportunity. Evidence can be found in the continued and costly expansion of the University of California, particularly the new and poorly justified research university at Merced and the plans for new medical and law schools.

A great strength of the Master Plan was its delineation of distinctive missions and governance of each sector, which proved to be effective in meeting the challenges of the 1960s and 1970s. As the systems grew and matured, however, the organizing principle has come to look more like "each train on its own track" or each higher education sector in its own "silo." The same structure that has reinforced differentiated missions may also impede needed collaboration and effective distribution of resources across the higher education systems—for example, the need to work collaboratively with public schools to strengthen college preparation; the need to assure adequate funding for the community colleges, which are the first-line responders in adjusting to changing demographics, population growth, and the weakness of public schools; the need to improve transfer and graduation rates; and the need to expand access and capacity collaboratively through electronic technology.[4]

After the Master Plan resolved the urgent planning issues of the early 1960s, additional measures for assuring statewide planning and coordination were perceived as unnecessary, and the mechanisms for these functions have always been weak. The ensuing vacuum in effective statewide policy and planning has contributed to the failure to set statewide priorities. There is a major gulf between the most urgent educational needs of California and the operating and capital priorities of educational and political leaders. This vacuum is partially responsible for the politicization of new campus locations and program allocations. In contrast to the expansion of the 1960s and 1970s, these decisions are not aligned with the educational needs of the state.

When initiatives are launched to address statewide educational needs, they are almost invariably confined to a single sector, which limits their impact even when they are effective. This has been the case with the impressive series of educational improvements initiated over the past decade by the State University under the leadership of the current Chancellor Charles B. Reed. These initiatives have included outreach to public schools to raise college aspirations, improve college readiness, and strengthen California's K-12 teaching force (Reed, 2006).

For at least the past three decades, California's governors and legislators have been reluctant to assert statewide priorities, particularly when confronted with fiscal problems. This deference of state leaders to each of the higher education systems has meant that overall public priorities, such as access, affordability, and the transfer function, have often been inadequately protected in hard economic times and overlooked in good ones.

Unless the erosion of the egalitarian provisions of the Master Plan are reversed, pressures on the organizational arrangements designed in 1960 are likely to mount. Californians may eventually be confronted with issues that have been "off the table" for the last half-century. If California's colleges and universities as configured by the Master Plan fail to deliver to the current and coming generations opportunities that are comparable to those provided for past generations, public pressure could demand fundamental changes in the structure and governance of higher education, which, after all, are *means* and not *ends.* Options that state and educational leaders have been reluctant to consider in the past may be revisited—for example, regional organization and governance of higher education—in order to find better ways to use scarce public dollars to address California's most pressing challenges.

The consequences of the reduction of college opportunity are manifested in the declining educational attainment of the young adult population. California's older population (ages 65 years and above) ranks eighth in the nation in the percentage that has attended some college or obtained an associate degree, and fifth in the percentage with a baccalaureate degree. In contrast, younger Californians (ages 25–35) are forty-first in the proportion with some college or an associate degree, and twenty-second in the percentage with a bachelor's degree (U.S. Bureau of the Census, 2008). There is also evidence of a growing public awareness of the erosion of college access and its consequences. In 2007, the Public Policy Institute of California found that almost two-thirds of Californians believe that college is necessary for success in the workplace; large majorities believe that getting a college education has become more difficult and is out of reach for many who are motivated and qualified; and 68 percent believe the state will need more college-educated workers in the future.

The bold policy blueprint developed for California in the mid-twentieth century has become increasingly out of alignment with the state's educational, economic, and demographic realities of this century. Despite rising public concern, governmental and higher education leaders have shown little motivation or capacity to develop a new framework or master plan better suited to the state's current needs and aspirations. It is ironic that the state that first put forth the principle of universal college access has reneged on that principle at a time of major demographic and economic transitions. For the foreseeable future, some California colleges and universities will continue to rank highly in national research ratings and other measures of reputational quality and prestige. However, these accomplishments will be small consolation if they exist in isolation in a state otherwise characterized by diminishing educational opportunity, declining levels of educational attainment, and reduced standards of living.

NOTES

1. Officially titled the Servicemen's Readjustment Act of 1944, the G.I. Bill offered college or vocational education to the returning World War II veterans.
2. The paucity of historical data precluded the inclusion of the private for-profit sector, which plays an increasingly important role in California and elsewhere.
3. See Breneman, Estrada, and Hayward (1995) for the mid-1990s projections, which were conservative. Community college enrollment for 2006 was more than 206,000 below projections of a 2000 study by the California Postsecondary Education Commission.
4. Issues and problems of collaboration are described in the following works: National Center for Public Policy and Higher Education (1997); Bracco and Callan (2002); Pickens (1999); and Richardson, Bracco, Callan, and Finney (1999).

REFERENCES

Academic Senate for California Community Colleges, Basic Skills Committee 2003–2004, *Issues in Basic Skills Assessment and Placement in the California Community Colleges*, p. 9 (adopted Fall 2004). Retrieved from http://www.asccc.org/Publications/Papers/Downloads/PDFs/ BasicSkillsIssuesAssessment.pdf, on April 30, 2008.

Bracco, K. R., and P. M. Callan. *Competition and Collaboration in California Higher Education.* San Jose, CA: National Center for Public Policy and Higher Education, 2002.

Breneman, D. W., L. F. Estrada, and G. C. Hayward. *Tidal Wave II: An Evaluation of Enrollment Projections for California Higher Education*, Technical Report #95–6. San Jose: California Higher Education Policy Center, 1995.

Brown, R. S., and D. N. Neimi. *Investigating the Alignment of High School and Community College Tests in California.* San Jose, CA: National Center for Public Policy and Higher Education, 2007.

California Department of Finance. *Governor's Proposed Budget, 1999–2007.* Sacramento: California Department of Finance, 1999–2007.

California Higher Education Policy Center. *Financing the California Master Plan: A Data Base of Public Finance for Higher Education in California 1958/59 to 1996/97.* San Jose: California Higher Education Policy Center, 1997.

California Postsecondary Education Commission. *Fiscal Profiles, 2010*, Report 10–21. Sacramento: California Postsecondary Education Commission, 2010.

———. *Custom Data Reports.* Retrieved from http://www.cpec.ca.gov/OnLineData/SelectFinalOptions.asp, on May 5, 2008.

———. *Fiscal Profiles, 2006*, Commission Report 06–13. Sacramento: California Postsecondary Education Commission, 2006.

California State Department of Education. "California NAEP." Retrieved from http:// www.cde.ca.gov/ta/tg/nr/caresults.asp, on March 20, 2008.

———. *A Master Plan for Higher Education in California, 1960–1975.* Sacramento: California State Department of Education, 1960.

California State University Analytic Studies. *Proficiency Reports of Students Entering CSU System.* Retrieved from http://www.asd.calstate.edu/performance/proficiency.html, on August 19, 2011.

———. *Proficiency Reports of Students Entering the CSU System.* Retrieved from http://www.asd.calstate.edu/performance/combo/2007/Combo_Prof_Sys_fall2007.htm, on April 30, 2008.

Carnegie Foundation for the Advancement of Teaching. *State Higher Education in California.* Sacramento: California State Printing Office, 1932.

Condren, C. *Preparing for the Twenty-First Century.* A Report on Higher Education in California Requested by the Organization for Economic Cooperation and Development, Report 88–1. Sacramento: California Postsecondary Education Commission, 1988.

Douglass, J. A. *The California Idea and American Higher Education.* Palo Alto: Stanford University Press, 2000.

EdSource, *Staff-Per-Pupil Ratios in California 2005–06.* Retrieved from http:// www. edsource.org/sch_schman_ratio2005–06.cfm, on May 21, 2008.

Governor's Committee on Educational Excellence. *Students First, Renewing Hope for California's Future.* Sacramento, CA: Office of the Governor, 2007.

Johnson, H. P., and D. Reed. "Can California Import Enough College Graduates to Meet Workforce Needs?" *California Counts: Population Trends and Profiles,* vol. 8, no. 4. San Francisco: Public Policy Institute of California, 2007.

Jones, D. "State Shortfalls Projected to Continue Despite Economic Gains." In *Policy Alert.* San Jose, CA: National Center for Public Policy and Higher Education, 2006.

Kerr, C. *The Gold and the Blue: A Personal Memoir of the University of California, 1949–1967.* Vol. 1: *Academic Triumphs.* Berkeley: University of California Press, 2001.

Kerr, C. *Preserving the Master Plan.* San Jose: California Higher Education Policy Center, 1994.

———. "The California Master Plan of 1960 for Higher Education: An *Ex Ante* View." In S. Rothblatt (ed.), *The OECD, the Master Plan and the California Dream: A Berkeley Conversation.* University of California Berkeley: Center for Studies in Higher Education, 1992.

Martinez, M., and T. Nodine. "California: Financing Higher Education Amid Policy Drift." In P. M. Callan and J. E. Finney, *Public and Private Financing of Higher Education.* Phoenix, AZ: American Council on Education/Oryx Press, 1997.

National Center for Higher Education Management Systems. *Information Center.* Retrieved from http://www.higheredinfo.org/dbrowser/index.php?submeasure =85&year=2005&level=nation&mod e=data&state=0, on May 5, 2008.

National Center for Public Policy and Higher Education. *Measuring Up 2008: The State and National Report Card on Higher Education, California.* San Jose, CA: National Center for Public Policy and Higher Education, 2008.

———. "Projected Drop in Income for California Most Severe in U.S." In California Supplement to *Policy Alert Income of U.S. Workforce Projected to Decline If Education Doesn't Improve.* San Jose, CA: National Center for Public Policy and Higher Education, 2005.

———. *A Promise Worth Keeping, a Special Roundtable Examines the Challenge of Renewing California's Historic Commitment to Access and Quality.* San Jose, CA: National Center for Public Policy and Higher Education, 1997.

National Education Association. *Rankings & Estimates, Rankings of the States 2006 and Estimates of School Statistics 2007*, NEA Research, December 2007. Retrieved from http://www.nea.org/edstats/ images/07rankings.pdf, on May 2, 2008.

Pickens, W. H. "The California Experience: The Segmented Approach." In Gerald Gaither (ed.), *The Multicampus System: Perspectives on Practice and Prospect.* Sterling, VA: Stylus, 1999.

Public Policy Institute of California. *Californians and Higher Education.* San Francisco: Public Policy Institute of California, 2007.

Reed, C. B. "The Future Cannot Wait." *Change,* November/December, 2006, 39: 28–34.

Richardson, Jr., R. C., K. R. Bracco, P. M. Callan, and J. E. Finney. *Designing State Higher Education Systems for a New Century.* Phoenix, AZ: American Council on Education/Oryx Press, 1999.

Rothblatt, S. *Education's Abiding Moral Dilemma.* Providence, RI: Symposium Books, 2007, p. 261.

Schrag, P. *California, America's High Stakes Experiment.* Berkeley: University of California Press, 2006.

———. *Paradise Lost, California's Experience, America's Future.* Berkeley: University of California Press, 1999.

Shulock, N. "2004 Postscript: The Impact of Recent Budget Reductions and Enrollment Pressures on Access and Quality." In G. C. Hayward, D. P. Jones, A. C. McGuinness Jr., and A. Timar (eds.), *Ensuring Access with Quality to California's Community Colleges.* San Jose, CA: National Center for Public Policy and Higher Education, 2004.

University of California Office of the President. *Analytical Writing Placement Exam Data.* Retrieved from https://uasother.ucop.edu/cgi-bin/awpe/county_detail. pl?countyid=001&year=2007&sor t=sch, on April 28, 2008.

US Bureau of the Census. *2007 American Community Survey,* Table C15001: Sex by Age by Educational Attainment for the Population 18 Years and Over, American FactFinder Downloadable Tables, Retrieved from www.factfinder.census.gov, in December 2008.

Zumeta, W., and D. Frankle. *California Community Colleges: Making Them Stronger and More Affordable.* San Jose, CA: National Center for Public Policy and Higher Education, 2007.

8

The Federal Government and Western Higher Education

David A. Longanecker

Mythology holds that the West is filled with independent types; that the struggle to settle the region was led by fierce individualists—cowboys, miners, ranchers, entrepreneurs, and such. This same mythology carries over to issues of public policy and is often used to explain the West's generally more conservative (and individualistic) approach to government. However, in one specific area of public policy—higher education—there is little evidence of this "independence." Indeed, one of the most exemplary models of "interdependence," the Western Interstate Commission for Higher Education (WICHE), has served the West for now 60 years and remains as vibrant today as it was at its inception.

Another example of where western higher education has been anything but independent has been in its relationship to the federal government. Indeed, western higher education would appear to have been more closely associated with federal higher education efforts than is the case elsewhere in the country.

Perhaps this is because the origins of western higher education coincided with the origins of federal involvement in higher education. For nearly the first 100 years of our nation's history, the federal government was not involved in higher education issues, for all practical purposes. Education was one of the important public missions relegated by the US Constitution to the states rather than to the federal government. This division of labor was honored absolutely during the early years of our nation.

In 1862, however, the federal government began its first foray into higher education with the passage of the Morrill Land Grant College Act. This federal legislation set aside resources, in the form of land, to help each state create a college or university that would extend access to higher education to the best and brightest sons of regular folks—farmers and mechanics. The passage of the Morrill Act coincided with the development of states—and state colleges and universities—in the West (Grubb and Lazerson, 2005, p. 3).

A handful of private colleges had been founded as early as the 1840s in the Far West. Willamette University in Salem, Oregon, was the first, established in 1842, and a few others were built in the late 1840s and 1850s. Virtually all of these institutions had a religious affiliation and were created in part to offer a spiritual ministry to the West, often providing education to the indigent, as well. Santa Clara University was created in 1851, in part to serve the sons of *caballeros*, as the Santa Clara Valley in 1851 was populated primarily by Mexicans.[1] However, private institutions were never as significant a part of higher education in the West, as they were in the rest of the country. In 2010 private colleges enrolled only 8 percent of the West's students, compared to 17 percent nationally (National Center for Education Statistics, 2010).

Just two public institutions existed in the West before the passage of the Morrill Act: the University of Utah, founded in 1850, and the University of Washington, established in 1861. One of the main reasons for this was that many of the western states had not yet been established. Only California and Oregon had been granted statehood before 1862. But before the turn of the nineteenth century, all but Arizona, Alaska, and Hawaii would receive statehood.[2] The passage of the Morrill Act, occurring as it did in the timeframe during which many western states were established, had a significant impact on the development of higher education in the region. Even the two public institutions that predated the Morrill Act ultimately would be shaped substantially by this, one of the first federal efforts in American higher education.

The growth of the federal role in higher education, along with the founding of so many western states, shaped higher education in the region in three distinct ways. First, the funds provided by the land grants to each state provided the financial wherewithal to create viable institutions in the emerging but not wealthy states of the West. These institutions, which would become known as land-grant colleges and universities, include some of the most prestigious public institutions in the world. The 2011 Academic Ranking of World Universities conducted by Shanghai Jiao Tong University's Center for World-Class Universities ranks 5 public western universities (the University of California campuses at Berkeley, Los Angeles, San Diego, and San Francisco, and the University of Washington) and 2 private western universities (Stanford University and California Institute of Technology) among the top 20 universities in the world. Had resources not been provided by the federal government, the states would have had to finance the development of their public systems of higher education with their own meager resources, which would have been extremely difficult. The West has never been a wealthy region, and its states had very modest resources in their early days. Without the land-grant act, higher education in the West would have grown much less rapidly and much less substantially.

Second, the Morrill Act, whether intentionally or not, created a bifurcated model of higher education that is unique to the United States but nearly universal in the West: a system in which one university within each state would focus on the applied sciences—in particular, on agriculture and engineering (then referred to as mechanics)—and another university would focus on everything else. Except in the most rural western states, where the population base simply couldn't support the two-university model, this design prevailed, beginning in the Far West, with California, Oregon, and Washington, and extending into the Southwest, the Rocky Mountain region, and the Great Plains.[3] Interestingly, the western universities that gained the greatest reputations were seldom the federally assisted land-grant institutions but rather institutions supported by the state. In fact, the University of California Berkeley is the only western land-grant institution ranked among the leading universities in the Shanghai rankings today, and for all practical purposes it has shed the land-grant role to its sister institution, the University of California Davis. Without doubt, however, support from the Morrill Act paved the way for this level of distinction from a region of the country that simply lacked the resources to achieve such excellence without federal assistance.

Third, the concurrence of federal involvement through the Morrill Act and the expansion of higher education in the West imbued institutions with a new spirit, unique to the region. Before the Morrill Act, most higher education institutions in the United States had focused on serving an elite few. These were not just the wealthy and privileged. Rather, students were drawn from society's educated class: John Adams, for instance, who came from a farming family of modest means, was accepted by Harvard because his father was well educated (McCullough, 2001). But in the West, higher education evolved at the same time as the new federal thrust to open the system to those who were not part of the well-educated elite. Even today, the West's strong public institutions ensure that higher education in the region remains more open and less elitist than elsewhere.

From its beginnings, then, the West's higher education realm was fundamentally different from that in the East. It presumed that a much larger share of the population could, should, and indeed *must* benefit from higher education. This new educational philosophy was not nearly as broad-based as the egalitarian movements in higher education in the twentieth century, which have brought us to the belief that virtually all people should have the opportunity to receive a postsecondary education. Rather, what initially evolved in the West was what might more appropriately be referred to as a meritocratic system of higher education: a system that made it possible for bright people to get a college education, even if they did not come from educated stock. It was, and is, a system where people can get ahead because of their merit, not their birthright.

Western higher education, following the concept behind the Morrill Act, provided much greater access to the best and brightest sons of regular farmers and mechanics. Yet this privilege did not generally extend to the daughters of these folks—or to the sons and daughters of those who worked for farmers and mechanics. Furthermore, this expansion was not driven by a belief in the inherent value of well-educated people but by a demand for more workers educated in the agricultural and mechanical sciences to satisfy the high-end labor needs of the agricultural and industrial revolutions. Economic and workforce development needs, therefore, were behind federal and state interest in higher education, much as they are today.

With the advent of World War II, however, the demographic composition of American higher education changed dramatically. In the early 1940s, the enrollment of males dropped precipitously as large numbers of young men went into the military. In 1943–1944, about one-half of the students in colleges were women (Snyder, 1993, p. 65). But when the war ended, the demand for higher education surged. Enrollment at public degree-granting institutions nationwide grew by 70 percent between 1940 and 1950, and 82 percent of this increase was due to enrollments by male students (NCES, 2011). The rising demand for a college degree, particularly from veterans, led to the second major federal influence on American higher education: the Servicemen's Readjustment Act, better known as the G.I. Bill.

The reasons for and results of the G.I. Bill have been somewhat romanticized over the years. Most descriptions hold it to have been the first major effort in the United States to make higher education available to the masses. In truth, that egalitarianism was secondary to—and a byproduct of—the bill's original intent. Actually, the G.I. Bill was another federal workforce management effort, although its thrust was much different than that of the Morrill Act. When the war ended, the United States had too many men returning home for the economy to absorb. The nation needed a way to keep many of these men out of the workforce until the economy was ready to assimilate them. Higher education seemed like the perfect solution. It offered a "twofer": the men were enticed to go to school instead of returning to the workforce and were getting enhanced skills that would help increase their productivity in the future (Greenberg, 1997, p. 11).

One unique feature of the G.I. Bill that has not received adequate attention is the impact it had on the overall finance of higher education in America. The G.I. Bill was the first government program to provide students rather than institutions with voucher-like payments to secure their education. And the payments were quite generous, covering full direct educational costs (tuition, fees, and books) and supporting students (even married students) in genteel poverty. The bill provided this level of support because that's what it took to achieve its purpose: to encourage students to attend college rather than to try to enter the workforce (Greenberg, 1997, p. 50).

In the West, the G.I. Bill had a powerful impact on higher education. Before the passage of the bill, the western states had modest systems of higher education. In addition to the institutions created under the two-university model in the late nineteenth century, a number of "normal schools"—colleges that trained teachers—had developed in the West. Other than that, there were relatively few public higher education alternatives. However, the huge influx of discharged servicemen ratcheted up higher education demand dramatically. That demand grew further thanks to a postwar population explosion, caused by heavy migration to the West, particularly the Far West (California's population, for example, grew by nearly 50 percent between 1950 and 1960—from about 10 million residents to 15 million).[4] Skyrocketing demand finally put higher education closer to the top of the agenda for many state governments in the West. At the same time, the G.I. Bill, by funding students so generously, gave states the ability to meet that need and grow their systems.

Interestingly, however, in one way, federal policy was less influential in the West than in the rest of the country. The generous nature of the G.I. Bill provided a strong incentive for institutions to increase tuition and fees,—which were covered in full for G.I. participants,—thus many institutions, particularly in the East and Midwest, used this opportunity to optimize their revenues. That did not happen in the West. Western higher education has had a strong tradition of low tuition. In fact, keeping tuition low is a mandate in many western states, required by state constitution or statute.[5] This tradition of low or no tuition prevailed, despite the financial incentive of the G.I. Bill to increase tuition; and it endured until the end of the past century.

At roughly the same time as the passage of the G.I. Bill, the federal government was beginning to provide major increases in funded research. This new federal infatuation with research would fundamentally shape the West's, and American, higher education. The creation of the National Science Foundation in 1950, the substantial enhancement of the military industrial complex (with much of its research to be contracted to higher education), and the substantial expansion of the National Institutes of Health (which had existed for more than 50 years but came to the forefront in the 1950s and 1960s) all helped to shape the establishment of the American research university. The Morrill Act may have fathered the American research university, but the federal infatuation with research that followed World War II was the mother lode.

One federal research effort would have a unique impact on the West: the establishment of the so-called national labs. Such labs—at Los Alamos and Sandia in New Mexico; Berkeley (Lawrence) and Livermore in California; and Richland (Northwest Labs) in Washington—would drive western higher education to move strongly on energy and environmental issues. Initially centered primarily on nuclear research, these labs—and the western universities that followed their lead—have helped sustain an exceptionally strong focus on environmental sciences in the region.

Many western states and institutions capitalized on the increase in federal research activity. In some cases this was because of a good match between institutional and federal research interests: the University of California Berkeley and Stanford University emerged as premiere American universities during this time partly because of a synergy between their particular strengths and the interests of the federal government.[6] Politics helped some states: the University of Washington emerged as a top-tier institution during this period, particularly in health sciences, in large part because US Senator Warren Magnuson of Washington was the chairman of the Senate Appropriations Committee (and made sure the university received its "fair share" of federal resources).[7] The legacy of this strong engagement in federal research continues in the present day. One-third of the top 50 universities receiving federal research funding in 2011 were public institutions in the West.

DEVELOPMENT OF THE REGIONAL CONCEPT

Another federal effort at about this time—the chartering of regional interstate compacts—also had a significant impact on higher education in the West as well as in the South. The first such compact in the United States was created in 1948 by the Southern Regional Education Board (SREB). The second compact, approved by Congress in 1951, created the Western Interstate Commission for Higher Education (WICHE). The interstate collaboration fostered by this federal compact made it possible for western states, particularly those with modest population bases, to provide a wide array of educational opportunities to their citizens that the states simply could not afford to offer. Through these interstate agreements, states could focus their precious resources on building a strong basic system of higher education, deferring to other, larger states the task of providing training in high-cost specialty areas, such as many of the medical fields. Not surprisingly, the impetus for establishing this interstate compact among the western states was initiated by the Mountain West states, which lacked the resources to establish high-cost professional programs but needed to provide professional educational opportunities to their college graduates and to build their professional workforce. The idea of regional collaboration in higher education was initially proffered by university presidents and governors in Wyoming, Colorado, and New Mexico, who were working with a fledgling national organization, the Council of State Governments (CSG). Within two years, the majority of western states had committed to the concept, with eight states ratifying the compact by the end of 1953 and the three states and two territories (which would subsequently become states) joining the compact by 1959 (Abbott, 2004).

The synergy proved advantageous for the West. Small states could have the best of both worlds: their citizens had access to strong colleges and universities that provided a basic undergraduate education within their own state as well as to exceptional professional programs in other states. Larger states could build stronger graduate and professional programs because of the support provided by neighboring states and the ability to draw "the best and brightest" students from those states.

For example, the University of Washington's health sciences center became poised for its future national stature, in part because it was able to build a talented student body in its medical professional schools in just this manner. Colorado State University's veterinary medicine program attained similar national prominence for the same reason: at one point, more than one-half of its student body hailed from partnering WICHE states. In addition, when the vet school needed a new hospital, 11 of the then 13 WICHE states contributed to building the facility. As the West grew in the latter half of the twentieth century and legislators demanded greater coherence in state higher education policy, WICHE's role expanded. It began to work more directly with states, both individually and collectively, as they developed policies consistent with WICHE's mission "to expand educational access and excellence for all citizens of the West."

From the federal perspective, the fact that WICHE and other interstate compacts worked as well as they did may have been to some extent a fortuitous accident. The federal government did not charter these compacts solely to foster interstate collaboration. These federally sanctioned interstate collaborative efforts were being created less than 90 years after the Civil War, which had left many within the federal government wary of letting states do their own thing (federal anxiety about state collaboration and the impact it might have on the cohesiveness of the United States is reflected clearly in the eighteenth-century Articles of Confederation and the later US Constitution).[8] Federally chartered compacts were one mechanism the government used, therefore, to contain state activity. The result, however, was to establish a robust partnership among many states, particularly in the West, albeit within the prescribed sphere of higher education.

The 1960s brought two new, substantial expansions of the federal role in higher education. The National Defense Education Act (NDEA) of 1958 was enacted in response to the Soviet Union's launching of Sputnik, the first satellite to circle the globe. The fear was that Sputnik demonstrated Soviet superiority over the United States in science and represented a Communist threat to our democratic society. The NDEA, building on the framework of the G.I. Bill, worked to ensure that there was sufficient civilian participation at our nation's colleges and universities in areas of particular national interest and need. Much of the focus of the NDEA was on encouraging students to enhance their science skills. Another major component—and another responsibility our colleges and universities took on—was to assure that there were enough well-trained science and math teachers in our nation's elementary and secondary schools. Again, however, this was not done for the sake of the individuals who were receiving the education but rather as an effort to protect national security by assuring that our citizenry was educated enough to allow the United States to stand up to the Soviet Union in the Cold War.

In 1965, the federal government pursued another major higher education initiative, a much more radical one. As part of his Great Society initiative, President Lyndon B. Johnson proposed, and Congress adopted, the Higher Education Act of 1965, which changed the landscape of American higher education forever. The act, combined with amendments adopted in 1972, moved away from previous federal efforts, which were focused on economic development, to the concept of "enabling" people to attend college. It promoted educational participation, because education was good and essential for citizens, as well as for society—an idea that began to change the face of the country. "Access" to higher education for all citizens who could benefit

Table 8.1 Distribution of Pell Grants by state and public institution, selected years

Year	1973–1974	1979–1980	1989–1990	1999–2000	2009–2010
US Pell recipients in Western states	19%	18%	21%	25%	24%
Percent of Pell grants awarded to students at public institutions					
United States	66%	67%	62%	69%	62%
Western states	73%	77%	66%	75%	59%
States where 75% or more of Pell grants awarded to students at public institutions					
United States	15	23	8	26	17
Western states	10	12	5	11	6
Western states, total percentage	67%	52%	63%	42%	35%

Source: US Department of Education, *Federal Pell Grant Program Annual Data Reports*, various years, Retrieved from www2.ed.gov/finaid/prof/resources/data/pell-data.html. on December 12, 2011. "US" refers to the 50 states and District of Columbia. "Western states" refers to Alaska, Arizona, California, Colorado, Hawaii, Idaho, Montana, Nevada, New Mexico, North Dakota, Oregon, South Dakota, Utah, Washington, and Wyoming.

from it became the goal of public policy, with federal and state governments working in sync to accomplish this objective.

At the federal level, the major new program designed to advance this new national interest was the Basic Education Opportunity Grant (BEOG) program, later renamed the Pell Grant Program. Through this program all students with assessed financial need (as determined by federal law) were provided with grants to cover a portion of their educational expenses, including both tuition and room and board. As noted in table 8.1, Pell Grant usage in the West differed substantially from use elsewhere in the country: the share of awards to students attending public institutions was much higher. Initially, two-thirds of the states in which more than 75 percent of Pell Grant recipients attended public institutions were in the West (a region that includes fewer than one-third of all states).

At the state level, a unique American invention—the community college—which had begun in modest form around the beginning of the twentieth century, came to prominence as the federal government began to focus on expanding access in the 1960s. These institutions became critical to achieving this mission. In addition, they became a more significant part of higher education in the West than in other regions. To some extent, this was a consequence of California's creation in 1960 of its Master Plan for Higher Education, which explicitly charged community colleges with being the entry point for all potential postsecondary students who came from the bottom two-thirds of their high school graduating class. Admission to the University of California was restricted to the upper one-eighth of each high school graduating class, while the California State University system reserved admission only to students in the top one-third of their class. Although few other western states established standards as stringent as California's, many western states established similarly tiered systems. The impact of this intentional segmentation remains evident even today in western higher education. While 53 percent of public higher education students attend community colleges nationally, the numbers in the West's four largest states exceed this percentage, in some cases substantially: 77 percent of public postsecondary enrollments are in community colleges in California, 72 percent in Arizona, 59 percent in Oregon, and 54 percent in Washington (NCES, 2010, Table 229).

Subsequent experience has demonstrated that these efforts to broaden access to higher education did not fully achieve their objectives. The vestiges of the elitism and meritocratic values imbedded early on in American higher education remain today, even in the West. Nevertheless, the federal and state efforts of the 1960s and 1970s to expand the concept of who could benefit vastly broadened the base of American higher education, changing it profoundly.

With the expanded federal role in enhancing access to higher education came, not surprisingly, a commensurate increase in federal oversight, including more significant regulation of the delivery of higher education to assure that institutions were serving their students well. For instance, in the late 1960s and early 1970s, the federal government heightened its focus on the management of higher education with the Higher Education Act of 1965 (Section 1202), encouraging states to establish state higher education planning and policy agencies. This led to the creation of state planning agencies in many western states and consolidated governance structures in others. About one-third of the western states, mostly the larger ones, established what became known as coordinating boards, which had responsibility for planning the growth of higher education and coordinating policy to deal with this growth. Smaller states were more likely to establish governing boards with responsibility for all or portions of higher education. Over time these governing and coordinating bodies have evolved, with some states eliminating one or the other, and others doing just the opposite. In fact, when it comes to planning and governance processes, the western states have been rather schizophrenic. Initially, they all followed the federal guidelines for establishing politically neutral state planning entities. Over time, however, both coordinating and governing structures have in general become more closely aligned with the states' political structures, particularly with governors' offices.

The federal government was not just concerned about the capacity of states to manage growth in the higher education sector: it was also focused on the ability of institutions to manage such growth. As a result, the US Office of Education and the National Science Foundation became interested in enhancing the "management science" of higher education.

The new federal focus on higher education management systems coincided with growing interest in the same topic in the West. WICHE, the region's interstate compact, had been developing a strong capacity in database development and the use of data for management purposes. The coincidence of federal interest and WICHE capacity led to the development of a national effort, based at WICHE and funded by the US Office of Education. Initially, this work fit comfortably within the WICHE organization, because of the prevalence of public higher education and the rapid growth in enrollments in the West. Over time, however, the activity began to overshadow WICHE's other core activities, while the national nature of the work challenged WICHE's proudly western role and mission. This conflict, or imbalance, led to the creation of a new entity, the National Center for Higher Education Management Systems (NCHEMS). Initially a unit within WICHE, NCHEMS became a stand-alone national organization in the late 1970s, allowing its parent to return to its western roots. However, the two organizations continue to work together: in fact, in 2005 they joined with the State Higher Education Executive Officers (SHEEO) to form the State Higher Education Policy Center (SHEPC), located in Boulder, Colorado.

The Challenges of a New Century

From the 1970s until the end of the twentieth century, the federal role in higher education increased and evolved, although the changes in policy were essentially incremental. Subsequent amendments to the Higher Education Act worked to refine and improve federal policy, but not to alter it radically. Likewise, in the area of research, new fields of endeavor evolved, while the general relationship between higher education and the federal government did not change substantially.

The financial challenges of the new century, resulting from two deep recessions coming in unprecedentedly close proximity and exacerbated by a painful legacy of excess (both in terms of escalating costs for providing higher education and prices charged via tuition and fees) have changed the landscape of American higher education as well as the federal role in this enterprise. This has been true for both of the major areas in which the federal government is significantly engaged in higher education—student financial assistance and research. In addition, through the American Recovery and Reinvestment Act of 2009 (ARRA), federal support for basic operations of public educational institutions increased significantly for a brief time (FY2009–FY2011). Despite increasing federal budget deficits and reductions in domestic funding, funding for federal student aid has grown rapidly since the turn of the century. Certainly, one primary reason for this has been the expansion of benefits to a much larger share of students. Most of the federal investment in student assistance goes into two federal programs: the federal Pell Grant Program, providing foundation grant assistance to students with assessed financial need and the federal student loan programs, which provide loan assistance to low- and middle-income students to help defray educational costs not covered by family assistance, savings, or grants. Both Pell and loan programs expanded greatly in the first decade of the new century.

One of the dilemmas of these programs has been their unpredictability over time. From 1986–1987 to 1996–1997, for example, the maximum Pell Grant increased only from $2,100 to $2,470, losing nearly 18 percent of its inflation-adjusted value. By 2002–2003, though, the maximum had increased to $4,000, bringing the inflation-adjusted value to virtually the same level it had been in 1986–1987. Since that time, the maximum award has continued to increase, rising to $5,500 in 2011–2012. The increase led to an expected rise in federal program costs. However, costs grew in another, unexpected way. From 2000 to 2010, the share of students receiving Pell grants rose from 20 percent of all enrollments to 35 percent; at the same time, enrollments jumped nearly 35 percent. These two factors combined to increase Pell Grant participation by nearly 50 percent. Without doubt a large portion of this increase resulted from the downturn in the economy, which caused the share of traditional students with assessed need to rise and enticed more students to attend college. A large share came also from growth in the ranks of eligible students resulting from the larger grant size, an unintended but significant effect of a poorly designed process for assessing student need. The result has been an increase in Pell Grant Program costs from $10 billion in 2000 to $36 billion in 2011. Similar increases in the federal student loan program have caused annual borrowing to rise from $37 billion in 2000 to more than $90 billion in 2010.

Not surprisingly, increased federal support has led to more oversight, including more regulatory requirements, greater interest in improving institutional efficiency and effectiveness in serving students, and more federal initiatives to improve accountability for the use of federal funds. The West has demonstrated leadership in responding to some federal oversight initiatives. Its regional compact, WICHE, has been working with western states to develop reciprocity between them in their response to federal initiatives designed to enhance state oversight of private institutions.

With respect to the federal role in research, the story line is essentially "more of the same"—or perhaps more accurately, "more of the same—but done for a little less." In 1998, Congress authorized doubling federal research and development funding for the National Institutes of Health. This ambitious agenda was based on the assumption that the economic growth of the 1990s would persist. Funding levels for health (though not for other areas of federal research) continued to rise until 2003. Since 2003 federal funding for academic R&D has remained roughly stable in the $30 billion range (in 2010 dollars), though federal research funding did increase substantially in 2010 and 2011, thanks to ARRA's largesse. And western institutions continue to rank high in the receipt of federal funds.

In the less populated western states, however, institutions have fared less well in federal research funding. To rectify this, the federal government established the Experimental Program to Stimulate Competitive Research (EPSCOR) within the National Science Foundation in 1979. EPSCOR has helped western frontier states with smaller populations a great deal. Now part of a national research initiative, it provides half a billion dollars annually to 29 states and territories, including 9 western states (Alaska, Hawaii, Idaho, Montana, Nevada, New Mexico, North Dakota, South Dakota, and Wyoming).

Many frontier state universities in the West have also benefited substantially from research funds garnered as earmarks by influential federal legislators. In 2010, 7 of the top 20 institutions receiving earmarked federal funds were western universities: University of North Dakota, North Dakota State University, University of Hawaii, Utah State University, New Mexico Institute of Mining and Technology, University of Utah, and Montana State University. And only 2 of these (University of Hawaii and University of Utah) would otherwise fall within the top 50 funded institutions in the country. These seven institutions received nearly 10 percent of the total amount provided in earmarks that year. But the era of federal earmarks appears to have come to an end. No resources for earmarks were provided in the FY2011 federal budget, and the federal political climate suggests that such funding will not be available in the future. Certainly, those institutions that benefited from this largess will miss this noncompetitively granted federal research funding.

The third and newest thrust of the federal government came with ARRA, which provided billions of dollars to states to shore up funding for education in the wake of the recession of 2009. These funds were provided on a short-term basis to help states "weather the storm" and allow them time to adjust to what has been termed "the new normal": a fiscal environment marked, in the long term, by lower revenue streams than were available in the go-go years at the close of the past century

With these funds, however, came additional federal expectations, including demands for improved higher education performance. Again, the West, in part through its regional compact, WICHE, took a leadership role in this federal initiative. One ARRA requirement was that every state accepting funds must also invest in developing a robust data system, including student-level data for all those enrolled in elementary, secondary, and postsecondary education as well as all employed individuals in the state. The goal is to provide states and the federal government with better information on the efficacy of state education efforts. WICHE has worked with four states to help build their federally funded and required database development projects (designed to provide better information for accountability purposes) into robust data networks that will allow states to garner information not only about their residents but also about individuals who migrate from one state to another.

The net result of all these national initiatives is that currently the federal government invests as much in higher education as do the states (if not more), although states retain the constitutional right to provide this public good and the responsibilities that go with it. Furthermore, the substantial shift in who pays for education, particularly undergraduate education—from states to students, through steadily increasing tuition and fees—creates a disconnect between authority, funding, and responsibility that is inconsistent with good public policy. While the West has always been heavily dependent upon federal support for higher education, it is becoming even more dependent upon it—and doing so at a time when the western states appear hell-bent on distancing themselves from federal intrusion. Time will tell, but it may well be that "this dog won't hunt."

Notes

1. Dates for the establishment of colleges and universities have been taken from the *2008 Higher Education Directory* (Burke, 2008).
2. Dates for statehood were gleaned from the official state websites of Alaska, Arizona, California, Hawaii, and Oregon. Retrieved from www.state.ak.us; http://az.gov/webapp/portal; www. state.ca.us; www.hawaii.gov/portal; and www.oregon.gov., on August 3, 2005.
3. Only two western states, Hawaii and Wyoming, failed to establish the dual university model. All others have sustained this model, except California, which evolved its dual system into the University of California system, with ten research universities.
4. Historical data are from the State of California website. Retrieved from www. state. ca.us., on August 3, 2005.
5. Arizona, California, Idaho, Nevada, and New Mexico have constitutional requirements that tuition not be charged or that it be kept as low as possible.
6. The University of California Berkeley, which at one time ranked among the top R&D-funded institutions, now ranks eighteenth in federal R&D funding, not including the funding it receives for the federal labs under its management. Other campuses of the University of California system, including University of California Los Angeles, University of California San Francisco (solely a health sciences university), and University of California San Diego, now surpass University of California Berkeley in federal R&D funding, but this is only because each of these campuses has a medical sciences mission, which Berkeley does not. Stanford University also remains a leader in attracting federal R&D, now ranking fourth.
7. The University of Washington ranks second in federal R&D funding today, above any other public university in the nation and any university in the West.
8. The Articles of Confederation stated in Article Six that "no two or more States shall enter into any treaty, confederation, or alliance whatever between them, without the consent of the United States in Congress assembled." While the US Constitution is less explicit about the limits of interstate collaboration, the federal angst remains evident in Article One, Section 10, which paraphrases the language from the Articles of Confederation, by stating, "No State shall enter into any treaty, alliance, or confederation."

References

Abbott, F. C. *A History of the Western Interstate Commission for Higher Education: The First Forty Years.* Boulder, CO: WICHE, 2004.

Burke, J. M. (ed.). *2008 Higher Education Directory.* Falls Church, VA: Higher Education, 2008.

College Board. *Trends in Student Aid, 2007.* Washington, DC: College Board, 2008.

Greenberg, M. *The GI Bill: The Law that Changed America.* West Palm Beach, FL: Lickle, 1997.

Grubb, W. N., and M. Lazerson. "Vocationalism in Higher Education: The Triumph of the Education Gospel." *Journal of Higher Education*, 2005, 76: 1.

McCullough, D. G. *John Adams*. New York: Simon and Schuster, 2001.

National Center for Education Statistics (NCES), US Department of Education. *Digest of Education Statistics*, 2010 (NCES 2011–015): Table 229. Retrieved from http://nces.ed.gov/ programs/digest/d10/tables/dt10_003.asp?referrer=report, on December 1, 2011.

National Center for Higher Education Management Systems. Retrieved from www .higheredinfo.org., on July 14, 2009.

National Science Foundation. "Master Government List of Federally Funded R&D Centers (FFRDCs)." Retrived from www.nsf.gov/statistics/ffrdclist/. on November 11, 2011.

National Science Foundation, Division of Science Resource Statistics. "Federal Science and Engineering Support to Universities, Colleges, and Nonprofit Institutions: FY 2007, Detailed Statistical Tables" (NSF 09–315, September, 2009).

Organisation for Economic Co-operation and Development (OECD). *Education at a Glance 2007.* Paris: OECD, 2007.

Snyder, T. D. (ed.). *120 Years of American Education: A Statistical Portrait.* Washington, DC: National Center for Educational Statistics, 1993.

Western Interstate Commission for Higher Education (WICHE). *Knocking at the College Door: Projections of High School Graduates by State, Income, and Race /Ethnicity, 1992–2022.* Boulder, CO: Western Interstate Commission for Higher Education, 2008.

Part III

A Concluding Commentary

Afterword

Understanding the First Regional History of American Higher Education: The Spirit of Innovation

Lester F. Goodchild

Higher education in the American West began with a small Catholic college in St. Louis in 1818. Grand hopes and dreams led the early educators to offer literary studies there, as the frontier exploded with new peoples ambitious to take western lands, especially after the 1848 discovery of gold in California. Generally, private religious-related colleges began first in most western states and territories in hopes of evangelizing the frontier population. After almost two centuries now, over 1,200 colleges and universities fill the western US region with world-class opportunities for higher education at prestigious research universities, land-grant universities, distinctive colleges, state colleges, numerous community colleges, and, importantly, tribal colleges and universities (TCUs) as well as Hispanic Seriving Institutions (HSIs).

This book offered a broad historical regional portrait of these social institutions that were founded to transmit knowledge and advance research in undergraduate, graduate, and professional studies that augmented America's quest for distinctive higher learning. This project dramatically extends our historical research on American higher education (Cohen and Kisker, 2010; Rudolph, 1962; Thelin, 2011; Wechsler, Goodchild, and Eisenmann, 2007). As the first regional history of American higher education, its editors and authors sought to capture the distinctive roles that its approximately 1,000 universities and colleges have played in providing higher learning to its citizens, advancing research that benefited the nation, and encouraging cultural expressions in the arts and literature. This project began in 1999 with an effort to mark the fiftieth anniversary of the Western Interstate Commission for Higher Education (WICHE) that was to occur in 2003. Its editors and contributors took much longer to achieve this definitive regional work in part due to 10 years of witnessing dramatic changes in growth and retrenchment of western higher education in the 15 WICHE states. Now, this volume and its companion work, L. F. Goodchild, R. W. Jonsen, P. Limerick, and D. A. Longanecker, *Public Policy Challenges Facing Higher Education in the American West* (2104), mark the sixtieth anniversary year of the interstate commission.

Patty Limerick, professor of history and director of the Center of the American West at the University of Colorado, Boulder, reminds us in chapter 3 that the "West is a place of bold innovation." These western territories were lands of conquest and conflict in the eighteenth and nineteenth centuries, as Native Americans lost their homelands in favor of more developed European colonists and eastern American immigrants. Innovation came after the displacement and subjugation of these indigenous populations. Appropriately, her more well-known and highly acclaimed groundbreaking works, *The Legacy of Conquest: The Unbroken Past of the American West* (1987) and *Trails: Toward a New Western History* (1991), call to mind how we have advanced in our thinking and understanding of peoples due precisely to these higher studies. This enlightenment led to the new federal laws in 1978 that funded the 32 land-grant tribal colleges and then in 1994 restorated the sovereignty of the Native American nations to redress some of the injustices done long ago.

Amid these tragic conquests, the Civil War seared these developing lands, as the nation was torn apart by sectional conflict and strife regarding the place of slavery in American society. Freeing African slaves led to the rebuilding of societal and government infrastructures that not only restored the union but also brought about institutions of higher learning for these persons of color with the rise of the 1890 land-grant universities. Such difficulties demonstrated a continuing determination to recognize the rights of peoples in an enlightened society, based on western legal traditions and freedoms. Eventually, western higher education became fully available for most peoples.

Importantly, Patty Limerick's chapter seeks to debunk the romanticism of university developments and acknowledges that the increase in the number of universities had much to do with the grand designs of wealthy capitalists who inadvertently struck societal good by creating institutions of higher learning. Even more so, one could add that state monies have founded and supported these institutions, producing greater good for its citizens. This realpolitik for western universities and colleges is interestingly later scaffolded on a textual dialogue pitting national dilemmas in higher education with western regional responses. The outcome of this literary construction points to the reality of a true western understanding of American higher education. As with all her works, such a tour de force claim invites the reader to grapple with a regional situationalism that is necessary for understanding the missions of the 1,229 institutions of higher learning in the 15 WICHE states. Overall, Limerick creates a bold and commanding justification for the value of a western regional history and policy study. Her 45 years in the academic saddle have produced a grounded "celebration of the power of higher education" in the American West.

Critically, this book opened with a chapter offering for the first time a geographical history of the rise of higher education in the trans-Mississippi West, by showing how college development followed three major migration paths close to the wagon trials, near larger rivers, or through general population movements both from the Pacific coast east or across the Mississippi west. New towns offered schooling and even higher education as quickly as possible. Such developments provided educational opportunities that reflected either the Christian churches' efforts to promote evangelization among these new settlers or the town peoples' hopes to advance their communities through economic and social boosterism. As Goodchild and Wrobel have shown, this early developing era from 1818 to 1859 led to an expansion era from 1860 to 1899 and then a service era from 1900 to 1940, as some 655 still-operating colleges opened in these western lands.

As these migrations expanded, statehood followed and public higher education blossomed. Now states sought to advance practical studies on the frontier, as land-grant colleges with the goals of agricultural and mining studies assisted these new populations in harvesting the lands better and extracting the mineral riches from their depths. Cohen's chapter underscores how these developing lands brought about a different focus to the studies among institutions of higher education than in the eastern, southern, or midwestern regions of the country. He noted how "it had become 'settled policy' among the western states" to create state social institutions of higher learning, the capital, the prison, and the mental hospital as soon as possible. Then after 1862, land-grant funding augmented these efforts in the western states as institutions, such as the University of California Berkeley, Oregon State University, Colorado State University, and the University of Arizona, between 1868 and 1885 respectively, gradually become more focused on the practical studies of agriculture and mining. From the middle to the end of the nineteenth century, early private universities and colleges, such as Santa Clara University (Catholic), University of the Pacific (Methodist), Brigham Young University (Mormon), Stanford University (nondenominational), University of Southern California (Methodist), and the all-women's Mills College (nondenominational) contributed a new distinctive spirit to developing western higher education. Importantly, junior and community colleges began in the 1900–1940 service era to provide more higher education opportunities to all groups in society.

One of the major contributions to the vitality of western higher education occurred with the beginnings of interstate coordination through the creation of the WICHE compact, the second of the four regional higher education compacts in the United States, devoted to coordinating opportunities across the 15 western states in 1952. Its early programs focused on promoting professional education, student tuition exchanges among states, and data gathering across the region. Later, these types of collaborations brought about further innovation in western higher education from the development of the Western Cooperative for Educational Technology, not-for-profit distance education (e.g., the Western Governors University, Regis University, and the National University in San Diego), and new for-profit higher education (e.g., University of Phoenix, Jones International University, and DeVry University).

Moreover, this regional story has great complexity as was explored in the four "quadrant" histories, representing the four major state areas in the region, that were presented in this book. Each chapter history sought to describe the developments in each area from 1940 up to the present. These now 74 years saw massive expansion of higher education student enrollments with the G.I. Bill after World War II, student revolts in the 1960s, and extensive federal research investment due to the Cold War and the Vietnam War. Throughout these decades, public and private higher education continued to play major roles in state development, scientific research, professional career education, and undergraduate studies as part of their missions to promote the transmission of knowledge and advancement of research to benefit the region and the country.

Each of these four areas in the region evolved as internal and external forces brought about changes in higher education. Our authors have written some of the first multistate histories of American higher education in our larger effort to produce a regional study. Chapter 4 describes how the middle border area states of Idaho, Montana, North Dakota, South Dakota, and Wyoming provided significant public higher education to the region with the founding of some 60 four- and two-year institutions, while private higher education added 27 and for-profit contributed 46 (with 12 four-year institutions)—totalling 133. Such predominant public concentration of institutions was reflected in student enrollments at state institutions, with Wyoming's 97 percent and South Dakota's 76 percent admissions. Moreover, this area enabled a greater number of Native Americans to attend college with seven tribal colleges in Montana, five in North Dakota, and four in South Dakota. WICHE played an important role in the subregion when it brought together state leaders in 1971 who created the University of Washington's Medical School Program called WWAMI—for each of the states involved—that enabled Idaho, Montana, Alaska, and Wyoming to send their medical students to the University of Washington at a reduced state tuition (Abbott, 2004, pp. 100–107). The Great Recession hit this area heavily as Idaho lost 19 percent, Montana some 14 percent, and South Dakota more than 5 percent of their public state funding from 2008 to 2011. On the other hand, North Dakota increased their public funding to higher education by 18 percent and Wyoming 15 percent—some of the brightest spots in the region.

In chapter 5, the Southwest area of the WICHE region offered extensive higher education in the states of Arizona, Colorado, Nevada, New Mexico, and Utah. All together they comprised 262 institutions of higher learning with some 99 public (or 38 percent), 32 private, and 131 for-profit (with 85 being four-year colleges or universities). The University of Colorado became one of the world's top research universities with its thirty-second ranking according to the 2012 Academic Rankings of World Universities (www.arwu.org). Moreover, Arizona provides distinctive Native American educational opportunities with Diné College and its seven branch campuses, founded in 1968. New Mexico also offers three unique opportunities for Native Americans and others at its Institute of Native American Arts, Southwest Indian Polytechnic Institute, and Navajo Technical College, founded in 1969, 1971, and 1977 respectively. Further, Fort Lewis College in Colorado enrolls 37 percent students of color, most of whom "come from 139 American Indian tribes and Native Alaskan villages" (www.fortlewis.edu). Overall, this WICHE region's institutions are 26.7 percent diverse with strong Latino and other persons of color student populations. WICHE also played a critical role in the development of medical education by aiding in the opening of the medical school at the University of Nevada Reno, with the Mountain States Medical Regional Program in the 1970s that Idaho, Montana, and Wyoming's students attended. It also encouraged undergraduate engineering studies across the region. The region's most innovative contribution to higher education became its distance education institutions, especially the online Western Governors University, sponsored by 19 western state governors in 1995 and enrolling 30,000 students by 2010, and the for-profit institutions with the University of Phoenix leading the three major institutions within the WICHE states and across the nation with some 470,000 enrolled students at the end of the 2009–2010 academic year. Similar to other subregions in the West, the Great Recession brought about significant state government retrenchments of operating budgets as Arizona lost 28 percent, New Mexico 21 percent, Utah 13.6 percent, Colorado 10.5 percent, and Nevada with 0.47 of their public funding from 2008 to 2011. Arizona trailed the country, as the most severely affected state system during these difficult times.

In chapter 6, the Pacific West, which comprises the states of Alaska, Hawaii, Oregon, and Washington, is analyzed. These states created 168 institutions of higher learning, with 84 (50 percent) being in the public sector. In addition, private higher education institutions contributed 49, while for-profit postsecondary institutions numbered 35 (with 22 being four-year institutions). The University of Washington became one of the world's top research universities with approximately $213 million in research funding and was ranked sixteenth according to the 2012 Academic Rankings of World Universities (www.argu.org). WICHE also facilitated the University of Washington's role in this area with its WWAMI program for medical students from Idaho, Montana, and Wyoming. Turning to some of the unique higher education efforts in this subregion, an Alaskan contribution to American higher education is the leading role the University of Alaska plays in delivering community college education at its three four-year campuses at Fairbanks, Anchorage, and Southeast, coordinating a total of 11 community colleges within the state. In the rest of the country, mission differentiation has meant that four-year and two-year campuses are usually physically separated—actually the only other example of this is in Denver, Colorado, where the Auraria Campus has the University of Colorado

Denver, Metropolitan State University, and the Community College of Denver. Distinctively, one of the two independent Alaskan community colleges, Ilisagvik, is for the indigenous Inupiat population. At the University of Hawaii-Hilo, its Ka Haka 'Ula O Ke'elikōlani (College of the Hawaiian Language) further offers the unique Hawaiian language and culture studies. The Great Recession forced the withdrawal of significant public funding of higher education in the area with Oregon losing 19 percent, Washington some 16 percent, and Hawaii more than 11 percent from 2008 to 2011. On the other hand, Alaska improved its public funding to higher education by 22 percent—the highest in the region.

Chapter 7 takes a more unusual subregional analysis with a focus on only one state; however, California represents the largest and strongest state higher education system in the United States with some 666 institutions,[1] as may be seen from various national and international rankings. Among the top 50 world universities according to the 2012 Academic Ranking of World Universities (see chapter 2, p. 63), 10 are from this state (in descending ranking order): Stanford University, University of California Berkeley, California Institute of Technology, University of California Los Angeles, University of California San Diego, University of California San Francisco, University of California Santa Barbara, University of California Irvine, University of Southern California, and University of California Davis (www.arwu.org). Patrick Callan in this chapter provides an extraordinarily helpful commentary on the rise of the 1960 Master Plan's "unified policy" for California that led to eight of these universities being part of this historic plan. Most importantly, the plan set a "principle of universal access as public policy" for higher education. Its three sectors accommodated California's massive postsecondary education need with 1.1 million students in the community colleges, 358,063 in the CSU state universities, and 232,613 in the UC research universities in fall 2010. Overall, this state in the WICHE region reflected the nation's most diverse populations in 2011 with 52 percent being students of color (i.e., Latino, Asian/Pacific Islander, Filipino, Black, and Native American), 33 percent White, and 15 percent unknown. Callan's current public policy focus in this chapter describes the state's public finance difficulties, demographic shifts, and problems with the state's public education during the past 30 years. Surprisingly, the state's retrenchment of funding for public higher education has resulted in only less than half a percent decline in FY2008–FY2011 (Zumeta and Kinne, 2011).

However, as the cost of higher education rose in the 1980s and 1990s, more calls to curb state government spending and reduce taxation began to embroil the western states as a center for the so-called American Tax Revolt. Proposition 13 in California in 1978 caused the curtailment of the public mandate for continued excellence in public higher education quality regardless of cost, as state budgets retrenched from their historic largesse given to higher education during the 1960s and 1970s. The growing cost of research and graduate education as well as the expansion of undergraduate education forced a reversal in the public mandate for higher education for all, called then by higher education researchers a quest for mass and universal higher education.

In place of state monies came federal government funding for student scholarships, loans, research (especially through the National Science Foundation), and the newest assistance to public higher education, the American Recovery and Reinvestment Act (ARRA), in the recession-reeling states. All of these changes are discussed in chapter 8, where David Longanecker's commentary points to the strategic role that Washington has played in providing federal monies to western higher education, especially its land-grant and research universities. These funds assisted the nation by keeping the region a center of postsecondary innovation, as its large number of globally ranked universities testifies. Nevertheless, this is a critical time in state support for its institutions of higher learning.

We stand now at an era of reassessment, as Arthur Cohen noted, with state governments withdrawing their funding of public higher education: recent annual retrenchments from the FY2008 to FY2011 amount to approximately –28 percent in Arizona, –25 percent in Oregon, –21 percent in New Mexico, and –19 percent in Idaho. Overall, in the 15 WICHE states, the average decline was –14 percent. Only three western states countered this trend, with Alaska, Wyoming, and North Dakota advancing their public state contributions (Zumeta and Kinne, 2011).

In discussing this rather current dark regional picture of state financial support for western higher education, it is important to point to the overall national trend, which is somewhat brighter. While such recent declines reflect the recession, there may be a developing underlying state policy movement toward cost shifting. As the higher education enterprise has become more expensive, states pressed by other societal demands are seeking higher student tuition and greater fee increases. This growing cost-sharing approach may signal a fundamental change in public funding of higher education. Historically, the picture reflects a great and supportive partnership. From FY1960 to FY1980, states' funding of higher education grew from an initial $1.4 billion to some $20.9 billion. This tripled by 2000, reaching $60.5 billion. State funding added another $28.3 billion in just eight short years to reach its highpoint at $88.8 billion in FY2008 (Chambers, 1960, 1980; Hines, 1990; Palmer and Gillian, 2000; Palmer, 2011).

As the recession took hold, the federal government recognized the states' problems in meeting all of their fiscal demands and passed ARRA. It supplemented declining state support for higher education by providing approximately $2.8 billion annually to the 31 states that participated. Nationally, the decline in public funding for higher education with ARRA funding has only been –3.8 percent from 2007 to 2011. Accordingly, the State Higher Education Executive Officers' (SHEEO) report (2012, p. 7) notes "state and local support in 2011 including ARRA funds totaled $87.5 billion, actually showing a 2.5 percent increase in funding for higher education over 2010 (although still below 2008 and 2009)."

Will this trend continue once the recession is over? In other words, do these shifts indicate a reduction of state investment in higher education in the American West? Unfortunately, the decline of ARRA monies and further erosion of state funding at the national level for FY2012 meant that states retrenched in funding public higher education: around $3.5 billion from $75.7 billion in 2011 to $72.2 billion in 2012. Thus "state support for higher education is down 7.9 percent" (SHEEO, 2012, pp. 7–8, 12). While the western state picture seems to differ little from the national one, there is some good news from California, where Governor Jerry Brown through significant tax changes under the new California legislature has been able to make state funding almost double from $1,503 to $2,491 per student over the next three years through 2016 (Schatz, 2013, p. A4). Other western states that show more positive expenditures than the national average the past fiscal year are Alaska, Hawaii, New Mexico, Nevada, North Dakota, and Wyoming (SHEEO, 2012, p. 37). However, only future analyses of higher education public policy's longer term trends and funding for FY2013 through FY2020 will provide a truly clearer picture of state funding of public higher education.

In part, the quest to understand and explore the public policy issues and their related difficulties that American western higher education faces is the project of our companion volume, *Public Policy Challenges Facing Higher Education in the American West.* After an initial extensive demographic chapter providing useful data on postsecondary institutions and constituencies in the 15 WICHE states, this book explores major public policy issues regarding: student access; federal government laws, mandates, and funding; state government governance of higher education; financial challenges in western public higher education; rise of higher tuition and fees among these institutions and its meaning for various constituencies; and the increasingly important role of distance education and technology in higher education. These major policy issues set the agenda for federal and state government leaders, 1,229 college and university campus leaders, and especially multicultural student groups, as each explores the possibilities for delivering high-quality and world-class higher education in the future.[2] These companion volumes represent the first efforts to explore the history of higher education and its public policy issues in one of the regions of American higher education. Higher education in the western states has played a leading role in enabling American society to advance its global leadership in higher education, scientific and humanities research, professional studies of law, business, engineering, and education, as well as educating its citizens to further an American perspective in the world.

How will western colleges and universities continue to hold their critical places at the increasingly complex and competitive global higher education table? This overall regional history of the WICHE West discloses how higher education has played an essential role in the transmission and the advancement of knowledge, provided new opportunities for most to participate in higher learning, and created various innovative means to extend education across the nation. Moreover, extraordinary public and private research universities have been recognized as being world-class universities, while at the same time other nations have created community colleges, for-profit institutions, and online education to meet the educational needs of various groups. Greater efforts to provide funding to all people through these and other distinctive institutions show promise. In many ways, western higher education thus has contributed greatly to the excellence of and innovation in American higher education. Nevertheless, challenges continue, as our companion volume attests.

NOTES

1. California Postsecondary Commission, *50 State Comparison—Postsecondary Education Data Table*, Number of Title IV Postsecondary Institutions, 2003–04 to 2009–10. Retrieved from www.cpec.ca.gov/StudentData/50StateTable.asp?Type=NumColleges) in January 2014.
2. The total number of 1,229 WICHE West higher education institutions that the authors of this book have determined comes from various 2010 sources—see individual quadrant subregional chapters or the Afterword for further research. This total is derived from the following: 133 from the Middle Border states, 262 from the Southwest states, 168 from the Pacific West states, and 666 from California.

REFERENCES

Abbott, F. *A History of the Western Interstate Commission for Higher Education: The First Forty Years.* Boulder, CO: Western Interstate Commission for Higher Education, 2004.

Academic Rankings of World Universities, 2012. Retrieved from www.arwu.org.

Chambers, M. M. *Grapevine: An Annual Compilation of Data on Fiscal Support for Higher Education*, 1960, 1980. Retrieved from http://grapevine.illinoisstate.edu/historical/index.htm.

Cohen, A. M., and C. B. Kisker. *The Shaping of American Higher Education: Emergence and Growth of the Contemporary System*, 2nd ed. San Francisco, CA: Jossey-Bass, 2010.

Goodchild, L. F., R. W. Jonsen, P. Limerick, and D. A. Longanecker (eds.). *Public Policy Challenges Facing Higher Education in the American West.* Higher Education and Society series. New York: Palgrave Macmillan, 2014.

Hines, E. R. *Grapevine: An Annual Compilation of Data on Fiscal Support for Higher Education*, 1990. Retrieved from http://grapevine.illinoisstate.edu/historical/index.htm.

Limerick, P. N. *The Legacy of Conquest: The Unbroken Past of the American West.* New York: W. W. Norton, 1987.

Limerick, P. N., C. A. Miller II, and C. E. Ranking (eds.). *Trails: Toward a New Western History.* Lawrence: University Press of Kansas, 1991.

Palmer, J. C. *Grapevine: An Annual Compilation of Data on Fiscal Support for Higher Education*, 2011. Retrieved from http://grapevine.illinoisstate.edu/historical/index.htm.

Palmer, J. C., and S. Gillian. *Grapevine: An Annual Compilation of Data on Fiscal Support for Higher Education*, 2000. Retrieved from http://grapevine.illinois-state.edu/historical/index.htm.

Rudolph, F. *The American College and University: A History.* New York: Alfred A. Knopf, 1962.

Schatz, A. "States Raise College Budgets after Years of Deep Cuts." *Wall Street Journal*, May 30, 2013, 261 (123): A-1, A-4

State Higher Education Executive Officers (SHEEO). *State Higher Education Finance, FY2011: A Project of the Staff of the State Higher Education Officers*, 2012. Retrieved from http://www.sheeo. org/finance/shef/SHEF_FY11.pdf.

———. *State Higher Education Finance, FY2012: A Project of the Staff of the State Higher Education Officers*, 2013. Retrieved from http://www.sheeo.org/sites/default/files/publications/SHEF%20FY%2012–20130322rev.pdf.

Thelin, J. R. *A History of American Higher Education*, 2nd ed. Baltimore, MD: Johns Hopkins University Press, 2011.

Wechsler, H. S., L. F. Goodchild, and L. Eisenmann. *The History of Higher Education*, 3rd ed. ASHE Reader Series. Boston, MA: Pearson, 2007.

Zumeta, W., and A. Kinne. "The Recession Is Not Over for Higher Education." *The NEA 2011 Almanac for Higher Education.* Washington, DC: National Education Association, 2011, pp. 29–42.

Contributors

Patrick M. Callan
President, Higher Education Policy Institute, San Jose, California
From 1992 to 1997, Patrick M. Callan was executive director of the California Higher Education Policy Center, and, from 1997 through 2011, president of the National Center for Public Policy and Higher Education. He previously served as executive director of the California Postsecondary Education Commission, the Washington State Council for Postsecondary Education, the Montana Commission on Postsecondary Education, and as vice president of the Education Commission of the States. Callan has written extensively on higher education policy, educational opportunity, public accountability, and financing of higher education. He is coauthor of *Financing American Higher Education in the Era of Globalization* (2012) and *Designing State Higher Education Systems for a New* Century (2001), and coeditor of *Public and Private Financing of Higher Education: Shaping Public Policy for the Future* (1997) and *The Learning Connection, New Partnerships between Schools and Colleges* (2001).

Arthur M. Cohen
Professor Emeritus, University of California Los Angeles, California
Arthur M. Cohen has been professor of higher education at the University of California at Los Angeles since 1964; he became emeritus in the Graduate School of Education and Information Studies in 2004. He received his BA and MA degrees in history from the University of Miami and his PhD degree in higher education from the Florida State University. He was director of the ERIC Clearinghouse for Community Colleges from 1966 to 2003 and president of the Center for the Study of Community Colleges from 1974 to 2007. Cohen's numerous professional honors range from *Change* magazine's naming him "One of the 44 Most Influential People in American Higher Education" (1974) to receiving the Association for the Study of Higher Education's "Research Achievement" award (2005). His most recent books are *The American Community College* (5th ed., 2008), coauthored with Florence B. Brawer, and *The Shaping of American Higher Education* (2nd ed., 2010), coauthored with Carrie B. Kisker.

William E. ("Bud") Davis
Chancellor Emeritus, Oregon State System of Higher Education, Salem, Oregon
William E. Davis served as chairman of WICHE in 1974 and 1975, and had been a WICHE commissioner for the states of Idaho, New Mexico, and

Oregon. He has a long and distinguished career in senior executive positions in western and southern higher education, beginning with the presidency of Idaho State University in 1965 and then at the University of New Mexico in 1975. Moving to the state system level, Davis was appointed chancellor of the Oregon State System of Higher Education in 1982 and then the Louisiana State University in 1989. Retiring in 2000, Davis moved to Corrales, New Mexico, where he served as regent for Western New Mexico University and as a member of the state student loan board until 2009. He began his academic career at the University of Wyoming as the head of student affairs and professor in 1963. Davis earned his BS degree and EdD from the University of Colorado, and was the university's alumni director, head football coach, and dean of men. His dissertation was published as a book, *Glory Colorado! A History of the University of Colorado, 1858 to 1963* (1965), which was followed by a second volume covering the years 1963 to 2000 in 2007. Later, he wrote *Miracle on the Mesa: A History of the University of New Mexico from 1889–2004* (2006). He has also published some 200 articles in his career.

Lester F. Goodchild
Distinguished Professor of International and Comparative Education and Advisor to the Provost, University of Massachusetts Boston, Boston, Massachusetts since September 2012; and Professor of Education, Emeritus, Santa Clara University, Santa Clara, California.
Lester F. Goodchild had served as dean of Santa Clara's School of Education and Counseling Psychology and director of its Higher Education Program. Previously, Goodchild was dean of the School of Education and Human Development at the University of Massachusetts Boston as well as earlier interim dean of education, director of the Higher Education Program, and associate professor of education at the University of Denver. His specialty is the study of higher education, with emphases on its history, public policy, administration, and professional ethics. He has coedited five books: *Advancing Higher Education as a Field of Study: In Quest of Doctoral Degree Guidelines—Commemorating 120 Years of Excellence* (2014); *The History of Higher Education* (1989, 1997, 2007); *Public Policy and Higher Education* (1997); *Rethinking the Dissertation Process: Tackling Personal and Institutional Obstacles* (1997); and *Administration as a Profession* (1991). He has written 61 refereed articles, book chapters, and other publications. Goodchild received his PhD in higher education from the University of Chicago, MDiv from St. Meinrad School of Theology, Indiana, MA in religious studies from Indiana University, and BA in sociology from the University of St. Thomas, Minnesota.

Richard W. Jonsen
Former Executive Director, Western Interstate Commission for Higher Education (WICHE), Boulder, Colorado
Richard W. Jonsen served in this position from 1990 until his retirement in 1999. Recently, he taught ESL at Front Range Community College in

Westminster, Colorado. He had been at WICHE since 1977, first as project director and then as deputy director. He served in previous administrative positions at the Education Commission of the States, Syracuse University (New York), and University of Santa Clara (California). He held faculty positions in higher education at Syracuse, University of Denver (visiting), and the Autonomous University of Tamaulipus, Mexico (visiting). Jonsen earned degrees in English from Santa Clara University and San Jose State University, and a PhD in higher education from Stanford University.

Francis J. ("Frank") Kerins Sr.
Former President, Carroll College, Helena, Montana
Kerins has served as the president at Carroll College in Helena, Montana for 22 years, and at the University of St. Francis in Joliet, Illinois, for 5 years. He has also served briefly in this capacity at other public and independent institutions. Earlier, Kerins was professor of philosophy and of higher education at Loretto Heights College in Colorado and at the University of Denver, respectively. He holds a BA from St. Francis College in New York and an MA from St. Louis University. He earned his EdD from the University of Denver and received several honorary doctorates from other institutions. He has been a board member and/or officer of many agencies including the American Council on Education, the Association of Catholic Colleges and Universities, the Council of Independent Colleges, the Council on Naturopathic Medical Education, the Montana Committee for the Humanities, the Northwest Commission on Colleges, and the Western Interstate Commission for Higher Education. In 1988, at a convocation in New Orleans, he was privileged to address Pope John Paul II on behalf of American Catholic higher education. He and Mary Costigan Kerins have been married for more than 50 years, and reside in Montana and Arizona.

Jason E. Lane
SUNY Provost Fellow and Deputy Director for Research at the Nelson A. Rockefeller Institute of Government as well as Associate Professor of Educational Policy and Senior Researcher at the Institute for Global Education Policy Studies, State University of New York (SUNY), Albany, New York.
Prior to arriving in New York, Lane was on the faculty at the University of North Dakota. Lane's research focuses on the organization and leadership of higher education institutions and their relationship to governments. Lane has written numerous articles, book chapters, policy reports, and authored or edited seven books, including *Higher Education Systems 3.0: Harnessing Systemness*; *Delivering Performance* (with Bruce Johnstone, 2013); *Academic Leadership and Governance of Higher Education* (with Robert Hendrickson, James Harris, and Rick Dorman, 2012); and *Colleges and Universities as Economic Drivers* (with Bruce Johnstone, 2012). He has served on the boards of the Comparative and International Education Society (CIES), Council for International Higher Education (CIHE), and the Gulf Comparative Education Society (GCES).

Patricia Nelson ("Patty") Limerick
Professor of History and Director of the Center of the American West, University of Colorado, Boulder, Colorado.
Patty Limerick received her PhD from Yale University in 1980, and has dedicated her career to demonstrating the benefits of applying historical perspective to contemporary dilemmas and bridging the gap between academics and the general public. She is the author of numerous books, most notably *The Legacy of Conquest* (1987) and *A Ditch in Time* (2012); she is also a prolific essayist and sought-after speaker. Her scholarship and her commitment to teaching have been recognized with a number of honors, including the MacArthur Fellowship (1995–2000), and she has served as president of several professional organizations, advised documentary film projects, done two tours as a Pulitzer Prize nonfiction jurist, and been a guest columnist for the *New York Times.* In 1986, Limerick was one of the principal founders of the Center of the American West, and since 1995 it has been her primary affiliation. Under her leadership, the center serves as a forum committed to the civil, respectful, problem-solving exploration of important, often contentious, public issues.

David A. Longanecker
President, Western Interstate Commission for Higher Education (WICHE), Boulder, Colorado
David A. Longanecker has served as the president of WICHE since 1999. He was appointed the assistant secretary for postsecondary education at the US Department of Education and remained in that position for six years. He was also the principal analyst for higher education for the Congressional Budget Office. He has been the state higher education executive officer in Colorado and Minnesota. Longanecker serves on numerous national boards and commissions. He writes extensively on higher education issues. His primary higher education interests are: expanding access to successful completion for students within all sectors of higher education, promoting student and institutional performance, assuring efficient and effective finance and financial aid strategies, and fostering educational technologies. These activities seek to sustain America's educational strength in the world and increase the quality of life for all Americans, particularly those who have traditionally been left out in the past. He holds an EdD from Stanford University, an MA in student personnel work from George Washington University, and a BA in sociology from Washington State University.

David A. Tandberg
Assistant Professor of Higher Education, Florida State University
David A. Tandberg's teaching and research interests center on state higher education policy and politics. He is particularly interested in the political antecedents of state higher education policy and finance decisions and broader issues involving state higher education finance, policy, governance, and economics. Tandberg also explores policy evaluation, particularly state policies meant to increase access and success in higher education. His research

has appeared in *Research in Higher Education*, *Educational Policy*, *Higher Education in Review* and the *Journal of Education Finance*. Previously Tandberg served as special assistant to the secretary of higher education in the Pennsylvania Department of Education, focusing on postsecondary policy development and implementation. He earned his BA from Adams State College in Colorado, MA in political science, and PhD in higher education from Pennsylvania State University. His dissertation on the politics of state higher education funding won dissertation of the year award for 2006–2007 from the Politics of Education Association. Tandberg was an associate with the National Center for Public Policy and Higher Education and a young academic fellow with the Institute for Higher Education Policy.

David M. Wrobel
Merrick Chair and Professor in Western American History, University of Oklahoma, Norman, Oklahoma
David M. Wrobel teaches undergraduate and graduate courses on the American West and modern American history. He is the author of *Global West, American Frontier: Travel, Empire and Exceptionalism from Manifest Destiny to the Great Depression* (2013); *Promised Lands: Promotion, Memory and the Creation of the American West* (2002); and *The End of American Exceptionalism: Frontier Anxiety from the Old West to the New Deal* (1993). He has coedited *Seeing and Being Seen: Tourism in the American West* (2001) and *Many Wests: Place, Culture, and Regional Identity* (1997). Wrobel coedits two book series: The Modern American West (University of Arizona Press) and The Urban West (University of Nevada Press). He is a participant in the Organization of American Historians' Distinguished Lecturer Program, and previously held the position of senior research fellow in Western American History at Yale University (2005–2006). He has served as president (2007–2008) of the American Historical Association's Pacific Coast Branch and Phi Alpha Theta, the National History Honor Society (2004–2006). His latest book project is titled "The West and America, 1900–2000: A Regional History."

Index

Printed and bound in the United States of America